Comparative criticism
A yearbook

3

Comparative criticism

A yearbook

3

Edited by
E. S. SHAFFER
READER IN COMPARATIVE LITERATURE
SCHOOL OF MODERN LANGUAGES AND EUROPEAN HISTORY
UNIVERSITY OF EAST ANGLIA

CAMBRIDGE UNIVERSITY PRESS
CAMBRIDGE
LONDON NEW YORK NEW ROCHELLE
MELBOURNE SYDNEY

Published by the Press Syndicate of the University of Cambridge
The Pitt Building, Trumpington Street, Cambridge CB2 1RP
32 East 57th Street, New York, NY 10022, USA
296 Beaconsfield Parade, Middle Park, Melbourne 3206, Australia

First published 1981

Printed in Great Britain at the
University Press, Cambridge

British Library cataloguing in publication data

Comparative criticism. – 3.
1. Literature, Comparative – Periodicals
I. British Comparative Literature Association
801'.95'05 PN851 80-41998

ISBN 0 521 23276 7
ISSN 0144-7564

CONTENTS

CONTRIBUTORS

Stephen Bann, historian and Reader in Modern Cultural Studies, University of Kent at Canterbury

Michael Caesar, Lecturer in Italian, University of Kent at Canterbury

Garland Cannon, Professor of English, Kuwait University and Texas A & M University

Terence Cave, Fellow and Tutor in French, St John's College, Oxford

Kenelm Foster, Reader in Italian, Faculty of Modern and Medieval Languages, University of Cambridge

Roger Fowler, Professor of Linguistics, School of English and American Studies, University of East Anglia

Peter France, Professor of French, University of Edinburgh

Charles Martindale, Lecturer in Classical and Medieval Studies, School of European Studies, University of Sussex

Alastair J. Minnis, Lecturer in Medieval English, University of Bristol

Arnaldo Momigliano, Fellow of All Souls College, Oxford, and Professor in the Humanities, University of Chicago

Edwin Morgan, Emeritus Professor of English, University of Glasgow

Göran Printz-Påhlson, Lecturer in Swedish, Department of Scandinavian Studies, Faculty of Modern and Medieval Languages, University of Cambridge

Michael Robinson, research student in the Department of Scandinavian Studies, Faculty of Modern and Medieval Languages, University of Cambridge

J. P. Stern, Professor of German, University College, London

Sheila Stern, translator

Brian Vickers, Professor of English Literature and Director of the Centre for Renaissance Studies, Eidgenössische Technische Hochschule, Zürich

ACKNOWLEDGEMENTS

Acknowledgements are made to Barthes' literary executors, and Editions du Seuil of Paris for permission to publish a translation of Roland Barthes, 'Le Discours de l'histoire', first published in *Social Science Information* in 1967.

For permission to publish correspondence of Sir William Jones, acknowledgement is owing to the Asiatic Society, Calcutta; Blackwell's Rare Books, Oxford; the Bodleian Library, Oxford; Controller of Her Majesty's Stationery Office; the Staatsbibliothek, Berlin; and the Trustees of the National Library of Scotland, Edinburgh.

EDITOR'S NOTE
Rhetoric, 'orientalism', and comparative method

Nothing in recent years has been more startling than the receding of the authority of the 'real', and of 'realism'. Fiction and history have gladly abandoned their pretence of telling it as it really was, and have strongly hinted that it wasn't, really. Fiction, and critics of fiction, have gloried in offering, and analysing, the rhetoric of the real, and the interpretation of the real, and interpretation *tout court*, or 'hermeneutics', often enough without reference to the real at all. All we have is interpretation; and this has been experienced as a liberation and a triumph, in the hands of its most effective practitioners, like the late Roland Barthes, who celebrated the euphoric pleasures of the text.

Hayden White, whose influential book *Metahistory* (1973) attempts to analyse the rhetorical tropes employed by the leading historians of the nineteenth century, approaches the problem of 'realistic' representation – '*the* problem for modern historiography' – through the work of Erich Auerbach, whose *Mimesis: the Representation of Reality in Western Literature* (1968) is a classic of comparative criticism, and, secondarily, through the work of recent French critics, including Barthes. Auerbach, taking the trope of realism to be the dominant one in Western literature, saw the Gospels as the source of it, especially the Passion narrative, the *sermo humilis* and model for the claim to be reporting actual events as observed by an eye-witness; Frank Kermode has recently used the Gospel of Mark to argue that as the Gospels are a tissue of 'fulfilments' of Old Testament texts, and the first written versions of the Gospels are 'testimonies' or citations of Old Testament passages bearing on the Messiah, the model for the trope of realism is itself proof that (in Morton White's phrase, from *Foundations of Historical Knowledge*, 1965) 'metahistorically motivated value judgements' govern the historian's choice of chronicle. All this, of course, is no more than Schleiermacher and Strauss argued early in the nineteenth century (Kermode cites no hermeneutical text earlier than Dilthey), and one could make a strong case for the sophisticated awareness of the German historians who followed them of the rhetoric they employed; this would strengthen Kermode's claim that a fifth, or 'Hermeneutic', model, should be added to Hayden White's four modes, 'Formist', 'Organicist', 'Mechanistic', and 'Contextualist', although in fact such an 'addition' would involve the re-casting of White's whole case. But now that it is no longer a question of religious faith that is at stake, the argument has been taken to have much wider application to other systems of belief: as Barthes put it in the article translated in this volume (and his statement is endorsed by Kermode in *The Genesis of Secrecy*, 1979), 'The fact can exist only linguistically, as a term in a discourse', although 'we behave as if it were a simple reproduction of something or other on another plane of existence altogether, some extra-structural "reality"'.

This far-reaching claim has occurred under the aegis of the transformation, still in progress, of 'literary criticism' into a general theory of reading, of which vol. 2 of this yearbook, 'Text and Reader', gives some telling illustrations. But 'reading' has ambitious overtones of 'intellectual interpretation', and in so far as it is taken in a philosophic sense involves the paradoxical overturn of traditional hierarchies, placing poetics at the pinnacle instead of the base, where it simply supplied techniques of troping to a rhetoric of persuasion and debate. Conjoined with a neo-Romanticism which sees poetics as a creative art of the imagination, and which long ago abandoned traditional rhetoric in favour of a few simple central tropes taken as functions of the imagination, this intellectual aspiration makes a heady brew which restores significance to the old German Romantic enterprise of a 'philosophical poetry'. This major shift in views of the nature of rhetoric can be best located in English in Coleridge (though Alastair Minnis in this volume shows that conceptions of the imagination were already present in late-medieval theory, and Brian Vickers regrets the loss of a fully fledged Renaissance rhetoric to the anti-rhetorical party). It is no accident that White's four tropes, the merest sampling of classical tropes, are drawn from Kenneth Burke, *A Grammar of Motives* (1945). The conjunction of the intellectual aspiration of the new 'art of reading' and a neo-Romantic poetics is powerfully represented in Geoffrey Hartman's *Criticism in the Wilderness: The Study of Literature Today* (1980), where the view still held by Arnold and Eliot of their critical function as sober handmaidens to literature (both, of course, were in their own eyes primarily poets, and as such defending their place in the pecking order of literary activity) is rejected in favour of the 'intellectual poetry' of critics like Friedrich Schlegel, Gyorgy Lukács, Ortega y Gasset, Walter Benjamin, and Jacques Derrida. If on the side of the intellectual claim, this impulse runs to the employment of literary categories in the conduct of other disciplines (which naturally causes more of a stir when, as in the case of Hayden White, it is carried out by exponents of the other discipline), on the imaginative side it runs to the production of 'critical fictions' such as Harold Bloom's quest of the gnostic psyche in *The Flight to Lucifer*, George Steiner's artfully pseudo-pop Nazi thriller, 'The Portage to San Cristobal of A. H.', and Herbert Lindenberger's *Saul's Fall*, a pale *Pale Fire*, in which an imaginary poet's drama is parodically manhandled by a variety of critics. All three authors, be it noted, are professional romanticists – as indeed is Hartman, who nevertheless reserves his praise for Derrida's *Glas*.

These ambitious claims for literary criticism, and the evident excesses in both directions, in an enterprise even the most formidably gifted of the Romantics found notoriously difficult to hold together, invites deflationary responses, and has been receiving them, especially from voices in this country, where the liberation experienced by vaunting critics has been widely experienced as a shameful abandonment of the actual text and its relation – so precious – to the context of its creation and the precise point of its application. Surely the author is not to be reduced, as in Foucault's brilliant essay, to the 'author-function', any more than the 'real' can be reduced to the Barthian 'effect of the real', nor character to what Kermode, following Greimas, calls 'actants' (originally a notion of Vladimir Propp, whose analysis of Russian folk-tales held that deep-lying plot-functions generated spheres of action in which the required actantial roles were carried out). In a lucid, committed and well-grounded book, *The Nouveau Roman and the Poetics of Fiction* (1980), Ann Jefferson shows that the guarantor of 'realism' in the modern novel is the narrative perspective; in short, that today the 'unreliable narrator' of yesteryear has become the last outpost of mimesis, and is rapidly being bundled out of sight. To the stalwarts of 'ordinary science', or business as usual, these results are unacceptable on the face of it. To others, willing to entertain new insights, they are nevertheless profoundly disturbing.

Yet a critic like Kermode uses the Barthian model to give himself the degree of freedom needed to enable him to offer a brilliant literary interpretation of that obscure and resistant text, hedged about with immemorial theological proscription, the Gospel of Mark. A degree of freedom for the critic was of course what Barthes meant to secure, and he put the case for it persuasively in *Critique et verité* and in his own works of renovation of the classic texts, notably *S/Z*, on Balzac's *Sarrasine*; his case rests primarily on the historical grounds of the nature of the French technique of *explication de textes*, in short, one internal to the conditions of the discipline in which he had been trained. The question that needs to be asked in any case, is, what degree of freedom is required to achieve a given end; one characteristic of the current critical euphoria is that so much freedom is claimed as sometimes to undermine the very case the critic wants to make, to abolish the terms in which in his discipline a judgement can have force.

It is just this that Arnaldo Momigliano argues so powerfully in his review of Hayden White's work, as represented by *Tropics of Discourse* as well as *Metahistory*. The retention of the aim of uncovering historical truth, of fact, is not a sign of simple-mindedness, vulgarity, or being out of tune with the current phase of the history of consciousness, it is the defining mark of the historical discipline. It is not an unexamined premise, but an axiom of the discipline. Any approach that abandons it, abandons the historical discipline. It would be useful to have an examination of the rhetoric of 'disciplines', and Michel Foucault, one of White's masters, has made a start at his, especially in *Les Mots et les choses* (*The Order of Things*), where he examines the notions of 'origin' and 'growth' of disciplines, as well as the participation of new disciplines in the eighteenth century (linguistics, economics, and biology) in the common *épistémè* of the time. Foucault, however, in trying to escape from the rhetoric of disciplines himself, especially in *The Archaeology of Knowledge*, has only succeeded in showing how indispensable it is. Momigliano's own *Studies in Historiography* form a masterly analysis of the emergence of the methods of the discipline to which he is committed. There is nothing which does the same job for literary theory and criticism; René Wellek's work perhaps comes closest to it. This, of course, is a major cause of the present disarray: it has never been clear that there is such a thing as a 'discipline' of literary criticism. Those who have insisted most on its existence, like the late F. R. Leavis, have been unable to define it articulately. It is tempting to think that this, not the challenge to 'realism', is the fundamental reason for the current revival of rhetoric studies explored in this volume by Peter France: for if there is to be a 'historiography' of the discipline, it must take into account its ancient roots and the long history of its skilled deployment and exposition. Brian Vickers' suggestions here for the writing of the history of *elocutio* move in this direction. As Peter France suggests, 'rhetoric' may now be seen as itself 'an art of reading', and a contribution to a 'science' of literature.

The current reinterpretation of rhetoric may of course itself be seen as a modernist, a Barthian undertaking. It relates to the development of sociological linguistics and communication theory, as Roger Fowler points out, and to the growth of the study of ideology, especially in Germany, among men of letters intensely preoccupied with the rhetorical devices that determine the social function of literature. Nearly all German criticism of the last thirty years, Victor Lange has emphasized in his succinct and precise introduction to *New Perspectives in German Literary Criticism* (1979), is concerned with 'the problem of the public effectiveness of literary works', the 'interlocking relationship between text and reader, and, altogether, the historical (and ideological) conditions of literature'. Peter Stern puts the case with his customary discriminating engagement. Michael Caesar and Göran Printz-Påhlson subtly display the impingement of the larger social world on the art of Manzoni and Strindberg respectively.

The analysis of disciplines and the critique of ideology come together in Edward Said's *Orientalism* (Routledge and Kegan Paul, 1978), which exhibits the riskiness of the undertaking. In considering the founding of our own discipline, comparative literary studies – if discipline it be – no name is more important than that of Sir William Jones. Indeed, the importance of Jones for the development of Oriental studies, for comparative mythology, philology, and law, as well as for the translation of literary masterpieces from the Arabic, Persian, and Sanskrit, is indisputable. If his work is still too little known, it is perhaps because the extraordinary range of his interests and accomplishments puts him beyond the means of assessment available to specialists in any one field. Jones is an immensely attractive figure, who combined the sensibility of a poet, the cultivation and liberal sympathies of an eighteenth-century man of letters, the erudition of a scholar, and the practical accomplishments of a legal emissary of the British Crown in Bengal. We are pleased to be able to present the five new letters that have been found since the publication of Garland Cannon's edition of *The Letters of Sir William Jones* by the Clarendon Press in 1970, together with a few of the many letters addressed to Jones by scholars, statesmen, and literati in all quarters of the globe. Many of his correspondents have not yet been traced, and we should be happy to hear of any letters lodged in smaller libraries or in private hands, with a view towards further exploration of the effective influence of Jones.

Jones' importance is recognized by Edward Said, for he can be seen as the founder of what Said has identified as the source not simply of new and objective knowledge about the Orient, its sacred and secular texts, and its languages, but of 'orientalism', a refurbished and secularized version of Western Christian strategies of annexing and subordinating the Orient to its own values and purposes, and, more specifically, to its imperialist presence. Oriental scholarship, Said argues, became an effective instrument of European domination of 85 per cent of the world by the end of the nineteenth century. Said attempts to analyse the rhetorical strategies by which this was carried out, and further views it as simply one of the more egregious examples of the ideological basis of all scholarly endeavour.

Jones and Anquetil-Duperron, the discoverer and translator of the *Zend-Avesta*, were the founders of modern oriental studies; Said sees their work as placed on a scientific and rational basis in the next generation by Silvestre de Sacy, Ernest Renan, and Edward Lane. He chooses to analyse Renan in the greatest detail as the outstanding example of full-blown 'orientalism', with its scholarly apparatus, its noxious religious and racial assumptions, and its romantic décor. Of all the possible examples of literary orientalism, he analyses Flaubert most fully, a relatively late inheritor of the romantic Orient, as he first adopts it and later (in *Bouvard et Pécuchet*) deflates it. Said tends to stress the later generation, partly because of his own avowed bias towards Islamic rather than Indian or Far Eastern studies (Said, now a literary academic with a considerable reputation in the United States, was born in Palestine and educated by the British in Egypt), but primarily for political reasons: he sees Napoleon's invasion of Egypt as the 'enabling expedition' for nineteenth-century oriental studies. He sums up Jones's role thus: 'Anquetil, Jones, the Napoleonic expedition define the tradition's earliest contours' (p. 156).

Jones, in fact, is let off relatively lightly, for it is only after him that the conjunction of British and French imperialism creates Said's 'orientalism' (he ignores German scholarship, which, considering the extent and depth of its contribution, is a damaging omission). The new literary mode of disregarding the intentions of authors has in this context a political consequence: the well-intentioned, the heroic, romantic, even therapeutic and sympathetic orientalist – and Said does not deny that these existed, and in plenty ('The East has prophets, the West doctors') – is nevertheless guilty. His work served the purposes of imperialism, whether he knew it or not. There is in fact a great deal of legitimate evidence that often orientalists did indeed directly and consciously serve their governments. But the suppression of the author in favour of the author-function makes it easier to have little compunction about seeing 'orientalists', as a group, as an enemy deserving no quarter. The personal qualities and the individual merits of a man like Jones become an irrelevance.

The analysis of a discipline that Said attempts to conduct on the model of Foucault too often employs not Foucault's rhetorical method, but Foucault's rhetoric merely. In his comments on the tendency of orientalists, from d'Herbelot's great Dictionnaire, to Dacier's *tableau générale* on the state and progress of the arts and sciences, and de Sacy's anthologies, to systematize and catalogue, Said draws on Foucault's insights in *The Order of Things* and in his preface to Flaubert's *La Tentation de Saint Antoine*; but where Foucault uses the correspondences thus obtained to illuminate the structures of nascent disciplines, Said sees them as signs of the imperialist nature of Western rationality. He writes:

> like all his learned contemporaries, Sacy considered a learned work a positive addition to an edifice that all scholars erected together. Knowledge was essentially the *making visible of* material, and the aim of a tableau was the construction of a sort of Benthamite Panopticon. Scholarly discipline was therefore a specific technology of power: it gained for its user (and its students) tools and knowledge which (if he was an historian) had hitherto been lost. And indeed the vocabulary of specialized power and acquisition is particularly associated with Sacy's reputation as a pioneer Orientalist. (p. 127)

Here Said is using an image from Foucault's *Surveillir et punir* (*Discipline and Punish*): the pervasive image of the model prison of Bentham, in which all the prisoners were at all times to be visible from a central tower. Foucault makes of this a very powerful rhetorical tool in his exposition of his central thesis that the Enlightenment invented, through its very liberal and reformist endeavours, new and more effective means of social discipline. Said uses the image simply in passing – indeed, his use of it is liable to have no effect whatever on the reader who has not read Foucault's book (for even familiarity with Bentham does not fully explicate the allusion) – and to this extent Said is merely slipshod; but assuming knowledge of Foucault, Said is slipping a sinister interpretation over the scholarly desire to acquire knowledge and the teacher's wish to make it accessible. At another point Said makes the step more explicit:

'acquisition' is replaced by the term 'accumulation'. Said writes: 'I am interested in showing how modern Orientalism, unlike the precolonial awareness of Dante and d'Herbelot, embodies a systematic discipline of *accumulation*. And far from this being exclusively an intellectual or theoretical feature, it made Orientalism fatally tend towards the systematic accumulation of human beings and territories' (p. 123). In one sense, this is to say no more than 'Knowledge is power' – and Bacon was a notable maker of tables such as *The Advancement of Learning*. But Said wishes to put off knowledge with power.

If his argument were less sweeping, Said might be able to justify his attack by specifying what was in the Tableau or in the systematic anthologies and chrestomathies of Sacy, or, perhaps more tellingly, what was left out of them, abridged, distorted, or misinterpreted. In ignoring content for structure understood in a superficial sense, he misses his chance to make good his case, and travesties Foucault.

Unlike Foucault, Said emphasizes rigidity rather than openness to possibility in the early phases of the development of a discipline, and connects this explicitly with comparative method:

> Like many academic specialities in their early phases, modern Orientalism held its subject matter, which it defined, in a vise-like grip which it did almost everything in its power to sustain. Thus a knowing vocabulary developed, and its functions, as much as its style, located the Orient in a comparative framework, of the sort employed and manipulated by Renan. (p. 149)

Said's on the whole well-founded indictment of Renan's racialism is converted into a wholesale charge against cultural comparatism, which is said to have 'spawned ethnocentrism, racial theory, and economic oppression' (p. 146). Said makes legitimate use of Foucault in his extension of Foucault's analysis of the parallel between linguistic and biological science in the eighteenth century to Renan's use of the parallel; and indeed, his analysis of this parallel in Renan's *Histoire générale et système comparée des langues sémitiques* is his major piece of sustained analysis of an orientalist text in the book. Renan drew on the comparative anatomy of Cuvier and Geoffroi Saint-Hilaire to support his distinction between the living, organic languages (Indo-European) and the inorganic, anomalous and teratological languages (Semitic), a distinction then extended to the cultures employing those languages. As Said remarks, 'We readily observe the way cultural generalization had begun to acquire the armor of scientific statement and the ambience of corrective study.' Yet in fact 'Such comparatism is rarely descriptive; most often, it is both evaluative and expository' (p. 149).

The misuse of a method in one instance does not, of course, disqualify it. Indeed, Said himself, in his earlier article, 'Renan's Philological Laboratory', severed from the polemics of *Orientalism*, and published in *Art, Politics, and Will. Essays in Honor of Lionel Trilling* (1977), showed his enthusiastic interest in the proliferation of philological studies in nineteenth-century Europe. Much more still needs to be said about Jones and the stimulus he gave to comparative philology. But throughout this book his argument is directed against comparative approaches of all kinds. The very specifying of what was meant by 'West' and 'East', he argues, instead of leading to empirical discriminations, led to the imposition of generalizations on geographical areas which might otherwise have had an independent life. 'The age-old distinction between "Europe" and "Asia" or "Occident" and "Orient" herds beneath very wide labels every possible variety of human plurality, reducing it in the process to one or two terminal, collective abstractions' (p. 155). For Said, 'generalization' (as an especially expeditious form of acquisition) tends to be equated with oppression and conquest; it is just one step in the loose association of terms leading from abstraction to acquisition to accumulation to imperialism. The very alphabetical order of a dictionary is enough to raise his hackles. Dante, with his hierarchical universe and his carefully calculated circles of infernal punishment, in which Mahomet is perpetually ripped from chin to anus in a circle very near the bottom circle of the devil himself, is an early but flagrant example of the kind of Western Christian systematization that in a later period becomes comparatism and still later, structuralism. Jones is singled out for blame as a systematizer: 'Whereas Anquetil opened large vistas, Jones closed them down, codifying, tabulating, comparing' (p. 77). All of Jones's wide-ranging efforts, which even today have an enlarging effect on the mind of the reader (see, for example, his splendid letters from India to his pupil, Viscount Althorp), for Said represent a 'course of personal study that was to gather in, to rope off, to domesticate the Orient and thereby turn it into a province of European learning' (p. 78).

It is clear that Said has succumbed to something very like the myth he is struggling against of 'Western rationalism' versus 'Eastern sensualism or particularity'. To the West is attributed not only a battery of unchanging stereotypes of the Orient that persist through centuries of scholarship, but a timeless, ahistorical, abstract and rigid mode of intellection. Perhaps we may detect here an ironic reversal of old notions of 'Oriental despotism', as well as of Renan's conception of the incapacity of semitic languages to regenerate themselves. His indictment of the West is so sweeping that it undercuts his own otherwise substantial case for pervasive bias in oriental studies down to the present day. His caricatural account of Western ratiocinative processes forces him to adopt an anti-intellectual stance that deprives him of the grounds of his own method. For all that he has learned from French criticism, he has attacked it (in his earlier book, *Beginnings*, and in an article in a recent collection editied by V. Harari) for the 'rigidity' of its structural thinking. Although he exempts Foucault from these charges (and of course Foucault has always denied being a structuralist), the repetitions and rigidities of his own accusatory mode disable him from employing Foucault's method.

Said uses Foucault's word 'discourse', but in a quite different manner. Where Said harangues 'orientalists' for rigidity, and sees them as, by 1880, 'mere copyists', Foucault strikingly holds that it is by 'le moutonnement indéfini des commentaires', the apparently repetitious unfolding of commentaries, that change takes place; and for Flaubert, the very collection and organization of *idées reçues*, and their reorganization in his notebooks for *Bouvard*, was a creative act.

Said is, nevertheless, a comparatist, and a literary critic, even if he is not, like Foucault, 'an analyst of discourse'. When he turns to the best French literary orientalism, Said displays his admiration for Nerval and Flaubert, who were 'thoroughly steeped in aspects of European culture that encouraged a sympathetic, if perverse, vision of the Orient'. We may be surprised that Said is prepared to embrace this perverse vision, including the imagery of exotic places, the cultivation of sado-masochistic tastes, a fascination with the macabre, with the Fatal Woman (Cleopatra, Salome, and Isis), and with secrecy and occultism. But finally, one perceives, neither a real Orient nor a counter-Orient is offered by Said in this book; this mythical Orient is his own. He modulates the traits of 'Eastern sensualism or particularity' only so far as to call for the recognition of 'existential human identities' (p. 155) – a plea, surely, with Western roots. Indeed, it is surprising that after his adverse comments on comparative approaches, he returns to its practice in a manner reminiscent of those nineteenth-century English comparatists whose views we traced in the 'Editor's Note' in vol. 2 – Posnett, drawing on Mill and Henry Maine (and behind him, Sir William Jones) – who explicitly rejected racialism, maintained their scepticism in the face of claims to found 'universal laws' on historical investigations, and insisted that moral scruple depended on the maintenance of such scepticism.

Said's ideological guns are silenced by the urgent claims of his own discipline; it is as a literary critic he responds to the art of Nerval and Flaubert. But only for a moment. The 'objective discoveries' of the Orientalists

> are and always have been conditioned by the fact that its truths, like any truths delivered by language, are embodied in language, and what is the truth of language, Nietzsche once said, but 'a mobile army of metaphors, metonyms, and anthropomorphisms – in short, a sum of human relations, which have been enhanced, transposed, and embellished poetically and rhetorically, and which after long use seem firm, canonical, and obligatory to a people: truths are illusions about which one has forgotten that this is what they are.' (p. 203)

With the invocation of Nietzsche, and the claim that 'all is language', Said returns to the fray: 'Orientalism was such a system of truths, truths in Nietzsche's sense of the word. It is therefore correct that every European, in what he could say about the Orient, was consequently a racist, an imperialist, and almost totally ethnocentic' (p. 204). Thus the severance from 'realism' may grant the critic needed degrees of freedom; but if more than the required degrees of freedom are appropriated, he may find himself enslaved to an ideological construct of his own design.

Let me express my warmest thanks to Stephen Bann for his unstinting and imaginative help at every stage of this volume, for his own genial contribution on Ranke, for, his lucid and graceful translation of Barthes' opaque prose, his fertile suggestions and practical interventions. I should also like to thank Brian Vickers for his many constructive suggestions, not least the notion of a specialist bibliography of the important work in rhetoric in the last ten years, an innovation we hope to continue in the succeeding volumes of *Comparative Criticism*. Many others have been of great help in the preparation of this volume, and I should like to thank Peter France, R. R. Bolgar and Richard Gordon. Once again thanks are owing to Paula Clifford for circulating and collecting bibliographical material on comparative literature in Britain. I am grateful for the dedicated and cheerful labour of Martin Aske as Editorial Assistant, who spared us time and thought even during the last phases of writing up his thesis; and for the good counsel and unremitting work of a number of people at the Cambridge University Press, in particular Terence Moore, Elizabeth O'Beirne-Ranelagh, and Helen Beddow; and, as ever, for Michael Black's scrupulous care for this among many enterprises.

The next four volumes of *Comparative Criticism* will be concerned with the following themes: vol. 4, 'The Languages of the Arts'; vol. 5, 'Biblical and Literary Interpretation', drawing in part on the proceedings of a conference on Hermeneutics to be held at King's College, Cambridge, in 1981; vol. 6, 'Translation: Theory and Practice'; vol 7, 'English and World Literature', which will follow our conference at Manchester in 1983. Translations of poetry and other literary works as well as of scholary and critical works, past and present, are welcome at all times, and especially for vol. 6. The BCLA has established an annual prize for the best translation, and all submissions will be considered. We shall continue to publish a selection of the best papers given at the conferences of the British Comparative Literature Association. The annual deadline for submission of manuscripts is 1 February; the annual press deadline is 30 June; volumes appear in the autumn of the following year. Submissions for vols. 5–7 are now welcome. All correspondence should be addressed to the Editor, *Comparative Criticism*, Cambridge University Press, P.O. Box 110, Cambridge CB2 3RL.

E. S. Shaffer

PART I
Rhetoric and history

The discourse of history

ROLAND BARTHES

TRANSLATED WITH AN INTRODUCTION BY STEPHEN BANN

INTRODUCTION: BARTHES' DISCOURSE

Roland Barthes' brief article on 'The Discourse of History', first published in 1967 in the multi-lingual periodical *Social Science Information*, is his most specific and technical contribution to the linguistic and rhetorical analysis of historiography. Falling roughly at the mid-way point of his career as a critic and theorist, it testifies to an interest in – even a fascination with – historians and historical representation, that was continually evident in his work. Barthes' second book, published in 1954, was a highly original presentation of Michelet for the series 'Ecrivains de toujours' (later to become the vehicle for his own autobiography, *Roland Barthes par Roland Barthes*). In 1959 he returned to Michelet, the 'discredited historian', with a Preface for a new edition of *La Sorcière*, and again in 1973 he wrote an article entitled 'Aujourd'hui Michelet' for a special edition of the magazine *L'Arc*. Apart from this consistent interest in an individual historian, he returned on more than one occasion to the problem of historical representation in drama, the novel and film: readers of *Mythologies* will certainly recall the delicate sarcasm with which he describes the raked forelocks and sweating brows of the conspirators in Mankiewicz's *Julius Caesar*. And History in the widest sense – the History that is, or is not, on our side – was never far from his concerns. As late as 1979, in his penultimate book *Sollers écrivain*, he thought it worthwhile to include a lengthy note on changing attitudes to History over the past few decades. From being 'a rather simplistic divinity to which we felt it necessary to sacrifice any consideration of forms', History had been rediscovered as 'a play of structures, just like language'. It could now be acknowledged as 'itself, also, a form of *écriture*'.

'The Discourse of History', probably among the least well-known of Barthes' occasional pieces, does not deal in such dizzying perspectives. It falls clearly within the stage of his career which he was later to identify as his 'petit délire scientifique'. It comes three years after the first appearance of his *Eléments de sémiologie* in *Communications*, and in the same year as the laborious *Système de la mode*. In other words, it forms part of a coherent programme of introducing the concepts of semiology and linguistics into the analysis of any and every type of discourse, from Herodotus to the fashion magazine. Broadly speaking, Barthes is applying the concepts of structural linguistics (in particular, those developed by Jakobson and Benveniste) to the particular conditions of 'utterance' which characterize the historical narrative. He makes a particularly apt use of Jakobson's concept of the 'shifter', asking 'under what conditions the classic historian is enabled – or authorized – himself to designate, in his discourse, the act by which he promulgates it'. And he advances for further development the interesting notion that the 'units of content' employed in historical discourse could be classed as 'collections' which differ considerably from historian to historian: those found in Herodotus being 'collections' of 'dynasties, princes, generals, soldiers, peoples and places', interpreted according to the lexicon of war; while the works of less archaic authors may be strongly structured by a personal thematic like Tacitus' *fama* or Machiavelli's opposition between the terms of energy and decadence (*mantenere* as opposed to *ruinare*). If these ideas can hardly be developed in the available space, Barthes does later extend the valuable concept of the 'realistic effect', which occurs right at the end of the article. In a contribution to *Communications* which was published in 1968, he takes it as the basis of a general discussion on the criteria of 'realism' in fictional and historical narrative.

It would be wrong to claim that, in either of these articles, Barthes was pioneering a decisive shift in attitudes to the analysis of historiography. As the closing sentence of 'The Discourse of History' makes clear, he had himself been attentive to the theoretical innovations of the *Annales* school, who had already defined a historical approach denying the primacy of the event, and by the same token drawn attention to the conventional nature of classic strategies of narration (see, for example, the 'Conclusion' to the new edition of Braudel's *The Mediterranean*, which is dated June 1965). Nonetheless, there are grounds for holding that Barthes was indeed one of the 'shifters' between the province of historiography – in its practical and critical manifestations – and the productive exploration of discourse in general which was associated with structuralism and semiology. Two of the most stimulating studies in historiographical theory to appear recently in France have been Paul Veyne's *Comment on écrit l'histoire* (1971) and Michel de Certeau's *L'Écriture de l'histoire* (1975). As the remarkable supplement to his 1978 edition makes quite clear, Veyne is overwhelmingly indebted to Michel Foucault, while Certeau shows strong affiliations both to Foucault and to Lacan's Neo-Freudiansm. Yet it is hard to account for the common emphasis on 'écriture' without mentioning the very personal inflection which Barthes gave to the term. Without doubt, the parallel lines of historiographical inquiry opened up in the United States by Hayden White's *Metahistory* (1973) testify both implicitly and explicitly to the influence of Barthes. In the significantly named *The Writing of History*, a collection of articles published in 1978, Lionel Gossman gives close attention to 'The Discourse of History'.

In the last resort, it must be conceded, Barthes' view of historiography, and indeed of History, was a sceptical one. His championing of Michelet was explicitly that of the 'discredited historian', whose achievement was to anticipate the merging of historiography within the general perspective of the human sciences. The linguistic and rhetorical analysis of historical narrative, as in this article, cannot grant to history, *a priori*, the mythic status which differentiates it from fiction. And indeed, the historian might not relish the distinctive status which Barthes eventually agrees to give to historical discourse in this article, since it is a distinction which he is obliged to share with the psychotic. For Barthes, historiography could no more effectively disavow its fictional status than any other form of discursive language. Yet in *La Chambre claire*, the work whose publication anticipated his tragic death by just a few days, Barthes managed to make even of the ontological insecurity of historiography a compelling and creative argument. One passage must be quoted at length:

Earlier societies made arrangements for memory, as a substitute for life, to be eternal and for at least the thing which told of Death to be itself immortal: that was the Monument. But in making Photography, which is mortal, the general and – as it were – natural witness of 'what has been', modern society has renounced the Monument. A paradox: the same century invented History and Photography. But History is a form of memory fabricated from positive recipes, a purely intellectual discourse which abolishes mythic Time; and Photography is a sure testimony, but a fleeting one; to such an extent that, today, everything tends to prepare our species for an incapacity, which will soon be with us: an incapacity to conceive, either affectively or symbolically, of *duration*: the era of Photography is also that of revolutions, contestation, assault and explosion – in short of different forms of impatience, of all that is opposed to the notion of maturing. – And no doubt, the astonishment of saying 'That has been' will vanish, that as well. It has already vanished. I remain, I don't know why, one of its last witnesses...and this book is its archaic trace.

For Barthes' almost posthumous work to strike this nostalgic, indeed rather mystic note is curiously appropriate. Against the 'fiction' of language, which Barthes so lovingly explored, the photograph offers the incontrovertible certainty of 'That has been': it is, as he strikingly expresses it, a 'certificate of presence'. But beyond the nostalgia and mysticism, beyond the adventitious solemnity which Barthes' death gives to *La Chambre claire*, we can perhaps discern a new programme for the 'purely intellectual discourse' of historiography: to recount the strange emergence of that 'certificate of presence' – to clarify the place of what Barthes called the 'anthropological revolution' of photography within the as yet unwritten history of representation.

THE DISCOURSE OF HISTORY

The formal description of sets of words beyond the level of the sentence (what we call for convenience *discourse*) is not a modern development: from Gorgias to the nineteenth century, it was the special concern of traditional rhetoric. Recent developments in the science of language have nonetheless endowed it with a new timeliness and new methods of analysis: a linguistic description of discourse can perhaps already be envisaged at this stage; because of its bearings on literary analysis (whose importance in education is well known) it is one of the first assignments for semiology to undertake.

This second level of linguistics, which must look for the universals of discourse (if they exist) under the form of units and general rules of combination, must at the same time obviously give an answer to the question whether structural analysis is justified in retaining the traditional typology of discourses; whether it is fully legitimate to make a constant opposition between the discourses of poetry and the novel, the fictional narrative and the historical narrative. It is the last point which gives rise to the reflections set down here. Does the narration of past events, which, in our culture from the time of the Greeks onwards, has generally been subject to the sanction of historical 'science', bound to the unbending standard of the 'real', and justified by the principles of 'rational' exposition – does this form of narration really differ, in some specific trait, in some indubitably distinctive feature, from imaginary narration, as we find it in the epic, the novel, and the drama? And if this trait or feature exists, then in what level of the historical statement must it be placed?[1] In order to suggest a reply to this question, we shall here be looking, in a free and far from exhaustive fashion, at the discourse of a number of great classic historians: Herodotus, Machiavelli, Bossuet and Michelet.

I. THE ACT OF UTTERING

First of all, we may ask under what conditions the classic historian is enabled – or authorized – himself to designate, in his discourse, the act by which he promulgates it. In other words, what, on the level of discourse – and not of language, are the *shifters* (in Jakobson's sense of the term)[2] which assure the transition from the utterance to the act of uttering (or *vice versa*)?

It would appear that historical discourse involves two regular types of shifters. The first type comprises what we might call the shifters of *listening*. This category has been identified by Jakobson, on the level of language, with the term *testimonial*, according to the formula C^eC^{a1}/Ca^{a2}: in addition to the event reported (C^e), discourse mentions at the same time the act of the informer (C^{a1}), and the speech of the utterer which is related to it (C^{a2}). This form of shifter thus designates any reference to the historian's *listening*, collecting testimony from *elsewhere* and telling it in his own discourse. Listening made explicit represents a choice, for it is possible not to refer to it at all; it brings the historian closer to the anthropologist, in so far as he mentions the source of his information. Thus we find an abundant use of this shifter of listening among historian/anthropologists like Herodotus. The forms vary: they range from phrases of the type of *as I have heard*, or *to my knowledge*, to the historian's use of the present tense which testifies to the intervention of the utterer, and to any mention of the historian's personal experience. Such is the case with Michelet, who 'listens to' the History of France as a result of an overwhelming personal experience (of the Revolution of July 1830) and takes account of this in his discourse. The *listening* shifter is obviously not distinctive to historical discourse: it is found frequently in conversation, and in certain expository devices used in the novel (such as anecdotes which are taken from fictional sources of information mentioned in the text).

The second type of shifter comprises all the explicit signs whereby the utterer – in this case, the historian – organizes his own discourse, taking up the thread or modifying his approach in some way in the course of narration: that is to say, where he provides explicit points of reference in the text. This is an important type of shifter, and there can be many different ways of 'organizing' discourse accordingly; but these different instances can all be subsumed under the principle that each shifter indicates a movement of the discourse in relation to its matter, or more precisely a movement in relation to the sequence of its matter, rather like the operation of the temporal and locational deictics 'here is/there is'. Thus we can cite as cases where the shifter affects the flow of utterances: the effect of immobility (*comme nous l'avons dit plus haut*), that of returning to an earlier stage (*altius repetere*, *replicare da piu alto luogo*), that of coming back again (*ma ritornando all'ordine nostro*, *dico come...*), that of stopping dead (*sur lui*, *nous n'en dirons pas plus*), and that of announcing (*voici les autres actions dignes de mémoire qu'il fit pendant son règne*). The organizing shifter poses a problem which is worthy of attention, though it can only be lightly indicated here: this is the problem arising from the coexistence, or to be more exact the friction between two times – the time of uttering and the time of the matter of the utterance. This friction gives rise to a number of important factors in historical discourse, of which we shall mention three. The first relates to the many ways of producing the phenomenon of acceleration in a historical account: an equal number of pages (if such be the rough measure of the time of uttering) can cover very different lapses of time (the time of matter of the utterance). In Machiavelli's *History of Florence*, the same measure (a chapter) covers in one instance a number of centuries, and in another no more than two decades. The nearer we are to the historian's own time, the more strongly the pressure of the uttering makes itself felt, and the slower the history becomes. There is no such thing as isochrony – and to say this, is to attack implicitly the linearity of the discourse and open it up to a possible 'paragrammatical' reading of the historical message.[3] The second point also reminds us, in its way, that this type of discourse – though linear in its material form – when it is face to face with historical time, undertakes (so it would appear) the role of amplifying the depth of that time. We become aware of what we might call a zig-zag or saw-toothed history. A good example is Herodotus, who turns back to the ancestors of a newcomer, and then returns to his point of departure to proceed a little further – and then starts the whole process all over again with the next newcomer. Finally there is a third factor in historical discourse which is of the utmost importance, one which bears witness to the destructive effect of organizing shifters as far as the chronological time of the history is concerned. This is a question of the way historical discourse is inaugurated, of the place where we find in conjunction the beginning of the matter of the utterance and the *exordium* of the uttering.[4] Historical discourse is familiar with two general types of inauguration: in the first place, there is what we might call the performative opening, for the words really perform a solemn act of foundation; the model for this is poetic, the *I sing* of the poets. So Joinville begins his history with a religious invocation (*Au nom de Dieu le tout-puissant, je, Jehan, sire de Joinville, fais écrire la vie de nostre Saint roi Louis*), and even the socialist Louis Blanc does not disdain the purificatory introit,[5] so evident is it that the beginnings of speech always carry with them a kind of difficulty, perhaps even a sacred character. Then there is a much more commonly found element, the Preface, which is an act of uttering characterized as such, whether prospectively in so far as it announces the discourse to come, or retrospectively in that it embodies a judgement on the discourse. (Such is the case with the Preface which Michelet wrote to crown his *History of France*, once it had been completely written and published.) Bearing in mind these different elements, we are likely to conclude that the entry of the act of uttering into the historical utterance, through these organizing shifters, is directed less towards offering the historian a chance of expressing his 'subjectivity', as is commonly held, than to 'complicating' the chronological time of history by bringing it up against another time, which is that of the discourse itself and could be termed for short the 'paper-time'. To sum up, the presence in historical narration of explicit signs of uttering would represent an attempt to 'dechronologize' the 'thread' of history and to restore, even though it may merely be a matter of reminiscence or nostalgia, a form of time that is complex, parametric and not in the least linear: a form of time whose spatial depths recall the mythic time of the ancient cosmogonies, which was also linked in its essence to the words of the poet and the soothsayer. Organizing shifters bear witness, in effect – though they do so through indirect ploys which have the appearance of rationality – to the predictive function of the historian. It is to the extent that he *knows* what has not yet been told that the historian, like the actor of myth, needs to double up the chronological unwinding of events with references to the time of his own speech.

The signs (or shifters) which have just been mentioned bear solely on the very process of uttering. There are other signs which refer no longer to the act of uttering, but to what Jakobson calls its protagonists (T^a): the receiver and the sender. It is a fact worthy of note, and somewhat mysterious at the same time, that literary discourse very rarely carries within it the signs of the 'reader'. Indeed we can say that its distinctive trait is precisely that it is – or so it would appear – a discourse without the pronoun 'you', even though in reality the entire structure of such a discourse implies a reading 'subject'. In historical discourse, the signs of the receiver are usually absent: they can be found only in cases where History is offered as a lesson, as with Bossuet's *Universal History*, a discourse which is explicitly addressed by the tutor to his pupil, the prince. Yet in a certain sense, this schema is only possible to the extent that Bossuet's discourse can be held to reproduce by homology the discourse which God himself holds with men – precisely in the form of the History which he grants to them. It is because the History of men is the Writing of God that Bossuet, as the mediator of this writing, can establish a relationship of sender and receiver between himself and the young prince.

Signs of the utterer (or sender) are obviously much more frequent. Here we should class all the discursive elements through which the historian – as the empty subject of the uttering – replenishes himself little by little with a variety of predicates which are destined to constitute him as a *person*, endowed with a psychological plenitude, or again (the word has a precious figurative sense) to give him *countenance*.[6] We can mention at this point a particular form of this 'filling' process, which is more directly associated with literary criticism. This is the case where the utterer means to 'absent himself' from his discourse, and where there is in consequence a systematic deficiency of any form of sign referring to the sender of the historical message. The history seems to be telling itself all on its own. This feature has a career which is worthy of note, since it corresponds in effect to the type of historical discourse labelled as 'objective' (in which the historian never intervenes). Actually in this case, the utterer nullifies his emotional persona, but substitutes for it another persona, the 'objective' persona. The subject persists in its plenitude, but as an objective subject. This is what Fustel de Coulanges referred to significantly (and somewhat naively) as the 'chastity of History'. On the level of discourse, objectivity – or the deficiency of signs of the utterer – thus appears as a particular form of imaginary projection, the product of what might be called the referential illusion, since in this case the historian is claiming to allow the referent to speak all on its own. This type of illusion is not exclusive to historical discourse. It would be hard to count the novelists who imagined – in the epoch of Realism – that they were 'objective' because they suppressed the signs of the 'I' in their discourse! Today linguistics and psychoanalysis have made us much more lucid with regard to privative utterances: we know that absences of signs are also in themselves significant.

To bring this section which deals with the act of uttering to a close, we should mention the special case – foreseen by Jakobson and placed within his lattice of shifters, on the linguistic level – when the utterer of the discourse is also at the same time a participant in the process described in the utterance, when the protagonist of the utterance is the same as the protagonist of the act of uttering (T^e/T^a): that is, when the historian, who is an actor with regard to the event, becomes its narrator; as with Xenophon, who takes part in the retreat of the Ten Thousand and subsequently becomes its historian. The most famous example of this conjunction of the *I* in the utterance and the *I* in the act of uttering is doubtless the *he* of Caesar's *Gallic War*. This celebrated *he* belongs to the utterance; when Caesar explicitly undertakes the act of uttering, he passes to the use of *we* (*ut supra demonstravimus*). Caesar's *he* appears at first sight to be submerged amid the other participants in the process described, and on this count has been viewed as the supreme sign of objectivity. And yet it would appear that we can make a formal distinction which impugns this objectivity. How? By making the observation that the predicates of Caesar's *he* are constantly pre-selected: this *he* can only tolerate a certain class of syntagmas, which we could call the syntagmas of command (*giving orders*, *holding court*, *visiting*, *having things done*, *congratulating*, *explaining*, *thinking*). The examples are, in effect, very close to certain cases of the performative, in which speech is inextricably associated with action. Other instances can be found for this *he* who is both a past actor and a present narrator (particularly in Clausewitz). They show that the choice of an apersonal pronoun is no more than a rhetorical alibi, and that the true situation of the utterer is clear from the choice of syntagmas with which he surrounds his past actions.

II. THE UTTERANCE

It should be possible to break down the historical utterance into units of content, which can then be classified. These units of content represent what is spoken of in the history; in so far as they are *signifieds*, they are neither the pure referent nor the discourse as a whole: their wholeness is constituted by the referent inasmuch as it has been broken down, named and rendered intelligible, but not yet made subject to a syntax. We shall not attempt to go deeply into the investigation of these classes of units in this article. Such an effort would be premature. We shall confine the discussion to a few preliminary remarks.

The historical utterance, just like the utterance in sentence form, involves both 'existents' and 'occurrents', that is beings or entities, and their predicates. Now an initial examination enables us to foresee that both of these categories, in their different ways, can form lists that are to a certain extent closed, and therefore accessible to comprehension: in a word, they can form *collections*, whose units end up by repeating themselves, in combinations that are obviously subject to variation. Thus, in Herodotus, the existents can be reduced to dynasties, princes, generals, soldiers, peoples, and places, and the occurrents to actions like laying waste, putting into slavery, making alliances, organizing expeditions, reigning, using stratagems, consulting oracles etc. These collections, in so far as they are (to a certain extent) closed, should observe certain rules of substitution and transformation and it ought to be possible to structure them – a task which is obviously more or less easy according to the historian. The units found in Herodotus, for example, depend largely on a single lexicon, which is that of war. It would be an interesting question to investigate whether, for more modern historians, we should expect to find more complex associations of different lexicons, and whether, even in this case, historical discourse would not turn out to be based, in the last resort, on strong collections (it is preferable to talk of *collections*, rather than of *lexicons*, since here we are discussing only the level of the content). Machiavelli seems to have had an intuitive understanding of this type of structure: at the beginning of the *History of Florence*, he presents his 'collection', that is to say the list of juridical, political and ethnic objects which will subsequently be mobilized and set in combination in his narrative.

In the case of less well defined collections (in historians who are less archaic than Herodotus), the units of content may nonetheless receive a strong structuring which derives not from the lexicon, but from the personal thematic of the author. These (recurrent) thematic objects are numerous in the case of a Romantic author like Michelet, but we can also find them without any difficulty in authors who are reputedly more intellectual. In Tacitus, *fama* is such a personal unit, and Machiavelli establishes his history on the thematic opposition between *mantenere* (a verb which refers to the basic energy of the statesman) and *ruinare* (which, by contrast, implies the logic of affairs in a state of decline).[7] It goes without saying that, by means of these thematic units, which are most often imprisoned within a single word, we can find units of the discourse (and not of the content alone). So we come to the problem of the naming of historical objects. The word can convey with economy a situation or a sequence of actions; it aids structuring to the extent that, when it is projected on to the level of content, it forms in itself a small-scale structure. So it is with Machiavelli's use of the *conspiracy* to save having to make fully explicit a complex datum, which designates the sole possibility of struggle remaining when a government has vanquished every form of opposition that can be displayed in the open. The very act of naming, which enables the discourse to be strongly articulated, is a reinforcement of its structure. Strongly structured histories are histories which give an important place to the substantive: Bossuet, for whom the history of men is structured by God, makes abundant use of substantives in sequence as a short-cut.[8]

These remarks are just as applicable to the occurrents as to the existents. The processes of history in themselves (however they happen to be developed through the use of terminology) pose an interesting question – among so many others, that of their status. The status of a process may be affirmative, negative or interrogative. But the status of historical discourse is uniformly assertive, affirmative. The historical fact is linguistically associated with a privileged ontological status: we recount what has been, not what has not been, or what has been uncertain. To sum up, historical discourse is not acquainted with negation (or only very rarely, in exceptional cases). Strangely enough, but significantly, this fact can be compared with the tendency which we find in a type of utterer who is very different from the historian: that is, the psychotic, who is incapable of submitting an utterance to a negative transformation.[9] We can conclude that, in a certain sense, 'objective' discourse (as in the case of positivist history) shares the situation of schizophrenic discourse. In both cases, there is a radical censorship of the act of uttering (which has to be experienced for a negative transformation to take place), a massive flowing back of discourse in the direction of the utterance and even (in the historian's case) in the direction of the referent: no one is there to take responsibility for the utterance.

To introduce another aspect, an essential aspect, of the historical utterance, we must turn to the classing of units of content, and the way in which they fall into succession. As far as a preliminary sample seems to indicate, classes of this kind are the very same as we have claimed to discover in the fictional narrative.[10] The first class comprises all the segments of the discourse which lead back to an implicit signified, through the process of metaphor; so we have Michelet describing the motley clothing, the garbling of coats of arms and the mixture of architectural styles, at the outset of the fifteenth century, as so many signifiers of a single signified, which is the disintegration of morality at the close of the Middle Ages. This particular class is therefore one of indices, or more exactly of signs (and it is a class very frequently found in the classic novel). The second class of units is formed by the fragments of discourse which are rational, or syllogistic by nature: it would perhaps be more accurate to call them enthymematic, since it is almost always a case of syllogisms which are approximate, or incomplete.[11] Enthymemes are not exclusive to historical discourse; they occur frequently in the novel, where bifurcations in the anecdote are generally justified in the eyes of the reader by pseudo-reasonings of a syllogistic type. The enthymeme confers upon historical discourse a non-symbolic intelligibility, and for this reason it deserves attention. Does it still exist in recent historical studies, where the discourse attempts to break with the classic, Aristotelian model? Lastly, there is a third class of units – which is by no means the least important – comprising what we have tended to call, after Propp, the 'functions' of the narrative, or the cardinal points whence the anecdote may adopt a different course. These functions are grouped together: they may be syntagmatically grouped in a closed succession, with a high degree of logical entailment or sequential order. Thus, in Herodotus, we can find on more than one occasion an *Oracle* sequence, composed of three terms, each of which presents an alternative (to consult or not, to answer or not, to follow or not); these may be separated one from the other by other units which are foreign to the sequence. The foreign units are either the terms of another sequence, in which case the schema is one of imbrication; or they are minor expansions (items of information, indices), in which case the schema acts as a catalyst which fills the interstices between the core elements.

To generalize – perhaps unwarrantably – from these few remarks on the structure of the utterance, we may offer the suggestion that historical discourse oscillates between two poles, according to whether it is indices or functions that predominate. When the indexical units predominate in a historian (testifying at every moment to an implicit signified), history is drawn towards a metaphorical form and borders upon the lyrical and symbolic. This is the case, for example, with Michelet. When, by contrast, it is the functional units which predominate, History takes on a metonymic form and becomes a close relation of the epic. A clear example of this tendency can be found in the narrative history of Augustin Thierry. There exists, it is true, yet another form of History: the History which tries to reproduce in the structure of the discourse the structure of the choices lived through by the protagonists of the process described. Here reasoning is dominant; the history is a reflexive one, which we might also call strategic history, and Machiavelli would be its best demonstration.

III. SIGNIFICATION

For History not to signify, discourse must be confined to a pure, unstructured series of notations. This is the case with chronologies and annals (in the pure sense of the term). In the fully formed (or, as we might say, 'clothed') historical discourse, the facts related function inevitably either as indices, or as core elements whose very succession has in itself an indexical value. Even if the facts happen to be presented in an anarchic fashion, they still signify anarchy and to that extent conjure up a certain negative idea of human history.

The signifieds of historical discourse can occupy at least two different levels. First of all, there is the level which is inherent to the matter of the historical statement. Here we would cite all the meanings which the historian, of his own accord, gives to the facts which he relates (the motley costumes of the fifteenth century for Michelet, the importance of certain conflicts for Thucydides). Into this category also fall the moral or political 'lessons' which the narrator extracts from certain episodes (in Machiavelli, or Bossuet). If the lesson is being drawn all the time, then we reach a second level, which is that of the signified transcending the whole historical discourse, and transmitted through the thematic of the historian – which we can thus justifiably identify as the form of the signified. So we might say that the very imperfection of the narrative structure in Herodotus (the product of a number of *series* of facts without conclusion) refers in the last instance to a certain philosophy of history, which is the submission of the world of men to the workings of the divine law. In the same way in Michelet, we can find that particular signifieds have been structured very strongly, and articulated in the form of oppositions (antitheses on the level of the signifier), in order to establish the ultimate meaning of a Manichean philosophy of life and death. In the historical discourse of our civilization, the process of signification is always aimed at 'filling out' the meaning of History. The historian is not so much a collector of facts as a collector and relater of signifiers; that is to say, he organizes them with the purpose of establishing positive meaning and filling the vacuum of pure, meaningless series.

As we can see, simply from looking at its structure and without having to invoke the substance of its content, historical discourse is in its essence a form of ideological elaboration, or to put it more precisely, an *imaginary* elaboration, if we can take the imaginary to be the language through which the utterer of a discourse (a purely linguistic entity) 'fills out' the place of subject of the utterance (a psychological or ideological entity). We can appreciate as a result why it is that the notion of a historical 'fact' has often aroused a certain degree of suspicion in various quarters. Nietzsche said in his time: 'There are no facts in themselves. It is always necessary to begin by introducing a meaning in order that there can be a fact.' From the moment that language is involved (and when is it not involved?), the fact can only be defined in a tautological fashion: what is noted derives from the notable, but the notable is only – from

Herodotus onwards, when the word lost its accepted mythic meaning – what is worthy of recollection, that is to say, worthy of being noted. We thus arrive at the paradox which governs the entire question of the distinctiveness of historical discourse (in relation to other types of discourse). The fact can only have a linguistic existence, as a term in a discourse, and yet it is exactly as if this existence were merely the 'copy', purely and simply, of another existence situated in the extra-structural domain of the 'real'. This type of discourse is doubtless the only type in which the referent is aimed for as something external to the discourse, without it ever being possible to attain it outside this discourse. We should therefore ask ourselves in a more searching way what place the 'real' plays in the structure of the discourse.

Historical discourse takes for granted, so to speak, a double operation which is very crafty. At one point (this break-down is of course only metaphorical) the referent is detached from the discourse, becomes external to it, its founding and governing principle: this is the point of the *res gestae*, when the discourse offers itself quite simply as *historia rerum gestarum*. But at a second point, it is the signified itself which is forced out and becomes confused with the referent; the referent enters into a direct relation with the signifier, and the discourse, solely charged with *expressing* the real, believes itself authorized to dispense with the fundamental term in imaginary structures, which is the signified. As with any discourse which lays claim to 'realism', historical discourse only admits to knowing a semantic schema with two terms, the referent and the signifier; the (illusory) confusion of referent and signified is, as we know, the hallmark of auto-referential discourses like the performative. We could say that historical discourse is a fudged up performative, in which what appears as statement (and description) is in fact no more than the signifier of the speech act as an act of authority.[12]

In other words, in 'objective' history, the 'real' is never more than an unformulated signified, sheltering behind the apparently all-powerful referent. This situation characterizes what we might call the *realistic effect*. The signified is eliminated from the 'objective' discourse, and ostensibly allows the 'real' and its expression to come together, and this succeeds in establishing a new meaning, on the infallible principle already stated that any deficiency of elements in a system is in itself significant. This new meaning – which extends to the whole of historical discourse and is its ultimately distinctive property – is the real in itself, surreptitiously transformed into a sheepish signified. Historical discourse does not follow the real, it can do no more than signify the real, constantly repeating that *it happened*, without this assertion amounting to anything but the signified 'other side' of the whole process of historical narration.

The prestige attached to *it happened* has important ramifications which are themselves worthy of historical investigation. Our civilization has a taste for the realistic effect, as can be seen in the development of specific genres like the realist novel, the private diary, documentary literature, news items, historical museums, exhibitions of old objects and especially in the massive development of photography, whose sole distinctive trait (by comparison with drawing) is precisely that it signifies that the event represented has *really* taken place.[13] When the relic is secularized, it loses its sacred character, all except for that very sacredness which is attached to the enigma of what has been, is no longer, and yet offers itself for reading as the present sign of a dead thing. By contrast, the profanation of relics is in fact a destruction of the real itself, which derives from the intuition that the real is never any more than a meaning, which can be revoked when history requires it and demands a thorough subversion of the very foundations of civilized society.[14]

History's refusal to assume the real as signified (or again, to detach the referent from its mere assertion) led it, as we understand, at the privileged point when it attempted to form itself into a genre in the nineteenth century, to see in the 'pure and simple' relation of the facts the best proof of those facts, and to institute narration as the privileged signifier of the real. Augustin Thierry became the theoretician of this narrative style of history, which draws its 'truth' from the careful attention to narration, the architecture of articulations and the abundance of expanded elements (known, in this case, as 'concrete details').[15] So the circle of paradox is complete. Narrative structure, which was originally developed within the cauldron of fiction (in myths and the first epics) becomes at once the sign and the proof of reality. In this connection, we can also understand how the relative lack of prominence (if not complete disappearance) of narration in the historical science of the present day, which seeks to talk of structures and not of chronologies, implies much more than a mere change in schools of thought. Historical narration is dying because the sign of History from now on is no longer the real, but the intelligible.

NOTES

'Le discours de l'histoire' was first published in *Social Science Information* (1967). See also the translation by Peter Wexler in Michael Lane, ed., *Structuralism: A Reader* (London, 1970), pp. 145–55.

1 Translator's note: Barthes makes frequent use in this essay of the linguistic terms: *énonciation/énoncé*. While the latter denotes a statement or proposition, the former is used to designate the act of making the statement or proposition, in speech or writing. Since this distinction is central to Barthes' purpose, and cannot easily be conveyed in any other way, I have used the two terms: act of uttering/utterance.

2 R. Jakobson, *Essais de linguistique générale* (Paris, 1963), Ch. 9.

3 Following Julia Kristeva, we designate by the term 'paragrammatism' (which is derived from the anagrams of Saussure) forms of double writing, which involve a dialogue of the text with other texts, and call for a new logic (Julia Kristeva, 'Bakhtine, le mot, le dialogue et le roman', *Critique*, 239 (April 1967), 438–65).

4 The exordium (in any form of discourse) poses one of the most interesting problems in rhetoric, to the extent that it is a codification of ways of breaking silence and combats aphasia.

5 'Avant de prendre la plume, je me suis interrogé sévèrement, et comme je ne trouvais en moi ni affections intéressées, ni haines implacables, j'ai pensé que je pourrais juger les hommes et les choses sans manquer à la justice et sans trahir la vérité' (L. Blanc, *Histoire de dix ans* (Paris, 1842)).

6 Translator's note: Barthes uses the term *contenance*, which combines the two senses of 'content' and 'countenance'.

7 Cf. E. Raimondi, *Opere di Niccolò Macchiavelli* (Milan, 1966).

8 An example: 'On y voit avant toutes choses l'innocence et la sagesse du jeune Joseph; ses songes mystérieux; ses frères jaloux; la vente de ce grand homme; la fidélité qu'il garde à son maître; sa chasteté admirable; les persécutions qu'elle lui attire; sa prison et sa constance' (Bossuet, *Discours sur l'histoire universelle*, in *Oeuvres* (Bibliothèque de la Pléiade) (Paris, 1961), p. 674).

9 L. Irigaray, 'Négation et transformation négative dans le langage des schizophrènes', *Langages*, 5 (March 1967), 84–98.

10 Cf. 'Introduction to the Structural Analysis of Narratives', in Barthes, *Image, Music, Text*, translated by Stephen Heath (London, 1977), pp. 79–124.

11 Here is the syllogistic schema in a particular passage of Michelet (*Histoire du moyen âge*, vol. III, book VI, chapter I): (1) To distract the people from revolt, it is necessary to occupy them; (2) now, the best way to do that, is to throw them a man; (3) so, the princes chose old Aubriot, etc. (Translator's note: the term 'enthymema' or 'enthymeme' has been used, from Aristotle onwards, to denote an argument based on merely probable grounds: i.e. a rhetorical as opposed to a demonstrative argument.)

12 Thiers expressed with great purity and naivety this referential illusion, or this confusion of referent and signified, thus fixing the ideal of the historian: 'Être simplement vrai, être ce que sont les choses elles-mêmes, n'être rien de plus qu'elles, n'être rien que par elles, comme elles, autant qu'elles' (quoted by C. Jullian, *Historiens français du XIX siècle* (Paris, n.d.), p. lxiii).

13 Cf. 'Rhetoric of the Image', in Barthes, *Image*, *Music*, *Text*, pp. 32–51.

14 No doubt this is the sense that we ought to give, over and beyond any case of strictly religious subversion, to the gesture of the Red Guards when they profaned the temple of the place where Confucius was born (January 1967); let us recall that the expression 'cultural revolution' is a (very bad) translation of 'destruction of the foundations of civilization'.

15 'On a dit que le but de l'historien était de raconter, non de prouver; je ne sais, mais je suis certain qu'en histoire le meilleur genre de preuve, le plus capable de frapper et de convaincre tous les esprits, celui qui permet le moins de défiance et laisse le moins de doutes, c'est la narration complète' (A. Thierry, *Récits des temps mérovingiens*, vol. II (Paris, 1851), p. 227).

The historian as taxidermist: Ranke, Barante, Waterton

STEPHEN BANN

I

What would be 'the most famous statement in all historiography'?[1] For Leonard Krieger, a recent commentator on the work of Leopold von Ranke, the answer lies unequivocally to the credit of his subject: 'History has had assigned to it the task of judging the past, of instructing the present for the benefit of ages to come. The present study does not assume such a high office; it wants to show only what actually happened (*wie es eigentlich gewesen*).'

Supplied with its appropriate glosses, and supplemented by other quotations, the 'statement' reads off the page unexceptionally enough, in spite of its celebrity. Yet we may find ourselves pausing momentarily at the point where the commentator brackets and italicizes the four-word phrase from the original German. Is this phrase included merely to recall us to the fact that the original language was indeed German? Does it hint maybe at a need for precision that is not entirely fulfilled by the English translation? Given that the latter is the case, why has this particular part of the 'statement' been singled out for special attention? Is it because it is even more 'famous' than the remainder and therefore deserves such special recognition?

These questions are not, I would submit, entirely frivolous. There are at present two accessible English versions of the full Preface from which this statement is taken. The first makes exactly the same parenthetic nod towards the original: 'It wants only to show what actually happened (*wie es eigentlich gewesen*).'[2] The second, however, diverges sharply from this practice, and leads us to conclude that the underlined 'dictum' has been singled out for special attention at the price of dismissing the real problem of interpretation which it poses. 'Indeed Ranke's oft quoted dictum, '*wie es eigentlich gewesen*', has generally been misunderstood in this country as asking the historian to be satisfied with a purely factual recreation of the past.'[3] Evidently, in the view of this authority, it is a matter of mere mistranslation. The 'dictum' is reabsorbed into the 'statement' once again. But the word *eigentlich* has been retranslated, and the prominence of this new reading is emphasized by flanking commas: 'To history has been given the function of judging the past, of instructing men for the profit of future years. The present attempt does not aspire to such a lofty undertaking. It merely wants to show how, essentially, things happened.'[4]

Let us make one tentative comment at this point. If the 'statement' or the 'dictum' within the statement is indeed so 'famous' (to take two further qualifications, 'classic',[5] and, *mea culpa*, 'time-honoured'[6]), then this is not necessarily because of what Ranke meant. It may be more accurately a question of what Ranke has been taken to mean. Our second translator stakes his case on the claim that the 'dictum', at least, has been widely misinterpreted 'in this country' – presumably America. Less circumspect opinion might go so far as to say that the misunderstanding has gone further afield. A recent attack on the premisses of traditional British historiography has used the 'dictum' to epitomize the positivism of late-nineteenth-century British historians: 'The task of the historian in Ranke's much quoted dictum, was "simply to show how it really was" – in other words to ascertain the facts.'[7] But if Gareth Stedman Jones is wrong in his translation and in his interpretation, and Messrs Iggers and Von Moltke right, then what conclusions must we draw? That Ranke's 'dictum' genuinely did become the slogan of positivist historiography, but that he himself intended something quite different? There would then be a neat distinction between the original intention and the falsifying myth, between Ranke the straw positivist 'satisfied with a purely factual recreation of the past' and the genuine Ranke who held that it is 'the emphasis on the essential that makes an account historical'.[8]

Any growing impatience of the reader at this stage may well be given expression through Herbert Butterfield's sage judgement on the matter. Without deeming it necessary to give additional currency to the 'statement' or the 'dictum', he rightly discerns that Ranke has served as a mythic repository for the attitudes of the 'new' historiography of the nineteenth century, and that his originality has in all probability been exaggerated for that reason:

> The world in general, when it discusses the basic ideas which are here in question, seems to find it useful to examine them as they are embodied in the work and views of Ranke; and possibly it is true that Ranke had the principal share in the development of the

nineteenth-century tradition. There would be grounds for saying, however, that some of the main ideas and decisions go back beyond Ranke: and this may be true to even a greater degree than is suggested below.[9]

The reminder is salutary, and impels us to define the scope of this investigation more precisely. At least since the publication of Meinecke's *Die Entstehung des Historismus* in 1959, it has been customary to view Ranke's work as the culmination of a mighty tradition of historical thinking, which arose within the specific intellectual and cultural circumstances of eighteenth-century Germany. Significantly enough, Meinecke leads us up to Ranke, through Möser, Herder and Goethe, but he does not actually discuss Ranke except as a 'supplement' to the main body of the text.[10] The inference to be drawn is clear enough. Meinecke's concern is with historical thinking, and with the nature of history itself. Ranke is the bridge through which 'Historism' passes from its period of incubation in eighteenth-century philosophy to its maturity in the historiography of the nineteenth-century. Yet, for all the importance that it accords to Ranke, this valuation tells us little about the character of Ranke's contribution to historiography. Meinecke himself admits, in the preliminary remarks which introduce his great work: 'I do not deal with the history of historical writing...but only with the history of the standards of value and formative principles in general lying at the back of all historical thought.'[11] Such a distinction is perfectly fair. But it leaves more than a mere 'supplement' for further consideration.

We thus have, on the one hand, Meinecke's Ranke, whose 'historical thought' is the culmination of an eighteenth-century German tradition. But we also have, as Butterfield implies, another very different image to contend with: that of the Ranke incorporated by Lord Acton into the British historical tradition, who has come to seem – if not to the 'world in general', at least to the historical profession – the exemplary progenitor of a 'new', professional historiography. Ranke's meta-historical pronouncements, such as they are, have had to bear the weight of this mythic load. And if we wish to understand their relevance, both to the placing of Ranke within the intellectual context of his times and to the singular tenacity of the Rankean myth, we cannot accept the alibi of Meinecke's 'Historism'. Meinecke's method, expressed in suitably Alpine imagery, was 'to undertake a kind of mountain journey along the ridges, attempting to get across from one high peak to the next, in the course of which it [would] also be possible to get glimpses of mountains and valleys that [could not] actually be visited'.[12] The present essay presumes less ideal weather conditions. It aspires simply to clear away the mist from one part of the mountain.

That there is mist around can easily be demonstrated. Let us go back to one of Ranke's most immediate and distinguished precursors, Wilhelm von Humboldt. When Humboldt lectured on 'The Historian's Task' in 1821 (three years, that is, before the publication of Ranke's Preface), he began with the following, strangely familiar statement: 'The historian's task is to present what actually happened.'[13] Our immediate reaction is to proclaim a direct source for Ranke's dictum. So – it was not even original! Yet recourse to the German text of Humboldt's lecture reveals this opening sentence: 'Die Aufgabe des Geschichtschreibers ist die Darstellung des Geschehenen.'[14] In other words, through the misleading approximations of the English translation, Ranke has succeeded in casting his shadow backwards, against time. 'What actually happened' – *wie es eigentlich gewesen*: even if we retranslate, or qualify it as mythic, we are not going to get rid of it so easily.

The interests of precision seem to dictate, at this stage, that there should be a full quotation from Ranke's original German, not merely of the 'dictum' but of the full 'statement' within which it occurs. The statement comes (as if that information were necessary) from the Preface to Ranke's first substantial historical work: *Geschichten der romanischen und germanischen Völker von 1494 bis 1514*. The Preface bears the date 'October 1824'.

> Man hat der Historie das Amt, die Vergangenheit zu richten, die Mittwelt zum Nutzen zukünftiger Jahre zu belehren, beigemessen: so hoher Aemter unterwindet sich gegenwärtiger Versuch nicht: er will bloss zeigen, wie as eigentlich gewesen.[15]

Certain obvious points arise from the detailed comparison between the original and the translation initially quoted. The 'statement' is indeed a coherent whole, not only because it is in effect a single sentence, divided by colons, but also because of the anaphora involved (and abandoned in the English) when the word *Amt* is picked up for a second time, made prominent by subject/object inversion. But the statement is also, beyond doubt, an ironical one. That is to say, the renunciation of 'so high an office' cannot fail to appear disingenuous when set in the context of Ranke's claims for the new methodology. The second part of the statement is moreover constructed as an oxymoron: *merely* to show what *essentially* happened. Is there not a piquant contrast here? And, finally, the concluding phrase can hardly be regarded other than as a conspicuous litotes. After rejecting the 'high office', Ranke proposes that he will show us 'merely' what 'essentially' happened. Is this in any way, or could it possibly be conceived as, a simple task?

That Ranke is a highly accomplished rhetorician is by no means a new case to be sustained. Indeed, attention has been specifically drawn to his use of the gap between 'books' of a work to obtain a specific rhetorical effect.[16] In an analogous, though more modest way, the closure of the paragraph with 'wie es eigentlich gewesen' here accentuates the daring of the (understated) claim. We catch in our breath, as it were, before picking up the thread of the argument: 'But whence the sources for such a new investigation?' And in that momentary interruption and resumption of discourse, we have been shifted from one realm of assertion to another. In the first paragraph, Ranke was claiming to 'show' (*zeigen*), in the second he talks about 'investigating' (*erforscht*). If Ranke has indeed taken note of the substance of Humboldt's lecture, then he has carefully ignored the fact that Humboldt is specifically making a point about representation:

> The historian's task is to present what actually happened. The more purely and completely he achieves this, the more perfectly has he solved his problem. A simple presentation [*Die einfache Darstellung*] is at the same time the primary, indispensable condition of his work and the highest achievement he will be able to attain. Regarded in this way, he seems to be merely receptive and reproductive, not himself active and creative. [*Von dieser Seite betrachtet*, *scheint er nur auffassend und wiedergebend*, *nicht selbstthätig und schöpferisch*.][17]

For Humboldt, therefore, the apparent paradox of the historian's self-effacement is resolved by the acknowledgement that it is a stylistic effect. The historian must *seem* to be 'merely receptive and reproductive'. His vocation is to aspire only to the modest fulfilment of a 'simple presentation'. We may glimpse Ranke's originality, by comparison, in the very movement from *darstellen* to *zeigen*, and in the effective elision of the question of representation which is involved.

Ranke's statement has thus become 'famous', we may be sure, not because of its explicit and understandable content, but because it represents in itself a form of evasion. It presents, with exemplary concision, the Utopia of historical discourse in the nineteenth century, which is to lie entirely outside the province of 'poetry' and of style – even in so far as style is envisaged in the self-immolating guise of Humboldt's programme. Naturally, as the century progressed, Ranke's commentators and translators were obliged to admit that the exemplary historian had, in effect, a style. But the very ways in which they make the concession indicate the paradoxical force of Ranke's formulation. Antoine Guilland, whose French *parti pris* helped him to dismiss the image of Ranke's political innocence, also took care to assert the disingenuousness of the famous statement: '"Je veux raconter simplement les choses, comme elles ont été réellement"...Il ne suffit pas, en effet, de le vouloir pour y arriver, il faut encore une grace particulière qui n'est accordée qu'à bien peu.'[18] Innocently or not, however, Guilland has re-positioned and remade his target before shooting. Ranke does not use the personalized formula of *Je veux raconter*; he chooses the impersonal *er will bloss zeigen*. To narrate, to tell a story, this is an activity which fits well within the traditional terms of representation. But what, we may ask again, is the force of *showing*? To answer this question, we must in the first place divest ourselves of the elaborate apparatus which the later nineteenth century employed to inspect the problem of truth. If Truth is, as Nietzsche like to imagine, a woman, then style is the sharp instrument which pierces the veils that conceal her.[19] Or, as Kipling put it in his clever short story 'A Matter of Fact', the only resource of the writer in possession of the remarkable story is to 'tell it as a lie': 'for Truth is a naked lady, and if by accident she is drawn up from the bottom of the sea, it behoves a gentleman either to give her a print petticoat or to turn his face to the wall and vow that he did not see.'[20] Against the orthodoxy of this position, Ranke raises up, in the days of his chivalrous youth, a redoubtable standard. For Truth, that abstract and over-extended lady, is substituted the homlier figure of Clio. And Clio, or History personified, will be revealed in untrammelled nakedness: is not the primary sense of *bloss* (*er will bloss zeigen*) precisely that of nakedness? *Eigentlich*, whether we translate it 'actually' or 'essentially', becomes no more than a means of assuring us that all the veils are off: there is not even a print petticoat for the sake of her modesty, and *a fortiori* no need of the probing style (*stylus*) to make intrusive jabs into her secret places.

Let us, however, return to the formulation of our own problem, which is, or has been up to this point, the progressive unveiling of an elusive Ranke – the Ranke of the 'statement' and the 'dictum'. There are at least two layers to be removed, it would appear, in the process of our attempt to attain that area of primary meaning. On the one hand, and clearly in view, is the Ranke of our contemporary manuals of historiography. Despite his benefit from the more exact interpretations and translations of the present period, he remains, in the last resort, problematic. After all, does it really advance us very far to replace the translation of 'actually' with 'essentially', to proffer the by no means self-explanatory statement that Ranke's concern is 'not factuality but the emphasis on the essential'?[21] Equally, we may ask if it is anything more than an outer layer of Ranke that is identified when a modern exploder of 'Historians' Fallacies' insists that the historian's business is 'not to tell what actually *was*, but what actually *happened*'.[22] Again there is the shift from 'show' to 'tell', and the consequent elision of the problem of representation, which appears crucial – by its very absence – in the celebrated statement.

A considerable further step is taken if we attempt to reconstruct a nineteenth-century viewpoint, in which it is precisely the obfuscation of this problem and the unvarnished nakedness of his Clio, that secures Ranke's standing. Tzvetan Todorov has written about the genre of the fantastic, that it is 'nothing more than the uneasy conscience of the positivist nineteenth century. But nowadays we can no longer believe in an external immutable reality, nor in a literature which would merely be the transcription of this reality. Words have gained an autonomy which things have lost.'[23] If the fantastic was the uneasy conscience of positivism, then clearly Ranke's historiography was its good conscience, held within exactly the same economy of fact and fiction but fulfilling an opposite role. This economic requirement is doubtless responsible for the fact that Ranke's highly rhetorical and indeed dramatic style, which cannot fail to strike us today, was interpreted wholly in the light of the discrimination between 'poetry' and 'fact'. As his first English translator insisted, 'A strict representation of facts, be it ever so narrow and unpoetical is, beyond doubt, the first law.'[24] Called upon further to explicate the positive characteristics of Ranke's style, the second translator made a valiant attempt to represent the *degree zero*: 'If Ranke's style was as transparent as water, it was said, it was also as tasteless.'[25] And then of course, there is the most elliptical and celebrated of all judgements on Ranke, which will require much further discussion at a later stage: Lord Acton's tribute to the historian who taught the age 'to be critical, to be colourless, and to be new'.[26]

Within the terms of this requirement, we may well find the 'primary meaning' of Ranke's modestly assertive phrase disappearing to a fine point of unintelligibility. *Er will bloss zeigen, wie es eigentlich gewesen.* Is there any way of disentangling the message from the loading which it has had to support? Certainly not, in my opinion, if we hold to the desperate project of trying to recover a meaning intended by Ranke, as if additional materal from letters and published statements would enable us to recover the plenitude of the enigmatic terms. And yet, a possibility of further inquiry does exist if we wholly reframe the questions which are asked about the Rankean text. Instead of asking: what did Ranke mean? we can pose the very different question: how was it possible for what Ranke says to be said at the time? What were the pre-conditions which made possible the emergence of this meta-historical claim at this particular period? In other words, it is not a question of vindicating a subject's 'originality' by crediting him with a 'new' formulation of the historian's task, but of asking how, within the overall economy of types of discourse, such a claim, as it happens on behalf of historiography, came to be put forward. More precisely, it is a question about the history of representation, and the singular place which 'historical' representation held within the web of representational possibilities open to the men of Ranke's time. And yet how singular a place was this? My concern is precisely to show that the apparent singularity, measured against classic notions of representation, conceals a close kinship with a stream of new, heterodox, non-mimetic forms of discourse which is already swelling by the 1820s and will have become a torrent by the end of the century.

A final point must be made, however, about the 'newness' of Ranke, or rather about the novel epistemological configuration within which his statement acquires its meaning. This study takes as its hypothesis the assumption that there is indeed a 'new history', but that its novelty cannot be assessed simply by contrast with the 'old history' of the eighteenth century. Michel Foucault has memorably argued, in *Les Mots et les choses*, that the early nineteenth century witnessed 'le grand bouleversement de l'*épistémè* occidentale',[27] and he has outlined the crucial position of historical consciousness in the radical recomposition of the map of knowledge. Above all, he has insisted that 'the lyrical halo which surrounded, at that epoch, the awareness of history, the lively curiosity for the documents of traces which time had left behind' was a reaction to an overpowering sense of loss: 'tout ceci manifeste en surface le fait nu que l'homme s'est trouvé vidé d'histoire, mais qu'il était déjà à la tâche de retrouver au fond de lui-même... une historicité qui lui fut liée essentiellement'.[28] It is the dialectic of this loss, and this retrieval, that the next section will seek to trace.

II

The question which arises could be put in the following form. At what stage, and in what domains, does the ideal of *life-like representation* achieve expression both in theoretical and practical terms? The student of the eighteenth century will instantly point out that the very notion of 'life-like representation' is a contradiction in terms. Representation is assumed, within the classicist aesthetic, to be a process of *mimesis* or imitation, in which we pass from the real to the simulated. *Vraisemblance* rather than *vérité* is the moderating criterion of this process. Nonetheless, if we examine the later eighteenth century, we find the tell-tale signs of a movement away from the paradigm of the *vraisemblable*. Étienne de Silhouette, prefacing his translations of Pope's 'Essay on Criticism' and 'Essay on Man' in 1737, expresses the aspiration 'de rendre fidèlement les pensées de M. Pope'.[29] By his death in 1767, his name has become famous throughout Europe to designate the cut-out black profiles, reduced mechanically from projected shadows, which had come into vogue. Both the ideal of 'fidelity' in translation and the technique of representation through a system which involves no mediating level of signs have this in common. They assume, at least as an ideal, the transparency of the signifier.

Of course in neither of these cases does the 'life-like' come into play. The translator's concern with a 'faithful' rendering, as opposed to the transposition from one set of conventions to another, must be largely a personal matter. Only the bi-lingual reader can judge the degree of 'fidelity' and acknowledge it with a remark like: 'This reads just like Pope.' Equally, the black cut-out of the silhouette is not likely to convince anyone of its life-like qualities, being so clearly devoid of all the characteristic features which we associated with a living person's image. But having made this point, we may well turn back and consider once again whether it is entirely convincing. Such a remark as 'This reads like Pope' – which is set within the terms of the *vraisemblable* – depends on our recognizing a functional homology between texts: the original and the translated. What if it were a question of a narrated action? In that case, the remark 'This reads like Pope' could well be replaced by the statement: 'I could really see it happening.' In the case of the silhouette, the reservation must be even stronger. We may grant that the remark 'This looks just like X' is equally applicable to the technique of the silhouette and to any other form of iconic representation, including the traditional drawing or portrait. But there is a further stage of credence which might be represented by the phrase: 'That really is X.' The example of the photograph is there to remind us that the dissimilarity between the image and 'real life' is not an obstacle to our perceiving it as more than merely *vraisemblable*: on the contrary, it is precisely the degree of abstraction in photographic reproduction, coupled with the automatic, non-mediated process involved, that establishes the image as more than a *simulacrum*. As far as the silhouette goes, it is useful to note that the physiognomic calculations of Lavater were made from the basis of silhouettes, which were thus recognized as having an epistemological status quite different from that of the conventional portrait.[30]

In both of these cases, therefore, the movement is tentatively towards a transgressive mode of representation. 'Fidelity', whether to the thoughts of an author or to the lineaments of a profile, implies a negation of the sign as sign. What is restored is not language but life, not the symbolic but the real. But it is worth asking at this stage why such a restoration is rendered necessary. What, on the anthropological level, necessitates the abandonment of the rule of mimesis, or mediated representation, so that this transgressive mode can be received? It would appear that Foucault's explanation, confronting 'le grand bouleversement de l'épistémè occidentale', is at least a plausible one. The restoration of the life-like is itself postulated as a response to a sense of loss. In other words, the Utopia of life-like reproduction depends upon, and reacts to, the fact of death. It is a strenuous attempt to recover, by means which must exceed those of convention, a state which is (and must be) recognized as lost.

A specific case from early-nineteenth-century historiography will be chosen to illustrate, in an unusually graphic way, the dynamic of this double movement. But first of all, and as a symmetrical pair to the example from historiography, there is even more striking example from another, quite different sphere. As Foucault suggests, man's sense of being 'dispossessed' of history is a response to the growing awareness that there is no unified, anthropocentric history, but rather a number of 'histories' – of language, of the natural world etc. – which do not place him at their centre. The attempt to recreate the 'life-like' in the natural world is therefore strictly analogous to the impulse towards historical recreation in the narrower sense. Both form part of the same programme, as it were, and disclose common structures of theory and practice.

In 1825, the Yorkshire Catholic squire Charles Waterton published his autobiographical account of *Wanderings in South America, the North-West of the United States and the Antilles, in the Years 1812, 1816, 1820 and 1824*; it bore the sub-title: 'With original instructions for the perfect preservation of birds etc., for cabinets of natural history'. Despite the dates given, Waterton's reminiscences go back to an earlier visit to South America, around 1808, when his system 'for the perfect preservation of birds' was first partially put into practice. Having secured, and wishing to preserve, a specimen of the toucan, he decided to take precautions against the fact that all specimens which he had previously seen had lost the brilliant blue bill which was the bird's most decorative feature in the natural state. He therefore attempted a dissection which would not merely remove the perishable parts of the bird's anatomy but would also perpetuate the brilliance of its bill. This followed two stages, which were reproduced as instructions in the text of 1825: 'You have rendered the bill transparent by the operation [of paring away the lower mandible], and that transparency must be done away to make it appear perfectly natural...[The lower mandible] must be painted blue inside. When all this is completed, the bill will please you; it will appear in its original colours.'[31] Waterton's recreation of the Toucan's beak in 1808 was, as his 1825 publication suggests, merely a prelude to the sustained and (as far as one can judge) entirely original investigation of the science of taxidermy, which indeed Waterton may be said to have pioneered. In his combative and admittedly eccentric way, he put before the early-nineteenth-century English reader the claim that all previous methods of preserving birds, insects and animals had resulted in grotesque travesties of the living original. In a fascinating paper, 'On Museums', which he published together with other essays in 1838, he asserted boldly: 'It may be said with great truth that, from Rome to Russia, and from Orkney to Africa, there is not to be found, in any cabinet of natural history, one single quadruped which has been stuffed, or prepared, or mounted (as the French term it), upon scientific principles.'[32]

Of Waterton's scientific principles, the essentials may be stated quite simply. Instead of mounting the dissected carcase on an internal frame, which would impede the natural shrinking of the skin and thus produce hideous distortions, he regularly soaked it in a solution of corrosive sublimate in alcohol. After this soaking, it was entirely manipulable, and his thorough knowledge of anatomy could be employed to reconstruct the carcase in its original state – no longer subject to shrinkage or deterioration but preserved by the invisible chemical. Yet even more fascinating than his technique, for our purposes, is the end to which this technique was directed. This was, quite simply, the end of life-like representation, the reconstitution of the beast or bird 'as it really was'. Other taxidermists had conspicuously failed at this (one wonders how incredulously they would have greeted the suggestion that they might attempt it!):

> Now should I call upon any one of these, who have given to the public a mode of preserving specimens for museums, to step forward and show me how to restore majesty to the face of a lion's skin, ferocity to the tiger's countenance, innocence to that of the lamb, or sulkiness to that of the bull, he would not know which way to set to work: he would have no resources at hand to help him in that operation...He could produce nothing beyond a mere dried specimen, shrunk too much in this part, or too bloated in that; a mummy, a distortion, an hideous spectacle, a failure in every sense of the word.[33]

By contrast, the new taxidermist could confidently attempt a hugely more impressive aspiration: 'It now depends upon the skill and anatomical knowledge of the operator (perhaps I ought to call him artist at this stage of the process), to do such complete justice to the skin before him, that, when a visitor shall gaze upon it afterwards, he will exclaim, "That animal is alive!"'[34]

Waterton's self-confidence is astounding, but his self-awareness is hardly less remarkable. Where other 'operators' have perpetuated sad *simulacra* of the natural world, Waterton claims to perpetuate the impression of life. But he can do so precisely because he has accepted the fact of death: the carcase has had to be recognized as mere malleable material for the taxidermist to work upon, and the natural colour replaced by the artificial. In this process, the guiding principle has necessarily been that of science: 'anatomical knowledge of the operator'. But it has been overtaken, with equal necessity, by the exigencies of art: 'perhaps I ought to call him artist at this stage of the process'. Waterton recognizes, however obliquely, that there is no inevitable link between the science of anatomy and the rhetoric of life-like recreation. They are bound together simply by the professional integrity of the man who is both scientist and artist. And in certain circumstances, where that integrity is outweighed by the temptation to cause mischief, the artist can have his head. He can create a monster.

While Charles Waterton was wandering in the forests of South America, and reconstituting the brilliant colouring of the toucan's bill, the young Napoleonic *sous-préfet* Prosper de Barante was making his home in the small town of Bressuire, in the depths of the Vendée. During his childhood, the events of the Vendée wars had made a strong impression on him and his arrival at Bressuire rekindled this enthusiasm. The inhabitants struck him by their conformity to 'l'ancien caractère français'.[35] In their stories, the various campaigns took on a chivalric character that made them seem closer to the period described by Froissart and his fellow chroniclers than to the contemporary devastation which Barante had witnessed as an imperial *intendant* in Germany. This interest was greatly intensified when he made the acquaintance of his country neighbour Mme de La Rochejaquelein, who had a double stake in the Vendée legend, both as the widow of Lescure and as the subsequent sister-in-law of his companion in arms, Henri de La Rochejaquelein. Writing to Mme de Stäel on 29 June 1808, Barante emphasized the pleasure which he experienced in hearing his neighbour's first-hand accounts of the campaigns. He added: 'Si je suis destiné à passer encore un an ici, je crois que j'écrirai l'histoire de la Vendée. C'est un projet qui me plait assez; celle qu'on a faite ne manque pas de vérité; mais elle n'a ni simplicité ni coloris local.'[36]

Whether Barante would ever have attempted a full-scale history of the Vendée wars is doubtful. At any rate, the opportunity soon presented itself for supplementing the existing history, published in 1806 by Alphonse de Beauchamp, with a narrative in which 'simplicity and local colour' abounded. Mme de La Rochejaquelein had contrived to escape to Spain after the defeat of her companions. There she had begun to write an account of the wars, but had left it unfinished. When she finally returned to France and married the brother of Henri, she resumed work on these *Mémoires*, taking advantage of the more settled conditions to request information and corrections from other survivors of the campaigns. As a result, the initial character of the *Mémoires* was transformed. It had begun as a strictly personal account, but the accumulating material gave it the potential to be a more accurate and comprehensive contribution to the history of the Vendée wars. Prosper de Barante, with his revived enthusiasm for the subject, presented himself as the ideal person to review the manuscript, incorporate the supplementary notes into the body of the work and generally undertake the conversion of an important primary source into a coherent historical account. But he did so while seeking to preserve the personal character of the manuscript. The qualities which Mme de La Rochejaquelein supplied were not to be cancelled out in the search for objectivity; on the contrary, they were to be enhanced. As he wrote to Mme Récamier on 24 December 1808:

> Je vous ai mandé que j'avais commencé à copier ces mémoires de la Vendée. C'est une excellente occupation; assez mécanique sauf qu'elle m'intéresse. Je n'y change rien. Je craindrais d'altérer en quelque chose la parfaite candeur et l'élévation toute simple qui y règnent. Ce n'est pas un ouvrage, c'est des sentimens et des faits, que ces mémoires. Il n'y a pas trace d'art, de but, de considération du public.[37]

In effect, Barante's modesty belies the importance of the task which he had undertaken. Work on the text of the *Mémories* was to occupy a large part of his spare time for almost a year, and the painstaking review of additional testimonies was especially time-consuming. In one sense, he had done nothing more than to counterfeit, with elaborate care, the memoir which Mme de La Rochejaquelein would have written if she had been preserved from the fallibility of an ordinary eye-witness. But in another sense – the only valid one from his point of view – he had aided the engenderment of a valid history. He had enabled the through passage of 'des sentimens et des faits', rather than overlaying them with the falsifying devices of historiographic convention. He was bearing constantly in mind the erroneous model which both he and his source of information identified in the history of Alphonse de Beauchamp, as the following letter from Mme de La Rochejaquelein makes clear:

[Beauchamp] n'a point changé sa troisième édition. Je doute que la quatrième puisse jamais être bonne dans le genre que vous préférez. Il ne descendra pas de son échafaudage. Il a fait le portrait d'Henri en médaille antique coiffé à la Titus, et, ne sachant comment le vêtir, il lui a coupé le col.[38]

Reference to the particular issue of the characterization of Henri de La Rochejaquelein makes it possible for us to consider, in more detailed terms, the issue which preoccupied both Barante and his correspondent. We may compare the 'entry', and brief description, of the Vendée hero in three distinct sources: the history of Alphonse de Beauchamp, the original, uncorrected account of Mme de La Rochejaquelein and the final text of the *Mémoires* after Barante's attentions:

Beauchamp
Un chef célèbre dans le parti royaliste parut alors sur ce théâtre de carnage.

La Rochejaquelein, fils de l'ancien colonel du regiment royal Pologne, demeurant à Saint-Aubin de Baubigné, près Châtillon, s'était mis à la tête des insurgés de son territoire. Jeune, d'un tempérament vigoureux, l'œil vif, le né [*sic*] aquilin, la mine guerrière, il semblait né pour les combats. Destiné à jouer un rôle brillant dans l'ancien régime, il crut pouvoir défendre le trône dans la garde constitutionelle de Louis XVI. Le 10 Aout renversa ses espérances. Ce fut alors qu'au moment de quitter Paris, il dit: 'Un royaliste n'a plus rien à faire ici, j'irai dans ma province, où bientôt on entendra parler de moi.' Il émigra, rentra peu après dans le Poitou, et enfin prit part à l'insurrection. Son coup d'essai fût une victoire.[39]

Mme de La Rochejaquelein
Je veux commencer par tracer le portrait d'Henri de La Rochejaquelein, que j'augmenterai dans la suite, son caractère s'étant singulièrement développé par la guerre. Il avait cinq pieds sept pouces; extrêmement mince et blond, une figure allongée, il paraissait plutôt Anglais que Français. Il n'avait pas de jolis traits, mais la physiognomie douce et noble. Dans ce temps-là il avait l'air fort timide; on remarquait cependant des yeux très vifs, qui depuis sont devenus si fiers et si ardents qu'on disait qu'il avait un regard d'aigle. Il était excessivement adroit et leste, montait à cheval à merveille. C'était un bon sujet, sévère sur ses devoirs.[40]

Mme de La Rochejaquelein/Barante
M. Henri de La Rochejaquelein étatit enfin parvenu à s'échapper de Paris; tout sa famille avait émigré; il se trouvait seul au château de la Durbelière... Henri de La Rochejaquelein avait alors vingt ans. C'etait un jeune homme assez timide, et qui avait peu vécu dans le monde; ses manières et son langage laconique étaient remarquables par la simplicité et le naturel; il avait une physiognomie douce et noble; ses yeux, malgré son air timide,

paraissaient vifs et animés; depuis, son regard devint fier et ardent. Il avait une taille élevée et svelte, des cheveux blonds, un visage un peu allongé, et une tournure plutôt anglaise que française. Il excellait dans tous les exercices du corps, surtout à monter à cheval.[41]

It will be clear from this comparison that much more is at stake, for Barante, than the implicit correction of an inaccurate source. He does, indeed, correct Beauchamp's inaccurate statement that La Rochejaquelein briefly joined the emigration. But his most evident concern is to preserve and enhance the invaluable personal reminiscence of Mme de La Rochejaquelein. As she perceptively described it, Beauchamp had constructed a Henri all of one piece, in a classical mould: 'médaille antique coiffé à la Titus'. Her own account, by contrast, stresses the crucial fact that Henri was changed by his very experience of the wars; his appearance and character, moreover, were made up of conflicting, even incongruous elements. Barante has taken care to extract the 'scaffolding' of this primary testimony: the *incipit* 'Je veux commencer par tracer' is missing, as is the equivocal and superfluous last sentence. But the nuances of his source are all there, and the composite 'portrait' finely and economically drawn.

It is not difficult to sketch in the immediate intellectual context of Barante's historiographic enterprise. In 1808, his close friend Benjamin Constant had been wrestling with the problem of translating Schiller's *Wallstein* for the French theatre, and lamenting the intolerable pressures of classicist convention: 'Je ne connais pas de naturel en tout que les nuances, mais, en France, il y a pour le théâtre un certain nombre de moules à caractères... Les couleurs locales ne leur plaisent pas du tout, et les moeurs de tous les siècles doivent être celles convenues au théâtre.'[42] In the reaction of Barante, Constant and other members of the circle of Mme de Stäel against the stereotypes of classicism, history had already come to have a particular value. It served, in the simplest terms, as a principle of *difference*, a panacea against the totalitarian oscillation 'from the same to the same'. Barante, the imperial official reconstructing the testimony of a die-hard royalist, put into the apparently self-abnegating role of the re-writer of the *Mémoires* the lessons of a thorough training in the Romantic school of 'le naturel'. But he also expressed there a deep sense of the necessity to conserve the otherness of the past. We have already considered the specifications for the ideal historian laid down by Mme de Stäel's friend and intellectual ally, Wilhelm von Humboldt: 'A simple presentation is at the same time the primary, indispensable condition of his work and the highest achievement he will be able to attain. Regarded in this way, he seems to be merely receptive and reproductive, not himself active and creative.' Whether or not Humboldt was aware of the *Mémoires*, it seems obvious that these words could have been applied directly to Barante's achievement. He had not only delighted his source by producing a new version which she still recognized as her own, but he had established the conditions under which he was finally to disappear completely from the authorial scene. As his friend Charles de Rémusat put it later in the century, 'Rien ne sent moins l'auteur que ces Mémoires.'[43] By this time, Barante's name had disappeared from the title-page and indeed ceased to be associated with the work.

The adventitious nature of my juxtaposition of the historian and the taxidermist will doubtless have already made its point. Waterton repudiates a method of reconstruction which has filled museums of natural history with travesties of natural life. Mme de La Rochejaquelein, and Barante, sense the incongruity of a historical style which constructs its heroes according to a preconceived pattern of what a hero should be. To Waterton's 'mere dried specimen, shrunk too much in this part, or too bloated in that' corresponds Mme de La Rochejaquelein's 'médaille antique coiffé à la Titus' whose throat has been cut for want of any principle of animation. Waterton's radical approach provides for the dissection and reduction of the living thing to a shapeless skin, and its reconstruction, through science and corrosive sublimate, to the point where the visitor will exclaim: 'That animal is alive!' Barante's technique is to animate from within, as it were, the fragmented text of Mme de La Rochejaquelein and to give it a life in which his own science is totally obliterated. Thus the critic Alfred Nettement writes in 1858 of the constantly republished work: 'Ces mémoires feront vivre éternellement l'époque et le pays qui y sont peints avec des couleurs si vives et des traits si naturels qu'on croit voir respirer les personnages, les mœurs, la Vendée toute entière...C'est la nature prise sur le fait, c'est la vérité dite sans reticence, sans ambages, sans ornement.'[44] The naked Clio, once again, and with a vengeance.

Let us, however, be circumspect about making too close an equation between Waterton and Barante. The taxidermist who parenthetically admitted the role of 'artist' to be more applicable to the process of reconstruction than that of simple 'operator' is indeed capable of engendering monsters. As a frontispiece to the *Wanderings*, he illustrates the most celebrated and bizarre of these: the so-called 'Nondescript' which consists of a monkey's carcase cunningly manipulated to ape the expression on the face of a learned judge. For Waterton, the exacerbation of his social and political life was at time too acute for the scientific conscience. Having possessed himself of the appropriate technique for making the dead live again, he could use this power to confute a political opponent or satirize the degeneracy of Hanoverian England. Indeed it is arguable that Waterton's veritable obsession with life-like representation has its pathological correlative in a fascination with monsters – with the composite, incongruous beast which yet simulated the seamless integrity of organic life. In this connection, it is worth pointing out that his most bitter polemic, which dogged his entire scientific career, was in defence of the claim that he had ridden on the back of a cayman: or more precisely, in defence of the authenticity of an illustration representing this feat, in which the naturalist and the reptile are incongruously clasped together.

No further reference is necessary to indicate Waterton's kinship with the pervasive Romantic fantasy of the human creator, who usurps the divine prerogative. The period which saw the publication of Mary Shelley's *Frankenstein* was well qualified to sense the ambiguities in any human preoccupation with the recreation of life. But we may well ask at this stage how the monstrous *double face* of the new taxidermy relates to the new history. How does the risk of monstrosity occur to the historian, if at all? Once the question is posed in this way, an obvious answer suggests itself. Let us grant that the historian, like the taxidermist, is conscious of the power which his technique offers him over the dissected carcase of the historic past: the precondition of his new concern with recreation is precisely the sense of being 'dispossessed' of history to which Foucault alludes. He will therefore have to situate somewhere, even if not in the historian's practice, the possibility of using the rhetoric of recreation to dubious ends. And a notorious culprit is there to be arraigned: the author of *Waverley*, Sir Walter Scott.

Considered in this way, the evident perturbation caused by Scott within a whole generation of historians acquires a full significance. Ranke relates in his autobiography that, after reading *Quentin Durward*, he 'took the resolution to avoid, in [his] works, all imagination and all invention and to restrict myself severely to the facts'.[45] The very anxiety to establish this distinction between 'all' imagination and invention, on the one hand, and on the other the facts, is of course the evidence of a desire to repress the rhetorical status of historical writing – a desire which Ranke so effectively transmitted to his successors. For Macaulay, on the other hand, the monstrosity is already an intertextual fact; contemporary readers are already obliged to look 'for one half of King James in Hume and for the other half in the Fortunes of Nigel'[46] (Scott's Jacobean novel). The historian's business is therefore to aspire, at least, to recovering the mythic wholeness of the historical *disjecta membra*. If the German and the English historians express their reserve in general terms, it is left to a French historian to meet Scott promptly on his own ground. Prosper de Barante, whose success in divesting Henri de La Rochejaquelein of his classical garb has already been mentioned, was already at work on his *Histoire des Ducs de Bourgogne* when he read the French translation of *Quentin Durward*. An exchange of letters with his fellow historian François Guizot resulted in unqualified agreement on Scott's misrepresentation of the character of Louis XI. As Guizot expressed it, Scott had committed the same fault as Beauchamp with the hero of the Vendée: 'Walter Scott a conçu un type plutôt qu'il n'a peint un individu.'[47] By contrast, Guizot's response to the successive volumes of Barante's history showed a ready acknowledgement of his success: 'Votre Louis XI m'a charmé; pour la première fois je l'ai vu tel que je l'avois un peu entrevu.'[48] The critic of the *Journal des Débats* went even further in proclaiming his achievement: 'Sous la plume de M. de Barante, la narration devient une action visible. Son Louis XI parle et agit comme sur le théâtre même où s'est accomplie sa haute destinée.'[49]

Our comparative pursuit of taxidermy and historiography therefore returns us to a more thorough investigation of the problem of life-like representation, whether enunciated by a historian or proclaimed in the press. To single out, as comparable cases, the 'mounted' specimen of natural history and the 'narrated' specimen of the illustrious past, is to pose in more insistent terms the question of the text in which the latter is inserted. For Waterton, after all, there is an institutional boundary. The museum of natural history (and indeed, in another way, the nature reserve which Waterton himself pioneered) defines the field within which the specimen must appear 'life-like'. For the collector of historical objects, as I have attempted to show elsewhere, the problem is strictly analogous. The creator of the Musée de Cluny, Étienne du Sommerard, rehabilitated the diverse historical objects of his collection through arranging them in separate rooms which evoked a complex picture of 'medieval life'.[50] But for the historian proper, the extrapolation is not possible. It is therefore a question of searching more diligently for the terms of representation as they are conveyed within the text: that is to say, within the intertextuality composed of the history, the 'meta-historical' essay and the article of critical response. As anticipated in the first section of this study, it is a question of scrutinizing the modes of representation to which the nineteenth-century historian declares his affinity, and rediscovering the undisclosed affinities which eluded his awareness.

III

Having begun this essay with an allusion to 'the most famous statement in all historiography', let me open its concluding section with the almost equally famous statement which characterizes Ranke's mythic status as the pioneer of modern historiography. In his 'Inaugural Lecture on the Study of History', delivered in June 1895, Lord Acton pronounced: 'Ranke is the representative of the age which instituted the modern study of History. He taught it to be critical, to be colourless, and to be new.'[51] A few years later, introducing his new translation of the *Latin and Teutonic Nations* to the British public, E. Armstrong gave what was no doubt intended to be a gloss on the 'colourless' aspect of the Master's teaching: 'Ranke probably never aimed at being a colourist; his natural gift was that of an artist in black and white, or at most in tinted line. Nevertheless, when he takes up the palette, he shows a fine and delicate sense for atmosphere and texture, the result less of technical skill than of imaginative indwelling in his subject.'[52] The translator's note is, at first sight, curiously incoherent. What exactly would be 'an artist in black and white'? How does this notion, or that of 'tinted line', square with the classical image of the painter taking up the palette, on which the full range of oil colours are conventionally arrayed? Again, what is the force of the antithesis between 'technical skill' and 'imaginative indwelling', if it is something more than the mere depreciation of technique and style which we have already witnessed as a cliché of the Romantic period? These questions can be answered indirectly, at least, if we assume that the apparent incoherence is a sign of endemic disturbance within the field of representation to which reference is being made. In short, the translator is taking his metaphors from a domain which has been rendered problematic by the intrusion of photography into the traditional spectrum of the visual arts. 'An artist in black and white' – did not the great painter Degas proclaim towards the end of his life, in 1906: 'If I could live my life again, I should do nothing but black and white.'[52] 'Colour' and 'tinted line' – it is worth bearing in mind that, until 1907 precisely, when the Lumière brothers pioneered a primitive form of colour photography known as the 'autochrome', photography could only acquire colour through tinting. 'Atmosphere and texture', 'less of technical skill than of imaginative indwelling in his subject' – are not the criteria close to those which defined the new method of capturing and perpetuating the image of the real world on a light-responsive plate?

What I would argue is that Armstrong's metaphors, and indeed Acton's adjective – applied as they are around the turn of the century – plunge us back once again into the ferment in representation which characterized the Europe of the 1820s: the decade of Niepce's first photographic image (1822) and Daguerre's historical diorama (1823) as well as of Ranke's Preface. But the connection between these disparate form of representation cannot, of course, be appreciated simply from the synchronic study of phenomena which appear to occupy the same epistemological space. We need to go back further into the history of representation if we are to understand in what sense to take the 'colour' references, whether admitted or repressed, in the historical or meta-historical text. As classic a formulation as we are likely to find, and one which is germane to the whole context which has been developed here, is the definition of types of perspective offered by Leonardo:

> There are three sorts of perspective: the first is related to the causes of diminution or, as it is known, the diminishing perspective of objects according to their distance from the eye. The second is the way in which colours are modified as they get further from the eye. The third and last consists in the definition of how objects must be depicted with less and less precision as they get further and further away.[54]

What must be stressed about the relation of colour to perspective implied in Leonardo's scheme is the fact that colour is necessarily conceived as subordinate. It is a property of bodies, which alters according to their respective placing within the perspectival recession. Yet, as Jean-Louis Schefer has argued, the history of painting since the eighteenth century has been that of the gradual emancipation of colour both from figuration and from perspective. Already in the eighteenth century, with Goya and Watteau, 'the quantum invested in colour displaces and tends to continually annul the quantum in implicitness, the system of figures'.[55] From playing a merely distinctive and differential role within the Renaissance system of representation, colour has itself come to characterize the modern reversal of that system: a reversal which is exactly conveyed in the contrast between Leonardo's repression of colour as such and the crucial value attached by Cézanne to his 'petite sensation colorante'.[56]

Yet what may appear at first sight as a specific trait of the history of painting turns out to have a much more pervasive influence within the development of representation in the more general sense, Post-Renaissance painting is, as Schefer has again argued, a scenography:[57] it therefore shares with theatrical representation the system of geometrical construction according to a unique vanishing point. Moreover, the vocabulary proper to painting plays, within the theoretical writings of classicism, a colonizing role. Consequently we find that the term 'colour' is a constellation which brings together the threads of the aesthetic conflict which, in the middle of the eighteenth century, already anticipated the battle of Classicism and Romanticism. Marmontel, seeking to identify the difference between Greek tragedy and that of his countrymen Racine and Voltaire, chooses his metaphors directly from painting: 'dans le grec, on verra des couleurs fortes, mais entières, sans reflets et sans demi-teintes; dans le français, mille nuances qui, loin d'affaiblir la peinture, ne la rendent que plus vivante, plus variée et plus sensible.'[58] Marmontel is, of course, speaking at this point of the literary text. But the priority of painting as an aesthetic pace-setter is also fully demonstrated in his concern with costume and *mise-en-scène*. Pursuing his mock dialogue with the exponent of classicist convention, he asks:

> Comment les habillerait un grand peintre? Il faut donner, dit-on, quelque chose au moeurs de son temps. Il fallait donc aussi que Lebrun frisât Porus et mit des gants à Alexandre. C'est au spectateur à se déplacer, non au spectacle; et c'est la réflexion que tous les acteurs devraient faire à chaque rôle qu'ils vont jouer: on ne verrait point paraître César en perruque carrée, ni Ulysse sortir tout poudré du milieu des flots.[59]

In making a catachresis out of Caesar and his wig, Marmontel pours ridicule precisely on the historical anomaly of conventional costume. And, through whatever vicissitudes of 'fidelity' Talma and his successors might lead it, the principle to be known as 'couleur locale' gained ground irreversibly throughout the revolutionary and imperial epochs. But it is important to note the force of Marmontel's succinct statement: 'it is for the spectator to be displaced, and not the spectacle'. Such an implication does not merely involve the search for authentic costume and *mise-en-scène* – which, after all, can only be judged by the ill-informed spectator in terms of their absolute divergence from his own experience of everyday life or of the stage. It also indicates, as a project, the possibility of exceeding the norms of *vraisemblance*, of literally taking the spectator out of his place through overpowering illusion. Confronted with Daguerre's diorama, the young spectator of the late 1820s can only exclaim his incredulity:

> 'I thought it was to be only a picture,' said Edward; 'but they must be real rocks and mountains, made on purpose!'

> '*It is only a picture*,' replied Mr Finsbury. 'To convince yourself of this, you have only to change your position in the room, and you will see the objects are seen in exactly the same way, go where you will. For instance, there is a projection *represented* of a piece of rock in front. If a real projection, by moving across the apartment, you will see a little this way or that of the object behind it; but you find that it is in vain that you rise from your seat, or stoop, or go from side to side; nothing different can be seen. It must, therefore, be a plain surface.'[60]

Edward is hardly convinced, for the scene shifts finally and he protests: 'Oh, this *must be* a real town!' His insistence, and the advice of Mr Finsbury on how to reassure oneself of the representational status of the image, recalls us to the ambiguities and indeed contradictions in the sequence of developments which has been traced. For Daguerre's diorama, so far from epitomizing the 'spilling' of colour within the representational system, is in effect the direct descendant of Leonardo's perspectival scheme. It is strictly dependent, as Mr Finsbury's advice demonstrates, on the establishment of a single viewpoint. It makes it a matter of intellectual proof for the image to be diagnosed as 'paper and colours' rather than 'posts, boards, tiles, stones, utensils, a roadway'. Through an extraordinarily ingenious combination of front and back illumination, it floods the image with an overall luminosity which contradicts the very principle of 'couleur locale' in its proper sense: '*Couleur locale*, en peinture, est la couleur propre à chaque objet, indépendamment de la distribution particulière de la lumière et des ombres.'[61]

We therefore arrive at a conclusion which appears, at any rate, to contradict the tentative conclusions of my first section. What may seem to be the 'heterodox' representation of the diorama turns out to be the reinforcement of traditional schemata through new techniques. And yet there is still the problem of colour, 'local colour' or 'spilling' colour, in the system. Obviously the definition just quoted represents an antithetical term: the object, in painting, will never have its own colour entirely to the exclusion of 'the distribution of light and shade', but will always be more or less 'local' in its colouring. But the use of the term as a slogan by the Romantics does at least involve a transgressive intention: to proceed as far as possible in the direction of the individual and the particular at the expense of the general. Equally, Schefer's concept, which of course anticipates the 'emancipation' of colour from figure and perspective in the present century, embodies the Utopia of a colour not merely local in the object, but asserting its own materiality irrespective of all systematic constraint. Is there any significant parallel to this sense within the field of representation which has been under discussion? More particularly, can we now return to the immediate province of historiography and find comparable distinctions which will enable us to place more exactly both the 'colourless' virtue of Ranke, and the epistemological configuration within which it has its place?

The prelude to any resolution of this question is, of course, a reference to the way in which historical representation was conceived in the eighteenth century. Here, again, the *encyclopédiste* Marmontel is revealingly explicit. Despite the conventional definition of the historian's role in the terms of Herodotus, he devotes most of his attention to spatializing the historical field according to the metaphor of pictorial perspective. Invoking 'les points de perspective que les écrivains se proposent', he conceptualizes the relation to the past in terms which echo Leonardo's definition: 'Plus la postérité pour laquelle on écrit est reculée, plus l'intérêt des détails diminue...Il n'y a que les peuples célèbres et les hommes vraiment illustres, dont les particularités domestiques soient intéressantes encore à une certaine distance.'[62] An immediate consequence of this model is the repression of colour, conceived as the positive and personal element of the historian's style, and the metaphor of transparency comes to hand: 'Quelqu'un a dit que pour *l'historien*, le meilleur style étoit celui qui ressembloit à une eau limpide. Mais s'il n'a point de couleur à soi, il prendra naturellement celle de son sujet, comme le ruisseau prend la teinture du sable qui forme son lit.'[63]

Prefiguring of historical space in terms of receding perspective, repression of colour as the trace of the author's style – what is the third element which, in Leonardo's terms, gives this conception its coherence? Clearly, it is the eye of the painter which, in a quasi-theological sense, ordains the perspectival system and enables the spectator to take his place there vicariously. Hence the subject who was expelled in the name of colourlessness returns to guarantee the system from his unique point of view. Marmontel can speak of the way in which the historical writer 's'impose la tâche pénible d'embrasser d'un coup d'oeil tout ce qu'un siècle lui présente d'intéressant pour l'avenir'.[64] Note that the criterion of 'interest for the future' sets the seal upon the coherence of the system. The receding perspective departs from, and returns to, the ordaining eye: the 'vanishing point' in the picture is no more than a necessary theoretical consequence of the external, ideal subjectivity.

It is indeed striking how tenaciously the young Macaulay, in his 1828 essay on 'History', holds to this traditional view of historical representation. Not only does he defend it, but he explicitly rejects the temptation to claim for historiography a more secure epistemological grounding. For him, history is not concerned with the naked Clio, truth as 'one' and admitting of 'no degrees'. It can observe only 'the truth of imitation in the fine arts'.[65] To illustrate this point, Macaulay chooses to compare the portrait of 'a handsome peeress' by Sir Thomas Lawrence with the same lady as revealed by 'a powerful microscope' which would disclose 'the pores of the skin, the blood-vessels of the eye'. Of course the example is disconcertingly revealing in its avoidance of the scientific paradigm. The subject (the peeress) is given, and the requirement is not for a critical instrument which will disturb this imaginary coherence in the interests of knowledge, but simply for a confirmation of a conventional status. Significantly, Macaulay develops his parallel in terms which juxtapose, as metaphors of historical representation, the avoidance of colour and the establishment of perspective:

A bust of white marble may give an excellent idea of a blooming face. Colour the lips and cheeks of the bust, leaving the hair and eyes unaltered, and the similarity, instead of being more striking, will be less so. History has its foreground and its background; and it is principally in the management of its perspective that one artist differs from another. Some events must be represented on a large scale, others diminished; the great majority will be lost in the dimness of the horizon; and a general idea of their joint effect will be given by a few slight touches.[66]

Of course, the necessary implication of this problematic of 'diminishment' and 'dimness' is the reinforcement of the single point of view as the guarantee of perspective: in Leonardo's words, 'Perspective comes to our aid where our judgement is at fault with regard to things which recede and diminish.' Such a remark may illuminate obliquely the significance of the 'Whig view of history'. By contrast, the problematic which Augustin Thierry develops in the Preface to his *Histoire de la conquête de l'Angleterre par les Normands* (1825) seems to be designed specifically to confute the traditional conception which Macaulay defends. The single-point perspective is superseded by the requirement of local colour:

In the present day, however, it is no longer permissible to write history for the profit of one single idea; our age will not sanction it; it requires to be told everything, to have portrayed and explained to it the existence of nations at various epochs; and that each past century shall have assigned to it its true place, its colour, and its signification.[67]

Thierry remains implicitly within the pictorial metaphor at this stage, causing a direct reversal of the perspectival scheme. But his concluding remarks go far beyond this rhetorical level. Simultaneously Thierry asserts the 'scientific' commitment which Macaulay disclaimed, and the need to place the problem of 'colour' on the level of the signifier, in the very names and linguistic forms which find their place in the historical narrative:

I have only now to mention one other historical innovation, of no less importance than the rest; the retaining the orthography of the Saxon, Norman, and other names, so as to keep constantly marked out the distinction of races, and to secure the local colouring which is one of the conditions, not merely of historic interest, but of historic truth. I have, in like manner, taken care not to apply to one period the language, forms, or titles of another. In a word, I have essayed thoroughly to reintegrate political facts, details of manners, official forms, languages, and names; so as, by restoring to each period comprised in my narrative its external aspect, its original features, its reality, to communicate to this portion of history the certitude and fixity which are the distinguishing characteristics of the positive sciences.[68]

Where then does Ranke belong within the polarity of Macaulay and Thierry? On the one hand, there is no doubt that he represses, as strongly as Macaulay, the question of 'colour'. Indeed this *lapsus*, which Thierry would legitimately lead us to associate with an attention to the historical name as signifier, causes him to repeat, towards the end of his life, the fantasy of evacuating the text of Scott which Macaulay disclosed in 1828. 'But a truly great historian', writes Macaulay, 'would reclaim those materials which the novelist has appropriated.'[69] Only a few weeks before his death (according to his first English translator), Ranke was regretting that Scott 'was not more available for the purposes of a historian than he is...What valuable lessons were not to be drawn from facts to which the great English novelist had the key; yet, by reason of the fault to which I have referred, I have been unable to illustrate many of my assertions by reference to him.'[70] The notion of a Scott with footnotes, sedulously split again in the apparatus of Ranke's own footnotes and references, is a comic but an intensely revealing one. The designation 'colourless' does indeed conceal an absolute dedication to the binary division between 'facts' and 'style', and a consistent repression of the signifying level of the historian's discourse.

Yet Ranke is not, quite evidently, espousing the categories of imitation and the metaphor of perspective as Macaulay does. The elliptical statement which with this essay began testifies beyond doubt to that fact. The 'high office' abjured is, at one level, the perspectival viewpoint.[71] The aim to 'show what actually happened' is breathtakingly free of the circumspection of *mimesis*. Indeed my references to the ideal of 'life-like' representation, in taxidermy, in the diorama and in the daguerreotype, have been largely devoted to establishing a representational space in which Ranke's claim could be seen to have meaning: a space in which new techniques were explicitly devoted to securing an overpowering illusion of presence. But I would wish to repeat here the reservation about the 'novelty' of this aim, which can more appropriately be seen as an intensification, through technique, of the conditions of representation implicit in Renaissance perspective. In this light, the 'colourless' virtue of Ranke can be seen as the denial of language, of the historical signifier, and his nineteenth-century reputation (which still persists) as the mythic enhancement of this denial. By comparison, the relative undervaluation of Thierry, despite his strict contemporaneity with Ranke, should be assessed in the light of his determination to assert simultaneously the claims of science and of language.

Such, at any rate, is the hypothesis of this essay. In so far as it attempts to demythologize the tenacious myth which has attached to Ranke's 'dictum', it must also embody a more constructive purpose: that of extracting Ranke from *Historismus* and the perspectival viewpoint, and giving him a central role (with Thierry, and Barante, and Scott) in the drama of the loss and retrieval of 'historicity' which Foucault outlines. Such a purpose would seek to understand historical representation more fully by considering its multiple affiliations and connections within the other strategies of representation – visual and linguistic – which are characteristic of the nineteenth century. But its efficacy would not be merely retrospective. The Oxford philosopher, Alan Montefiore, once remarked that it was impossible to account for the deep divergence between contemporary philosophers in Britain and France without returning to the source of the divergence in two alternative readings of Kant. In a similar way, we can best understand the character of current French historiography – the *Annales* school which, with Le Roy Ladurie's *Montaillou*, has recently usurped our market – by retracing their descent from Thierry and Michelet, among many others. 'To show how, essentially, things happened' was a noble undertaking, which anchored its author within the epistemological context of his times, and continues to merit our most careful study. But the phrase has now become, in its mythic fixity, a head of Medusa, petrifying the impulse to meta-historical inquiry. One has only to look at the many-sided, but coherent, achievement of the *Annales* school to realize how much more various are the claims of a creative modern historiography.

NOTES

1 Leonard Krieger, *Ranke: The Meaning of History* (Chicago and London, 1977), p. 4.
2 Fritz Stern (ed.), *The Varieties of History from Voltaire to the Present*, second edition (London, 1970), p. 57.
3 Georg C. Iggers and Konrad von Moltke (eds.), *The Theory and Practice of History: Leopold von Ranke* (New York, 1973), p. xix.
4 *Ibid.*, p. 137.
5 David Hackett Fischer, *Historians' Fallacies* (London, 1971), p. xix.
6 Stephen Bann, 'Historical Text and Historical Object: The Poetics of the Musée de Cluny', *History and Theory*, 17:3 (1978), 265.
7 Gareth Stedman Jones, 'History: The Poverty of Empiricism', in *Ideology in Social Science*, edited by Robin Blackburn (London, 1972), p. 97.
8 Iggers and von Moltke, *Theory and Practice*, pp. xix–xx.
9 Herbert Butterfield, *Man on his Past: The Study of the History of Historical Scholarship* (Cambridge, 1969 reprint), p. xv.
10 The 'supplement' consists of a 'Memorial Address' concerning Ranke, which was originally given on 23 January 1936 at the Preussische Akademie der Wissenschaften.
11 Friedrich Meinecke, *Historism: The Rise of a New Historical Outlook*, translated by J. E. Anderson (London, 1972), p. lx.
12 *Ibid.*, p. lviii.
13 Wilhelm von Humboldt, 'The Historian's Task', translated in *History and Theory*, 6:1 (1967), 56–71.
14 Humboldt, *Werke*, 5 vols. (Darmstadt, 1960), I, 585.
15 Leopold von Ranke, *Geschichten der romanischen und germanischen Völker von 1494 bis 1514*, second edition (Leipzig, 1874), p. vii.
16 Cf. Peter Gay, *Style in History* (London, 1975): chapter 2 is devoted to Ranke.
17 Humboldt, 'The Historian's Task', p. 56. I am aware that I may be accused, at this point, of creating an artificial distinction between the approaches of Humboldt and Ranke, and allowing my case to rest upon selective quotations and dubious linguistic distinctions. This hypothetical accusation requires a clear statement in response. On the one hand, I would not wish to minimize the indebtedness of Ranke to Humboldt, and the significance of their common adherence to the German tradition of historical thinking. It would not be difficult to select passages from Humboldt's address, for example those which relate to the poetic and creative vocation of the historian, which Ranke would have assented to with enthusiasm. My concern, however, is not to emphasize the common elements, but to identify what seem to me to be the significant, even if apparently minute, points of difference. This is where the difference between *darstellen* and *zeigen* comes in. Evidently these words could, in a particular circumstance, be used as synonyms. The dictionary, however gives as meanings for *darstellen*: represent, depict, delineate, exhibit, limn, portray, and for *zeigen*: show, point out, indicate, exhibit, display. *Darstellen* is thus a term whose shades of meaning adhere, for the most part, to a traditional mimetic formula of representation. *Zeigen* is more appropriately used for direct *showing*, unmediated by a code or system of transcription. In terms of Peirce's semiotics, we could say that *darstellen* covers the 'iconic' and 'symbolic' sign, whereas *zeigen* involves also – and preeminently – the 'indexical' dimension.

Nevertheless, I would not wish to lay too much emphasis on the assertion that Ranke *intended* to load his dictum with this new significance. What I am arguing is that, in 1824, the difference between *darstellen* and *zeigen makes sense* – provided that we relate it to the crisis in representation which is perceptible in other, related fields of expression. I am also arguing, moreover, that the 'mythic' status of Ranke's dictum is closely bound up with this *implication* of transgressive meaning.

18 Antoine Guilland, *L'Allemagne nouvelle et ses historiens* (Paris, 1899), p. 71. Guilland is described on the title page as 'Professeur d'Histoire à l'École Polytechnique Suisse'.

19 Cf. Jacques Derrida, *Éperons: les styles de Nietszche* (Paris, 1978). pp. 43ff.

20 Rudyard Kipling, *Many Inventions* (London, 1898), p. 171.

21 Iggers and von Moltke, *Theory and Practice*, p. xx. I should emphasize that I am not disputing the accuracy of this new translation. I have no doubt that 'essentially' is a more appropriate way of translating *eigentlich* than 'actually'. But I question the epistemological dividend that accrues from this change. After all, the distinctiveness of the 'dictum' does not reside in the fact that it implied an emphasis on 'factuality' rather than the 'essential'. What person could have been misled into thinking that Ranke aspired to a 'factuality' untouched by selection? The distinctiveness lies in what could be made of the claim that Ranke aspired to 'show how...things happened'.

22 Fisher, *Historians' Fallacies*, p. 160.

23 Tzvetan Todorov, 'The Fantastic in Fiction', *20th Century Studies*, 3 (May 1970), 91–2.

24 Ranke, *History of the Latin and Teutonic Nations*, translated by P. A. Ashworth (London, 1887), p. vi.

25 Translated by E. Armstrong (London, 1909). p. x. Both translations omit the Preface.

26 Lord Acton, *Lectures on Modern History* (London, 1969), p. 32.

27 Michel Foucault, *Les Mots et les choses* (Paris, 1966), p. 379.

28 *Ibid.*, p. 380.

29 Quoted in Stephen Bann, 'Postscript: Three Translators, Silhouette, Barante, Rossetti', *20th Century Studies*, 11 (Sept. 1974), 89.

30 *Ibid.*, pp. 91–2.

31 Charles Waterton, *Wanderings in South America* (London, 1825), p. 122.

32 Charles Waterton, *Essays on Natural History chiefly Ornithology* (London, 1838), p. 300.

33 *Ibid.*, pp. 300–1.

34 *Ibid.*, p. 304.

35 Prosper de Barante, *Letters to Mme de Stäel* (Clermont-Ferrand, 1929), p. 289.

36 *Ibid.*, p. 293.

37 Prosper de Barante, Letters to Mme Récamier, Bibliothèque Nationale, Paris, naf 14099, 24 Dec. 1808.

38 Letter from Mme de La Rochejaquelein to Barante, 10 March 1809, in *Andegaviana*, fifth series (Paris/Nantes, 1906), p. 357.

39 Alphonse de Beauchamp, *Histoire de la Guerre de la Vendée et des Chouans*, 3 vols. (Paris, 1806), I, 154.

40 Mme de La Rochejaquelein, *Mémoires* (Paris, 1889), p. 94. This edition, published by the author's family, reproduces the original text, before Barante's revisions.

41 Mme de La Rochejaquelein, *Mémoires* (Paris, 1817), p. 52.

42 Letter from Benjamin Constant to Barante, 25 Feb. 1808, in *Revue des deux mondes*, 34 (July 1906), 249–50.
43 Charles de Rémusat, *Mémoires de ma vie*, 4 vols. (Paris, 1958), I, 309, note 1.
44 Alfred Nettement, *Vie de Madame la Marquise de La Rochejaquelein* (Paris, 1858), p. 340.
45 Quoted in Guilland, *L'Allemagne nouvelle*, p. 71.
46 Stern, *Varieties of History*, p. 87.
47 Letters of François Guizot to Barante, Archives Nationales, Paris, 42 AP 200, 14 June 1823.
48 Letter of Guizot to Barante, Archives Nationales, 21 Nov. 1825.
49 *Journal des Débats*, 20 Feb. 1826.
50 Cf. Bann, 'Historical Text and Historical Object'.
51 Acton, *Lectures*, p. 32.
52 Ranke, *Latin and Teutonic Nations*, trans. Armstrong, p. xi.
53 Quoted in Douglas Crimp, 'Positive/Negative: A Note on Dégas' Photographs', *October*, 5 (Photography special issue) (Summer 1978), 100. There can be little doubt that by 'black and white' Dégas was referring to photography.
54 Quoted in Jean-Louis Schefer, 'Spilt Colour/Blur', translated by Paul Smith, *20th Century Studies*, 15/16 (Special issue on Visual Poetics) (Dec. 1976) 99. Cf. also Schefer, *Scénographie d'un tableau* (Paris, 1969).
55 Schefer, 'Spilt Colour/Blur', p. 90.
56 Cf. Marcelin Pleynet, 'La Lettre de l'incarnation', *Documents sur* 2/3 (1978), 84–92.
57 Cf. Schefer, 'Spilt Colour/Blur', pp. 82 ff.
58 Quoted in S. Lenel, *Marmontel* (Paris, 1902; reprinted 1970), p. 373.
59 *Ibid.*, p. 375.
60 Quoted in Arthur Gill, 'The London Diorama', *History of Photography*, 1:1 (Jan. 1977), 33: the source is Jeffreys Taylor, *A Month in London* (London, 1832).
61 Definition from the Dictionary of the Academy quoted in J. Hovenkamp, *P. Merimée et la couleur locale* (Nijmegen, 1928), p. 4, note 3.
62 Marmontel, *Elémens de littérature*, vol. IV (*Oeuvres complètes*, vol. VIII) Paris, 1787), p. 113.
63 *Ibid.*, p. 118.
64 *Ibid.*, p. 116.
65 Stern, *Varieties of History*, p. 75.
66 *Ibid.*, pp. 76–7.
67 Augustin Thierry, *History of the Conquest of England by the Normans*, translated by William Hazlitt (London, 1856), p. xxi.
68 *Ibid.*, p. xxx.
69 Stern, *Varieties of History*, p. 87.
70 Quoted by Ashworth in *Latin and Teutonic Nations*, p. vi.
71 It is worth quoting here, as a reminder of Ranke's relationship to *Historismus* and its Enlightenment origins, the following passage from Meinecke's *Idee der Staatsräson* which explicitly relates the perspectival view of history to the changes in thought consequent upon the Renaissance and the Reformation. 'This was perhaps the greatest revolution of thought the West had ever experienced...All history now began to take on a different aspect. It no longer looked to be one simple flat level that could easily be surveyed; it was seen to be a matter of perspective, and to possess infinite depths of background.' (Quoted in Meinecke, *Historism*, p. xliii.)

Literature and ideology

J. P. STERN

TRANSLATED BY SHEILA STERN

The times are gone when we could happily accept that 'a political song is a horrid song':[1] that only such plays as Schiller's *Wilhelm Tell* or certain aspects of *Wallenstein* have anything to do with politics, or that human relations can ever be purely private. After a long period of that ostensibly unpolitical literary history and scholarship that enjoyed its St Martin's summer in post-war Germany under the slogan of *werkimmanente Wissenschaft* (uncommitted study, resembling the New Criticism in the English-speaking world), our time is one in which the interpretation of literature, if not literature itself, is becoming increasingly political and ideological. This means, first, the shifting into the foreground of those works of the past which convey a more or less explicit political message – a process which changes the literary canon in favour of some works hitherto reckoned to be of secondary value (I am thinking, for instance, of the political comedy of the *Vormärz*). Secondly, it means that works (like those of the 'classical' period in German) from which it is impossible, or nearly so, to extract an overt political message are interpreted as having implicit political tendencies, and these nearly always of a conservative and repressive kind. And thirdly it means that works which show undesirable tendencies are re-interpreted in such a way as to serve to confirm quite different political aims or poetic intentions, on occasion directly opposed to those of the original; I am thinking, for instance, of the fundamentally anti-political anarchism of *Dantons Tod* or of Shakespeare's *Coriolanus*, the strikingly anti-proletarian tone of which offended the tender conscience of many German intellectuals until Brecht rewrote it. Literary historians are familiar with similar practices from the twenties and thirties, that is from a time when literature and criticism were supposed to be unpolitical; whereas in those days the re-interpretation proceeded from left to right, it is now usually the other way round. This development might be demonstrated by the history of the 'reception' of almost any author. An obvious and fairly recent example would be the treatment of Kleist's dramas, from August Sauer and Friedrich Gundolf up to present-day performances of them on the West German stage.

The fundamental question arises whether literature is bound in every case to contain an explicit or implicit political message; whether the political dimension is an *a priori* of literature. In looking for an answer we may begin by noting that, as a general rule, works of literature are by their nature datable, that is, they cannot help manifesting the linguistic constellation, the social and temporal dimension of their place of origin. Every work of literature has its *parole*. A glance at the first stanza of Matthias Claudius' 'Kriegslied' ('War-song') should make this clear:

> 'S ist Krieg! 's ist Krieg! O Gottes Engel wehre,
> Und rede Du darein!
> 's ist leider Krieg – und ich begehre
> Nicht schuld daran zu sein![2]

> 'Tis war! 'Tis war! O be our ward, God's angel
> And speak thou to be heard!
> 'tis war, alas – and my desire
> Is not to bear the guilt of it!

Even if we were ignorant of the historical connection of the poem with the period of the Frederician wars, we could arrive at a date in the late eighteenth or early nineteenth centuries from the construction 'rede Du darein!', no longer in use, and almost synonymous with the preceding 'wehre'; still more conclusive is the strong use of the little word 'leider', now merely a casual 'alas', a weak survival, which for Claudius has the power to express a full measure of 'lament, regret, distress' (as the word is defined in Adelung's Dictionary of 1796). So much for the specifically linguistic aspect of this poem's datability. Our argument could be rounded off by pointing to the political or (it comes to the same thing) ideological attitudes expressed in the poem; starting under the sign of civic passivity, timidity and resignation to the will of God, which form *one* important structure of the poem, the story of civic conformism and political backwardness (of the onset of what Marx will eventually call 'die deutsche Misere') could then be unfolded. The only doubt that remains is whether this is the right way to approach this particular poem; whether its specific mood and meaning can be communicated to the reader in this way. That meaning and mood are profoundly private and anti-worldly. The moment we acknowledge this, the political analysis, without becoming entirely superfluous (for we may assume that all private concerns are interwoven in a dialectic with the public and the political), is none the less seen to be quite marginal to any critical commentary that could illuminate the poem. Admittedly such an analysis points to the occasion and some of the circumstances in which the poem originated, but the poem itself is barely touched by it.

My example is meant to show only that there are degrees of relevance, and therefore that there is a possibility of entirely irrelevant criticism; that while all criticism is necessarily 'aspectival',[3] some aspects of a text are more important than others, and some are perfectly useless. (Uselessness and irrelevance of evidence are possibilities which professional critics and other persons interested in literature are reluctant to acknowledge, for in their heart of hearts they believe that every interpretation and thus every aspect of a text is 'bound to come in handy' in some way.) In other words, to recognize that language is a public or common medium (Nietzsche often complains of its excessive 'commonness')[4] and that it always bears some relation to the public sphere is by no means the same as to say that the detailed working out of this relationship necessarily assists the better understanding of any and every text. Ludwig Wittgenstein once remarked[5] that the answer to the question whether a set of chessmen is carved out of oak or deal in no way affects or explains the rules of chess. Every hermeneutic, especially that of literary texts, remains inadequate as long as it contains no theory of the irrelevant. Thus a true illumination of the text by reference to its political and public dimension is only to be expected in cases where the text itself touches on or perceptibly suppresses political themes, and so in either case arouses the expectation of political solutions. This is not a tautology: the immediate origin of a legitimate literary expectation is not of a politico-ideological kind but one of literary form. As the competent speaker of a language expects from his collocutor a certain conformity in the observance of syntactic rules and semantic conventions, or else the express rejection of them in favour of new forms, so the spectator or the good reader expects that certain formal presuppositions with which he comes to the theatre or approaches the text will either be fulfilled or replaced by others that justify themselves on their own terms. What seems to me irreconcilable with the idea of literary effectiveness is the incidental or unintended disappointment of literary expections; that is, a non-fulfilment by inadvertence.

The problem posed by literary expectation is particularly clear – or particularly crass – in the case of the writings of the German classicists. Thus in Goethe's *Götz von Berlichingen*, in *Egmont*, and in *Die Natürliche Tochter* there are situations, of fundamental importance for the action of the plays, which demand political solutions. (I mean solutions such as we find in Shakespeare at the point where Caesar is murdered or Prince Hal crowned; in Racine, where Titus renounces Bérénice, or in Sophocles, where the fatal dialectic between Antigone and the *raison d'état* is carried out and leads not only to Antigone's personal doom but also to the threat to Creon's rule.) In situations of this kind Goethe avoids the political solution, abandons the plane of dramatic and political action and replaces it by purely private episodes which lead on to a lyrical mood. Götz von Berlichingen's loyalty to the Emperor is unshakeable only because it is never shaken either by an actual confrontation with the Emperor or by a clear understanding of the real circumstances in the Empire. Goethe never allows Götz or Egmont an insight into the real conflict of their parallel situations – the conflict between personal glory and social responsibility – and thus to arrive at a conscious decision, for any politically clear-sighted action is condemned in advance as unheroic politicking, not only by them but by the characterizations and the slant of the play itself. Neither Götz nor Egmont is conscious of responsibility for the popular movement he has brought into being. What they are really concerned with is not the political freedom germane to their task as popular leaders, but the purely personal freedom appropriate to their heroic or 'daemonic' personality; that is, they are concerned with 'freedom' in a situation in which 'liberty' would be the primary legitimate aim. And so there is nothing left for Egmont but the experience of that celebrated vision which substitutes dream symbolism for the real chance missed, and an erotic apotheosis for the political component of liberty.

It might now be asked why Goethe was apparently not capable of taking the political course of his plays to a rigorous conclusion and thus satisfying the *literary* expectation he himself had aroused – a question usually answered with an allusion to the historic conditions in which he worked. I am not referring to his everyday personal interest as expressed for instance in his conversations with contemporary statesmen. But when, in a play as politically inspired as *Die Natürliche Tochter* was to have been according to his plan,[6] he contents himself with dark allusions to nameless powers and 'necessary unjust deeds',[7] and sacrifices his heroine to these powers, then we may well see this as an indication that his imagination is constrained by the unpolitical and anti-political ideology of his time and place. 'The due seriousness' of his poetic creativeness is devoted to the private and personal sphere on the one hand and the cosmic and metaphysical on the other, but not at all to what he himself called 'the middle altitude of life', the sphere of the social and political, from which certain fundamental decisions proceed which affect our daily lives. (Nietzsche too, with his notorious lack of positive concern with all social and institutional questions, is in a similar predicament.)

'It were easier to turn the wind or stop it blowing than to imprison the minds [*die Gesinnungen*] of men', says Lichtenberg:[8] there is nothing impenetrable about the limitation imposed on people and poets by the ideology of their time. The tremendous lyrical (and partly irrelevant) last act of *Egmont* contains not only the bewildering apotheosis of the dream of freedom, but also the dialogue between Egmont and Ferdinand, the son of his arch-enemy Alba, in which Egmont becomes aware of the meaning of his sacrificial death: his existence and something of his message of freedom will survive him as an effective national example and future political message. It goes against the grain for Goethe to draw these conclusions, rooted in the theme of this play – 'political' still means for him, as it did in *Werther*,[9] something of unpleasant shrewdness and prudence – and yet Egmont's last words to the people are more than empty rhetoric.

A recurring pattern emerges. The ideology or, to use Lichtenberg's more modest expression, 'the system of convictions'[10] of an age is not *a priori* limiting. On the contrary: in their initial stages, before they have petrified into clichés, the convictions of an age form the very staple of its literature. They come to impose themselves as a system of intellectual bondage on a literary work or on a man's imagination in any of its forms when they become embattled in dogma (the stage which Goethe recognized and warned against, 'damit sichs nicht zum Starren waffne'). Only then does a writer's intellectual and affective horizon become restrictive, but even then it is not absolutely limiting. It may be forced open, transcended, and may lead to new insights and creative solutions, which will not however be characterized by the same conviction and stylistic assurance as were the thoughts and motives that were part of the original system.

An example from the late nineteenth century is Theodor Fontane, who occupies himself again and again with the question of who wields power in Wilhelminian Germany. He never comes nearer to it than in *Der Stechlin*, his last novel, in the words addressed by the young Countess von Barby to Pastor Lorenzen:

You used the word 'Régime'. Who is this Régime? A person or a thing? Is it the old machine inherited from past times, with its clock-work clattering away automatically, or is it the fellow who stands at the machine [Bismarck]? Or again, is it rather a particular limited multiplicity [*eine bestimmte, abgegrenzte Vielheit*] that tries to determine and direct the hand of the man at the machine?[11]

The subject of *Der Stechlin*, once chosen, makes questions of this kind inevitable: it seems that, as a German of the post-1870 era, Fontane cannot avoid posing them; and it is certain that, as a novelist, he is not in a position to answer them.

Nietzsche, and the ideology prevailing in German literature in the first half of the twentieth century, offer a further example, which moreover has the advantage of being almost immediately accessible to us. From his first work, *The Birth of Tragedy* (1872), to the very last notes made in the months and weeks before his breakdown in January 1889, Nietzsche embarked on countless attempts to confront his existential morality of values – that is, his philosophy of evaluations and judgements – with an aesthetic, non-judging, playful attitude to the world. The motto of this aesthetic attitude is to be the sentence that occurs three times in the *Birth of Tragedy* – 'Only as an aesthetic phenomenon is the world and existence eternally justified'[12] – yet his attempts to elaborate this aesthetic attitude all fail. His lack of consequentiality, here too, is notorious. It may be objected that the systematization of his existential morality of values, that is the elaboration of a philosophy of 'the will to power', also remains fragmentary. But from the surviving fragments we may clearly see what such a moral system would have been like and why it suffered an internal collapse. Nietzsche's notes for a comprehensive aesthetic or metaphysic of play, on the other hand (which extend from his earliest Basle lectures[13] on the pre-Socratics to the last jottings of the *Nachlass*), are so rudimentary, so fragmentary, that we are justified in assuming that to complete and work them out in full would have been a task beyond the creative gift inherent in his philosophical imagination – beyond his historical horizon.[14] Like Egmont's vision of freedom, Nietzsche's aestheticizing of the world remains a dream contained in a realistic scenario.

It is hardly possible to overestimate Nietzsche's influence on German literature and ideology in the first half of the twentieth century; Gottfried Benn, Rilke and Brecht dedicate poems to him; Stefan George writes unconvincing disclaimers and Thomas Mann critical essays about his influence; other writers bear witness to the overwhelming attraction of his thought. What our century inherits from Nietzsche, however, is not his aesthetic theodicy, but in the first instance his moral philosophy, by which I mean his philosophy of moral and existential strenuousness and sacrifice; that ideology which in *Zarathustra* is given the name of 'the Spirit of Heaviness'.

In all the phases of his philosophical career, brief as it was, Nietzsche vows allegiance to this philosophy. The way he comes to formulate 'the most difficult ideal of the philosopher', his insistence on truths which are true only by being 'in the highest degree harmful and dangerous' to the very existence of man, the value he sees inherent in insights which offer the greatest possible resistance to man's cognitive powers, his refutations of any possible harmony between true insight and comfort – all these components of his philosophy of strenuousness and sacrifice have been assembled and considered at length in another context.[15] Here I wish merely to assert that they are the constitutive elements of the ideology which Nietzsche bequeathed to our century. Thomas Mann's *Doktor Faustus* and its central theme, the ineluctable costliness of 'authentic' artistic experience, is the most obvious example of the way the Nietzschean heritage is applied and thematized in the era that follows his death. Hardly less obvious (to choose another example) is the peculiar dichotomy from which Hermann Hesse's *The Glass-Bead Game* (a precise analogue, in Hesse's oeuvre, to Mann's *Doktor Faustus*) is built – 'the Game' versus 'Reality'. This dichotomy comes to a head in that peculiar confession of Josef Knecht's when he resigns from his magisterial office in order to choose what he calls 'The Absolute' (*das Unbedingte*) as the aim of his life, and equates 'reality' not only with 'risk, weightiness and danger', but even more emphatically with 'deprivation and suffering'.[16] Of this concept of 'reality' it has been well said that it ceases to be a concept, that it merely generates an appearance of understanding and befogs thought.[17] This attack is well-founded; but unfortunately it does not ask why this non-concept is so flourishing in the *parole* of our century. One hardly thinks of Shakespeare as being short of the words he really needed, yet the word 'reality' does not occur in his works. To the writers of the post-Nietzschean era it seems indispensable. For all its ambiguity, for all its fuzziness and squidlike amorphousness, it is impossible to banish it from the vocabulary and the ideology of that age.

Reversing the meaning of a seventeenth-century sonnet, I have called it the ideology of *the dear purchase.*[18] Every important work of German literature in the first half of this century places the redemption and justification of man at its centre. No doubt this is a wholly unorthodox valuation, and yet this 'redemption', which is unthinkable without Nietzsche's critical anti-religious reflections and his 'philosophy of strenuousness', stands in a partly antagonistic, partly dependent, partly parodistic relationship to the traditional Christian values and concepts. The redemption and justification which we encounter in that literature is attempting to break through the dualism of world and transcendence, of the here and now and the beyond, and often it is in the no-man's-land between finite and infinite that the just attainable or finally unattainable act of redemption takes place. Every major writer of the time forms his work from the experience of a redemption or a valuation of man which is only to be obtained at the highest price; the highest price that the author, and also the hero whose fate is described, is capable of paying. Again and again (I am thinking of the great works of the time, from Stefan George through Rilke, Trakl, Benn, Kafka, Brecht, to Thomas Mann and Hesse, to sketch out a possible canon) it is an almost inconceivably costly ransom that alone can ensure a human being's validity, his 'reality', selfhood and significance. We encounter fictional situations in which this exaction is still further heightened, where more is demanded of the characters than they can possibly pay. And finally we come to the most radical of all conceivable situations, in which the impossibility of paying the price as such is the very token and confirmation of the redemptive act and its validity – the more impossible, the truer, more authentic, more 'real'.

Turning the argument around, we see that the age is one in which all easy, flowing solutions and liberations are suspect; in this ideology all values that are to be had at a lesser price are suspected or rejected as 'unreal' and invalid. And it is significant that many lesser authors of the time either ignore this theme or, if they do take account of it, fail to acknowledge its scope or to exhaust its profundity, or else evade it by undertaking traditional and less costly bargains.

In the poetry, drama and prose of this age the theme of the dear purchase is not confined to characterization and plot, however, but also manifests itself in the style and attitude towards language which these works display. The time is past when 'the language of the market place' and the language of poetry were mutually comprehensible, and when a linguistic consensus informed literature. 'Nothing but misunderstandings' might well be the motto of Hofmannsthal's finest comedy, *Der*

Schwierige. Fear of misinterpretation and an acute feeling for the inadequacy of linguistic formulation go hand in hand with an extraordinary virtuosity in the realm of language; and we can see that this linguistic creativeness (sometimes acrobatic in its allusiveness and originality) is nothing other than the linguistic correlative to the theme of the dear purchase. Franz Kafka is one of the few writers of the period who restricts himself exclusively to everyday language and avoids any linguistic innovation or idiosyncrasy. Are we then to conclude that after all here is an example of harmony between popular speech and literature? On the contrary: on page after page and in scene after scene Kafka entangles his heroes and his readers in a net of crushing contradictions and annihilating misinterpretations.

Here I must interrupt this description of the period from the point of view of literary history in order to avert a possible suspicion that may have arisen in the reader's mind: that I am using the word 'ideology' here in some special, merely literary sense, and trivializing it by depriving it of its political overtone. Again *Doktor Faustus* is our seminal text. The allegorical relation between Leverkühn and Germany, stressed by Thomas Mann himself, mainly through his *locum* Serenus Zeitblom, is an indication of the interlocking of art and politics. This allegory leads to conclusions which neither the novelist nor his worthy narrator were intending and which they would not approve, for seen in the perspective of the 'dear purchase' the story of the Third Reich takes on a new and in a sense even more terrifying meaning: is the central allegory of the novel, or rather the reader's interpretation of it, to be interrupted before the final justification and salvation of Leverkühn through his striving after 'the difficult', or is there some other way to prevent it from yielding a certainly unintentional justification of National Socialism?

All this is mentioned here to show that we are not concerned with a merely neutral system of thought, indifferent to questions of power, but with ideology in the accepted sense of the word, ideology as a means toward the attaining, stabilizing and maintaining of political power in the world. There is no space here for more than the assertion that this *Gesinnungensystem*, this ideology of 'the dear purchase', characteristic of a whole period at least in respect of its salient features, is by no means a purely literary matter but also typifies and determines politics and all *its* means, including the language of which politics availed itself in the era under discussion. It is possible to demonstrate that the inherent attraction, indeed the lure of National Socialism would be inexplicable were it not that the system of values of that regime possesses certain striking 'family resemblances' with the ideology of the 'dear purchase' and with the theme of the inconceivably, even mortally difficult salvation and justification at its centre. The usual reply to this statement (which I have endeavoured to give grounds for elsewhere)[19] is that it applies only to certain phases and aspects of national socialist propaganda, and that in any event we know this propaganda was full of lies. Such a reply fails, however, to explain why it was precisely that vocabulary of the wager requiring every kind of sacrifice, that language of 'Gemeinschaft' and 'Not' (the language of a community formed by a common need, real and imagined, and requiring ever-new emergencies for its survival as a community), which the regime made use of from the beginning and more and more exclusively as time went on, and from which the language of National Socialism drew its stock of metaphors.

At this point a warning is necessary. The fact that the National Socialists availed themselves of this ideology and that it was indispensable to their evil ends does not necessarily imply that there was anything evil about it in its literary uses; nor was it necessarily restrictive in its initial stages, where it is conveyed to us as a major literary theme and with the passionate seriousness of a new discovery about the being of man in the world. The works which are informed by it belong among the major contributions of German to world literature. Yet the moment of some of that literature's greatest achievements is also the moment when we can see the theme impose itself on the imagination as an intellectual bondage – though even then it can never be the monolithic scheme which political propaganda and counter-propaganda would make of it.

Ideology connotes not an identity but a family resemblance of ideas within one period. (The phrase 'family resemblance' I take from Wittgenstein's critique of the traditional language of universals.[20] Phenomena which seem to us to have something in common are referred to and subsumed, since Aristotle, under a single conceptual heading, one common denominator. Inherent in this method is the danger of the 'contempt for the individual case' – a kind of totalitarianism, if not of perception, at least of description. How can we avoid this totalitarianism? All great generalizing laws are suspect, says Lichtenberg: 'They give me no joy...: at close quarters none of it is true.'[21] In most cases, says Wittgenstein, things are in fact very different. Thus we may think, for example, of the various particular attitudes and convictions collectively subsumed under the heading of 'ideology': 'In reality [such phenomena] form a *family*, the members of which have family likenesses. Some of them have the same nose, others the same eyebrows and others again the same way of walking; and these likenesses overlap.') There is no doubt that this family resemblance of ideas is recognizable in writers who are totally uninterested in politics and indifferent to party allegiance; and when we observe its presence even in actual opponents of the regime (here too Thomas Mann and his *Doktor Faustus* are the type of many others) this resemblance of ideologically related ideas which apparently suspends moral contradictions gives our argument the deceptive form of a paradox which must be resolved.

This is the question we are trying to answer: if the prevailing mental attitude of an age is really so comprehensive and all-determining, even to stylistic nuances, as is here, if not demonstrated, at any rate asserted; if scenes and moods, whether in literature or outside it, in political or daily practice, can be so closely identified with an ideology and at the same time determined and restricted by it; if finally, as we said at the beginning, we draw all the consequences from the fact that literature (and every other form of cultural life) is datable, what then becomes of the possibility of opposition and protest, what (not to mince matters) happens in that case to human freedom? That it exists and is no chimera we know from our daily experience, in particular from our capacity to consider and arrive at decisions, and to convert them into actions; but we also know it by way of hindsight, for the very possibility of historicizing the politics, literature or thought of the past, however inadequately, argues some degree of liberation from the present. Moreover, to know one kind of past is to know that it was not of another kind. Any attempt to describe *or* explain the Third Reich in any detail at all is to show that life in that society, as in every other, was made up of numerous individual decisions, and this in turn is to show a society which might have chosen to live differently; historical theories which operate with notions of 'catastrophe', 'fate' and 'preordainment' find themselves short of material with which to demonstrate the difference between the natural and the human, a difference which those who hold such theories do not usually regard as chimeric.

How then is our practical experience of the possibility of decisions and of freedom to be reconciled with the recognition (without which there would be no historical continuity in literature, ideas or institutions) that men belong to their time and that no man can jump over his own shadow? Nietzsche never succeeded in freeing himself entirely from the system of values and morality (the system of 'the Will to Power') which he had composed and tried to live out in his endless *agon* with Schopenhauer; yet Nietzsche's aesthetic reflections (they too, incidentally, are deeply influenced by quasi-Christian redemptive ideas) point the way toward personal and reflective freedom. How is this possible? We need a model to embody and perhaps explain this paradox: the possibility of nonconformism in the face of the ideological dominant; moreover, this is to be a functional nonconformism, not mere caprice.

One of the metaphors we have used here will help us on: I am thinking of the phrase (almost a cliché) 'the language of National Socialism', in which the literal meaning of 'language' is not sharply divided from the metaphorical. What enables us to regard such a 'language' (which, as we can easily discern, is not really a self-contained and entire language at all) as a conceptual unity and to subject it to examination? Whether we are acquainted with it or not, it is the theory of language of Ferdinand de Saussure, the basis of modern linguistics. Fundamental to Saussure's theory is his claim (illustrated by means of a good many philological details) that the connection between a linguistic sign (e.g. a word) and the thing signified is arbitrary or conventional. This claim need not concern us here beyond saying that on it are based the two cardinal distinctions with which Saussure operates thoughout. (Both of them are not physical facts, but working hypotheses or 'methodological fictions'.)[22]

First (and central to our argument) is his distinction between the concept of *langue*, a system of signs coextensive with the whole potential, the totality of a natural language, and the concept of *parole*, which refers to that part of a natural language which is activated at a particular moment by an individual speaker.

There are several ways of paraphrasing Saussure's distinction: actualization of linguistic phenomena within a system of rules and potentials, or again *praxis* within theory – these and other formulations are not sanctioned by Saussure himself yet they are faithful to his basic idea and show something of its far-reaching significance. Nor is it doing violence to it if (for the sake of the present argument) we disregard Saussure's own insistence that *parole* denotes a strictly *individual* use of language and apply the distinction to the linguistic usage of a *group* defined in social, geographical, professional or some other terms. What must not be abandoned is the part-within-a-whole relationship.

Equally important (though ancillary to our argument) is Saussure's second distinction, between the study of language as an inquiry into its state at any one time (a synchronic study – the horizontal cross-section of a tree), and as an inquiry into the history of a language (a diachronic study – the longitudinal cut along the fibres); and this is a particularly clear-headed piece of the argument, seeing how frequent, in Saussure's day and ours, in linguistics and elsewhere, is the habit of confusing what a thing is with how it came to be what it is.

There is no need to demonstrate at length the usefulness of the *langue–parole* distinction: most modern linguistics is based on it, including Chomsky's antithesis between linguistic 'competence' and 'performance'; and Roland Barthes' notion of *écriture* is an extended application of it to literary history. The question that concerns us here is that of the relationship between the two concepts. Clearly, some relationship there must be and, equally clearly, it cannot be simply cumulative. As a first step towards establishing such a relationship we may note that both *langue* and *parole* are aspects of language which may be examined both synchronically and diachronically. Now it seems self-evident that a large number of individual *paroles* considered synchronically can never make up the totality of *langue*. (The totality of a natural language is not simply the sum total of the linguistic usages of its speakers; when Shakespeare or Dickens arrives on the scene something *new* happens to that language which, nevertheless, continues to be English.) If there is to be a connection, it can only be effected on a diachronic view of *parole*. The connectedness of the two phenomena (as opposed to the working-hypothesis separation with which we began) becomes manifest in the recognition that *parole*, viewed diachronically, is capable of expanding in the direction of *langue*, to the point where the one – actualization – comes close to becoming coextensive with or growing into the other – the full theoretical potential of a natural language. (Thus an author might discover, after a lifetime of writing, an area of language that was not available to him when he began.) One is tempted to continue the pattern, albeit in a speculative metaphysical vein, by tracing the expansion or growth of *langue* (seen diachronically) into that totality of linguistic systems which Saussure calls *langage*. And beyond that? (All these are merely ways of suggesting that what Saussure got hold of looks like the empirical end of an archetypal movement within human experience, a leapfrog pattern not confined to the sphere of language; and from that one might venture two further guesses: that most of what Saussure has to say is capable of translation into non-linguistic terms, and that whatever is really interesting in linguistic thinking contains the possibility of a translation beyond the linguistic.)

Now we are in a position to return to the main subject of this paper. Here is the model we needed in order to characterize the relationship between an individual and his age, or rather between the ideologically determined outlook of an individual or a group of individuals and the full potential of an age.

Of course we speak the *parole* that belongs to our age and no other. Of course we see and evaluate the past that the modern world has taught us to see. Certainly 'man is doomed to the state of *seeing his own system* everywhere he looks', as Lichtenberg observed.[23] But neither our speech nor our seeing is determined once and for all. Every living language, every living organ of experience changes and develops. Just as, on the diachronic view, it is a condition of their connectedness that *parole* should be capable of expanding in the direction of *langue* without yet ceasing to display those features which characterize it as belonging to that particular *langue* and no other, so an individual outlook is capable of transcending its own ideologically determined limitations in the direction of a fuller consciousness (it would be too sanguine to speak, as the Marxists do, of a 'total' one), without yet ceasing to show its membership of a particular era and no other; and nowhere is this more patently and abundantly true than in that area of experience where the dialogue between the individual self and the age to which it belongs is at its most conscious and articulate: the area of literature. The condition of such transcending, however, is not the synchronic view – consciousness as a state, as an aesthetic phenomenon – but the diachronic – the self-understanding of consciousness as an historical phenomenon not fearful of change. In this sense, then, it should no longer be paradoxical to claim that 'the language [= *parole*] of National Socialism' belongs to the same age and displays at least some of the same features – significant features – as the writings of the major poets and novelists of the age, though only the poets and novelists attempt to transcend the limitations of their *parole*, only they strive for a fuller consciousness.

Parole and *langue* never overlap completely, nor do ideological and potential consciousness. Liberation from the embrace of ideology can never be complete or definitive. (Works of literature are always datable.) Through one feature or another the products of the mind always remain bound to the style of their time, indeed it is in them that this style is exemplified. Nietzsche made fun of 'the Spirit of Heaviness' and yet could not avoid continually boasting of his tremendous mental exertion, and making a virtue, not only in his letters but also in the main stream of his philosophizing, of the dreadful loneliness which was the price of it. Part of our inheritance from him is that the first half of our century became a time in which ease was extremely difficult to achieve. Stefan George's striving for grace and élan embarrasses us. There is little or none of this striving in Trakl's dark poetry or in the *weltanschaulich* poetic cycles of Rilke's maturity. How unintentially comic it seems to us when Hofmannsthal concludes a heavy and amorphous tragedy with a miraculous peace-bearing infant king. Can we imagine Ernst Jünger's 'Worker' dancing? And yet Thomas Mann succeeds in his *Felix Krull*, his con-man's memoirs, in which Nietzsche's projected aesthetic justification of man is parodied and carried out; many of the poems Rilke wrote in the last four years of his life, after the completion of the *Duino Elegies* in February 1922, are filled with a lightness of touch and a grace of poetic expression that do not so much overcome the ideology of 'the dear purchase' to which the great cycles were devoted (each overcoming is an exertion), as seem rather to have forgotten all about it. And Bertolt Brecht confesses in his poem 'To Posterity':

> Still we know:
> It is hatred of the base thing too,
> That distorts our features.
> Anger at injustice too
> Makes our voices hoarse. Alas, we
> Who desired to prepare the way for friendliness
> Could not be friendly ourselves.[24]

It would have been hard to foresee the author of these lines in the Bert Brecht of the early thirties, preoccupied with ideological aridities. However much of a party henchman he could be when it seemed necessary, in poems such as these he speaks not as an ideologue but as a free man. His death and that of his great literary contemporaries bring to an end an age that believed more than any other in the determining power of ideology, furthered the dominance of ideology by this belief, and yet – at least in the case of some of its creative minds – succeeded in breaking through this dominance. Whatever was, in *one* generation, thematically marginal and only realized with great effort, becomes, in the succeeding generation, less problematic and more easily accessible, and can be made use of with less exertion. A new style comes into being. In a popular novel of the late 1960s (a work of decent sentiments though no great originality), a habitually intimidated son describes his father:

> Him – what a performance he made out of sitting there, wrapped in deep significance. I detect this overweening manner of sitting, I fear this silence that pretends to importance, I hate this laconic solemnity, the eye transfixed in that far-off gaze and the gesture that is hard to describe, and I fear, I fear our habit of listening inwardly and dispensing with words.[25]

(Even a much better novel written before 1945 would be bound to mention 'silence', 'the far-away gaze' or 'the all but indescribable gesture' with bated breath.) It seems as though the author of that scene had actually read and was taking issue with the following passage from the last of Nietzsche's *Thoughts Out of Season*:

When on that May day in 1872 the foundation-stone had been laid on the hill at Bayreuth in drenching rain and under a dark sky, Wagner drove back to the town with a few of us. He was silent and was all the time gazing into himself with a look which no one word could possibly describe.[26]

This is a text that is characteristic in every detail, and to the point of parody, of the prose and characterology of the ideological age, but from which it would scarcely be gathered that this silent man with the deep introspective glance, this paragon of inwardness, was capable of behaviour that would make a mountebank look respectable. We can certainly find headlong attacks on 'the Spirit of Heaviness' in Nietzsche's later books – passages of exhortation to and in praise of laughter, the light touch – but not the attitude of that (less than outstanding) novel of the 1960s, its combination of unemphatic irony and discretion:

And I ask myself why our people can see more deeply and more penetratingly in the evening than in the daytime, and why they are so totally absorbed in the pursuit of a task undertaken. The wordless lust for food, the self-righteousnes, the talk of ancient folklore which they prefer to going for a swim: these too I question...

and in this almost entirely unsentimental form an attitude to the preceding age is developed which is new – that is, critical and different.

Certainly the analogy I have chosen, between the structure of language and the structure of ideology, is not accidental. It is indicative of the fact that the rules of the linguistic activity are such that they relate it to other cultural activities; for language does not (as most of the nineteenth-century writers believed) only describe the world, without at the same time forming a part of it. It does not stand separate in some chimeric relationship to 'life'. The superior status and greater depth of wordless experience (in which Nietzsche believed) is part of that very ideology which no longer holds sway. Our argument confirms the fact that language and ideology are both forms of life. It is intended as a paradigm. A similar analogy could be drawn between the relationship of any text to the critique of it, between almost any experience and the subsequent account or evaluation of it, and in respect of every attempt to historicize a private or public event. The attainment of any new perception, any new knowledge, is only possible from the perspective of a wider view – a view beyond the frontiers of the old. Sentimental theories of alienation will not get us very far: *every* wider view and every fuller consciousness – that is, every new knowledge – implies a relative alienation. A true knowledge of the past is no less attainable for being disturbing. To affirm that the past is inaccessible is on a par with affirming the inescapable dominance of ideology. Both are forms of a solipsistic attitude to the world which one might have supposed had lost its least claim to validity.

It is no homage to the past and its victims to say of it that it is indescribable or inexplicable. But can it then really be said that the period here described *is the past*, that it has now come to an end and can thus be historicized – known as history and experienced as such? This much at least seems certain: the proposed relativization of the concept of ideology, the Wittgensteinian theory of family resemblances, the dissolving of the polarity between world and language, the suspicion with which we regard the concept of the 'embattled personality' – all these belong to a new style of thinking, a new *Gesinnungensystem*.

And thus, finally, the question may be asked whether the model I have sketched here of the relationship between literature and ideology can also be of use in other periods, or whether it only applies to the nineteenth and twentieth centuries, that is to periods in which the concept of ideology was invented and became modish, and which believed in ideological determination. 'And I saw too', St Augustine writes, 'that all things are fit and proper not only to their places, but also to their times.'[27] Every work of literature – this was our point of departure – is essentially datable (if not always with the same accuracy), not only according to its historical content, but also by its language and style; and this (as we have seen) throws a light on a variety of connections between literary works of art and other expressions of human society. Are there alternative solutions to this relationship, more appropriate to other, 'non-ideological' ages? Were there such ages, or were they merely less articulate about their beliefs? But is not this articulateness itself part of the ideological system of an age? However we answer these questions, the hypothesis that literature might be completely independent of the contemporary state of the language and ideology (and thus independent of society, whose manifestations they are) must surely seem to us today as absurd as its opposite, the hypothesis of the necessary determination of man, his language and his literature as well as his every thought process, by the prevalent ideology of the time.

NOTES

This is a revised version of *Über Literatur und Ideologie: als öffentlicher Vortrag der Jungius-Gesellschaft gehalten am 24. Mai 1977 in Hamburg* (Veröffentlichung der Joachim-Jungius Gesellschaft der Wissenschaft, No. 30) (Göttingen, 1977). I am very grateful to Ursula Riniker for a number of critical observations which led me to reconsider some of the arguments of the original German lecture.

1 'Ein garstig Lied! Pfui! ein politisch Lied!/Ein leidig Lied ' (*Faust* I. 2092–3.)

2 First published by Matthias Claudius in Voss' *Musen-Almanach auf 1779*, then in his own *Wandsbecker Bote: Vierter Teil* [1782].

3 See Peter Jones, *Philosophy and the Novel* (Oxford, 1975), ch. 5.

4 E.g. in *The Twilight of the Idols* (1889), 'Skirmishes...' §26. In *The Portable Nietzsche*, edited by W. Kaufmann (New York, 1968), pp. 530f.

5 *Philosophical Investigations* (Oxford, 1953), I.108; the chess metaphor is used extensively by Ferdinand de Saussure in his *Course in General Linguistics*, held c. 1906–11; see third (English) edition (New York, 1966), pp. 88f.

6 *Tag- und Jahreshefte* for 1799; see E. Staiger, *Goethe*, 3 vols. (Zürich, 1956), vol. II, p. 373 ('due seriousness' is intended to distinguish *Die Natürliche Tochter* from the farcical *Der Bürgergeneral*), and J. P. Stern, *Re-Interpretations: Seven Studies in 19th Century German Literature* (London, 1964), p. 34.

7 Act IV, scene I: 'Ich schelte nicht das Werkzeug...'

8 G. C. Lichtenberg, *Schriften und Briefe*, edited by W. Promies (Munich, 1968), vol. I, *Sudelbücher*, C148.

9 See the narrative following his letter of 20 December, where he is said to call a remark of Wilhelm's 'politisch! sehr politisch!' *Jubiläumsausgabe*, XVI, 119.

10 *Gesinnungensystem*, see Lichtenberg, *Schriften und Briefe*, vol. I, B22, 159 etc. The subsequent quotation, 'lest it should arm itself into rigidity', comes from Goethe's poem 'Eins und Alles', of 1821.

11 *Der Stechlin* (1898), ch. 29.

12 *Die Geburt der Tragödie* (1872), §§5, 24 and preface of 1886.

13 'Die Philosophie im tragischen Zeitalter der Griechen' (1873), beginning of §7. I pass over the notorious quandary of how to translate 'Spiel'.

14 The metaphor of a cultural and historical horizon is generally attributed to the Frankfurt School; in fact it comes from the second of Nietzsche's *Unzeitgemässe Betrachtungen*.

15 See J. P. Stern, 'Living in the Metaphor of Fiction', *Comparative Criticism* I (Cambridge, 1979), 3–16. See also J. P. Stern, *A Study of Nietzsche* (Cambridge, 1979). On the question of influence, see *Nietzsche und die deutsche Literatur*, edited by Bruno Hillebrand, 2 vols. (Tübingen, 1978).

16 Hermann Hesse, *Das Glasperlenspiel* (1943), last chapter ('Legende') of main part (Frankfurt/Main, 1973, pp. 434f); cf. also 'Der Regenmacher' (*ibid.*, pp. 503f): 'es war alles Wirklichkeit, war getränkt und voll von Wirklichkeit wie ein Brotteig von Hefe'.

17 See Johannes Kleinstück, *Wirklichkeit und Realität* (Stuttgart, 1971), pp. 61, 66.

18 See J. P. Stern, 'The Dear Purchase', *German Quarterly*, 41 (1968), 317–37; for the title see Andreas Gryphius' sonnet of 1663 for the third Sunday in Advent: 'hier

wird ohn teuren Kauf/*Den* Trost geschenkt/die vor in Tränen schier ersoffen'; in Andreas Gryphius, *Lyrische Gedichte*, 'Sonn- und Feiertags-Sonette', 1/3, edited by H. Palm (Tübingen, 1884), pp. 22f.

19 See J. P. Stern, *Hitler: the Führer and the People* (London, 1975).

20 See Ludwig Wittgenstein, *The Blue Book and the Brown Book* (Oxford, 1964), pp. 17f.

21 G. C. Lichtenberg, *Physikalische und mathematische Schriften*, 4 vols. (Göttingen, 1803–6), IV, 145f.

22 See above, note 6, and J. Culler, *Saussure* (London, 1976), pp. 37f and *passim*.

23 Lichtenberg, *Schriften und Briefe*, vol. I, B365.

24 'An die Nachgekommenen', in Bertolt Brecht, *Gesammelte Gedichte*, 4 vols. (Frankfurt/Main, 1967), II, 722–5: 'Dabei wissen wir doch: Auch der Hass gegen die Niedrigkeit/Verzerrt die Züge./Auch der Zorn über das Unrecht/Macht die Stimme heiser.'

25 Siegfried Lenz, *Deutschstunde*, (Hamburg, 1968), ch. 5, pp. 92, 292, 395.

26 'Richard Wagner in Bayreuth' (1876), end of §1.

27 *Confessiones*, VII, cap. XV.

Langland's Ymaginatif and late-medieval theories of imagination

ALASTAIR J. MINNIS

Recent scholarship has defined the basic problem of Langland's Ymaginatif as follows: if the imagination is a 'relatively unimportant faculty of the soul in scholastic philosophy',[1] why is a personification of imaginative power (*virtus imaginativa*) afforded a prominent position in *Piers Plowman*? Various solutions have been suggested. Some incline towards the view that Langland, far ahead of his time, believed in the creative powers of the imagination;[2] others hope that eventually an answer will come to light in some medieval treatise on psychology.[3] The most recent claim is that the Dreamer is in fact disappointed by Ymaginatif, and is forced to seek edification elsewhere.[4] Here I wish to suggest that the Ymaginatif episode, which begins at Passus XI.320 and ends with Passus XII (B-text), plays a positive role in *Piers Plowman* as a whole and, in particular, in the most academic dream-vision within the poem, Passus VIII–XII.[5]

At the beginning of Passus XIII Langland provides a summary of Passus VIII–XII, ending with a resumé of the Ymaginatif episode: this may be taken as evidence of his conception of that part of the poem as a discrete unit, brought to completion by the Ymaginatif episode. Therein Langland considers scholastic questions, questions of a type not raised elsewhere in the poem, namely the relative functions of faith and reason, of natural intelligence and revelation; more specifically, the problem of predestination, which involves the issue of the salvation of 'good pagans'. Moreover, Langland's idiom in Passus VIII–XII is a distinctive one: he employs the vocabulary of scholastic *disputatio* throughout.[6] In Passus XIII the idiom changes, as we are brought back to the world of the Fair Field full of Folk. The Dreamer no longer wishes to dispute with everyone he meets; the scholastic questions mentioned above no longer seem to trouble him. I believe that here Langland moves away from scholastic questions and changes his idiom precisely because he has offered positive answers of a particular kind to those questions, and the resultant shift of emphasis entails a change of idiom. This opinion will be substantiated by reference to late-medieval discussions and examples of the operation of *virtus imaginativa* in speculative thought. One aspect of Ymaginatif's positive role merits special attention, namely his production of 'ensamples and termes' for the Dreamer's benefit. This will involve an investigation of the operation of *virtus imaginativa* both in the formation of literary imagery and in the effect such imagery was supposed to have on an audience.

I. THE FUNCTION OF *VIRTUS IMAGINATIVA* IN SPECULATIVE THOUGHT

Most late-medieval thinkers accepted the basic triad of *imaginatio*, *ratio* and *memoria*, although it was much elaborated and amplified. Objects perceived by the five exterior senses were believed to cause separate sensations, these sensations met in the *sensus communis*, and the imagination, stimulated by these sensations, formed the mental pictures (*imagines* or *phantasmata*) necessary for thought. Images thus produced were handed over to the reason, which employed them in the formation of ideas. These ideas were in turn handed over to the memory, the store of ideas of past things. As Langland's contemporary John Trevisa puts it in his translation of *De proprietatibus rerum*:

> in þe brayn beþ þre smale celles. þe formest hatte *ymaginatiua*, þerin þingis þat þe vttir witte apprehendiþ withoute beþ i-ordeyned and iput togedres withinne, *vt dicitur Iohannicio I.* þe middil chambre hatte *logica* þerin þe vertu estimatiue is maister. þe þridde and þe laste is *memoratiua*, the vertu of mynde. þat vertu holdiþ and kepiþ in þe tresour of mynde þingis þat beþ apprehendid and iknowe bi þe ymaginatif and *racio.*[7]

In their attempts to describe precisely the various operations of imagination, medieval thinkers employed various terms in different ways. *Imaginatio* and *phantasia* could designate a single faculty or two distinct faculties; other faculties were believed to serve the imagination or to be served by it, depending on their relative status. Vincent of Beauvais O.P. (c. 1190–1264), who compiled many *auctoritates* on imagination without harmonizing them, quotes Avicenna as saying that the *phantasia* (which Avicenna identifies with the *sensus communis*) receives all the forms imprinted by the five exterior senses, while the imagination acts as a respository of images of things no longer present to the senses.[8] *Imaginatio vel imaginativa* is defined as a vis ordinata in extremo anterioris concavitatis cerebri, retinens quod recipit sensus communis a quinque sensibus, et remanet in ea post remotionem ipsorum sensibilium.[9]

The cogitative power (*vis cogitativa*) then takes images and combines or divides them, an activity which involves the will. This means that it can create new images from sensory inages, these being images of things not perceived by the five external senses. It is this faculty which, for example, feigns a golden mountain (by compounding the image of gold with the image of a mountain) or a chimera (by compounding the images of a lion's head, a goat's body and a serpent's tail).[10]

Albertus Magnus O.P. (c. 1200–80), regarded by Vincent of Beauvais as the great interpreter of Avicenna, rejected Avicenna's identification of *phantasia* and *sensus communis*. For Albertus, *phantasia* was a power between imagination and memory, with the prime function of comparing, compounding and dividing: thereby he dispensed with Avicenna's appeal to the *vis cogitativa*.[11] According to Albertus, it is *phantasia* which enables one to fancy a man with two heads, or a being with a human body, the head of a lion and the tail of a horse.[12]

Albertus was aware that not everyone would agree with his division and description of the inner senses. He admitted that, broadly speaking, the terms *imaginatio*, *opinio* and *phantasia* were often used interchangeably, and that Aristotle had not made a precise distinction between *imaginatio* and *phantasia*.[13] Thomas Aquinas O.P. (c. 1225–74), the great interpreter of Aristotle, believed that the terms *imaginatio* and *phantasia* designated one and the same faculty:

Ad harum autem formarum retentionem et conservationmen ordinatur phantasia sive imaginatio, quae idem sunt; est enim phantasia sive imaginatio quasi thesaurus quidam formarum per sensum acceptarum.[14]

Aquinas also rejects Avicenna's definition of the *vis cogitativa* as the power between the estimative power and the imaginative power, which combines and divides imaginary forms. It is the *virtus imaginativa* which creates the mental picture of a golden mountain.

ista operatio non apparet in aliis animalibus ab homine, in quo ad hoc sufficit virtus imaginativa.[15]

The *virtus imaginativa* is not merely passive, as Avicenna says. It has an active capacity of forming images of things not perceived by the senses. This point of view was reiterated by Bartholomaeus Anglicus:

By þe vertu ymaginatif þey he be absent we apprehendiþ liknes and schappis of þingis þat we apprehendid raþir and venge bi þe vttir witte; as whanne it semeþ þat we seeþ goldene hilles oþir when we metiþ of þe hil mount Parnasus for þe liknes of oþir hilles and mounteynes.[16]

However much the late-medieval thinkers disagreed in details of vocabulary and definition, in general they regarded the imagination as a 'low' and 'inferior' faculty within the mental hierarchy. It is of crucial importance to realize precisely what this means within the (basically Aristotelian) scientific systems so popular in the period. One of the basic tenets of medieval Aristotelianism was the belief that there was a place for everything and that everything has a place. Each thing was either an 'end' or a 'means' to some end. 'Subordinate' sciences were regarded as the handmaidens of 'superior' sciences; 'subordinate' faculties were the servants of 'superior' faculties'.[17] Usually, without the 'subordinate' the 'superior' could not function, and vice-versa. For example, a military commander cannot operate unless he has an army to command; an army cannot operate unless it is controlled by a military commander.[18] This reciprocal relationship of 'superior' and 'subordinate' was of equal importance in psychology.[19] Although, technically speaking, the imagination was 'subordinate' to the reason and to the memory, without the imagination no human reasoning could take place nor could the memory employ images of the past. Yet the imagination also needs its 'superiors': without the reason, images would be of little use to the mind as no ideas could form; without the memory, ideas could not be remembered and hence the *virtus imaginativa* would not be required to produce images of the past.

Albertus Magnus certainly accepted these principles.[20] He tells us that the reason may have recourse to *imagines* in, for example, the study of mathematics. Moreover, *imagines* may be combined or separated for the purpose of producing the effect of the terrible, the helpful or the harmful: thus imagination serves the faculty which produces opinions. Imagination also plays an important role in memory by recalling images of the past:

Quandoque autem deservit memoriae, ut dicit Aristoteles, quando scilicet per imagines praeparatas in anima recursus est in rem quae accepta fuit in praeterito per sensus.

An active imagination allows the memory to work to its full capacity, since ideas are more easily remembered if they are attached to images.[21] *Imagines* may even be exploited by the Holy Spirit, in revelations received in dreams.[22] The imagination, then, performs many functions in respect of many faculties; it enables its 'superiors' to function properly.

This interest in 'subordination' may help to explain the continued popularity of a twelfth-century account of the mental hierarchy, the *Benjamin minor* of Richard of St Victor.[23] Richard allegorized the wives of Jacob, Rachael and Leah, as reason and affection respectively. Rachael takes Bilhah (= imagination) as her handmaiden, while Leah takes Zilpah (= sensation) as hers. Imagination serves reason just as sensation serves affection: 'the reason would know nothing without the imagination and the affections would feel nothing without sensation'.[24] It is difficult for the carnal mind still untaught in spiritual studies to raise itself to the understanding of unseen things.[25] So far it knows nothing but bodily things; nothing presents itself to its thoughts but what it is accustomed to thinking about, namely visible things. The soul must do what it can, and think of higher things as it is able: it must think through the imagination since it cannot yet think by the pure intelligence.

Sed quis nesciat quam sit difficile, imo quam pene impossibile mentem carnalem, et adhuc in studiis spiritualibus rudem, ad invisibilium intelligentiam assurgere, et in illis contemplationis oculum figere? Nulla quippe novit adhuc, nisi corporalia; nil aliud adhuc cogitanti occurrit, nisi quae cogitare consuevit sola visibilia. Quaerit invisibilia videre, et nil occurrit nisi formae rerum visibilium; desiderat intueri incorporea, et nil somniat nisi imagines rerum corporalium. Quid igitur faciat, quid agat?...Facit tamen quod potest, intuetur ea quomodo potest. Cogitat per imaginationem, quia necdum videre valet per intelligentiae puritatem.

[Bot who is þat þat wote not how hard it is & niȝhond inpossible to a fleschly soule, þe whiche is ȝit ruyde in goostly studies, for to rise in knowyng of vnseable þinges, & for to set þe iȝe of contemplacioun in goostly þinges? For whi a soule þat is ȝit ruyde & fleschly knowiþ nouȝt bot bodely þinges, and noþing comeþ ȝit to þe mynde bot only seable þinges. And neuerþeles ȝit it lokiþ inward as it may, and þat it may not se ȝit cleerly by goostly knowyng, it þinkiþ by ymagynacioun.][26]

It is sweet for a man to think of spiritual things through the imagination when he cannot yet have an understanding by the reason:

dulce est ei saltem imaginando eorum memoriam retinere, quorum intelligentiam nondum valet ratiocinando apprehendere...Suadet ergo ratio commodius esse qualicunque modo vera bona cogitare, et imaginaria quadam saltem pulchritudine ad eorum desiderium animum accendere, quam in falsis et deceptoriis bonis cogitationem figere...

[And so it is þat þof al a mans soule may not ȝit gete þe lyȝt of goostly knowying in þe reson, ȝit it þinkeþ it sweet to holde þe mynde on God & goostly þinges in ymagynacioun...reson schewiþ þat it is more profitable for to þink on goostly þinges in what maner so it be – ȝe, ȝif it be in kyndelyng of oure desire wiþ som fayre ymagynacion – þan it is for to þink vanitees & diseyuable þinges of þis woreld.]

Richard distinguished between the animal imagination and the rational imagination.[27] The animal imagination occurs when, without deliberation, the mind runs vaguely this way and that on anything which we have seen, heard or done. This is carnal and the animal can do it. The rational imagination operates when a human mind creates some imaginary thing from what is known through the bodily senses. For example, we see gold, and we see a house, but we have never seen a golden house: however, the imagination can create the mental image of a golden house (clearly, this anticipates thirteenth-century discussions of the comparing, compounding and dividing action of the imagination, and the common example of the golden mountain). This kind of imagination is exploited when we wonder what good or evil things there may be in the future life. When, from the many good and evil things which we experience in this life we infer what and how great the highest good or evil in the afterlife can be and by imagination of these things create for ourselves an image of future things, then we are using the rational imagination and are in the company of Bilhah and Rachael. The sons of Bilhah were Dan and Naphtali: Dan is allegorized as the sight of future pains, Naphtali as the sight of future joys.

It would appear then, that the imagination, serving as the handmaiden of reason, can be of considerable use in speculation about such future things as the joys of heaven and the pains of hell. The imagination is not solely responsible for such thinking because the reason is also involved; however, such thinking could not occur without the operation of the imagination.[28] Therefore, Richard's term *imaginatio rationalis* is particularly apt.

All the theologians quoted above shared the belief that imagination is an essential part of the normal process of human thinking. They certainly did not interpret their authorities' sporadic warnings of the occasional fallibility of imagination as being an indictment of the faculty in general. The imagination was supposed to perform a necessary task in providing those images of absent things which are necessary for thought, and in forming composite images from sensory images. Thus, the *virtus imaginativa*, operating in conjunction with one or more of the other mental faculties, could produce far-reaching and far-seeing thought;[29] 'invention', 'scheming' or 'devising'.[30] The commonplace nature of this belief, the fact that it could be taken for granted on many occasions, may now be demonstrated by a range of examples from texts of different kinds, and including examples both in Latin and *in vulgari*.

In the prologue to his commentary on the Sapiential Books, Nicholas of Lyre O.F.M. (c. 1270–1340) seems to regard imaginative thinking as a means of gaining some knowledge of eternity.

aeternitas a nobis non capitur in praesenti, nisi secundum imaginationem temporis infiniti.[31]

A similar example occurs in *The Chastising of God's Children*, which was written between 1382 and 1408. The anonymous writer describes how some men

wolen imagyne of predestinaciouns, and of the prescience or of þe foreknowynge of god; and suche men sum tyme bien dredful for synnes don bifore, and sum tyme to dredeful. Wherfor sum bien in poynt to falle in dispeir: sum aȝens hir wil bien traueiled wiþ dispeir, natwiþstondynge þei knowen wele oure lordis mercy passiþ al her synnes. Summe also bien traueiled wiþ poyntes of þe feiþ,...and douten what god wil do wiþ hem.[32]

Apparently the imagination, working from knowledge of past sins, can enable one to form hypotheses about their future consequences. This passage reads like a particular application of Richard of St Victor's notion that from the many good and evil things which are experienced in this life the rational imagination can infer what and how great the highest good or evil in the afterlife can be. The problems and doubts mentioned here are very much those of Langland's Dreamer. Ymaginatif, as he says himself, has often 'meued' the Dreamer – by reminding him of past sins and noting the spiritual implications of evils as they occur – to 'mynne of þyn ende' (XII.3–12).

Geoffrey Chaucer, who so often displays his understanding of the principles of Aristotelian psychology,[33] provides us with several interesting statements concerning the profitable operation of the imagination. In the *Franklin's Tale*, Aurelius fails to conceive of the possibility that, during his long absence, someone might have spoken of love to his wife:

No thyng list hym to been ymaginatif,
If any wight hadde spoke, whil he was oute,
To hire of love; he hadde of it no doute. (V. 1094–6)[34]

The implication is that, had Aurelius been more astute, his *virtus imaginativa* would have played an important part in this far-sighted conception.[35] In the *Summoner's Tale*, we are told of a 'cherl' who confounded a master of theology with the difficult *quaestio*, how may a fart be divided into twelve equal parts? The local lord seems to regard active imagination as an important component of 'subtiltee/And heigh wit' (III. 2290–1).

The lord sat stille as he were in a traunce,
And in his herte he rolled up and doun,
'How hadde this cherl ymaginacioun

To shewe swich a probleme to the frere?
Nevere erst er now herde I of swich mateere'. (III. 2216–20)

The lord's exaggerated praise of the 'cherl' is of course ironic, but this does not impinge on his apparent belief that the imagination can be of considerable assistance in scholastic debate.[36] John Lydgate would have agreed with him. In the *Troy Book*, the narrator explains that his powers of imagination are too dull to cope with complicated matters, whether practical or speculative:

For-dullid is myn ymaginatif,
To deme in practik or in speculatif.[37]

John Gower also recognized this positive aspect of *virtus imaginativa*. In the *Confessio amantis*, he tells the story of King Alphonse, a young and wise king who loved to dispute 'depe ymaginaciouns' and difficult problems:

A king whilom was yong and wys,
The which sette of his wit gret pris.
Of depe ymaginaciouns
And strange interpretaciouns
Problemes and demandes eke
His wisdom was to finde and seke;
Wherof he wolde in sondri wise
Opposen hem that weren wise. (I.3067–74)[38]

Moreover, an active imagination was supposed to be necessary for the historian. Froissart explains how he often speculated about the state of prowess, its origin and development:

Or ay je eu pluseurs fois imagination sus l'estat de proèce, et penset comment et où elle a regnet et tenu signourie et domination, et salli d'un pays en aultre.[39]

Throughout the *Croniques*, Froissart uses the verb *imaginer* to denote the consideration of possible courses of action and military tactics.[40] The adjective *imaginatif* implies a prudence based on far-sighted grasp of a situation, and the initiative which accompanies that prudence. It is often associated with the adjective *sage*, as in this example:

Aucun *sage signeur et imaginatif*...qui estoient dou conseil le dit prince...li avoient dit fiablement, quant il en avoit rusé et parlé à yaus...'Monsigneur, vous avés oy dire et recorder par pluiseurs fois: Qui trop embrace, mal estraint.'[41]

It would seem that a knight could learn a lot about his trade through his imagination. This is the basic idea behind the French treatise entitled *Imaginacion de vraye noblesse* which, although much later than *Piers*

Plowman, is of some interest because here also the imaginative faculty is personified.[42] Imagination, 'in the person of a woman' (the influence of Boethius' Dame Philosophy is obvious), appears to a knight in 1440 near the town of Hals in Hainault, to which he was going on a pilgrimage. Dame Imagination gives him the choice of bearing an edifying message to the clergy, or to the nobility, or to the commons. The knight chooses the second of these estates, whereupon Imagination discourses on true nobility and chivalry.

By Langland's day the *virtus imaginativa* was commonly believed to be of considerable value 'in practik or in speculatif'. However, on occasion the far-reaching imagination could over-reach itself. It is significant that the Gower passage quoted above forms part of an *exemplum* which warns against intellectual pride. There are many examples of the verb *imaginare* being used to designate the thinking of one's academic opponents, and here the implication of 'far-fetched' thinking is often present. For instance, Nicholas of Lyre describes a point of view which he cannot share as follows:

> Item isti imaginantur quod istae literae non sint de integritate versuum sed quasi quidam tituli eis praepositi, quod non est verum...[43]

A similar example occurs when, in a quodlibet on the subject of baptism, Robert Holcot O.P. (d. 1349) refers to the opinion of an unnamed *socius* as *ymaginatio sua*.[44] Although Holcot and Lyre cannot accept their opponents' views, they do not reject them out of hand. The point seems to be that their opponents' thinking was ingenious and worthy of attention, with the definite implication that it was perhaps over-ingenious. While the subtle and far-reaching qualities of imagination rendered it an immensely valuable kind of thinking, it had to be recognized for what it was: thinking which produced not certainties but possibilities (often in areas where certainty could not be reached). Apparently, the philosopher was advised to handle his 'depe ymaginaciouns' with discretion and humility; if over-indulged, the imagination could go too far. The implications of these facts for *Piers Plowman* may now be considered in detail.

Langland first mentions Ymaginatif in Passus X.119. Studie has been telling the Dreamer about high-ranking laymen who presume to talk and 'dispute' about Christ and his powers as if they were clerics. The examples of such arguments which Studie provides all indicate a deplorable gap between faith and reason (lines 108–14). It seems irrational ('Reson wolde it neuere!') that we who are alive now should have to pay for the ancient sins of Adam. Moreover, the reason can point to apparent discrepancies in holy Scripture concerning this and related subjects (lines 112–14). Men who take such arguments seriously, the Dreamer is warned, are led into false beliefs. Then Studie encourages the Dreamer by promising that Ymaginatif will help him with his problems:

> 'Ymaginatif herafterward shal answere to youre purpos.
> Austyn to swiche Argueres he telleþ þis teme:
> *Non plus sapere quam oportet.*' (x.119–21)

The Dreamer should not attempt to be more wise than is fitting for him: he should not seek fully to understand ('Wilneþ neurere to wite...') the lore of holy Church but rather to believe it steadfastly ('bileueþ lelly'). Faith is as important as reason. Everything in the world happened as God chose, and this will always be true no matter how much any man may dispute (lines 127–39). This passage anticipates the Ymaginatif episode, and prepares us for the kind of answer offered therein.

In Passus xi.140ff the *exemplum* of Trajan the 'good pagan' is used to explain the fact that 'lawe wiþouten loue' is not worth a bean. All branches of learning, including the Seven Liberal Arts, are a waste of time unless they are undertaken for the love of God (xi.171–82). Once again, we are being reminded that faith is as important as reason. Christ told a common woman that *fides sua* would save her and salve her of her sins. Faith is above law and logic (xi.209–29). After this, Ymaginatif proceeds to 'answere to' the Dreamer's 'purpos'. At Passus xi.320 there is a clear change of direction in the poem:

> Ac muche moore in metynge þus me gan oon dispute,
> And slepynge I seiȝ al þis, and siþen cam kynde
> And nempned me by my name and bad me nymen hede,
> And þoruȝ þe wondres of þis world wit for to take. (xi.320–3)

Here one might envisage the chapter-heading *De Virtute Imaginativa*, for Ymaginatif presides over the entire portion of the poem which begins at this point and ends with Passus xii. The Dreamer remembers, *inter alia*,

> how þat Ymaginatif in dremels me tolde
> Of kynde and of his konnynge, and how curteis he is to bestes,
> And how louynge he is to ech lif on londe and on watre –
> Leneþ he no lif lasse ne moore –
> For alle creatures þat crepen or walken of kynde ben engendred;
> And siþen how ymaginatif seide '*vix saluabitur iustus*',
> And whan he hadde seid so, how sodeynliche he passed. (xiii.14–20)

The last two lines of this passage refer to the end of Passus XII; the rest is a summary of the significance of Passus XI.320–72 and Passus XII.217–69 taken together. In Passus XI.320–72 the Dreamer is indeed told 'of kynde and of his konnynge'. It remains to explain how Ymaginatif figures in the mental process described therein.

In a dream, Nature ('Kynde') shows the Dreamer's imagination the 'wondres of þis world'. The Dreamer's mind is supposed to move from known and visible things to things which are unknown and invisible, from the natural to the supernatural:

> I was fet forþ by forbisenes to knowe
> Thorugh ech a creature kynde my creatour to louye. (XI.325–6)

Impressed by the order which animals and birds observe in their eating, drinking, nesting and engendering, he proceeds to wonder about their maker and master:

> Muche merueilled me what maister þei hadde,
> And who tauȝte hem on trees to tymbre so heiȝe
> Ther neiþer burn ne beest may hir briddes rechen. (XI.360–2)

According to St Bonaventure's *Itinerarium mentis in Deum*, the universe is a ladder whereby we may ascend to God: we must begin with God's footprints (*vestigia*) in empirical nature and so enter on the way that leads to him.[45] In created things the contemplative can see mode, species and order, as well as substance, virtue and action, from which the mind may arise – as if from footprints – to knowledge of the power, wisdom and boundless goodness of the creator.[46] The *Benjamin minor* (as quoted above) states that the earthly mind must raise itself to the understanding of unseen things as it is able: it must think through the imagination when it cannot yet think by the pure intelligence. Aquinas made the same basic point in stating that the intellect rises to the limited knowledge it has of invisible things by way of the natures of visible things.[47] It must employ *imagines* or *phantasmata* to look at universal natures existing in particular things. Something can be known of incorporeal realities, which themselves have no phantasms or images, by comparison with sensible things of which there are phantasms.

> dicendum quod incorporea, quorum non sunt phantasmata, cognoscuntur a nobis per comparationem ad corpora sensibilia, quorum sunt phantasmata.

We know God as the cause about which we ascribe the utmost perfection and negate any limit. Other incorporeal substances are known by comparison and contrast with corporeal realities: when we understand anything of such spiritual beings we have to employ imagery derived from our sensory experience of bodily things.

Et ideo cum de hujusmodi aliquid intelligimus, necesse habemus converti ad phantasmata corporum, licet ipsorum non sint phantasmata.

These discussions provide the key to Langland's conception of the relationship between empirical nature and *virtus imaginativa*.

In XI.327–72 the exterior senses of the Dreamer are bombarded with sense-data, and he begins the mental process of moving from the known to the unknown through *imagines* formed from known things. Langland is not explicit here about this function of Ymaginatif, although his recapitulation in Passus XIII shows that certainly he had it in mind. Perhaps he felt that it was perfectly implicit in the context: after all, he was invoking a perfectly commonplace notion of imaginative power. The Dreamer's imagination offers its *imagines* to the reason, and soon ideas are formed concerning the universal natures of things. The Dreamer becomes aware especially of the universal principle of order which appears to govern all things. The next step seems obvious: from his observations of natural order the Dreamer should proceed to imagine divine order; from natural love he should proceed to imagine divine love. But he is not yet ready for this step. Having encountered the problem of man's inclination to wander without order or reason, he proceeds to accuse Reson. Reson, here a personification of the human faculty of reason in the abstract and not of the Dreamer's personal and very limited power of reason, replies that the disorder of men's lives is due to human weakness. Everything that God made was good, but man, being made of flesh, is bound at times to follow the flesh (XI.376–404). The Dreamer is ashamed, and awakes. At this point a personification appears who is later to be identified as Ymaginatif: having silently presided over the poem since line 320 he now appears in person.

The Dreamer's accusation of Reson has proved that his soul 'may not se þit cleerly by goostly knowyng', and so Ymaginatif has appeared to show him how he can 'think by imagination'. Ymaginatif does not offer himself as an alternative to Reson but as a colleague and helper. What Richard of St Victor called the rational imagination can be of considerable assistance to a person like the Dreamer who is still at an elementary stage of contemplation. Ymaginatif will assist the understanding of this 'ruyde & fleschly' man: yet the Dreamer is to some extent representative of men in general, for – as Aquinas' discussion makes clear – all men are rude and fleshly in their attempts to understand divine things. The Dreamer is told that Adam had paradise to enjoy until he began to pry into 'The wisedom and þe wit of God' – one remembers Clergie's criticisms of those noble laymen who presume to dispute of Christ and his mights, and her recommendation of Ymaginatif as an advisor in such matters (x.104–19). Likewise, the Dreamer has presumed to judge things which are beyond his powers (xi.420–2).

The Dreamer having accepted his help, Ymaginatif proceeds to define himself:

> 'I am ymaginatif', quod he; 'ydel was I neuere
> Thouȝ I sitte by myself in siknesse ne in helþe'. (xii.1–2)

As Aquinas and others say, understanding through *imagines* is the proper operation of the soul as long as it has the body united to it.[48] For the intellect actually to understand (not only in acquiring new knowledge but also in using knowledge already acquired), acts of imagination are required. Therefore, Ymaginatif is never 'ydel'. He sits by himself, presumably in the foremost chamber of the brain: the imagination is a distinct faculty, different in kind and in activity from the other mental faculties. The imagination operates in sickness and in health, while one is awake or asleep. Various clerics had warned of the misleading illusions which the imagination can produce when the body is sick,[49] but Langland is concerned rather with the positive point that the imagination never ceases to operate. In Passus xi, we watched the Dreamer's imagination operate in his sleep; in Passus xiii this activity is described with obvious approval:

> Ymaginatif in dremels me tolde
> Of kynde and of his konnygne, and how curteis he is to bestes,
> And how louynge he is to ech lif on londe and on watre – (xiii. 14ff)

Langland chooses to ignore the common criticism that in sleep the imagination, freed from the control of the reason, can run riot:[50] instead he shows how in sleep it can produce images of a beautiful and phantasmagoric world, and that through these images men can conceive of divine order and divine love.

Moreover, the *virtus imaginativa*, through *imagines* of things both present to the exterior senses and absent from them, can move the will to stimulate the reason to consider the future and one's fate:

> 'I haue folwed þee, þise fyue and fourty wynter,
> And manye tymes haue meued þee to mynne of þyn ende,
> And how fele fernyeres are faren and so fewe to come' (xii. 3–5)

Sometimes the *virtus imaginativa* operates in the service of memory by producing images of the past:

'And of þi wantownesse whiles þow yong were
To amende it in þi myddel age, lest my3t þe faille
In þyn olde elde, þat yuele kan suffre
Pouerte or penaunce...' (XII. 6–9)

Sometimes it forms images based on present experience, offering them to the reason in order that the spiritual implications may be noted:

'Amende þee while þow my3t; þow hast ben warned ofte
Wiþ poustees of pestilences, wiþ pouerte and with angres;
And wiþ þise bittre baleises god beteþ his deere children:
Quem diligo castigo.' (XII. 10–12)

The many operations of the *virtus imaginativa* are being described and shown in action. Throughout Passus XII, Ymaginatif teaches the Dreamer by means of *exempla*, including the stories of the swimmers in the Thames, the repentant thief on the cross, and the 'good pagan' Trajan. This is a particularly appropriate teaching-method for him to use, in view of the way in which *exempla* were supposed to stimulate the imagination (a point to which I shall return). Moreover, Ymaginatif reviews the whole of the *Vita* to date, reminding the Dreamer of what he has been taught since the beginning of Passus VIII. Here the *virtus imaginativa* is operating in the service of memory by helping to recall past experience (lines 155–297). In these lines the *virtus imaginativa* is shown also to be operating in the service of the reason in so far as it compares, divides and compounds images of past and present experiences to allow a new rational interpretation of the Dreamer's condition to emerge. The Dreamer is told where he went wrong, and is offered practical solutions to the problems which have been troubling him throughout the main scholastic section of *Piers Plowman*.

These practical solutions may now be examined. Ymaginatif states that 'þe trewe kny3t' Trajan did not dwell deep in hell, so our Lord could draw him out quite easily, and that the penitent thief dwells in the lowest part of heaven. These are matters of faith, not of reason:

'And ri3t as Troianus þe trewe kny3t tilde no3t depe in helle
That oure lord ne hadde hym li3tly out, so *leue I* by þe þef in heuene.
For he is in þe loweste of heuene, *if oure bileue be trewe...*'
(XII. 210–2. Italics mine)

One need not ask why one of the crucified thieves was saved rather than the other: 'Alle þe clerkes vnder crist' are unable to provide a rational answer. This is a matter of faith: 'Whatsoever the Lord willed, that willed he' (Psalm 135.6). Likewise, the question of the salvation of pagans and virtuous Jews who lived before the advent of

Christ is also a matter of faith. In this area, devout imaginations may be of assistance – and Ymaginatif proceeds to offer some. We cannot *prove* that Aristotle and the others are saved, but – since we believe by faith in the goodness and grace of God – we can *hope* that he will give them rest:

'And wheiþer he be saaf or noȝt saaf, þe soþe woot no clergie,
Ne of Sortes ne of Salomon no scripture kan telle.
Ac god is so good, I hope þat siþþe he gaf hem wittes
To wissen vs wyes þerwiþ þat wisshen to be saued...
That god for his grace gyue hir soules reste...' (XII. 270–5)

The Dreamer then protests that baptism is surely necessary for salvation. Ymaginatif replies by taking a syllogism:

'*Contra*!' quod Ymaginatif þoo and comsed to loure,
And seide, '*Saluabitur vix Iustus in die Iudicii*;
Ergo saluabitur' (XII. 280–2)[51]

and supporting it with the authority of 'þe book' (presumably the *Legenda sanctorum*, which tells of Trajan's release from hell). We are then informed that there are various kinds of baptism: by water, by shedding of blood, and by fire, i.e. by steadfast faith ('ferme bileue'). Trajan's faith ('bileue') was great: the implication is that he may have been 'baptized by fire', human merit and divine grace operating together to effect his salvation.

'Ne wolde neuere trewe god but trewe truþe were allowed.
And wheiþer it worþ of truþe or noȝt, þe worþ of bileue is gret,
And an hope hangynge þerinne to haue a mede for his truþe...'
(XII. 290–2)

This fideistic argument is persuasive, if not provable in a purely rational way. It is therefore appropriate that it is delivered by Imaginatif and not Reson.

In the three Langland passages quoted above, the tentative and speculative nature of Ymaginatif's arguments is stressed. The emphasis is on faith, hope, and love, on belief in God's goodness and truth: there is no suggestion that we are being offered certain knowledge or indubitable wisdom. Ymaginatif has provided plausible hypotheses rather than necessary truths. As has been explained above, imaginative thinking produces not certainties but possibilities, often in areas of thought where a mere mortal cannot expect to reach absolute certainty. Anyone who makes too large a claim for his 'depe ymaginaciouns' is in danger of falling into that sin of intellectual pride which Langland was so concerned to castigate throughout Passus VIII–XII.

In the idiom of Albertus Magnus, one might say that in Passus XII the *virtus imaginativa* has operated in the service of *opinio*: we have been given opinions concerning predestination and the salvation of men who lived before the time of Christ, opinions which may be true or false. Following idioms attested by *The Chastising of God's Children* and passages from Chaucer, Gower and Lydgate, one could also say that Ymaginatif has engaged in far-reaching and far-seeing thought about things which are beyond ordinary knowledge. A man who is full of 'subtiltee and heigh wit' has many 'depe ymaginaciouns'; he can 'deme' well 'in speculatif' – and what could be more speculative than thought about predestination? Finally, in the idiom of the *Beniamyn*, one could say that Langland was concerned to kindle 'oure desire wiþ some faire ymaginacion'. Whichever idiom is preferred, it would seem that the answers offered to the Dreamer's scholastic problems are both positive and pragmatic. We cannot have absolute certainty in the matters he has raised, but we can imagine how things may be, and hope and pray that this is in fact how they are.[52]

II. *VIRTUS IMAGINATIVA* AND THE USE OF IMAGERY

Passus XII raises another major problem for the modern reader. Ymaginatif takes the Dreamer to task for playing with 'makynges' instead of saying his Psalter and praying for others (lines 16–19). As the *virtus imaginativa* was supposed to play an important part in the composition of poetry and in its effect,[53] it may seem odd that Ymaginatif should call in question an imaginative activity. However, Ymaginatif is questioning not the use of imagination *per se* but rather a use of it which *some* men might regard as trivial:[54] later in the Passus he will demonstrate how important a role he can have 'in speculatif' (as has been suggested above). The Dreamer must therefore admit that Ymaginatif's criticism has some point: 'I seiȝ he seide me sooþ'. To exonerate himself, the Dreamer offers a two-fold defence of poetry: poetry can teach and delight.[55] Cato, a man of learning, would please his son by composing poetry as the Dreamer does (lines 20–2).[56] The implication may be that Cato's son and Langland's poetic 'son', the Dreamer, are on the same level: both must be weaned on poetry before proceeding to stronger fare.[57] Moreover, 'pleye' is important for mature men, even for those holy men who played in order to be more perfect (lines 23–4).[58]

In lines 25–8 Langland moves from discussing delight to consider the didactic function of poetry. The Dreamer wants to know about, to be taught about, Do-Well, Do-Better and Do-Best.

> 'Ac if þer were any wight þat wolde me telle
> What were dowel and dobet and dobest at þe laste,
> Wolde I neuere do werk, but wende to holi chirche
> And þere bidde my bedes but whan ich ete or slepe.'

These lines have encouraged certain critics to speculate on the possibility that Langland had devised an original theory of poetry, a theory which approximates to the Romantic notion of poetry as a medium for the personal discovery of truth. I suggest that we are dealing with a confusion caused by Langland's attempt to do justice to both functions of the Dreamer: the Dreamer as surrogate audience (requiring instruction of the kind appropriate to an untutored soul) and the Dreamer as surrogate poet (providing that instruction). To a limited extent, the Dreamer is a self-portrait of Langland the poet who 'medles wiþ makynges'. More importantly, he is a portrait of a typical member of Langland's audience: the Dreamer's main function is as an Everyman figure who receives Langland's teaching on behalf of the audience. Langland, we may assume, is perfectly familiar with the many meanings of Do-Well, Do-Better and Do-Best. The Dreamer is not, and – despite his intellectual pretentions – needs a poem like *Piers Plowman* which will encourage in him that faith which is necessary for understanding. There is a 'wight þat wolde telle' the Dreamer what he wants to hear in the way that he needs to hear it – the poet William Langland.

The Dreamer's defence of poetry, although highly condensed and cryptic in the form in which he expresses it, can be recognized as deriving from a typical late-medieval justification of *exempla* technique and 'imaginative writing'. Because lines 20–8 are spoken by the Dreamer, Langland had to curtail his defence, to express it in a form which was in keeping with the Dreamer's character. The fact that Ymaginatif does not contradict the Dreamer's stumbling justification but makes it a point of departure may be taken as an indication that it is basically valid. Eventually Ymaginatif provides his fuller version of the same justification of 'ensamples and termes'.

In Passus XII. 217–69 Ymaginatif reviews the beginning of the Ymaginatif scene (Passus XI. 320–end), where the Dreamer had failed to move from natural order to imagine divine order, from natural love to imagine divine love. The importance of investigating nature is affirmed. Questions such as why some birds breed in the ground and others in the trees, and why the fallen Adam covered his loins and not his mouth, must be referred back to the mysterious divine will which works through nature. The ancients rightly found in the behaviour of birds and beasts *exempla* and tokens of spiritual truths (XII. 236–69).

Langland is describing here the popular practice of moralizing the properties of things as found, for instance, in the *De proprietatibus rerum* of Bartholomaeus Anglicus. Bartholomaeus, as translated by Trevisa, explains how knowledge of 'þe kyndes and propirtees of þinges' can help us

to vndirstonde redels and menynges of scriptures and of writinges þat þe holy gost hath iȝeue derkliche ihid and wrapped vndir liknes and fygures of propirtees of þinges of kynde and craft; as seint Denys scheweth in Ierarchia angelica, and seith þat þe beme of God ȝeueth to vs no liȝt but iveyled and ihid by dyuerste of holy veylynges and wrappinges, menynge what we schal hope and desire. For it is not possible to oure witte to stye vp to þe contemplacioun vnmaterial of þe ierarchies of heuene but by material ledynge þat longith thereto; as þey he wolde mene þat oure wit may not stiȝe vnto þe contemplacioun of vnseye þinges but it be ilad by consideracioun of þinges þat beþ iseye.[59]

Romans 1.20 is then quoted: 'from the foundations of the world men have caught sight of God's invisible nature, his eternal power and his divineness, as they are known through his creatures'.

This *auctoritas* was used in a similar way in another 'moral encyclopaedia', the *Repertorium morale* of Pierre Bersuire O.S.B. (d. 1362).[60] Bersuire finds in it support for his belief that men should take great delight in reading the 'book of creation'. Created things or worldly creatures are, as it were, a book in which God has painted and described his goodness, wisdom and power.

Res enim creatae seu creaturae mundi sunt liber in quo Deus depinxit et descripsit bonitatem, sapientiam, et potentiam suam, quia scilicet sicut dicitur Roman. 1. Inuisibilia enim Dei per ea, quae facta sunt intellecta conspiciuntur. Sempiterna quoque eius virtus, et diuinitas.

Those *philosophi* who lived before the advent of Christ, not having the *liber Scripturae* to read, were able to perceive the virtues latent in things, the order and manner of creatures, and the beauty of the entire universe.[61] Therefore, they contemned all else, and dedicated themselves to the deep study of this *liber naturae*. It is not enough, Bersuire continues, to appreciate the 'words' in their literal sense, i.e. the beautiful appearance of natural things. One must proceed to the spiritual sense, to awareness of the divine mysteries hidden in nature. Whoever has the necessary understanding will find therein past, present and future, except for those things which proceed solely from the divine will – Bersuire seems to have in mind those divine interventions which are beyond the ordinary operations of nature. Human intelligence can lead us a considerable way from knowledge of creatures to knowledge of the creator, but there comes a point at which divinely revealed truth is necessary. This explains the plight of the pagan philosophers and *poetae*, so well summed up by Langland in Passus XII. 270–6. Various pre-Christian thinkers were able to find in nature many 'ensamples and termes' of spiritual truths and therefore Christian science owes them a considerable debt. However, there is considerable doubt concerning the salvation of Aristotle, Solomon, Socrates and the others.

Langland, Bartholomaeus and Bersuire were obviously confident of the efficacy of the *via positiva* in gaining some knowledge of God.

> Via positiva proceeds by way of affirmation and describes God in terms of human attributes, raising them, of course, to an infinite power. He is love, light, life, might, majesty, and everything else that can be given a positive content. Though inexpressibly beyond all human understanding of these terms, there is still a connexion between the human significance and the divine, and the difference is quantitative rather than qualitative.[62]

If 'þe vnseye þinges of God beth iknowe and vndirstode by thinges þat beth iseye',[63] it follows that an author can convey spiritual and unseen things by means of likenesses and similitudes derived from visible things. Bartholomaeus explains how spiritual writings employ such similitudes to express their meaning in a figurative way.

> þerfore diuynyte vsith holy informacioun and poesies þat myistik and dirk vndirstondinge and figuratif speches, menynge what we schall trowe, may be itake of þe liknes and þpinges þat beþ iseye, so þat spiritual þinges and þinges vnseye may be couenabliche ordeyned to fleisschliche and to þinges þat beþ iseye.

The *virtus imaginativa*, the power which can form the image of a golden mountain, was supposed to play an important part in the formulation of such 'figuratif speches'. Richard of St Victor regarded this as one of the ways in which the human soul can 'think by imagination'. He explained that often the holy Scriptures describe unseen things by the forms of visible things and impress them upon our memories by the beauty of desirable forms.[64] Thus they promise a land flowing with milk and honey; sometimes they name flowers or odours and describe the harmony of celestial joys either by human song or by the harmony of bird-song. Moreover, in St John's Apocalypse the heavenly Jerusalem is described as being adorned with gold and silver, pearls and other gems.

None of these things exist in heaven, but we can easily imagine such things, and so turn our minds towards heavenly things.[65]

When defending the usefulness of their writings, the compilers of *exempla* often appealed to this profitable operation of the imagination. To take but one instance, in his *Tractatus de diversis materiis predicabilibus* (compiled not later than 1261), Étienne de Bourbon O.P. explains that *exempla* are of great use in the instruction of the simple and rude man because they imprint themselves on his memory the more easily, and he retains them the longer.[66]

maxime valent exempla, que maxime erudiunt simplicum hominum ruditatem, et faciliorem et longiorum ingerunt et imprimunt in memoria tenacitatem.

One thinks of the statements of Albertus Magnus and Thomas Aquinas to the effect that ideas are more easily remembered if they are attached to images.[67] Étienne quotes St Gregory as saying that things teach better than words and *exempla* teach better than preachings. Therefore, Jesus Christ, the sum of divine wisdom, first taught by things rather than by words and rendered the subtlety of his doctrine in a basic way, as it were in corporeal and visible fashion, equipping and clothing it with diverse similitudes, parables, miracles and examples. Thus his doctrine was the more firmly grasped, the more easily understood, the more strongly retained in the memory and the more efficaciously implemented. Indeed, although Christ was eternal wisdom, incorporeal and invisible, because of the limitations of men he became incarnate and clothed himself in flesh. Therefore, men could know him more easily and he could be comprehended more readily by human senses. 'Saint Dionysius' states that the wise philosophers made their sayings corporeal by clothing them in similitudes and examples. Corporeal discourse moves more easily from the sense to the imagination and from the imagination to the memory:

'Verbum caro factum est et habitavit in nobis', etc. [John 1.14]. Ad hec dicit beatus Dionysius: 'Sapientes philosophi incorporant sermones suos vestiendo eos similitudinibus et exemplis. Sermo enim corporeus facilius transit de sensu ad ymaginativam et de ymaginacione ad memoriam.'

Étienne proceeds to defend his use of verse summaries of doctrine (placed at the beginning of each *materia et titulus*) on the grounds that by this means his teaching is 'the better and the more readily imprinted on the memory'. Belief in the mnemonic power of verse was quite commonplace in the later Middle Ages.[68]

This brings us to consider the conception which Langland may have had of the didactic function of *Piers Plowman*. The charge that another book on Do-Well, Do-Better and Do-Best is superfluous (XII. 17–18) may be met with the argument that Langland's intention was to convey well-established doctrine in a way which, through the medium of memorable poetry and by appeal to the *virtus imaginativa*, would stir the devotion of men. Therefore, the poem was directed primarily at the *affectus* or will and not the intellect:[69] certainly, Langland seems concerned with knowledge of God in so far as to know him is to love him.

The suspicion that in Passus XII. 25–8 Langland just might have been promulgating a view of creative writing as an individualistic means of reaching truth lacks historical plausibility because it ignores the quite strict principles of literary decorum followed by late-medieval clerics. The same is true of the suggestion that Langland's conception of the imagination is an unusually elevated one which may have its (as yet unidentified) source in some recherché commentary on Aristotle's *De anima* or some other psychological work.[70]

If one wishes to assess *Piers Plowman* in terms of medieval genres, it must be noted that vast areas of the work read as a *compendium theologicae veritatis*;[71] that Passus XVI–XVIII have some features in common with a 'meditation on the life of Christ'. Such writings aimed not at the promulgation of new ideas but at the communication of well-established doctrines in a way that was comprehensive, pre-digested, attractive and easily accessible. Similarly, *Piers Plowman* was probably intended for an audience of parish priests and literate laymen,[72] people with a limited education and limited knowledge of Latin works. Langland chose his material to suit their needs and capacities; he made his Dreamer in their image. It is perfectly fitting that the abstruse theological questions raised in the scholastic section of the poem should be given answers which are characterized by pragmatism and circumspect piety rather than by intellectual rigour. One remembers Langland's criticism of those nobles who at table presume to dispute about Christ and his mights; the whole Ymaginatif episode can be read as a warning against intellectual pride. A compilation of theological truths (and especially a work written in the vernacular) was not the place for a daring proposition or controversial statement. Traditionally, these were reserved for commentaries on Peter Lombard's *Libri sententiarum*, *summae*, and quodlibets, works written by and for academics within the intellectual sanctuary of the schools. (Wyclif, who 'told tales out of school', is the exception that proves the rule.) Because of such tacit decorum, modern interpretations of problem passages of *Piers Plowman* may be well advised to take as their touchstone the doctrine channelled by popular compilations. The notions which, in my opinion, are relevant to Langland's use of Ymaginatif seem to have been widely disseminated in various reference books. This may be taken as an *a priori* reason supporting the plausibility of the interpretation offered above.

In sum, the role afforded to Ymaginatif in *Piers Plowman* is, within carefully determined limits, a positive one. By 'positive' may be understood both a role which is significant and commendable and one which is in keeping with the 'positive way' (*via positiva*) of gaining knowledge of God. When Langland describes the never-idle Ymaginatif, the ever-present stimulus for devout thinking, he is describing a faithful follower whom the soul 'þat is ȝit ruyde & fleschly' and 'knowiþ nouȝt bot bodely þinges' cannot do without. Because the Dreamer has such a soul, Ymaginatif is able to satisfy him. The Ymaginatif episode is therefore the fitting climax of the most academic section of *Piers Plowman*.

APPENDIX: YMAGINATIF AND *VISIO IMAGINARIA*

The following note is offered as an addendum to Professor Bloomfield's important observation that 'the manner whereby imagination could be elevated is through the medieval theory of prophecy';[73] in particular, through the theory concerning prophetic dreams.

All the major late-medieval compilations contain statements to the effect that the imagination is responsible for dreams, and that in dream-visions some external force (God, an angel, the devil) can determine which images it produces.[74] A comprehensive account is provided in the *Speculum naturale*. First, Vincent of Beauvais gives the opinions of the *philosophi*, Aristotle being the most-quoted.[75] The essence of a dream is said to consist in imaginary forms and phantastic species, which are mixed with some degree of intelligence. A dream is not, except *per accidens*, intellectual: it is essentially of the phantasy or sense. Then Vincent proceeds to the opinions of the theologians. John of La Rochelle, following St Augustine, explains that a good angel can instruct the soul through visions or images: figurative similitudes can be imprinted on the *virtus imaginativa*, and by this means the soul may be raised to knowledge of mysteries.[76] St Augustine defined three kinds of *visio*: corporeal, spiritual and intellectual.[77] In a spiritual or imaginary vision images of absent things are seen; in an intellectual vision, intelligible truths are revealed directly without recourse to corporeal images or similitudes. The lesser prophet sees in his spirit only images which are the signs of things, the greater prophet is granted understanding alone, while the greatest prophet excels both in images and in understanding.[78] Vincent goes on to explain that there can be intellectual vision without spiritual or imaginary vision, but not vice-versa, because spiritual vision always includes a certain amount of intellectual vision.

The ultimate source for this distinction between three basic kinds of vision is Book 12 of St Augustine's *De Genesi ad litteram*. It was very widely disseminated in the Middle Ages through its occurrence in exegesis of the most important of the biblical dream-visions, St John's Apocalypse. A summary of Augustine's definitions was incorporated into the *Glossa ordinaria* on that scriptural text.[79] In the thirteenth century a prologue to the Apocalypse, ascribed to Gilbert de la Porrée, became one of the standard set of prologues in the 'Paris Bible'.[80] It contains the following version of Augustine's distinction:

Cum autem Ioanni haec in visione fuerit revelata, et sunt tria genera visionum, sub quo genere contineatur videndum est. Visio enim alia corporalis, quando videlicet corporalibus oculis aliquid videmus. Alia spiritualis seu imaginaria, cum videlicet dormientes, vel etiam vigilantes, imagines rerum cernimus, quibus aliquid aliud significatur. Sicut vidit Pharao spicas, et Moyses rubum ardere, ille dormiens, iste vigilans. Alia intellectualis, quando videlicet spiritu sancto reuelante, intellectu mentis veritatem mysteriorum sicut est capimus. Quomodo vidit Ioannes quae in libro referuntur. Non enim figuras tantum vidit spiritu, sed et earum significata mente intellexit.[81]

[Ac for þat seint Iohan seiȝ it in gost. holy chirche distynkteþ þre manere of siȝttes. Good is to vnderstonden hou he seiȝ hym in gost. for oo. siȝth is bodilich whan he sent it. þat oþere is gostlich als it were a semblaunce whan we seen it in sleep oþere makyng semblaunt of any þing þat oþere þinges ben bitokned by. As pharao seiȝ in Egipte in slepe as it telleþ in Genesis. And Moyses seiȝ wakande a grene bussh brennande. & ne brent nouȝth as it is written in Exodi. þe þrid manere of siȝth is cleped intellectuel. þat is whan þe gost aliȝtteþ þe vnderstondyng of þe soules. & dooþ hem seen on niȝttes þe spirites & þe priutes of god als mychel as his wille is to shewen hem. As seint poule was rauisht in to þe þrid heuene & seiȝ þe priuetes of god þat it falleþ to noman to seien And seint Iohan seiȝ in þis manere nouȝth onlich þe figures ac he vnderstood what it was to menen...][82]

Because of its privileged position in the 'Paris Bible', this version of the *triplex genus visionum* received the attention of successive generations of exegetes. Nicholas of Lyre raised the interesting issue of the status of St John's vision: because he saw images, was not his vision imaginary rather than intellectual?[83] Lyre's reply is that it was both: imaginary in so far as images were seen; intellectual in so far as understanding of those images was granted by divine grace.

Responsio secundum diversos respectus imaginaria fuit et intellectualis: quia mentis intellectu illuminato a spiritu sancto veritatem cognovit, per hoc patet quod verissime fuit prophetia.

This belief in the dual nature of St John's vision explains why in *The Chastising of God's Children* the Apocalypse is discussed under the heading of 'spiritual vision or imaginatif'.[84] There are two details found in this account which are not in Gilbert's prologue, namely Elisha's vision of Elijah ascending to heaven in a fiery chariot as an example of corporeal vision, and St Peter's vision of the dish full of diverse beasts as an example of imaginary vision.[85] Both these examples are provided in Lyre's glosses,[86] and one wonders if the Middle English author got them from there.

There is considerable evidence that, in the later Middle Ages, clerics came to appreciate more and more the literary qualities of scriptural texts.[87] For example, certain exegetes were so impressed with the literary qualities which many prophetic writings seemed to have that they came to regard the *modus prophetialis* as a possible genre or style of writing.[88] In such an intellectual climate, a writer could imitate biblical 'modes of treatment' without in any way offending against the great authority of the Bible, or appearing to claim divine inspiration of the kind possessed by the authors of holy Scripture. Therefore, there seems to be no *a priori* reason against regarding *Piers Plowman* in the light of the *triplex genus visionum*. The poem can be described as a 'spiritual vision or imaginatif' in so far as the Dreamer sees images and figures of various things; it can be said to have an element of *visio intellectualis* in so far as Langland's personifications explain their significance. If this suggestion be accepted, then the Ymaginatif episode has a special relationship with Langland's dream-vision form. Because the *virtus imaginativa* is the medium through which everything in the poem has passed, it seems perfectly appropriate that a personification of this mental power should offer solutions to many of the most difficult problems raised therein. In absolute terms, the imagination may be a relatively 'subordinate' faculty of the soul, but as the human power largely responsible for the kind of dream-vision which Langland is describing it deserves an exalted position in the poem.

ACKNOWLEDGEMENTS

I wish to thank several scholars who read versions of this paper and offered helpful comments, in particular M. B. Parkes, É. Ó Carragáin, J. W. W. Bennett and the late Elizabeth Salter. I owe a special debt to Pamela de Wit for valuable discussion. Her thesis *The Visual Experience of Fifteenth-Century English Readers* (unpublished D. Phil. thesis, Oxford, 1977) includes an examination of the relevance of late-medieval theories of imagination for an understanding of fifteenth-century readers' visual experience of books. I am grateful to the Queen's University of Belfast for the research grants which made my work possible.

NOTES

1 M. W. Bloomfield, *Piers Plowman as a Fourteenth-Century Apocalypse* (New Brunswick, 1962), p. 170.

2 For example see E. D. Kirk, *The Dream Thought of Piers Plowman* (Yale Studies in English, 178) (New Haven and London, 1972), pp. 140–5.

3 For example see Bloomfield, *P.Pl. as Apocalypse*, p. 172.

4 See B. J. Harwood, 'Imaginative in Piers Plowman', *Medium Aevum*, 44 (1975), 249–59. Harwood concludes that 'the dreamer's quest to believe "kyndeli on criste" is not to be satisfied by Imaginative'. Of course the Dreamer carries on questing after his encounter with Ymaginatif, but this does not rule out the possibility that *some* of his problems have been resolved in Passus XII. The fact that in Passus XIII. 1 the Dreamer wakens 'witlees nerhande' cannot be interpreted as meaning that he is wildly dissatisfied with Ymaginatif's answers, for the poem will never again return to the issues which came to a head in Passus XII. The point is rather that the Dreamer has learnt something, and is eager to learn more: thanks to Ymaginatif's persuasive discourse he can now move away from academic theology to ask questions of a different kind, questions which require answers different in nature from those which Ymaginatif supplied.

5 All Langland references are to *Piers Plowman, the B Version*, edited by G. Kane and T. Donaldson (London, 1975). I have confined my attention to the B-text as a matter of convenience, since the same attitude to imagination seems to be involved in the C-text.

6 For discussion of Langland's use of *contra* and *disputen* in this context see Bloomfield, *P.Pl. as Apocalypse*, p. 164.

7 *De proprietatibus rerum*, III, cap. 10, in *On the Properties of Things*, edited by M. C. Seymour *et al.* (Oxford, 1975), I, 98. For general discussion of this triad see M. W. Bundy, *The Theory of Imagination in Classical and Medieval Thought* (University of Illinois Studies in Language and Literature, XII, 2–3) (Urbana, 1927), pp. 179–80.

8 *Speculum naturale*, XXV, cap. 86. Quotations from the *Speculum maius* are from the Venice edition of 1591.

9 This definition of Avicenna's was very popular: see for example the use made of it by John of La Rochelle O.F.M. (d. 1246) in his *Tractatus de divisione multiplici potentiarum animae*, edited by P. Michaud-Quantin (Paris, 1964), p. 75.

10 Compare Bundy, *Theory of Imagination*, pp. 182–3. See further M.-D. Chenu, '*Imaginatio*: Note de lexicographie philosophique médiévale', *Studi e testi*, 122 (1946), 599ff; F. Rahman, *Avicenna's Psychology* (London, 1952), pp. 38–56.

11 *Speculum naturale*, XXV, cap. 90.

12 *Summa de creaturis*, pars II, qu. 37 and 38, in *B. Alberti Magni opera omnia*, edited by S. Borgnet, 38 vols. (Paris, 1890–9), XXXVI, 323–35. Compare *Liber de apprehensione*, pars. III, 6–9; pars. IV, 1–6 in *Alberti opera*, V, 579–81, 583–5. Similar distinctions between *imaginatio* and *phantasia* were made by, among others, Peter of Spain, the compiler of the popular *Compendium theologicae veritatis*, and Reginald Pecock. See *Pedro Hispano scientia libri de anima*, edited by M. A. Alonso, second edition (Barcelona, 1961), pp. 259–64; *Compendium theologicae veritatis*, II, capi 37–9, in *S. Bonaventurae opera omnia*, 11 vols. (Rome, 1588–96), VII, 759–60; *The Donet by Reginald Pecock*, edited by E. V. Hitchcock (EETS OS 156) (Oxford, 1921), p. 10.

13 *Summa de creaturis*, pars. II, qu. 37, art. 1 (pp. 324–5).

14 *Summa theologiae*, Ia 78, 4, responsio, in the Blackfriars edition (London and New York, 1964–), XI, 138. See further G. P. Klubertanz, *The Discursive Power; Sources and Doctrine of the 'Vis Cogitativa' according to St Thomas Aquinas* (St Louis, 1952), pp. 242–6; R. E. Brennan, 'The Thomistic Concept of Imagination', *The New Scholasticism*, 15 (1941), 149–61. Robert Kilwardby O.P., who derived his theory of imagination mainly from St Augustine, also identified *imaginatio* with *phantasia*: see M.-D. Chenu, 'Le "De Spiritu Imaginativo" de R. Kilwardby O.P., d. 1279', *Revue des sciences philosophiques et théologiques*, 15 (1926), 507–17 (p. 510).

15 *Summa theologiae*, Ia 78, 4 (XI, 140).

16 *De proprietatibus rerum*, III, cap. 11 (ed. Seymour, I, 99).

17 For recent discussion of the principle of 'subordination' see M.-D. Chenu, *La Théologie comme science au XIIIe siècle*, third edition (Bibliothèque Thomiste, 33) (Paris, 1969), pp. 71–85; U. Köpf, *Die Anfänge der theologischen Wissenschaftstheorie im 13. Jahrhundert*, (Beiträge zur historischen Theologie, 49) (Tübingen, 1974), pp. 145–9, 168–71; also the appendix to the first volume of the Blackfriars edition of Aquinas' *Summa theologiae*, pp. 73–4.

18 See Aquinas' commentary on Aristotle's *Metaphysica*, in lib. primo, lect. 2, 41–2, in the Marietti edition (1935), p. 15; compare the beginning of his commentary on the *Ethica*, translated by C. I. Litzinger (Chicago, 1964), I, 6.

19 For example, see Aquinas' discussion of the *ordo* of the powers of the soul: *Summa theologiae*, Ia 77, 4 (XI, 102–5). In *De consolatione philosophiae*, V, prosa 5, Boethius had explained how the imagination relates to sense and reason respectively; medieval glosses on this text expounded the mental hierachy: see for example the comments of William of Aragon and Nicholas Trivet, in Paris, Bibliothèque Nationale, MS Lat. 11,856, fol. 122^{r}–122^{v}. William of Auvergne (c. 1180–1249) compared the will to a king, the external senses to messengers who make known the king's decrees, and the interior senses (*sensus communis*, *imaginatio*, *memoria*) to closets or book-chests which contain all that is necessary for the king. The intellect is the counsellor and the reason the judge who together advise the king to act rationally and justly. See *Guilielmi Alverni opera omnia* (Venice, 1591), p. 118.

20 *Summa de creaturis*, pars. II, qu. 37, art. 4 (pp. 328–9).

21 Albertus fully explains this notion in *De bono*, tr. IV, qu. 2, art. 2, de arte memorandi, in *Alberti Magni opera omnia* (Aschendorff, 1951–), XXVIII, 246–52. For discussion of

his view see F. A. Yates, *The Art of Memory* (reprinted Harmondsworth, 1969), pp. 73–80.

22 *Summa de creaturis*, pars. II, qu. 37. art. 4 (p. 329); compare the *Liber de apprehensione*, pars. VI, 13–16 (pp. 611–15). See further my Appendix.

23 Text in Migne, *PL*, 196, cols. 1–64. On Richard's influence see *Richard of St Victor: Selected Writings on Contemplation*, translated and introduced by C. Kirchberger (London, 1972), pp. 57–74. See further St Bonaventure's (largely favourable) reaction to Richard's views in *De septem itineribus aeternitatis*, art. 2, dist. 2, in the Rome edition of Bonaventure's *Opera*, VII, 155. By the middle of the fourteenth century, the *Benjamin minor* had been translated into Middle English (nine fourteenth-century manuscripts survive). Through his omission of certain materials, the anonymous translator turned Richard's work into a precise account of the relationship between 'reson' and 'affeccioun or wille'. Text in *Deonise hid Diuinite and Other Treatises on Contemplative Prayer*, edited by P. Hodgson (EETS OS 231) (Oxford, 1955), pp. 12–46. The significance of Richard's treatise for an understanding of Langland's Ymaginatif was first realized by H. S. V. Jones, 'Imaginatif in *Piers Plowman*', *Journal of English and Germanic Philology*, 13 (1914), 583–8. Unfortunately, Jones failed to support his argument with an analysis of Langland's text.

24 *Benjamin minor*, cap. 5 (col. 4).

25 *Benjamin minor*, cap. 14 (col. 10).

26 *Beniamyn*, ed. Hodgson, p. 23.

27 *Benjamin minor*, cap. 16 (col. 11).

28 A similar view concerning the imagination was held by Richard's teacher, Hugh of St Victor (d. 1141). 'Chez l'homme elle [l'imagination] pénètre jusqu'à la partie raisonnable et éveille le jugement, *eadem imaginatio ipsam animae rationalis substantiam contingit et excitat discretionem*...Le champ de l'imagination n'est pas seulement celui de l'imagination reproductrice, mais aussi celui de *l'imagination créatrice*': R. Baron, *Science et sagesse chez Hughes de Saint-Victor* (Paris, 1957), pp. 58–9. Hugh's main contribution is in his *De unione corporis et spiritus*: see Migne, *PL*, 177, cols. 287–9. Vincent of Beauvais quotes this treatise in *Speculum naturale*, XXV, cap. 97: compare Migne, *PL*, 177, col. 288ff.

29 Compare N. Davis' interpretation of such passages as Thomas Usk's 'be fals compassement & ymaginacion to-forn cast' and Chaucer's 'malice ymagined, avised, and forncast', in which 'ymaginacion' means 'scheming, contrivance', while 'forncast' means 'planned or arranged beforehand, premeditated': review of *A Book of London English 1384–1425*, edited by R. W. Chambers and M. Daunt (reprinted Oxford, 1967) in *Medium Aevum*, 40 (1971), 75–80 (p. 79). Doubtless this sense of *ymaginacion* owes something to late-medieval theory of dream-vision; in particular, to discussion of the imaginative dream: for discussion see my Appendix; also V. M. Hamm, 'Chaucer's "Heigh Ymaginacioun"', *Modern Language Notes*, 69 (1954), 394–5.

30 I borrow these terms from the Ann Arbor *Middle English Dictionary*, s.v. *imaginacioun*, 3. R. Quirk refers to this same positive activity of the imagination as 'calculative and deliberative' thought, 'creative reflection': see 'Vis Imaginativa', *Journal of English and Germanic Philology*, 53 (1953), 81–3. It is impossible to find a modern term or group of terms that does not have some unwanted connotations: cf. the most

helpful discussion of Ymaginatif to date, by J. S. Wittig, '*Piers Plowman*, B, Passus IX–XII: Elements in the Design of the Inward Journey', *Traditio*, 28 (1972), 211–80 (pp. 264–6).

31 *Super libros Salomonis praefatio*, in *Biblia sacra cum glossa ordinaria et postilla Nicolai Lyrani* (Lugduni, 1589), III, col. 1598.

32 *The Chastising of God's Children*, edited by J. Bazire and E. Colledge (Oxford, 1957), pp. 119–20.

33 See M. W. Stearns, 'A Note on Chaucer's use of Aristotelian Psychology', *Studies in Philology*, 43 (1946), 15–21.

34 *The Works of Geoffrey Chaucer*, edited by F. N. Robinson, second edition (Oxford, 1957), p. 139. All Chaucer references are to this edition.

35 Here Chaucer seems to have in mind the notion that the imagination assists one to think of the unexpected, or remote possibilities, but it should be noted that the imagination was supposed to play an important part in thoughts of love. For example, one can imagine the behaviour of one's lady or recall her beauty, or speculate about the future of the affair. See *Troilus and Criseyde*, I. 365–78; V. 453–5, 1440–2; perhaps also *The Book of the Duchess*, lines 14–15. Compare John Gower's *Confessio amantis*, VIII.842–50, in *The English Works of John Gower*, edited by G. C. Macaulay, 2 vols. (EETS ES 81–2) (Oxford, 1900–1), II, 409; also Dante's *Vita Nuova*, II, IX and XV, in *La Vita nuova di Dante Alighieri*, edited by M. Barbi (Florence, 1932), pp. 4–11, 33–7, 60–4. This may be related to the *Summa theologiae*, Ia 2ae 80, art. 2, where Aquinas expounds Aristotle's statement that 'even the faintest resemblance attracts the lover to the beloved'. In his very popular commentary on Wisdom, Robert Holcot discusses Aristotle's statement that 'the insane, lovers, and the melancholy' frequently have significative and imaginative dreams: quoted by R. A. Pratt, 'Some Latin Sources of the Nonnes Preest on Dreams', *Speculum*, 52 (1977), 538–70 (p. 567). Such themes as they appear in Old French love-poetry are examined exhaustively by Douglas Kelly, *Medieval Imagination: Rhetoric and the Poetry of Courtly Love* (Madison and London, 1978).

36 Compare *The House of Fame*, II. 725–8, and note also Chaucer's use of the form *ymagined* throughout his *Treatise on the Astrolabe*, in *Works*, pp. 548, 549, etc.

37 *Troy Book*, I. 3577–8, in *Lydgate's Troy Book*, part I, edited by H. Bergen (EETS ES 97) (Oxford, 1906), p. 118. Lydgate may be alluding to Chaucer's *Wife of Bath's Prologue*, III. 187, where the Wife is asked to instruct those ignorant of love in her 'praktike'.

38 *English Works*, I, 119. It is interesting to note that, when Gower describes a dubious or reprehensible operation of the imagination, he feels obliged to use a qualifying epithet: 'fals ymaginacion' (I. 958), 'fol ymaginacion' (I. 2269), etc. This suggests that his usual attitude was one of approval.

39 *Croniques, tome premier 1307–1340*, edited by S. Luce (Libraire de la Société de l'Histoire de France) (Paris, 1869), p. 5. 'Now I have often had imagination on the state of prowess, and thought how and where it has reigned and held lordship and domination, and passed from one country to another.'

40 See L. Foulet, 'Études sur le vocabulaire abstrait de Froissart: *Imaginer*', *Romania*, 68 (1945), 257–72.

41 *Croniques*, VI, 201, quoted by Foulet (Froissart), p. 271. 'Some wise and imaginative lords who belonged to the council of the said prince...had rightly said to him, when

he had considered and spoken to them... "My lord, you have heard said and related many times, 'He who grabs very much, holds very little.'"'

42 I consulted this work in two manuscripts, London, British Library, MSS Royal 19 C. VIII and Additional 15,469.

43 *Biblia Sacra*, IV, col. 925.

44 *Roberto Holcot, Dottrina della Grazia e della Giustificazione*, edited by P. Molteni (Pinerlo, 1967), pp. 200–1.

45 *Itinerarium mentis in Deum*, cap. I. 2, in *S. Bonaventurae opera omnia* (Quaracchi, 1882–1902), V, 297.

46 Compare *Itinerarium mentis*, cap. I. 14, where Bonaventure argues that aspects of God are reflected by the origin, magnitude, multitude, beauty, plenitude, action and order of all created things (p. 299). Similar statements are made by St Edmund Rich in *Le Merure de Seinte Eglise*: we are edified when we see in creatures the wonderful works of our creator; one must think of the great power with which everything was made out of nothing and given its existence, of the great wisdom which ordered created things in such great beauty, of the great goodness with which they are multiplied every day for our use. See the Middle English texts in C. Horstman, *Richard Rolle and his Followers*, 2 vols. (London, 1895–6), I, 222–3, 245.

47 *Summa theologiae*, Ia 84, 7. This should be compared with Aquinas' *In librum Boethii de trinitate*, quaestio 6, art. 2, where it is explained that knowledge sometimes terminates in the senses, sometimes in the imagination, and sometimes in the intellect alone. When our knowledge of images is impeded, we are incapable of knowing anything with our intellect, even about divine things. In this life the imagination is necessary in all our knowledge of the divine, but our knowledge of divine matters must go beyond the imaginative. See *St Thomas Aquinas, The Division and Methods of the Sciences: Questions V and VI of his Commentary on De trinitate*, translated by A. Maurer (Toronto, 1963), pp. 68–72.

48 From Aristotle was derived the notion that 'the soul never thinks without an image'; *Summa theologiae*, Ia 84, 7, sed contra; compare Ia 85, ad 2um.

49 For example see Bartholomaeus Anglicus, *De proprietatibus rerum*, VI, cap. 27 (ed. Seymour, I, 337–8); Robert Holcot, *In librum sapientiae*, lectiones 103 and 202, cited by Pratt, 'Latin Sources of the Nonnes Preest', pp. 543–6.

50 For example see *De proprietatibus rerum*, VI, cap. 25 (ed. Seymour, I, 334).

51 Compare the words of Chaucer's eagle in *The House of Fame*, II. 725–8:

> 'Now herkene wel, for-why I wille
> Tellen the a proper skille
> And a worthy demonstracion
> In myn ymagynacion.'

52 This method of interpreting Langland's Ymaginatif is supported by the materials cited in Kelly's *Medieval Imagination*: appropriate imaginations were supposed to give 'access to ideas and sentiments which ultimately defied rational scrutiny and analysis' (p. 28).

53 See Isidore of Seville, *Etymologiae*, I, 40. In fourteenth-century England, interest in poetry as image-making was stimulated by the theological interpretation of *fabulae*: see B. Smalley, *English Friars and Antiquity in the Early Fourteenth Century* (Oxford, 1960), pp. 112–21, 165–83, 209–11, etc.; see further John Ridevall's *Fulgentius metaforalis*, edited by H. Liebeschutz (Leipzig, 1926), pp. 65–71, etc. As far as

late-medieval England is concerned, the major discussions of imagery are found in the works of theologians. For an examination of the sparse theory of imagery found in *artes poeticae* see J. Richardson, *Blameth Nat Me; A Study of Imagery in Chaucer's Fabliaux* (The Hague and Paris, 1970), pp. 18–54. It must be added that the Arabian interpreters of Aristotle were champions of the belief that poetry is based on image-making. For Al-Farabi's views see J. J. Murphy, *Rhetoric in the Middle Ages* (Berkeley Cal., 1974), pp. 91–2. Averroes, as translated by Hermannus Alemannus in 1256, stated that 'sermones poetici sunt ymaginativi' and that the art of poetry seeks the level of pleasure which moves an audience to virtue through stimulation (*commotio*) of the imagination: see *Averrois Corubensis commentarium medium in Aristotelis poetriam*, edited by W. F. Boggess (Ph.D. thesis, University N. Carolina, 1965), pp. 3, 41, 43, etc. An abridged version of Hermann's translation seems to have circulated in the University of Paris; extracts were widely disseminated: see W. F. Boggess, 'Aristotle's Poetics in the Fourteenth Century', *Studies in Philology*, 67 (1970), 278–94; see further O. B. Hardison, 'The Place of Averroes' Commentary on the Poetics in the History of Medieval Criticism', *Medieval and Renaissance Studies 4*, edited by J. L. Lievsay (Durham, N.C., 1970), pp. 57–81; J. B. Allen, 'Hermann the German's Averroistic Aristotle and Medieval Literary Theory', *Mosaic*, 9 (1976), 67–81. For Avicenna's definition of poetry as 'imaginative speech' see *Avicenna's Commentary on the Poetics of Aristotle*, edited by I. M. Dahiyat (Leiden, 1974), pp. 31–58, 61–4, etc.

54 Considered from a purely rational point of view, the *poeticus modus* was the weakest of the philosophical modes: see Albertus Magnus, *Summa theologiae*, pars. I, tract. I, qu. 5, membrum 2, in *Alberti opera*, ed. Borgnet, XXXI, 24; Thomas Aquinas, *Summa theologiae*, Ia I, 9, ad Ium. E. R. Curtius stresses this supposedly low scholastic evaluation of poetry in *European Literature and the Latin Middle Ages*, translated by W. R. Trask (London, 1953), pp. 223–4. For a more balanced summary of Aquinas' reservations see P. Dronke, *Fabula: Explorations into the uses of Myth in Medieval Platonism* (Mittellateinische Studien und Texte, 9) (Leiden and Cologne, 1974), p. 3, note I.

55 See E. R. Curtius' discussion of 'Jest and Earnest in Medieval Literature' in Trask, *European Literature*, pp. 417–35. For medieval commentators' use of the related terms *prodesse* and *delectare*, or *utilitas* and *delectatio*, see *Accessus ad auctores; Bernard d'Utrecht; Conrad d'Hirsau*, edited by R. B. C. Huygens (Leiden, 1970), pp. 22, 26, 36, 45, 63, 84, etc.; F. Ghisalberti, 'Medieval Biographies of Ovid', *Journal of the Warburg and Courtauld Institutes*, 9 (1946), 10–59 (pp. 42–3, 46, 58). Horace's sentence about mixing 'grave and gay' was well known in the later Middle Ages: see for example the statements by Stephen Langton and Robert Holcot quoted by Smalley, *English Friars and Antiquity*, p. 158. In view of Langland's interest in beast fables it is interesting to note that *fabulae* were generally supposed to both teach and delight: see for example John of Wales' *Florilegium philosophorum*, pars. VIII, cap. 6, in the Rome edition (1655), pp. 391–8; compare the 'Prolog' to Robert Henryson's *Morall Fabillis of Esope*, edited by H. H. Wood (Edinburgh, 1958), pp. 3–5.

56 Generations of Christian commentators had emphasized the moral *utilitas* of the *Liber Catonis*. 'Censorius Cato cum videret iuvenes et puellas in magno errore versari, scripsit hunc libellum ad filium suum, insinuans ei rationem bene vivendi et per eum docens cunctos omines ut iuste et caste vivant...utilitas est hunc librum legentibus

ut vitam suam sapienter instituere agnoscant': Huygens, *Accessus ad auctores*, p. 21. See further R. Hazelton, 'The Christianization of Cato', *Mediaeval Studies*, 19 (1957), 157–73.

57 A *locus classicus* of this medieval commonplace is Boethius, *De consolatione philosophiae*, I, metrum I–prosa I. The poetic muses, described as the glory of Boethius' youth, must give way to Dame Philosophy.

58 See Curtius' description of 'The Church and Laughter' in *European Literature*, pp. 420–2.

59 *De proprietatibus rerum*, prohemium (ed. Seymour, I, 41).

60 *Repertorium morale*, s.v. *legere*, in the Venice edition (1583), p. 389; compare Bersuire's discussion of *liber*, p. 401. For other uses of Romans I. 20 in this way see Richard of St Victor, *Benjamin minor*, cap. 5, in Migne, *PL*, 196, cols. 4–5; St Bonaventure, *Itinerarium mentis in Deum*, cap. 2, 12 (V, 302–3); Aquinas, *In librum Boethii de trinitate*, quaestio 6, art. 2 (trans. Maurer, pp. 67, 71).

61 Compare *Itinerarium mentis in Deum*, cap. I. 14 (V, 299), where St Bonaventure describes the order to be found in the *liber creaturae*, the *liber Scripturae* and the *corpus Ecclesiae* respectively.

62 C. Wolters, *The Cloud of Unknowing* (Harmondsworth, 1961), p. 15. By contrast, the *via negativa* asserted the 'unknowability' of God, and the inadequacy of earthly terms and concepts in face of the divine 'otherness'. In *The Cloud of Unknowing* the contemplative is urged to 'forȝete alle þe creatures þat euer God maad & þe werkes of hem': *The Cloud of Unknowing*, edited by P. Hodgson (EET OS 218) (Oxford, 1944), p. 16. Therefore, the vigorous working of the imagination must be suppressed (pp. 22, 117–8). If it is not restrained by the reason, it will never cease, waking or sleeping, to suggest diverse and perverted ideas about the empirical world, or some hallucination, which is only a spiritual idea conceived in material terms, or a material one conceived in spiritual terms (p. 117).

63 *De proprietatibus rerum*, prohemium (ed. Seymour, I, 41).

64 *Benjamin minor*, cap. 15, in Migne, *PL*, 196, cols 10–11.

65 Compare Aquinas, *Summa theologiae*, Ia I, 9, responsio. 'Holy Scripture fittingly delivers divine and spiritual realities under bodily guises'; 'holy Scripture delivers spiritual things to us beneath metaphors taken from bodily things'.

66 *Anecdotes historiques, legendes et apologues tirés du recueil inédit d'Étienne de Bourbon*, edited by A. Lecoy de la Marche (Société de l'Histoire de France) (Paris, 1877), pp. 3–5. Compare the prologue to Arnulf of Liège's *Alphabetum narrationum*: 'Narraciones siquidem et exempla facilius in intellectu capiuntur et memorie firmius inprimuntur et a multis libencius audiuntur.' Quoted in *The British Museum Catalogue of Romances in the Department of Manuscripts*, vol. III, edited by J. A. Herbert (London, 1910), p. 428.

67 For Albertus see *Isagoge in libros de anima*, cap. 17, in *Alberti opera*, ed. Borgnet, V, 521; *De bono*, tr. IV, qu. 2, art. 2, solutio, 16–18, in the Aschendorff edition, XXVIII, 251. Aquinas says that one may invent mnemonic similitudes and images because spiritual intentions slip easily from the soul unless they are linked to corporeal similitudes: *Summa theologiae*, IIa 2ae, qu.49, art. I. Yates comments, 'It is extremely curious that those in search of scholastic justification of the use of imagery in religious art should have missed the elaborate analyses of why we use images in memory': *Art of Memory*, p. 89.

68 See L. Thorndike, 'Unde Versus', *Traditio*, 11 (1955), 163–93; see further D. Gray, *Themes and Images in the Medieval English Religious Lyric* (London and Boston, 1972), pp. 39–41; S. Wenzel, 'The English Verses in the *Fasciculus morum*', in *Chaucer and Middle English Studies in Honour of R. H. Robbins*, edited by B. Rowland (London, 1974), pp. 230–48 (p. 241).

69 St Bonaventure explains that our *affectus* is moved more strongly by *exempla* than by ratiocinative argument, by promised rewards than by reasoning, by devotion than by dogma. Therefore, holy Scripture fittingly employs all these literary modes. See his *Breviloquium*, prologus, 5, in *Bonaventurae opera*, v, pp. 206–7. For discussion of scholastic justifications of 'affective' writing see A. J. Minnis, 'Literary Theory in Discussions of *Formae tractandi* by Medieval Theologians', *New Literary History*, 11 (1979–80), 133–45. For an attempt to relate the distinction between *affectus* and *intellectus* to *Piers Plowman* see Wittig, '*Piers Plowman*'.

70 Suggested by Bloomfield, *P.Pl. as Apocalypse*, p. 172.

71 Indeed, Langland's basic mode of procedure throughout *Piers Plowman* is very similar to that found in a moralized 'properties of things' (like the *De proprietatibus rerum* of Bartholomaeus Anglicus or Bersuire's *Reductorium morale*) or a tropological compendium of the type used by preachers (like Bersuire's *Repertorium morale* or John Bromyard's *Summa praedicantium*), the main difference being that Langland has personified the chapter-rubrics or subject-headings. For discussion of the genre of *compilatio* see A. J. Minnis, 'Late-Medieval Discussions of *Compilatio* and the Role of the *Compilator*', *Beiträge zur Geschichte der deutschen Sprache und Literatur*, 101 (1979), 385–421.

72 For speculation concerning the intended audience of *Piers Plowman* see J. A. Burrow, 'The Audience of *Piers Plowman*', *Anglia*, 75 (1957), 373–84.

73 Bloomfield, *P.Pl. as Apocalypse*, p. 172.

74 For example see *De proprietatibus rerum*, VI, cap. 27 (ed. Seymour, I, 336–8); *Speculum naturale*, XXVI, capi 56 and 75.

75 *Speculum naturale*, XXVI, capi 32–59.

76 *Speculum naturale*, XXVI, cap. 64. Vincent's source is John's *Summa de anima*, II, cap. 25: see the edition by T. Domenichelli (Prato, 1882), p. 266. John's *Summa* is quoted extensively in this section of the *Speculum*.

77 *Speculum naturale*, XXVI, cap. 75. For an excellent discussion of thirteenth-century debate on the three kinds of vision see J.-P. Torrell, *Théorie de la prophétie et philosophie de la connaissance aux environs de 1230* (Spicilegium Sacrum Lovaniense, Études et documents, 40) (Louvain, 1977).

78 *Speculum naturale*, XXVI, cap. 81.

79 See the *Prothemata in Apocalypsim*, in *Biblia sacra*, VI, cols. 1451–4.

80 See S. Berger, *Les Préfaces jointes aux livres de la Bible dans les manuscrits de la Vulgate* (Mémoires présentés par divers savants à l'Académie des Inscriptions et Belles-Lettres, première série, 11) (Paris, 1902), pp. 1–78 (p. 28). For the 'Paris Bible' see H. Denifle, 'Das Exemplar Parisiense', *Archiv für Litteratur und Kirkengeschichte des Mittelalters*, 4 (1888), 277–92.

81 *Biblia sacra*, VI, cols. 1449–50.

82 *An English Fourteenth-Century Apocalypse Version with a Prose Commentary*, edited by E. Fridner (Lund Studies in English, 29) (Lund and Copenhagen, 1961), pp. 3–4.

83 *Biblia sacra*, VI, col. 1450.

84 E. Wilson, in 'The "Gostly Drem" in Pearl', *Neuphilologische Mitteilungen*, 69 (1968), 90–101, seems to regard this classification in *The Chastising* as the usual one, and thinks that the Apocalypse prologue (which he cites only in the English translation) is out of line in classifying the Apocalypse with St Peter's vision of 'the third heaven' as intellectual visions. Actually, this latter classification is the usual one. Moreover, it should be noted that in calling the Apocalypse a 'gostly drem' the *Pearl* poet may mean simply 'visionary dream'. There is no reason to equate 'gostly drem' with *visio imaginaria*: it could even mean *visio intellectualis* (following Gilbert's description of the Apocalypse). The *Pearl* poet's use of the word 'ravish' does not throw any light on the issue, as 'ravishing' can take place in either imaginary vision or intellectual vision.

85 *The Chastising of God's Children*, p. 169.

86 *Biblia sacra*, VI, col. 1449.

87 See A. J. Minnis, 'Discussions of "Authorial Role" and "Literary Form" in Late-Medieval Scriptural Exegesis', *Beiträge zur Geschichte der deutschen Sprache und Literatur*, 99 (1977), 37–65.

88 Minnis, 'Discussions of "Authorial Role"', pp. 58–9.

Rhetorical and anti-rhetorical tropes: On writing the history of *elocutio*

BRIAN VICKERS

I

In the study of rhetoric, as with all other disciplines, a narrow conception leads to narrow thinking, facile rejections, and hasty abandonment of the subject. Give rhetoric a trivial function and you trivialize it; conceive of it as widely as it originally existed, and you may begin to do justice to it.

Rhetoric as the art of persuasion, or communication, was an integrated system dealing with the whole process of composition: finding material, arranging it, giving it expression, memorizing it, delivering it effectively. While the last two stages had less relevance outside its original context in spoken oratory, they continued to have important effects in unexpected ways. But the first three, *inventio*, *dispositio*, and *elocutio* form an *inseparable* unit. So one would have thought, at least, working directly from the primary texts. But, using some influential modern histories of rhetoric one is struck time and again by the grudging status granted to *elocutio* with its detailed techniques, or, in some cases, a thorough-going rejection of this part of rhetoric. Even the most learned and intelligent historians of rhetoric are occasionally guilty of this wish to be rid of the details. George Kennedy, who has revolutionized the study of Greek rhetoric, nevertheless writes of the 'increasingly important role' played by the figures of rhetoric in Hellenistic times, and says that 'Theophrastus is probably responsible for elevating the subject to a level equal to diction and thus encouraging the process of identification of figures which led to the almost interminable lists in later rhetorical handbooks.'[1] Nancy Stuever, in her stimulating study of rhetoric and Renaissance historiography, while showing in many places a profound understanding of rhetoric's goals and its ambivalent position in society, nevertheless refers to the details of style with fatigue: the late classical rhetorical treatises are mostly 'exhaustive but repetitive and stale', and she refers dismissively to Cicero's *De inventione* and *Topica* and to the *Ad Herennium* as 'the more mechanical treatises'.[2] Similarly, J. J. Murphy, in his pioneer work of synthesis, *Rhetoric in the Middle Ages*,[3] several times refers disapprovingly to the fact that Roman rhetoric uses what he calls 'highly developed, rather mechanistic theories of style (*elocutio*) based upon a Hellenistic proliferation of *figurae*' (pp. 8f). The *De inventione* is said to have a 'severely arid textbook quality' (p. 17n), to be 'highly schematized' (p. 109), lacking humanity. Murphy is avowedly writing a history of rhetorical theory, and like other modern historians of rhetoric seems to prefer a 'philosophical' approach, lamenting the failure of all the 'great pleas' for 'philosophical and psychological breadth' (pp. 63f). One reason for their failure may well be that 'each demands...more than is usually found in a single man' (*ibid*), but whatever the truth of that speculation (one could also suggest that the 'broader' views of Cicero and Quintilian demanded something inimical to rhetoric), there can be no doubt about the success of practical rhetoric. For two thousand years virtually every rhetoric-book printed included a list of the tropes and schemes, ranging from a dozen to five thousand, and some books consisted of only such lists.

Murphy's treatment of these works exemplifies the difficulties facing the historian, who naturally tends to assume that, as time goes by, things will change. But they did not. For the period A.D. 400 to 1050, for instance, he notes the existence of a group of rhetorical treatises 'devoted solely to *figurae*. Parroting as they do the familiar Roman rhetorical doctrines, these works present nothing new. In fact, their only importance lies in their absolute acceptance of the ancient system' (p. 44). Their continuance during a period of cultural and intellectual disorder and confusion may be an instance of the unthinking persistence of tradition, but it may also point to a need. The practical treatises of Cicero, and the *Ad Herennium*, had an enormous influence in the Middle Ages (pp. 104f), and rhetoric was important both in grammar (in the tradition deriving from Donatus) and in its own right, as in the arts of poetry (pp. 140f), so that an eleventh- or twelfth-century student 'would have been exposed to the lore of the *exornationes*' twice over (p. 141). The details of rhetoric would have been inescapable in any worthwhile medieval education, as we can see from the lists of figures included in grammars and rhetorics which Murphy conscientiously reproduces.[4]

In general Murphy seems disturbed by the practical nature of these treatises: one is 'nakedly pragmatic' (p. 221); another, however, is 'no nakedly schematic handbook' (p. 230). Yet it was precisely their practicality that rendered these treatises so popular: they provided would-be writers, poets, or preachers with models for imitation or re-creation. At times one may wonder whether medieval writers merely imitated these figures loyally, out of a spirit of unthinking dedication to the doctrine of classical rhetoric (a rather improbable suggestion), or whether they were aware of their poetic and psychological functions. Murphy gives very little attention to the question of whether his authors pronounced on function. Classical rhetoric undoubtedly did, as I have shown in some detail,[5] so it is misleading of him to write that 'The available rhetoric of Cicero – the *De inventione* and *Rhetorica ad Herennium* – fastened entirely on technique without an explicit rationale for the use of rhetoric' (p. 360). Admittedly, medieval rhetoric is fragmented in every sense, including this, but one can find a number of passages where rhetoricians describe a specific device as arousing the feelings, say, or enforcing agreement in the audience. The sign of the originality of Renaissance rhetoric is that it restored this theoretical dimension, and vastly increased the coverage of the tropes and schemes.

Learned and helpful as Murphy's book is, one looks in vain for any enthusiasm about *elocutio*, or any commitment to the value of this doctrine, passed down so carefully from generation to generation. Part of the vacuum may derive from his decision to write a history of the theory of a practical art. Yet medieval rhetoric understood by theory 'a set of rules that provide a definite method and system of speaking' (p. ix): we see that attention was immediately directed to the practical plane, there being very little discussion of theoretical issues (as we would understand them) throughout the whole period. Further, medieval rhetoric made no demand that these 'rules' be original to any 'theorist'. The figures classified by the author of *Ad Herennium*, or Donatus, can be traced for thousands of years across Europe, re-used and touched up, 'newly set forth', with or without acknowledgement to, and often in ignorance of, the ultimate source. The issue of originality, indeed, can hardly be raised in rhetoric, for if it were, 'who would 'scape whipping?' The authors of later rhetoric books who really did something original are few: Longinus and Vives are the only ones that come to mind. Puttenham tried to be original with anglicized terminology, but with unconvincing results.

The whole problem is that writing the history of rhetoric is an extremely odd and perhaps even impossible task. The compiler of a rhetoric-book in any period, re-shuffling his ingredients, trying to find a new and better system of arrangement, more famous or more recondite illustrations, does not write for later historians: he writes for budding writers, and it is in the poetry, drama, fiction, history, or cultural life of the age that his function and effect are to be found. He seldom feels the need to make the final product a work of literature, or philosophy, or entertainment. He is producing a guide to be used by other men, seldom by himself – how few, if any, authors of rhetoric-books have ever produced original creation – for the purposes of composition. He doesn't know how to write; he only knows how to teach others to write...A rhetoric-book is not an artefact but a tool, which claims that it can show you how to move and persuade, defend, convince, impress, deceive, whatever you wish. A rhetoric-book, an *ars* or *techne*, is a handbook on how to practise a discipline according to a set of tried and tested operations. The closest modern analogy might be with a book on tennis, or ballet. Reading an account of how to execute the different types of forehand, passing shots, lobs, cross-court volleys; or the pirouette, or leap, or entrechats, might indeed be rather dull: but watch Borg or Nastase, Nureyev or Margot Fonteyn, and the system is justified by the graceful, purposeful and expressive movements it makes possible. To write the history of music merely on the basis of the printed theory, manuals of harmony and counterpoint, is always possible, but it makes more sense to listen to the music also. To write the history of rhetoric merely from the text-books may be deeply misleading: the plays of Shakespeare, the poetry of Donne and Sidney, are better guides to the potentialities of rhetoric than all the text-books put together. Yet they could not have been written without those text-books. A *full* history will involve both theory and artefact. Those who write a partial history must be aware that they may be missing all the action.

Another issue that the historian of rhetoric has to face is the success of systems and models, where the chronological survey approach can produce severe distortions. To follow the *ars dictaminis* from its apparent beginnings at the abbey of Monte Cassino in the 1080s to Bologna some three hundred years later, and to see few changes, must be depressing for the historian,[6] who tends to read in expectation of change. Yet in terms of cultural history the continuity is proof that the system worked to everyone's satisfaction. To evaluate the situation properly one would have to look at each cultural context separately, and with the *ars dictaminis* and its elaborate system of address, based on precise distinctions of rank and status, one would soon be led into cultural history, as several medieval historians have found. The arts of letter-writing exist to serve not only a compositional situation but a social situation, so that a mere history of the text-books could never establish their true significance. One must turn to life to understand rhetoric.

Again, it is one of the characteristics of systems to evolve with increasing complexity until they reach a point of saturation. Looking at rhetoric-books one must realize that it is in the nature of the beast to want to address itself to as many possible situations as it can. The ideal of the compiler of a total-rhetoric-book (an idea worthy of one of the *Fictions* of Jorge Luis Borges, such as 'Funes the Memorious') would be to devise a form, and a name, for every conceivable linguistic, or psychological, situation or effect. Some writers realized the impossibility of the task: 'Words are limited; realities infinite', wrote Juan Luis Vives.[7] But others went to incredible lengths to cover every possible eventuality. Murphy reports on a *Summa grammaticalis* written around 1220, 'which provides about three thousand examples of names to illustrate the four Latin declensions' (p. 235). Guido Faba apparently devoted four complete works to the subject of 'letter openings' (p. 257): words fail me. Lawrence of Acquilegia's *Practica* (c. 1300) reduces the whole issue of writing a letter to a series of horizontal charts, from which the user can merely pick out what he needs, thus making 'letter-writing a skill that is possible to any person capable of copying individual letters of the alphabet' (pp. 258ff). I have chosen some of the most stupefying examples deliberately, because they dramatize my point: even here the rhetoric-book is simply fulfilling its role of providing practical assistance, performing what it had promised. The more rhetoric-books one reads without referring to the literary or cultural mileu, the more one is bound to notice the weakness of the genre. The paradoxical difficulty of writing its history is that rhetoric was meant to be done, not contemplated.

II

Historians of Renaissance and modern rhetoric will meet the same problems as J. J. Murphy has faced, and it is to be hoped that they will reveal the same balance and catholicity of interest, the same fairness in noting the work of others. The most extensive studies of British rhetoric for the period 1500 to 1800 so far produced have come from W. S. Howell,[8] whose work raises some of the fundamental problems in writing the history of rhetoric. To begin with, rhetoric is seen here in isolation from literature. I do not say that Howell should have moved from the history of theory to practice, but this narrowness of reference has some disabling effects. Although rhetoric has pervaded literary criticism from the time of Horace's *Ars poetica* onwards, Howell ignores literary criticism, either that written in the period, or that written about the period in modern times, both sources of many important discussions of rhetoric and poetics. The critical debates on Elizabethan and neo-classic criticism, Augustan poetic diction, the concepts of 'wit' or 'imagination', the work of several generations of critics – all this is left out of the picture. The result is not merely parochial or 'over-specialized': the history of a major literary force is written from within a vacuum.

When Howell comments on wider issues, he can forget elementary facts in the history of rhetoric. So he professes to be astonished by a Tudor rhetorician's conventional definition (as old as Cicero and Quintilian) of a trope as a deviation from normal speech: 'the implication is plain not only that tropes involve the use of words in some orbit outside of their usual ones', but that the motive for doing so is 'ornament rather than necessity' (p. 130). But we know that Aristotle's recommendation of the use of 'foreign' words in his *Rhetoric*, or other writers' definition of metaphor as a *translatio* from one field of knowledge to another, point to phenomena that have a far greater significance than the brief introductory statements of a text-book writer may suggest. Of Puttenham's standard distinction that prose is one step above ordinary conversation, and that poetry is a step above prose, Howell observes with indignation that

> This view amounts to a denial that the language of ordinary life can be a medium for oratory or poetry. It also amounts to an affirmation that the medium for oratory and poetry can be found only by dressing-up the language of ordinary life with such violations of our daily speech as the tropes and figures represent. (p. 328)

It is surprising that a scholar of rhetoric should appear to overlook the fact that from Aristotle's *Rhetoric* on through Cicero, the *Ad Herennium*, Quintilian, and in countless other authors over virtually two thousand years, it was held that the language of art could not and should not be the language of ordinary life. To give one example only, Book 3 Chapter 2 of Puttenham's *Arte of English Poesie* has the title: *How our writing and speaches ought to be figurative, and if they be not doe greatly disgrace the cause and purpose of the speaker and writer.*[9] Far from being 'violations of our daily speech', they are perfections of it: language reaches the highest degree of formalization and expressivity in the tropes and figures of rhetoric. Indeed, as I have shown elsewhere, a number of theorists held that rhetoric is only a systematization of ordinary speech, for men in passion or grief would naturally use certain verbal forms which the first authors of rhetoric noted and codified. The rhetoricians expressing this concept of a natural rhetoric include Aristotle, Quintilian, Longinus, Puttenham, and Abraham Fraunce.[10]

Howell's avoidance of the rhetorical tradition in its wider sense reduces the value of his work. But he adds to it an animus against the details of *elocutio* which is even more damaging. Discussing a standard text on the tropes and figures he breaks off impatiently:

> It may seem strange that human energy should be applied so diligently to this interminable enumeration of stylistic devices, when the subject of communication offers more philosophic and more humane approaches. [Such an interest is] more concerned with the husks than with the kernels of style. (pp. 33–4)

Despite this dismissive gesture, the fact is that the doctrine of the tropes and figures grasped not only the husks of style but the kernels also. It was a systematization of structures of language and structures of feeling which went into minute particulars since only at this level could language properly represent the movements of the mind and feelings. It seems odd for a historian to be rejecting the element to which his texts devoted so much energy and inventiveness, and it is a prejudice that Howell persists in. Continuing his history fifteen years later, now stretching on through the eighteenth century,[11] he reveals even more hostility to *elocutio*. He seems to judge the rhetorical tradition and its views on style not in their terms, nor neutrally or dispassionately, but in terms of his own beliefs. He is an exponent of the plain style; he believes that there is a common norm of language, deviation from which, or ornamentation of which, is pernicious. His is a utilitarian, materialistic view of language, his favourite text being Locke's statement that language ought to communicate 'Thoughts or *Ideas*...*with* as much ease and *quickness*, as is possible... Thereby to *convey* the *Knowledge* of Things'.[12] So he paraphrases approvingly Locke's 'prophetic indication of the direction in which a reconstructed rhetoric might develop out of the necessity to recognize that language is abused or deficient when it fails to convey with ease and quickness a knowledge of things between one man and another' (p. 284). The consequences of this reification of language to the level of the exchange of objects had been exposed with brilliant satire as early as 1726 by Jonathan Swift, in Book 3 Chapter 5 of *Gulliver's Travels*, where the sages of the Grand Academy of Lagado, believing that 'Words are only Names for Things', have reduced themselves to the stage of carrying 'about them such *Things* as were necessary to express the particular Business they are to discourse on'. Gulliver is so enraptured with this invention that it is with some reluctance that he admits the disadvantage of the new Scheme of expressing themselves by *Things*; which hath only this Inconvenience attending it; that if a Man's Business be very great, and of various kinds, he must be obliged in Proportion to carry a greater Bundle of *Things* upon his Back, unless he can afford one or two strong Servants to attend him. I have often beheld two of these Sages almost sinking under the Weight of their Packs, like Pedlars among us; who when they met in the streets would lay down their Loads, open their Sacks, and hold Conversation for an Hour together; then put up their Implements, help each other to resume their Burthens, and take their Leave.

But, for short Conversations a Man may carry Implements in his Pockets and under his Arms, enough to supply him, and in his House he cannot be at a Loss; therefore the Room where Company meet who practice this Art, is full of all *Things* ready at Hand, requisite to furnish Matter for this Kind of artificial Converse.[13]

That devastating parody is almost enough to settle the fallacy of reducing words to objects, of ignoring the semiotic functioning of language. Between 'words' and 'things' we must introduce 'ideas' or 'concepts', as in traditional language-theory, or draw a line, as in Saussure's. The distinction between signified and signifier cannot be collapsed, nor can they be regarded as interchangeable objects.

Those writers who do not share Howell's concept of language as the 'transferring accurate ideas of things' are either ignored or criticized. Rhetorical figures belong 'in the world of learning' but 'never in the world of everyday life' (p. 106); rhetoricians 'endlessly repeat' them (p. 120), or indulge in 'elaborate and endless analysis' of them (p. 112). Any style that uses the figures must be 'ornate, intricate... showy, extravagant' (p. 446: Dante? Racine? Shakespeare?). These 'natural perversions' are 'ancient machinery' (p. 446f: 'modern' is Howell's favourite term of praise); they are 'extravagant, self-regarding' (p. 491), 'ritualistic', 'contrived', 'largely useless' (pp. 514, 506).[14] He repeats verbatim the passage from his earlier book on the concept of artistic language representing a 'violation' of 'everyday speech' (p. 515).

All this animus derives from a misunderstanding of rhetoric. Historically one can observe time and again the need, in every generation from about 84 B.C. to 1820, at least (from the *Ad Herennium* to Fontanier), for lists of the figures, with definitions and illustrations. Evidently students, teachers, and writers found the systematization of the expressive resources of language of the highest interest. John Holmes, for example, writing in 1755, proudly announces that he has included 'about 250 *Figures*, &c. That is all, and indeed many more than all that are treated of in any other One Book' (p. 128). This was the very kernel of rhetoric, and anyone wishing to understand the literature of the past must share that readiness to go into the details of *isocolon* or *hyperbaton* or *metonymy*. The techniques must be learned.

Howell's distrust of rhetoric concerns also its function or goal. *Elocutio*, he says, not only violates everyday speech but dares to address itself towards our feelings. With two thousand years of the concept of rhetoric as the art of persuasion, whose practical efficacy in life was due to its ability to influence the human passions and affections, Howell still writes as if this power of rhetoric were reprehensible and illicit. Here again he follows Locke in distrusting emotion, and expresses with Utopian naiveté the belief that any appeal to the emotions, whatever the rightness of the case being made, involves 'distorted ideas, misdirected judgments, and highly coloured expressions' (p. 492). The appeal to the feelings is to be suppressed in favour of 'logical, scientific, rational' discourse. But the idea that a non-emotional use of language will be automatically 'true' or 'rational' is a myth, and those who believe in the possibility of communication as a value-free, neutral 'data-swap' might be referred to Gregory Bateson's demonstration that 'the logician's dream that men should communicate only by unambiguous digital signals has not come true and is unlikely to'.[15] The effect that such a theory has on history is, once more, to distort it. Believing that persuasion is illegitimate, Howell not only attempts to dismiss discussion of *elocutio*, to which more attention was given than to all the other parts of rhetoric put together, but he ignores or apparently misreads the significance of statements which he himself quotes, from rhetoricians of whom he approves. Fénelon, whose *Dialogues Concerning Eloquence* he has labelled 'the first modern rhetoric' (p. 505), summarizes the classical doctrine that 'an Oration is so far eloquent as it affects the Hearer's Mind', moves his passions, persuades him to action (pp. 507ff). Howell says that Fénelon shows the orator making 'deeply human truth visible' (p. 507), and this becomes a fixed point in the discussion, although Fénelon continues to stress that 'the whole Art of Oratory may be reduc'd to *proving*, *painting*, and *raising* the *Passions*' (p. 516). Adam Smith also said that appeal to the feelings is basic to the success of oratory (pp. 550f), as did George Campbell, who restated the traditional concept that the figures were the best way to arouse the passions (p. 589). John Lawson wrote that 'Figures are the Language of the Passions' (p. 620), and Joseph Priestley described the power of literature to move the emotions (p. 635). Yet all four are said to be exponents of what Howell calls the 'New Rhetoric', which, he claims, scorns appeals to the feelings and makes 'truth visible' (p. 615). None of these rhetoricians introduced the Platonic appeal to truth in such a way, and none of them rejects the feelings. Howell does not see the persistence of traditional ideas that rhetoric influences the reason by moving the passions.

This approach to 'the Language of the Passions' affects both the content and the structure of his book, as well as its argument. It has five main chapters, in turn discussing Aristotelian logic from 1615 to 1825; Ciceronian rhetoric from 1700 to 1759; elocutionary rhetoric from 1702 to 1806; 'New Logic' from 1690 to 1814; and 'New Rhetoric' from 1646 to 1800. At first sight this chronology seems confused and pointless: Howell splits logic from rhetoric, and divides his account of logic into two chapters covering much the same time span; Locke on logic is found on pp. 264ff, Locke on rhetoric on pp. 489ff; the Royal Society appears for the first time on p. 448, long after discussions of late-eighteenth-century logic and rhetoric. A second reading reveals that the displaced chronology is intentional, suggesting that the shape of the book's thesis is the shape of history. The arrangement expresses the author's pre-determined division of his material into two parts, 'old' (240-odd pages) and 'new' (450-odd). 'Old' logic is Aristotelian, topical, syllogistic; 'new' logic is inductive. 'Old' rhetoric is supposedly concerned with *elocutio*, the figures of speech, the five parts of an oration; 'new' rhetoric is supposedly plain-style, truthful, sincere. In other words, 'old' rhetoric represents all the things that Howell dislikes, 'new' all those that he approves of.

Yet the re-arrangement of chronology cannot disguise the fact that 'old' and 'new' ran side-by-side throughout this period. Further, the designating a 'new tradition' merely by the attack on an old one is of doubtful validity, as is the related assumption that such attacks actually destroyed or displaced their targets. Thus Locke's criticism of the topics in logic is said to have made them 'utterly meaningless' (p. 504), yet the topics, like the syllogism, continued to be taught up to the nineteenth century and beyond. If the so-called New Logic is to be measured by its success in dislodging the Old, then its history is a history of failures.

Attacks on rhetoric are as old as rhetoric, are indeed part of rhetorical teaching, carefully formulated, such as affirmations of sincerity, or disclaimers of skill by one who is about to manifest his skill (as with Chaucer's Franklin, and his 'I lerned nevere rethorik, certeyn'). Sometimes they are made in order to distract attention from rhetorical activity in another area, sometimes – as with Fénelon (pp. 512ff) – they are directed against bad rhetoric. Such distinctions are ignored by

Howell, who holds Fénelon up as new, and good, even though much of what he says is old, and good. The weakness of the thesis is visible even in the accounts of the heroes of 'New Rhetoric', who are revealed as simply confused, on Howell's terms. Adam Smith attacked the figures (pp. 545ff), but approved of appeals to the feelings (p. 550f); he attacked the process of invention and judgement in one place, yet praised them in another (p. 568); he is a 'New Rhetorician' since he advocates not a five-part but a two-part structure for an oration, yet in so doing – as Howell himself observes – he is merely reviving Aristotle (p. 573). The 'New Rhetoric', a phrase constantly repeated (seven times in one paragraph), is revealed merely as a claim for simplification, a disagreement about some of rhetoric's constituent parts. Many elements in this supposedly new discipline are entirely traditional: Fénelon is supposed to have 'expanded rhetorical theory to the point where it embraced not only oratory but poetry' (p. 511), but this idea is as old as classical antiquity;[16] Campbell also says that poetry is a branch of oratory (p. 590), Lawson goes back to Aristotle (p. 626), Blair is even conceded to be both 'traditional' and 'modern' (p. 665). But it is not the rhetoricians who are confused. When Howell hails Witherspoon as a model of the 'New Rhetoric' because he recommends a three-part oration, not a five-part one (p. 684), the reader, having seen this point already urged on behalf of Adam Smith (p. 573) and John Lawson (p. 626), and having seen that in each case Aristotle himself is the model, is led to a certain scepticism about the claims for novelty or innovation. The fact is, there was no such thing as a 'New Rhetoric', only a continuing debate about the relative importance of some rhetorical processes.

The emotive nature of the thesis which informs it means that Howell's book is an instance not of deliberative, nor of judicial oratory, but of epideictic oratory, with its opposed modes of praise and blame, *laus* and *vituperatio*. The proclamation of a 'New Rhetoric' is followed by the elevation of Adam Smith and George Campbell (pp. 602f) to the status of pioneers and heroes; both are over-praised. Although worthy, they are neither profound nor especially original. To say of Smith that in his work 'rhetoric for the first time measured itself against the needs of the modern world and became fully and triumphantly responsive to those needs' (p. 556), is to lose objectivity. The villains are the Old Rhetoricians, with their tropes and schemes. One of the leading and most highly respected writers in this tradition was Henry Home, Lord Kames, whose *Elements of Criticism* (1762) had a great influence in the eighteenth century and after (ten editions by 1800, twenty-seven by 1840). Even

Dr Johnson, who disliked Kames, pronounced it an essay that 'deserves to be held in some estimation', and said on another occasion that 'The Scotchman has taken the right method in his *Elements of Criticism.* I do not mean that he has taught us anything; but he has told us old things in a new way', a fair comment on Kames' application of traditional topics to modern literature, including Shakespeare.[17] In one of several footnotes listing stylistic rhetorics which he has dismissed from consideration, Howell states that he has not considered this book 'as a contribution to rhetorical theory' (pp. 613–14n), preferring to follow a biographer of Kames who (in 1814) classified it as 'philosophical criticism' (p. 377). Yet it is evidently a work on rhetoric and poetics, dealing with *elocutio* as 'Beauty of language', and many of Kames' contemporaries found it a major contribution: indeed, among the tributes are several from Howell's New Rhetoricians, such as Joseph Priestley (p. 644), and especially Hugh Blair, who urges us to read Kames' treatment of the figures of speech (p. 652). Blair's own discussion of the figures is alluded to only briefly by Howell (pp. 652f), who has in effect denatured rhetoric by excising all discussion of style, the schemes and tropes, and the appeal to the passions.

This approach affects not only the internal history of rhetoric, but its relations with the outside world, especially with education. Howell asks himself why so many of his authors spent so much time on teaching and imparting *elocutio*, and his explanation is as follows. The reason why, of all the parts of rhetoric, 'elocution was the greatest favorite in classrooms of European grammar schools of the sixteenth and seventeenth centuries and in the literary studies that the precollege student of those days was required to undertake' – we note that he has omitted the universities – is 'not hard to explain':

> It was more obviously within the capacities of lower school children to be able to identify the tropes and figures of style in the poems of Horace or Virgil and in the orations of Cicero than it would have been for them to comment upon the state of the controversy in one of Cicero's forensic speeches or to show how Cicero had derived one of his arguments from such a topic as adjuncts or contraries. The tropes and the figures, in the Latin and Greek terminology that was assigned to them in textbooks on rhetorical style, must have appealed mightily to the mentality of the pedagogue. Here were long lists of definitions that students could be made to memorize in Greek and Latin and to illustrate from the classics... (p. 106)

Howell concludes rightly that 'it would be impossible to overrate' the importance of the tropes and the figures 'as a factor in determining Latin literary style and taste in Western Europe during the Middle Ages and the Renaissance', and he adds that the vernaculars were also influenced (*ibid.*). Howell's explanation for the popularity of such teaching, that it was convenient for hard-pressed or unimaginative schoolmasters, fails to engage the true importance of this topic, and is part of an unfounded conception of the history of education between the sixteenth and eighteenth centuries.

Howell's claim now is that *elocutio* was taught only in the lower schools (it is not clear whether he means the 'lower school' within a grammar school – the first three forms, usually – or the whole of the grammar school; either way, 'elementary' seems intended to minimize the importance of these studies). As he puts it in a later collection of essays,[18] rhetoric consisted of 'five compositional procedures': 'Style and delivery were of course the more elementary of these procedures, in the sense that they could be taught effectively in the lower schools. Memory has also to be counted one of the more elementary of these procedures.' Invention and disposition were 'always regarded as the more difficult' stages. By 'elementary' and 'difficult' Howell must mean, in his view, 'worthless' and 'valuable' respectively, since otherwise one cannot understand how he should have got the sequence of teaching rhetoric back to front. No school teacher would have taught *elocutio* or *memoria* without having first introduced *inventio*, the finding of materials, and *dispositio*, their arrangement. As to *elocutio* being an elementary subject, on the authority of Quintilian, no less, innumerable Renaissance rhetoricians taught that *elocutio* was the part of rhetoric that was hardest to master, and to which most time must therefore be devoted. As rhetoric became a written, rather than a spoken genre, *memoria* and *pronuntiatio* inevitably lost their importance, but the first three stages were, and are, a unity. If the Ramists assigned *inventio* and *dispositio* to logic, that was in the nature of a tidying-up operation, for they of course expected logic and rhetoric to be studied side-by-side. And they, as vigorously as other schools, and more efficiently than most, encouraged the study of *elocutio*, to which they – like other rhetoricians in the sixteenth and seventeenth centuries – devoted whole treatises.

Howell's attitude is shown by his comment that sixteenth-century rhetoric-books contained a 'long' list of schemes and tropes, 'as English schoolboys knew to their dismay' (p. 158), suggesting that they were merely there as a nuisance for schoolboys. As an admirer of the 'modern', Howell observes with satisfaction that 'in present-day American education students no longer memorize tropes and schemes' (p. 159). In its context this remark sounds like a rejection of past educational principles on the grounds that they are no longer practised. He goes on to state that rhetoric has thus 'purified' itself 'of some of the rhetorical mechanisms which no longer meet the needs of the modern world – invention by resort to commonplaces, for example, or style that grows from the exploitation of the tropes and figures...' (p. 255). This new state of affairs seems to him satisfactory, for 'ordinary speech as a medium of communication better reflects the needs of a businessman's culture' while 'tropes and figures were better for a culture of landed aristocrats' (p. 160). Such are Howell's ventures into social and intellectual history. In general, his work seems to be the product of a tradition in American departments of speech and rhetoric whereby only those aspects of rhetoric were taught which could be easily applied to the contemporary speech situation. While testifying to the persistence of the rhetorical tradition, this approach tended in fact to be non-historical, or anti-historical: the end of the tradition could no longer understand its beginnings. The work of other, and younger, American scholars suggests that the historical approach has been reinstated.[19]

III

When we turn to the pronouncements about *elocutio* made during the Renaissance, and to its place in grammar school and university education, we will see just how false is the impression given by Howell's summary accounts. If that massive survey of English Renaissance education by T. W. Baldwin is consulted,[20] it will be seen that it was in the senior, or more advanced classes that rhetoric, especially *elocutio*, was most studied. It is in the fourth, fifth, and sixth forms that the systematic memorizing of rhetorical figures was concentrated, and the triad of learning processes recommended in *Ad Herennium* – art, imitation, exercise – carried out with a thoroughness that ensured that no pupil could have passed through those schools without being indelibly marked with their lore. This can be seen from Baldwin's analysis of the grammar school curricula, starting from John Colet's organization of St Paul's in 1512, inspired by Erasmus' *De ratione studii* (Baldwin, vol. I, p. 78), which was taken over bodily by other schools (e.g. vol. I, pp. 118, 134). In the fourth form, at the age of ten, they might use Erasmus' seminal work *De copia*, in the fifth they would graduate to Susenbrotus' popular *Epitome troporum ac schematum* or to the list of figures in Book 4 of *Ad Herennium*. They memorized a certain number of figures each day, were trained to identify them in the Latin poetry or prose that they read, and to re-use them in their own compositions, Latin or English. The stress in the curricula is on mastery of the details of *elocutio* 'by daily practice' (vol. I, p. 349). At Rotherham in the early seventeenth century a Ramist rhetoric was used, Charles Butler's *Rhetoricae libri duo* (1597), and the progress of the fifth-form class was noted in this way: 'Their fore-noone Lessons were in Butler's *Rhetorick*, which they said *memoriter*, and then construed, and applyed the example to the definition' (vol. I, p. 427). Archbishop Laud's account of Westminster School in the early 1630s – the poet, dramatist, and critic John Dryden attended that school a decade later – noted of the pupils that 'Betwixt 4 and 5 they repeated a leafe or two out of some book of Rhetoricall figures' (vol. I, p. 360).

Baldwin's findings are supported by other authorities. Foster Watson analysed Archbishop Wolsey's curriculum for the Ipswich Grammar School, dated 1 September 1528. The school is divided into eight classes, and only in the eighth or highest were the students to be introduced to rhetoric, via the figures of Donatus, with the master being instructed to point out 'any figure of speech, uncommon beauty of style, rhetorical ornament', or the like.[21] John Brinsley's model curriculum, outlined in his *Ludus Literarius or the Grammar School* (1612) would begin rhetoric earlier, in the third form, spending a quarter of the year learning the figures: but the study of rhetoric, he maintained, should be continued through the fourth, fifth, and sixth forms, as part of the students' 'constant employment'.[22] Another English schoolmaster, Charles Hoole, in his *A New Discovery of the Old Art of Teaching School* (1660; written c. 1636–7),[23] begins rhetoric in the fourth form, three mornings a week, with William Dugard's *Elementa rhetorices* as the text. The pupils, having 'throughly learnt that little book' (pp. 132–3), should copy it out, collect examples, and continue to learn and revise rhetoric through the fifth and sixth forms (pp. 167, 179, 191). In the highest class they would read Horace in the afternoons, 'wherein they should be emploied... in construing and parsing, and giving the Tropes and Figures' (p. 197).

If Erasmus left his mark on English education, the same stress on absorbing *elocutio* can be found in the other great theorists of education in the sixteenth century. In his *De tradendis disciplinis* (1531) Vives advised teachers to begin with Erasmus' *De copia*, then proceed to the treatment of the figures in Quintilian.[24] He recommends a practical guide produced by Mosellanus, 'a table of figures of speech which can be hung on the wall so that it will catch the attention of the pupil as he walks past it, and force itself upon his eyes'. Vives puts rhetoric in the last but one place in the curriculum, just before mathematics, and sees its function – in a profound observation on the learning process – as being to help in the development of individuality through the imitation of models.[25] The great German educationalist Melanchthon also placed rhetoric late in the curriculum. In his school at Eisleben, founded in 1525 and divided into three classes, the principles of rhetoric were introduced in the third class, through works by Erasmus and Aphthonius. For the important and influential Obere Schule which he inaugurated at Nuremberg, the first class – that is, the continuation from the Latin school – studied rhetoric and dialectic (*De copia*, Cicero, Quintilian) before completing their studies with Latin poetry and verse composition, mathematics, and Greek.[26]

Turning to France, the great educational reformer Andrea de Gouvéa[27] was invited by the corporation of Bordeaux in 1534 to reorganize their boys' school, and in his work of transforming the Collége de Guyenne he was aided by such distinguished teachers as Budin, Grouchy, and Mathurin Cordier; later teachers included George Buchanan, Muretus, and Élie Vinet, whose *Schola aquitanica* of 1583 is a curriculum as drawn up on the basis of the school's traditional practice. In it we have the same pattern as in Germany or England: not until the fourth form (out of nine) 'did the pupils attack an oration of Cicero, with which was used a little manual of rhetoric such as that of Barzizza, or of Sulpicius, or the *De copia*'. In the third form following, the boys (now aged thirteen to fourteen) spent two terms on 'one of the speeches of Cicero and a substantial manual of rhetoric by "some good author"' – Despauterius on figures is mentioned.[28] Finally, in the 'Classe de Rhétorique, or highest form' – the very name shows that rhetoric was regarded as being the apex of education – the 'gradually increased stress... on rhetoric' noticeable in the three last classes reached its high point. The position is expressly said to be based upon 'the usage of the Roman schools of the time of Quintilian'. Each day began 'with an hour's lesson upon the precepts of the art of oratory after Cicero or Quintilian, followed at nine by one of the speeches of Cicero in illustration, and as a model for exercises in declamation and forensic prose' (p. 150). Logic is left to subsequent courses in the Faculté des Arts (p. 151).

One of Gouvéa's associates, Mathurin Cordier, was invited in 1536 by his former pupil, Calvin, to join him in Geneva to reorganize the Collége de la Rive, and spent the remaining twenty-eight years of his life 'in Switzerland, always teaching, organising, or reforming schools'. In his curriculum there are seven classes, and unlike most educationalists, who put logic after rhetoric, Cordier put logic in the last-but-one form, and introduced 'the elements of rhetoric' and 'elocution' only in the final class. The 'whole doctrine of rhetoric' was 'illustrated from Cicero's speeches, and from Demosthenes (the *Olynthiacs* and *Philippics*)' – Greek was also begun earlier than usual here – while Homer and Virgil were 'analyzed for rhetorical purposes' (pp. 159f).

Alex Gordon's survey of rhetorical education in sixteenth-century France[29] reaches, independently, the same conclusions. At the Collége de Guyenne, 'De la cinquième jusqu'à la première [classe] la rhétorique prenait une place de plus en plus importante dans les cours' (pp. 24f). In the Jesuit schools the pattern is the same: divided into a five-year curriculum, 'Dans la quatrième et dans la cinquième année des études, la rhétorique tenait une place importante' (p. 25). Instruction in France, as in the rest of the European Renaissance, was not merely theoretical. 'On l'enseignait d'une façon plutôt pratique que théorique.' The Jesuits, as one might expect, were remarkably systematic and detailed in their planning to achieve a practical mastery: 'Il s'agissait, en somme, de toute une éducation du style, visant à la perfection des moyens d'expression' (p 26). The attention to detail is common to all students of rhetoric in the sixteenth-century, and quite cuts across the artificial barriers set up by some modern historians of rhetoric. The system practised by the Jesuits was exactly the same as that urged by Erasmus, or Vives, or indeed by Ramus, who in his *Praelectiones* on Virgil's *Georgics* (1578) goes into great detail to analyse and identify the rhetorical components of Virgil's style. As Gordon rightly notes, 'Bien entendu, il ne néglige pas le fond (il explique toutes les allusions obscures), mais son grand souci demeure le style' (p. 27). Evidently the care which the Renaissance expended on style must have been devoted to some end higher than the 'mere ornament' to which modern historians disparagingly refer.

The seventeenth century in France may see, later, some controversies about rhetoric, but in the schools its importance did not dwindle; was, rather, consolidated. The Jesuits' *Ratio studiorum*, and the rapid spread of their schools throughout Catholic Europe, ensured a key position to rhetoric. In their system, Peter France[30] notes, rhetoric appears 'as the culmination of the basic cycle of studies. The Jesuit pattern was followed with variations in most of the other teaching establishments. Thus most boys who went to school had a thorough grounding in rhetoric by the time they were fifteen.' As Father François de Dainville has shown in a number of studies,[31] the Jesuits' reform established a solid base of grammar for three years of the curriculum. Then, 'Une quatrième année, la classe de poésie ou d'humanités, préparait ensuite les matériaux nécessaires pour la rhétorique: langue élégante, vocabulaire de choix, première étude de la composition.' In the fifth and final class, 'La rhétorique couronnait la formation littéraire. Son objectif propre était de former à la parfaite éloquence latine... qui comprenait, avant tout, l'art oratoire, secondairement l'art poétique.' This mastery was achieved by the daily study of Cicero's *Partitiones*, the *Ad Herennium*, Quintilian, and by the new standard text of Soarez, *De arte rhetorica*, which was the single manual recommended up to 1659, when it was partially replaced by Pomey's *Novus candidatus rhetoricae*.[32] No teacher in the Jesuit schools was ever afraid of going into detail, witness the enormous scope of many of the later treatises, nor did they regard the acquisition of rhetoric as the proper activity of small boys. It was so important that it demanded maturity, and application.

IV

As for the universities, Howell's account suggests that *elocutio* was studied only by 'the precollege student of those days'.[33] In fact the reverse is the case. At the University of Wittenberg, another foundation inspired by Melanchthon, the pre-matriculation student had to 'attend elementary courses in logic and rhetoric'. Yet, once matriculated, he would take further courses in logic, rhetoric and poetry, reading Cicero, Quintilian, and certain Latin poets.[34] As with all European universities in the sixteenth century we can trace the gradual influence of humanism on the curriculum, with a tremendous revival of rhetoric. Melanchthon was instrumental in reviving the humanities, Camerarius being invited to lecture on Quintilian in 1522, and re-establishing the humanist disciplines. There were four chairs for law, three for medicine, and ten for the liberal arts. At the Sorbonne,[35] for so long the bastion of scholasticism and the enemy of the newer learning, the revival of humanism had begun as early as the fifteenth century, through the person of Guillaume Fichet, himself the author of a *Rhetorica* (1471) and a professor of rhetoric, who could say by 1472 that the muses flourished in Paris. Other rhetoric teachers in Paris at that time were Robert Gaguin and Guillaume Tardif (author of a *Rhetorice artis...compendium*, 1475), who was authorized to teach rhetoric at the Sorbonne in 1484. One student who followed the courses of Gaguin and Tardif in 1473 was Reuchlin. As Alex Gordon has shown, rhetoric established itself firmly at the Sorbonne in the sixteenth century: in 1535 the professors of grammar and rhetoric got the same rights as those in philosophy. Ramus' reforms were in the humanist tradition of practicality, imitation and exercise, while once the Sorbonne adopted the *Ratio studiorum* in 1598 it aligned itself with the most efficient rhetoric-teaching system ever devised.

In England the position is identical. An early forerunner was Traversanus, whose *Nova rhetorica* was written at Cambridge and published by Caxton in 1479.[36] As Roberto Weiss has shown, humanism established itself in England thanks to the efforts of a few energetic and far-sighted patrons, such as Humphrey, Duke of Gloucester.[37] The changes in the curriculum occurred at much the same time as those made in Europe: when Bishop Fox founded Corpus Christi College, Oxford, in 1517, he laid down that lectures should be given on Cicero's *Orator*, *Partitiones*, Quintilian's *Institutes*, and the *Declamations* attributed to Quintilian. Trinity College, Oxford, adopted these texts into its statutes in 1555, adding Valla's *Elegantiae*; in the same year St John's College, Oxford, accepted the list and added to it further works by Cicero, Hermogenes, Isocrates, Demosthenes, and two Renaissance compilations, those by Trapezuntius and Cassander.[38] As a recent historian[39] of Oxford and Cambridge in the sixteenth century has shown, the elevation of rhetoric and grammar to the same place as logic, and the increasing time spent on rhetoric, had the effect of making rhetoric – including *elocutio* – more central to the student's education, which was once again practical, not theoretical. At Cambridge, the curriculum was reformed on similar lines: as Joan Simon sums up,[40] 'humanist studies had been absorbed into the old framework, the arts course being adapted to make way for rhetoric and the study of classical authors while grammar was delegated to the schools'. The teaching of logic on the old lines was swept away in the new statutes given to the university in 1544, as a result of a government visitation. Now the first year of the arts course was devoted to mathematics (comprising cosmography, arithmetic, geometry, astronomy), while the second year of that course 'was to cover dialectic and rhetoric, with texts of Aristotle, Cicero, Quintilian, and Hermogenes'. Rhetoric rose at the expense of other subjects besides logic, for 'one of the few changes made in the Edwardian statutes at the outset of Elizabeth's reign was to eliminate mathematics in favour of rhetoric' (one reason, perhaps, why Francis Bacon accorded mathematics so little function in his re-shaping of the sciences). In no sense, then, can rhetoric be thought of as the province of schoolboys. The vigour of rhetoric teaching in the English universities can be gauged from the traditions surrounding Sir John Cheke, and the extant published treatises of John Rainoldes, Gabriel Harvey, as well as some unedited manuscript material. The historian contemplating the spread of rhetoric at this time would be justified in quoting 'Wider still and wider/Shall thy bounds be set'.

V

The dominance of rhetoric in the European Renaissance, and the great prestige awarded to *elocutio*, were due to rather more than the efforts of unimaginative lower-school pedagogues. The Renaissance took the classics seriously, at times too reverently, perhaps, and were impressed by the praise of speech that they read in Isocrates, or Cicero.[41] If speech is a God-given faculty, which distinguishes men from beasts, and is the bond of all civil society, then the study of speech, and its practical mastery, must be occupations of the highest value, and of the greatest use to life. The ideology of the *vita activa*, that urge towards man's creative involvement with his fellow-men, was based on the concept of speech as communication, exchange, praxis. The importance of *elocutio* had been made clear by classical rhetoricians from the amount of space they devoted to it, and by their explicit pronouncements. The most frequently quoted of these during the Renaissance was Quintilian's, in the Preface to Book 8 of his *Institutes of Oratory*. Having devoted the preceding five books to *inventio* and *dispositio*, both 'absolutely necessary' to the orator (8. Pr. 1), he moves on to *elocutio*:

> The points which follow require greater care and industry. For I have now to discuss the theory of style, a subject which, as all orators agree, presents the greatest difficulty. For Marcus Antonius, whom I mentioned above, states that he has seen many good, but no really eloquent speakers, and holds that, while to be a good speaker it is sufficient to say what is necessary, only the really eloquent speaker can do this in ornate and appropriate language.[42] (8. Pr. 13–14)

The reference is to *De Oratore* (1. xxi. 94), and Quintilian adds that if Antonius considered neither himself nor Lucius Crassus to possess this gift, the reason why they lacked it 'was its extreme difficulty of acquisition'. With a reference to *Orator* (xiv. 44) he goes on:

> Again, Cicero holds that, while invention and arrangement are within the reach of any man of good sense, eloquence belongs to the orator alone, and consequently it was on the rules for the cultivation of eloquence that he expended the greatest care. That he was justified in so doing is shown clearly by the actual name of the art of which I am speaking. For the verb *eloqui* means the production and communication to the audience

of all that the speaker has conceived in his mind, and without this power all the preliminary accomplishments of oratory are as useless as a sword that is kept permanently concealed within its sheath. Therefore it is on this that teachers of rhetoric concentrate their attention, since it cannot possibly be acquired without the assistance of the rules of art: it is this which is the chief object of our study, the goal of all our exercises and all our efforts at imitation, and it is to this that we devote the energies of a life-time; it is this that makes one orator surpass his rivals, this that makes one style of speaking preferable to another. (8. Pr. 14–17)

Of course, Quintilian continues, he does not mean that 'we should devote ourselves to the study of words alone': it would be futile to disregard 'the subject matter which, after all, is the backbone of any speech' (8 Pr. 18). We must join *res* and *verba*, cultivate *elocutio* as the crowning-point, indeed the realization of *inventio* and *dispositio*.

There, with proper care for a balanced and nuanced position, Quintilian delivered one of his most influential pronouncements. Its echo in the Renaissance can be traced through German Baroque rhetoric, as Joachim Dyck[43] has shown; through the Pléiade poets – Peletier and Du Bellay repeat the point verbatim;[44] the great educationalists, such as Melanchthon and Budé,[45] state and develop it; for the sixteenth-century Italian critics, as Bernard Weinberg points out, poetics was essentially equated with *elocutio*, so that the greatest attention of all was given to style, diction, the concept of the three styles, and the appropriate decorum of ornament and figure.[46] This applied to their reading of ancient and modern authors: Speroni stated in 1581 that Virgil's merit rested exclusively in *elocutio* (p. 170); Pagano cites Aristotle's *Rhetoric* to account for Petrarch's use of rhetorical figures (p. 188). Parassio in 1531 states that 'elocution... is more important than invention' (p. 98), while rhetoric dominates the poetic theory of Tasso (p. 646), and is equally important in that of Vida (p. 715), Speroni (p. 342), Salutati,[47] and many others. The inheritors of the Italian sixteenth century were the French theorists and writers of the following century. Peter France has traced this tendency in theory and in practice, above all in the theatre: 'But it is clearly *elocutio* which is most useful to the dramatist, *elocutio* the use of language and, in particular, the use of language to simulate passion or, as we might say, to create character.'[48]

The rhetoricians themselves frequently declared that *elocutio* was the most important part of rhetoric: Trapezuntius[49] did so; in England Sherry, Puttenham, and Webbe do so.[50] This belief is shared by all writers on rhetoric, whatever the category modern historians try to force them into, Ciceronian, or Ramist, formulary or stylistic, secular or sacred, Catholic or Protestant: all believe in the importance of *elocutio*, that is of mastering the details of language in order to master the audience's feelings. Thus Soarez, in his vastly influential *De arte rhetorica*, gives most space to *elocutio* and quotes Quintilian's metaphor of the sheathed sword to explain his emphasis: 'Consequently, as this third book, which contains rules for expression, is more serviceable than both preceding books, it will have to be somewhat longer.' For 'Eloquence is so great, so distinguished, and such a wonderful thing that it contains almost everything.'[51] Vives' *De ratione dicendi* (1533) devotes itself entirely to *elocutio*, transforming rhetoric into literary criticism by giving the first modern treatise on stylistics. Some writers stress other parts of rhetoric more, for their own special purposes or interests: the logician Rudolph Agricola[52] put *docere* above *movere* and *delectare*, and was almost unique in doing so; Melanchthon stressed *inventio*, partly as the necessary first stage in composition, but partly because it could be applied directly to theology.[53] But Book 2 of his treatise is devoted to *elocutio* (given roughly the same space as *inventio*), and includes the standard points that *res* cannot be understood without the help of *verba*, and without their help all the arts would be taught 'in a confused and obscure way' (pp 218–19). To Melanchthon 'care in speaking well should be taken as a liberal art and one most worthy of a man', and if there is anyone to whom such speech does not give pleasure 'he has degenerated a long way from human nature' (p. 221). Thereafter Melanchthon draws on Book 3 of *De oratore* and Books 8 and 9 of Quintilian to provide the obligatory list of figures, which are related not to art or ornament but to life (e.g. p. 261).

It is true, as E. R. Curtius[54] stated, that the teaching and prestige of Quintilian is perhaps the main reason why, up to the French Revolution at least (and recent studies of Stendhal, Flaubert, and Hugo would continue it beyond that point), 'all literary arts rest upon school rhetoric'. Yet, to understand the importance of *elocutio* in classical antiquity, the Middle Ages, the Renaissance and after, it is not enough to read Quintilian. The history of rhetoric cannot be written from the rhetoric-books alone. It was an art that drew on life, and had for its main justification its promise of success in life. Words were there to arouse feelings, to move men to action. The major justification of *elocutio* was its efficacy in practical affairs. Admittedly, many works of rhetorical theory contain at some point the concept of the figures as ornament, and modern readers tend to understand such statements in the light of their own concept of ornament as something extraneous, applied after the event, not inherent in the process of composition and creation. Yet as long ago as 1897 W. H. Woodward,[55] that pioneer in the historiography of Renaissance education, gave the proper conception of *elocutio*, and why it was so vital to the Humanists, being

> manifest in all that they said and wrote. Style is the indispensable condition of permanence, almost indeed of credibility, in a literary work; in society it is accepted as the obvious mark of an educated man. The functions of eloquence...are of supreme dignity. For whilst it is the end of philosophy to exhibit canons of excellence in thought and character, and the use of history to illustrate them, it belongs to eloquence alone, by fitting stimulus, to enforce their application.

To the Renaissance, in particular, *elocutio* did not mean superficial ornament but the power of expression, and the result of expression: the written or spoken word. As Woodward wrote in another work,[56] to the Humanists it would be futile to attempt to define Truth without using language. In Rudolph Agricola's letter to a friend, written in 1484, and sometimes called *De formando studio*, the study of Philosophia has three divisions: moral philosophy, or the art of behaviour; *rerum cognitio*, or the liberal arts (including nature, history, letters, politics); and *ars commode eloqui*. This third section is

> the art of *expressing* truth. To every humanist truth was, in the first place, inconceivable unless defined in exact terms, and in the next, useless to man unless communicated and recorded. Eloquentia, then, with Agricola as with others, was much more than the ornamental garb of 'eruditio', it was an essential condition of its utility.

This position is one on which the Renaissance prided itself – not without reason – on having gone beyond medieval philosophy. Thus Budé in his tract *De l'institution du prince* (1516) attacks the scholastics of the University of Paris, because they

> will not understand that the function of eloquence is to serve as the instrument of knowledge in its relation to life, without which truth cannot be translated into action; just as a mechanic engine which no one knows how to work is no engine at all but a mere mass of metal... For all their Faculties, deprived of the aid of Letters, are scabbards without swords, which may serve to scare children but nothing else.[57]

Elocutio, the command of language, is especially necessary to a king, who 'must cultivate "sapientia", practical wisdom, rather than "contemplatio"'.[58]

To Vives rhetoric was 'necessary for all positions in life'. Men's emotions and reason can be swayed by speech, which 'holds in its possession a mighty strength which it continually manifests'. Students should declaim on 'matters which may afterwards be useful in life': 'let all eloquence', Vives urges, 'stand in full battle array for goodness and piety, against crime and wickedness'.[59] The Jesuit Perpinian, in a work *De oratore*, still in manuscript, 'conceives eloquence as extending beyond the senate and the court, so that it includes all affairs, public and private, civil and religious'.[60] The gap between theory and practice, between intellect and will, was to be bridged by speech. Since, as Cicero had taught, all virtue consists in action, and since the end of learning must be virtue, then, as Salutati put it, 'Eloquence is essential to the *studia humanitatis* because of the necessity of moving the will to action.'[61] With the increased emphasis in Renaissance philosophy on the nature of the will, *elocutio* was seen as the link between thought and deed. Nancy Struever has quoted the perceptive argument of George of Trebizond, that since "reason itself lies hidden in the obscure processes of the intellect before it has been drawn forth by speech", like "the fire hidden in the flint", then thought without speech would be a form of darkness, blindness or ignorance.[62] The orator, therefore, is a symbol of knowledge and power and virtue and of the practical realization of them all.

Melanchthon, 'the teacher of Germany', invoked the classical accounts (Horace, Cicero) of the function of language in creating human society, and in establishing its most vital processes:

> It has been said, with good reason, that when men were still dispersed and nomadic they were gathered together by eloquence, and that by it states were founded; by it rights, religions, legitimate marriage, and the other bonds of human society were constituted. In fact, it is by speech (*oratio*) that these things are maintained in commonwealths... Cultivated speech (*elocutio*) is not an empty adornment, but necessary for the right and proper exposition of matters of every sort.[63]

Introducing his survey of 'Rhetoric, or Art of Eloquence' in *The Advancement of Learning*, Bacon concisely stated its practical importance with a quotation from the Bible:

> For though in true value it is inferior to wisdom,... yet with people it is the more mighty: for so Salomon saith, *Sapiens corde appellabitur prudens, sed dulcis eloquio majora reperiet*, [the wise in heart shall be called prudent, but he that is sweet of speech shall compass greater things]; signifying that profoundness of wisdom will help a man to a name or admiration, but that it is eloquence that prevaileth in an active life.[64]

No less convinced of the need for 'well doing', Sir Philip Sidney, in the most compact and eloquent of all the Renaissance defences of poetry, invoked the tradition of language as God's gift to man to distinguish him from the beasts: 'For if *oratio* next to *ratio*, speech next to reason, be the greatest gift bestowed upon mortality, that cannot be praiseless which does most polish that blessing of speech.'[65] Eloquence is second only to the reason, and it is the means by which the reason can communicate itself.

What Hegel[66] said about mental impact – 'The force of mind is only as great as its expression' – may be matched by Puttenham's question, 'what els is man but his minde?'[67] and by Ben Jonson, translating Vives: 'Language most shewes a man: speake that I may see thee. It springs out of the most retired, and inmost parts of us, and is the Image of the Parent of it, the mind. No glasse renders a mans forme, or likenesse, so true as his speeech.'[68]

Mind, knowledge, truth; action, power, conviction: *elocutio* provided the passage from potentiality to realization, via the control of language and the force of feeling. If *elocutio* was the hinge around which the whole of Renaissance moral and civic philosophy turned, then it can only be fully understood by reference to life. This is why its study was not the property of lower-form schoolboys, and unimaginative pedagogues, but of all who wished to be fully human.

NOTES

1 Kennedy, *The Art of Persuasion in Greece* (London, 1963), p. 277; cf. also pp. 290, 321–2. For other modern historians rejecting the figures see Brian Vickers, *Classical Rhetoric in English Poetry* (London, 1970), pp. 88ff.

2 Struever, *The Language of History in the Renaissance. Rhetoric and Historical Consciousness in Florentine Humanism* (Princeton, 1970), pp. 33, 34; also 46f.

3 Murphy, *Rhetoric in the Middle Ages. A History of Rhetorical Theory from Saint Augustine to the Renaissance* (Berkeley and Los Angeles, 1974).

4 See pp. 149–52, 164–7, 170–2, 177–80, 182–91, 204–5, 238, 342. Murphy gives these lists without enthusiasm, or elucidation, or comment, except occasionally that he will attempt a 'brief listing of the items' (p. 151); or gives 'a long list of figures' (p. 179), or 'a lengthy section' (p. 205).

5 Vickers, *Classical Rhetoric*, ch. 3.

6 This is Murphy's claim, *Rhetoric in the Middle Ages*, p. 211, although not every scholar agrees with him.

7 Vives, *De ratione dicendi*, translated by J. F. Cooney (unpublished doctoral dissertation, Ohio State University, 1966; University Microfilms Order no. HUJ67-06303), p. 266.

8 Howell, *Logic and Rhetoric in England, 1500–1700* (Princeton, 1956).

9 Puttenham, *Arte of English Poesie*, edited by G. Willcock and A. Walker (Cambridge, 1936; 1970), p. 138.

10 Vickers, *Classical Rhetoric*, pp. 87, 94–6, 100–5, 107–8, 110–15. This tradition extended to the 1750s, at least. In his *Essai Sur les Bienseances Oratoires, Tome Second* (Paris, 1753), Edmé Mallet asks whether anyone has failed to notice the occurrence of tropes and figures in the natural language of the passions: 'Est-il quelqu'un de ceux qui se mêlent de parler en public, que le commerce de la vie n'ait mis à portée de remarquer tous les jours dans eux-mêmes ce langage de la nature, ou de l'étudier dans les autres? Un homme d'esprit a dit qu'il se faisoit plus de figures de Rhétorique

à la Halle en un jour de marché, qu'à l'Académie en plusieurs Séances' (pp. 198f). The author cited is Dumarsais, *Traité des Tropes* (1730). I owe this reference to Professor Dene Barnetto.

11 Howell, *Eighteenth-Century British Logic and Rhetoric* (Princeton, 1971).

12 Locke, *An Essay concerning Human Understanding*, Bk III, ch. 10, §23; edited by Peter H. Nidditch (Oxford, 1975), p. 504.

13 *Gulliver's Travels*, edited by Herbert Davis (Oxford, 1941: *The Works of Jonathan Swift*, vol. XI), pp. 185f.

14 For further instances of bias against *elocutio* see pp. 90, 113–15, 119, 138, 140f, 142, 145f, 202f, 243, 458, 489, 631, 712.

15 Bateson, 'Redundancy and Coding', in *Steps to an Ecology of Mind* (London, 1973), p. 388.

16 On the identification of poetry and oratory within rhetoric see Brian Vickers, *Francis Bacon and Renaissance Prose* (Cambridge, 1968), pp. 96ff, 141f, 281ff, 288f.

17 Boswell, *Life of Johnson*, edited by R. W. Chapman (Oxford Standard Authors) (Oxford, 1952), pp. 279, 414. For Kames' application of classical rhetoric to Shakespeare's style see Brian Vickers (ed.), *Shakespeare: the Critical Heritage*, vol. IV: *1753–1765* (London, 1976), pp. 471–97.

18 Howell, *Poetics, Rhetoric, and Logic. Studies in the Basic Disciplines of Criticism* (Ithaca and London, 1975), p. 85.

19 See, in the Bibliography of Rhetoric Studies below, the work of Harry Caplan, George Kennedy, James J. Murphy, Nancy Struever, Giles Constable, G. L. Kustas, Aldo Scaglione, Charles Faulhaber, Samuel Jaffé, Ernesto Gallo, Carol Lanham, John Monfasani (see my review in *Quarterly Journal of Speech* (December 1977), 443–8), J. S. Chamberlin, J. W. O'Malley, and Traugott Lawler.

20 Baldwin, *Shakespere's 'Small Latine and Lesse Greeke'*, 2 vols. (Urbana, Ill., 1944).

21 Watson, *The Old Grammar Schools* (Cambridge, 1916), pp. 16–18.

22 In Watson, *Old Grammar Schools*, pp. 99–109.

23 I quote from the facsimile edition of the Scolar Press (London, 1969, 1973).

24 Vives, *On Education*, translated by Foster Watson (Cambridge, 1913), pp. 134ff.

25 See W. H. Woodward, *Studies in Education during the Age of the Renaissance 1400–1600* (Cambridge, 1906), pp. 197, 200–1. This important book has not been replaced by any modern studies, and remains indispensable reading.

26 Woodward, *Studies in Education*, pp. 221, 225.

27 For Gouvéa and the Collège de Guyenne see Woodward, *Studies in Education*, pp. 139–54.

28 *Ibid.*, p. 149.

29 A. L. Gordon, *Ronsard et la rhétorique* (Geneva, 1970), ch. 2, 'L'Enseignement de la rhétorique', pp. 22–7. Gordon also disproves Howell's thesis: 'C'est dans les classes avancées des écoles que les notions fondamentales de la rhétorique sont transmises au public littré' (p. 227).

30 France, *Rhetoric and Truth in France. Descartes to Diderot* (Oxford, 1972), pp. 4f.

31 Dainville, *Le Naissance de l'humanisme moderne* (Paris, 1940), pp. 83–5; 'L'Évolution de l'enseignement de la rhétorique au XVIIe siècle', *XVIIe Siècle*, nos. 80–1 (1968), 19–43, at p. 20.

32 Dainville, *Naissance*, pp. 25, 29.

33 Howell, *Eighteenth Century British Logic and Rhetoric*, p. 106.

34 Woodward, *Studies in Education*, pp. 230–4.
35 On the Sorbonne, cf. Gordon, *Ronsard et la rhétorique*, pp. 22–4.
36 Howell, *Logic and Rhetoric in England, 1500–1700*, pp. 79–81.
37 Weiss, *Humanism in England During the Fifteenth Century*, second edition (Oxford, 1957).
38 Baldwin, *Shakespere's 'Small Latine and Lesse Greeke'*, I, 103ff.
39 M. H. Curtis, *Oxford and Cambridge in Transition, 1558–1642* (Oxford, 1959), p. 94.
40 Joan Simon, *Education and Society in Tudor England* (Cambridge, 1966), pp. 358, 252–3, 358n.
41 Cf. Isocrates, *Nicocles*, 5–9; in *Works*, translated by G. Norlin, 3 vols. (Loeb Library), and Cicero, *De oratore*, I. 8. 30ff.

On Isocrates' influence see H. I. Marrou, *Histoire de l'education dans l'antiquité* (Paris, 1948); English translation by G. Lamb, *A History of Education in Antiquity* (New York, 1964); and S. IJsseling, *Rhetoric and Philosophy in Conflict* (The Hague, 1976), pp. 16–20, 28.
42 Quintilian, *Institutes of Oratory*, translated by H. E. Butler, 4 vols. (Loeb Library), III, 185–7.
43 Dyck, *Ticht-Kunst. Deutsche Barockpoetik und rhetorische Tradition* (Bad Homburg, 1966; rev. 1969), pp. 66–112: 'Rhetorische Stillehre'.
44 Du Bellay and Peletier in S. John Holyoake, *An Introduction to French Sixteenth Century Poetic Theory. Texts and Commentary* (Manchester, 1972), pp. 122, 145. Du Bellay: 'l'eloquution [est] la partie certes la plus difficile, & sans la quelle toutes autres choses restent comme inutiles & semblables à un glayve encores couvert de sa gayne.' Also Gordon, *Ronsard et la rhétorique*, pp. 42–4: in the French poetics there is little on *inventio* and *dispositio*, much on *elocutio*; the poets are encouraged to borrow from rhetoric all the figures of speech: 'without them', Du Bellay writes, 'poetry is naked'.
45 For Melanchthon, see Plett, *Rhetorik der Affekte. Englische Wirkungsästhetik im Zeitalter der Renaissance* (Tübingen, 1975), p. 18: in the *Elementa rhetorices* (1531) Melanchthon says that *elocutio* was the original realm of rhetoric. For Budé, see Woodward, *Studies in Education*, p. 134.
46 Weinberg, *A History of Literary Criticism in the Italian Renaissance*, 2 vols. (Chicago, 1961), I, 109, 152, 804–5: passages of the greatest importance to an understanding of Renaissance literature.
47 B. L. Ullman, *The Humanism of Coluccio Salutati* (Padua, 1963), p. 61.
48 France, *Racine's Rhetoric* (Oxford, 1965; 1970) p. 32; also *Rhetoric and Truth*, p. 10.
49 J. Monfasani, *George of Trebizond. A Biography and a Study of his Rhetoric and Logic* (Leiden, 1976), pp. 282, 332n.
50 Plett, *Rhetorik der Affekte*, pp. 77f, 79, 105.
51 Soarez, *De arte rhetorica* (1568), translated by L. J. Flynn, S.J. (University of Florida, Ph.D., 1955; University Microfilms Order no. HUJ100-16926), pp. 265–6, 260.
52 Monfasani, *George of Trebizond*, p. 331.
53 Sister M. J. La Fontaine, 'A Critical Translation of Philip Melanchthon's *Elementorum Rhetorices Libri Duo*' (1542), University of Michigan, Ph.D., 1968; University Microfilms Order no. HUJ69-12161.
54 E. R. Curtius, *European Literature and the Latin Middle Ages*, translated by W. R. Trask (New York, 1963), p. 436. For the rhetorical tradition and the education of

Stendhal, Vigny, Lamartine, Sainte-Beuve, and Victor Hugo, see Basil Muntéano, *Constantes dialectiques en littérature et en histoire* (Paris, 1967), pp. 157–9, and the literature cited there.

55 Woodward, *Vittorino da Feltre and other Humanist Educators* (Cambridge, 1897; 1912), p. 230. Of the many modern historians of rhetoric who have noted the dominant place of *elocutio* in the Renaissance, let me cite only W. G. Crane: "In the Renaissance, style (*elocutio*) was regarded as the most important division of rhetoric. Frequently this branch included nearly everything which was considered worth attention in the entire subject." *Wit and Rhetoric in the Renaissance* (New York, 1937), p. 58.

56 Woodward, *Studies in Education*, p. 101.

57 Cit. *ibid.*, p. 134.

58 *Ibid.*, p. 132.

59 Vives, *On Education*, pp. 180, 185, 186.

60 Cf. Soarez, *De arte rhetorica*, p. 78.

61 Salutati, cit. Struever, *The Language of History in the Renaissance*, p. 59.

62 *Ibid.*, p. 61.

63 Melanchthon, *Reply to Pico* (1558), translated by Quirinus Breen, *Christianity and Humanism* (Grand Rapids, Mich., 1968), pp. 56–7.

64 *Works of Francis Bacon*, edited by J. Spedding *et al.*, 14 vols. (London, 1857–74), III, 409.

65 Sidney, *An Apology for Poetry*, edited by Geoffrey Shepherd (London, 1965), pp. 121f.

66 Hegel, *Phenomenology*, translated by J. B. Baillie (London, 1931), p. 74; cit. Struever, *The Language of History in the Renaissance*, p. 73.

67 Puttenham, *Arte of English Poesie*, p. 197.

68 Jonson, *Timber: or Discoveries* (a notebook kept during the 1630s); Jonson's *Works*, edited by C. Herford, P. and E. Simpson, 11 vols. (Oxford, 1925–52), vol. VIII, lines 2031ff, p 625; see vol. XI, p. 270 for the text of Vives' *De ratione dicendi*, Book 2.

The epic of ideas: Lucan's *De bello civili* and *Paradise Lost*

CHARLES MARTINDALE

The index of the Columbia edition of Milton's works contains only seventeen references to Lucan. It lists ten passages in *Paradise Lost* that are supposedly imitations of lines in the *De bello civili*, Lucan's unfinished epic on the Civil War between Julius Caesar and Pompey and the decline and fall of the Republican system of government that the poet admired.[1] Moreover only four of these suggested allusions seem to me completely certain, although there are in fact one or two omissions.[2] Thus when one considers that the Columbia index has six and a half columns under Virgil, more than four each under Homer and Ovid, and two under Horace, one might be tempted to conclude that Lucan was not a major influence on Milton. Nevertheless there seems no reason to doubt that Milton was thoroughly familiar with the *De bello civili*, or *Pharsalia* as Lucan's poem was then improperly called, since he seems to allude to lines in five of Lucan's ten books and not just to more famous passages. In due course I shall examine some of these allusions, but my main purpose will be to try to demonstrate and account for certain broad similarities of poetic strategy in *Paradise Lost* and the *De bello civili* that arguably arise essentially from similarities of purpose, and which thus might have existed even if Milton had not read a word of Lucan's epic. Whether in the circumstances we are entitled to assume an explicit indebtedness is a matter that I shall leave until towards the end of my discussion.

First, however, it will be useful to give, by way of context, a short sketch of Lucan's reputation and influence in this period. Lucan was, at least until the end of the eighteenth century, widely held in great esteem.[3] Some even preferred him to Virgil, our own Horace Walpole, together 'with that great judge Corneille and with that perhaps no judge Heinsius', among them.[4] In the nineteenth century, at least in this country, false distinctions between poetry and rhetoric led to a great decline in his reputation, despite the initial enthusiasm of Shelley. Lucan's poetry, as Robert Graves saw,[5] might have been expected to appeal to modern sensibilities, but the enormous decline in the prestige of classical studies, together with the notorious conservatism of classical scholarship, have until recently prevented the re-valuation that one might have thought probable. At all events in the late sixteenth and early seventeenth centuries the *De bello civili* was widely read, and was imitated by, among others, Daniel, Drayton, Chapman and Jonson.[6] Verse translations appeared by Marlowe (first book only), Sir Arthur Gorges and Thomas May, the last later a staunch parliamentarian who wrote *The History of the Parliament of England* (1647). May's popular translation was first published in 1627, with the title *Lucan's Pharsalia: or the Civil Warres of Rome.* Milton knew this version and took from it the phrase 'adamantine chains' in the first book of *Paradise Lost* (48). In a poem *To My Chosen Friend, the Learned Translator of Lucan, Thomas May, Esquire* Ben Jonson pours lavish praise on both the translator and on Lucan's poem.[7] That, of course, was in a panegyric; William Drummond of Hawthornden reports his true opinion: 'Lucan taken in parts excellent, altogether nought.' There is no positive evidence, so far as I know, that Milton knew Marlowe's fine translation into blank verse of *Lucan's First Book*, but it seems likely enough. In his discussion of this rendering A. L. Rowse goes so far as to say that 'it would seem obvious that if we are to look for the origin of Milton's blank verse style, we shall find it in Marlowe'.[8]

During the Civil War period the *De bello civili* must have assumed an unusual relevance, and poets turned to it for inspiration. Cowley's unfinished epic on the English Civil War, published in full for the first time by A. Pritchard,[9] owes a great deal to Lucan. The work is competent, rather than inspired, but certain passages would give a Latinless reader quite a good idea of Lucan's style,[10] particularly the account of the battle on the Thames near Brentforth with its fire and water conceits (1.325ff), and the grisly description of the effects of disease on Essex's army (2.159ff). Cowley ends his account of the siege of Lichfield with a paradox of the sort with which the *De bello civili* abounds. Of the brave parliamentary defenders Cowley writes:

> Unhappy men! who can your curses tell?
> Damn'd, and infam'ed for fighting *ill soe well!* (2.135–6)

We may compare this comment of Lucan's on the mutiny of Caesar's troops at Placentia:[11]

So let it goe, ye gods, since piety
Forsakes us, and our hopes on vice rely,
Let discord make an end of civill war.

(May's translation of 5.297–9)[12]

Elsewhere Cowley's epic seems closer in spirit to the brilliant partisan invective of Claudian than to the bitter irony of the *De bello civili*.

Marvell's *An Horatian Ode upon Cromwell's Return from Ireland* is formally modelled on Horace's patriotic lyrics, especially the Cleopatra Ode (1.37), whose imagery and movement Marvell's poem to some extent reproduces. But Marvell also alludes to a number of passages in the first book of the *De bello civili*, which he apparently knew in May's translation.[13] This dual background contributes to the ode's much admired poise or ambivalence, whereby to a degree Marvell holds an even balance between Cromwell and Charles I, and is certainly surprisingly objective in his assessment of the former. R. H. Syfret makes the useful suggestion that Marvell uses Horace to reflect his hopes and Lucan his fears about Cromwell.[14] This is perhaps an over-simplification, since Cromwell's abnormal energy, which is the main quality he shares with Lucan's Caesar, is seen by Marvell as an essential part of his effectiveness. Nevertheless we may say that in broad terms Cromwell is welcomed as a modern Augustus, feared as the heir of Lucan's Caesar. The *De bello civili* was in fact difficult to claim directly for either king or parliament, since, although Lucan's Republican sympathies were not in doubt, it was difficult to avoid casting Cromwell as Caesar, clearly the villain of Lucan's poem as the subverter of the Republic.

If we turn now to Milton we find a clear instance of an allusion to the *De bello civili* in *Paradise Lost* 10, which will serve as a convenient starting point to illustrate some of the qualities that the two epics have in common, and also to show something of the obvious difference between a good poet (as critics are increasingly again recognizing Lucan to be) and a great one. Satan, his mission successfully completed, returns to Hell to announce his success, but, before he can enjoy the fruits of his triumph, he and the other fallen angels are changed into snakes and forced to eat bitter ashes (410ff). *De bello civili* 9 contains the *locus classicus* for snakes in Latin literature. After the defeat at Pharsalus, Cato, the senatorial commander in Africa, marches his men through the Sahara, and, as the last of a series of trials, they are attacked by a host of venomous serpents (607ff), an episode much admired by Dante and Shelley.[15] Milton's list of snakes comes from Lucan (among other sources):[16]

dreadful was the din
Of hissing through the hall, thick swarming now
With complicated monsters head and tail,
Scorpion and asp, and amphisbaena dire,
Cerastes horned, hydrus, and ellops drear,
And dipsas (not so thick swarmed once the soil
Bedropped with blood of Gorgon, or the isle
Ophiusa) (521–8)

Like Lucan he uses *s* sounds to evoke the hissing of the snakes, although he nowhere attempts to rival the virtuosity of such lines as

stabant in margine siccae
aspides, in mediis sitiebant dipsades undis. (609–10)

Dry asps stood on the edge, dipsades thirsted in the midst of the waters.[17]

Here the *figura etymologica dipsades* (from διψάω the Greek word for 'thirst') *sitiebant* is the sort of stylistic trick that, as we shall see, Lucan (like Milton) loves.

The whole episode in *Paradise Lost* 10, for all the tremendous actuality of the description, has, of course, allegorical significance. Lucan's snakes too can be seen as part of an extended allegory.[18] Lucan's account of Cato's desert march owes little to the historical tradition. According to Plutarch, for example, Cato made a journey of a week (*Life of Cato the Younger* 56), whereas in Robert Graves' words 'Lucan sends him on a two-months' march for thousands of miles in a wide semi-circle through the waterless Sahara; meanwhile the troops battle day and night, apparently without any food but sand, against fantastically unzoological serpents'.[19] In fact Lucan uses the incident to develop his own Stoic ideas. In his hands the desert march becomes a test of virtue, a Stoic obstacle race. Its allegorical significance is made clear in the initial speech of Cato, who in the poem is the spokesman for Stoicism. *Durum iter ad leges*, he tells his men, 'hard is the way to legality' (9.385). They must prepare their minds *ad magnum virtutis opus summosque labores*, 'for virtue's great work and utmost hardships' (381). For the moral sluggard there is always an easier way:

Let onely those
My followers be, whom dangers doe invite,
Who think it brave, and Roman, in my fight
T'indure the worst of ills. He that would have
A surety for his safety, and faine save
His loved life, let him be gone from me,
And find an easier way to slavery. (390–4)

Stoics believed that adversity was a necessary test of a man's virtue. In Cato's words *gaudet patientia duris*, 'endurance rejoices in hardship' (403). Cato, the Stoic sage, guides his men through a series of trials (storms by sea and land, thirst, heat and deadly snakes) in which they prove themselves the true possessors of spiritual freedom.

Both the episodes under consideration, the metamorphosis of Satan and the fallen angels into snakes and the snakes' attack on Cato's army in the desert, combine an overwhelming sense of immediacy with an underlying allegorical significance. There is, however, this important difference. Lucan makes no attempt to harmonize his local rhetorical effects, in particular the virtuoso descriptions of the various deaths by snake bite that so fascinated Shelley, with his overall conceptual scheme. In Milton, on the other hand, the surface meaning coheres superbly with the allegorical framework, and the imagery has more than local significance. Satan, first described as 'the infernal serpent' (1.34), takes the form of a snake to tempt Eve. His undignified exit from the poem is thus magnificently apt: his true nature is laid bare.

I turn now to broader similarities of poetic strategy in the two epics. In the *Iliad* and *Odyssey* interest is centred on plot and to a lesser extent on character, as Aristotle saw. Since so much recent criticism has concentrated on the many distinctions between the epics of Homer and Virgil, it is worthwhile emphasizing a basic similarity. Virgil, like Homer, has a story to tell. It is a story, of course, of considerable ethical and other consequence, but any meaning or significance it may have is left largely to the reader (or listener) to determine. W. A. Camps describes the *Aeneid* thus: 'In essence it is a story consisting of splendid and moving episodes, organized in a strongly shaped architectural pattern, and told in language of great expressive and emotive power. This story is centred on examples of intense and important human experience.'[20] This may not seem a particularly exciting formulation, but it is surely a reasonable one. *Paradise Lost* and the *De bello civili* fall into a rather different category, which may be termed, if largely for convenience, the 'epic of ideas'. This is not of course to imply that there are no ideas in the *Iliad*, let alone the *Aeneid*. Indeed some might argue that one of Virgil's main achievements lay precisely in recreating Homeric epic along more obviously thematic lines. But Virgil maintains on the whole the traditional anonymity of the epic bard, and his attitude to his characters and their actions is often hard or impossible to determine. In the 'epic of ideas', theme has overtaken the creation of character for its own sake and sheer storytelling as the poet's dominant concern. It has become explicit: the poet is more open about his ideas and the reader is simply not allowed to escape the significance of the story. Most readers would probably agree that this is true of *Paradise Lost*. Milton gives an account of the Fall and its significance, which constitutes the poem's 'great argument'. The actual narrative content of the poem is in fact rather slight, a point emphasized by Waldock,[21] but the implications of the narrative are immense. Nor is Milton slow to make his own viewpoint plain. The poet has become in other words not merely the storyteller but also the interpreter of the story, a point to which we shall return.

The description of the *De bello civili* as an 'epic of ideas' will need justifying at rather greater length. This will involve combating the view, which has had some adherents in modern times, that Lucan was engaged in writing a verse chronicle, and is hardly to be accounted a poet at all. It might seem that this view can claim the support of some of Lucan's ancient critics.[22] Thus Servius in a note on *Aeneid* 1.182 remarks that 'Lucan did not deserve to be numbered among the poets, because he seems to have composed a history, not a poem', *quia videtur historiam composuisse*, *non poema*. It is important to be aware of the limited scope of such an observation. As with so much ancient literary criticism the point is essentially stylistic, and concerns decorum. We can see this from Petronius' *Satyricon*, where the poetaster Eumolpus launches what is a thinly veiled attack on the *De bello civili* (ch. 118).[23] Eumolpus implies that Lucan treats his subject matter like a historian: the true poet ought rather to immerse himself in the Greco-Roman literary tradition, and in particular should employ *deorum ministeria*, the traditional 'divine machinery' which Lucan had wisely omitted. Eumolpus then declaims a poem on the Civil War, which is intended by him to show the correct way to write historical epic, and in which the gods play an important part. Servius too accuses Lucan of ignorance of the law of poetry, *lex artis poeticae*. Lucan in other words did not approach the subject in the correct way: it was Virgil who for Servius and the traditionalists supplied the model and the norm.

It is clear, however, that Lucan was not writing versified history. Aristotle in the *Poetics* (1451^a 36ff) says that poetry is more philosophical than history, since history deals with τὰ γενόμενα, things that have been, brute fact, while poetry is concerned with οἷα ἂν γένοιτο, the kind of things that might be, universally observable truths. In Aristotle's terms Lucan belongs with the poets rather than the historians.[24] Historical facts may provide the raw material or most of it for the poem, but Lucan seeks the universal in the particular. One might say that civil war is as much his concern as the Civil War. Moreover the war is regarded as a paradigm of the incessant struggle between freedom and tyranny. As Lucan himself puts it, 'it was the never ending struggle between Freedom and Caesarism', *par quod semper habemus, libertas et Caesar* (7.695–6). A historical event has become part of a cosmic struggle with Caesar and Liberty as perpetual combatants (the image is of a gladiatorial match). In consequence Lucan felt no more qualms than Shakespeare in his Histories in inventing some incidents and embroidering others almost out of recognition. Thus it is almost certain that Lucan simply invented the splendid episode in which Sextus Pompey consults the witch Erictho about the outcome of the battle of Pharsalus in a grisly séance that is a sort of parody of Aeneas' visit to the Underworld. (6.413ff).[25] Other apparently equally unlikely episodes are in fact derived from the historical tradition. For example the attempt by Caesar to sail across the Adriatic in a fisherman's boat during a violet storm was recorded by historians, but Lucan uses the storm to symbolize the tryant's superhuman pride (5.497ff).[26] The poet, in other words, wanted not so much to give a historically accurate account of the war between Caesar and Pompey as to say some important things about the eternal human condition. Moreover, like Milton, he wanted to say them explicitly.

In the *Poetics* (1460^{a}7) Aristotle laid down that the epic poet should not give his point of view *in propria persona*. This prescription, based on Homeric practice, was in the main observed by Virgil, and became part of neoclassical epic theory.[27] Milton, however, had no qualms about transgressing the Aristotelian canon, most notably in the prologues of books 3, 7 and 9. Dr Johnson was too much of a classicizer not to feel some theoretical misgivings about these passages, although he was too honest a critic to allow dogma to override his more immediate response. 'The short digressions at the beginning of the third, seventh and ninth books might doubtless be spared', he writes in the *Life of Milton*, continuing disarmingly, 'but superfluities so beautiful who would take away? or who does not wish that the author of the *Iliad* had gratified succeeding ages with a little knowledge of himself? Perhaps no passages are more frequently or more attentively read than those extrinsick paragraphs; and, since the end of poetry is pleasure, that cannot be unpoetical with which all are pleased.'[28] A number of critics have shown that in fact the autobiographical passages should not be regarded as 'extrinsick paragraphs' at all. For example L. Martz writes: 'These personal touches are no mere self-indulgence: they have a function – to remind us, intimately, that this poem is an action of thoughts within a central, controlling intelligence that moves with inward eyes toward a recovery of Paradise.'[29] In particular the images of light and darkness and the contrast between external blindness and inner illumination are clearly central to the poem.

More importantly in the 'epic of ideas' the poet, as already noted, serves as both narrator and interpreter, and thus his personality and views are not peripheral, but central. The ideas have become too important to be left merely implicit. To some this seems like manipulation. Thus Waldock complains of what he calls 'the running fire of belittling commentary'[30] in books 1 and 2 of *Paradise Lost*, where the speeches of the fallen angels are continually undercut by explicit authorial comment. In fact, as Martz observes, the 'voice of the bard' is to be heard throughout 'advising, exhorting, warning, praising, denouncing, lamenting, promising, judging, in all ways guiding us'.[31] In addition to the invocations we have numerous passages of a satiric, didactic or moralizing character (a good example is the 'Paradise of Fools', significantly censured by Johnson). Such passages are generally superbly integrated into the narrative which they interrupt. It is, however, fair to say that the introduction of such material involved Milton in problems which he did not always manage to solve. An example is provided by the lines that describe Satan's entry into Paradise:

As when a prowling wolf,
Whom hunger drives to seek new haunt for prey,
Watching where shepherds pen their flocks at eve
In hurdled cotes amid the field secure,
Leaps o'er the fence with ease into the fold:
Or as a thief bent to unhoard the cash
Of some rich burgher, whose substantial doors,
Cross-barred and bolted fast, fear no assault,
In at the window climbs, or o'er the tiles;
So clomb this first grand thief into God's fold:
So since into his church lewd hirelings climb.
Thence up he flew, and on the tree of life
The middle tree and highest there that grew,
Sat like a cormorant. (4.183–96)

Here the interruption of the leisurely epic narrative by one line of invective (prepared for though it has been by the traditional allegorical image of the wolf and the sheep, and by the 'low' language of the second simile) is perhaps a little too abrupt and consequently jars somewhat. Milton likewise puts into Raphael's mouth the sort of material, for example the discussion of angelic sex and digestion, that Aristotle would probably have regarded as inappropriate in an epic (nor is Aristotle without his modern followers in the twentieth as in the eighteenth century).

Milton's technique had, to a large extent, been anticipated by Lucan in the *De bello civili*. Addison, in an essay first published in the *Spectator* in 1712, actually draws attention to the similarity:

If the Poet, even in the ordinary Course of his Narration, should speak as little as possible, he should certainly never let his Narrative sleep for the sake of any Reflection of his own... *Lucan*, who was an Injudicious Poet, lets drop his Story very frequently for the Sake of his unnecessary Digressions... *Milton*'s Complaint for his Blindness, his Panegyrick on Marriage, his Reflections on *Adam* and *Eve*'s going naked, of the Angels eating, and several other Passages in his Poem, are liable to the same Exception, tho' I must confess there is so great a Beauty in these very Digressions that I would not wish them out of his Poem.[32]

W. E. Heitland, in an essay published in 1887 which until quite recently was the fullest discussion of the *De bello civili* available in English, regards the presence of moralizing passages as one of 'the four characteristic defects' of the poem:

The poet's business is surely to develope his moral by the simple interaction of characters and circumstances. The reader should be left to judge: half the pleasure and most of the profit of poetry lies in the discovery of the moral significance of the characters and the meaning of the story, not by direct statement, but from the story and characters themselves. Now Lucan is always thrusting himself forward to tell us what it all means: and, whatever Roman audiences may have thought of the practice, on us the effect is simply to destroy the illusions of poetry and bring us face to face with an orator.[33]

The shadow cast by the *Poetics* is, it seems, a long one.

Lucan's interventions fall into the same general categories as Milton's. There are personal passages, as when the poet prays that he may be allowed to bring back Pompey's headless corpse to Italy for proper burial:

> Oh too too happy I, if Rome would chuse
> My hand to open that base sepulcher,
> And his deare ashes hither to transfer. (8.843–5)

There are satiric and moralizing observations. For example, when Caesar knocks at the hut of the poor fisherman Amyclas to ask him to take him across the Adriatic in his boat, Lucan comments ironically on the peace of mind that poverty brings:

> Oh safe blest poore mans life, oh gift of all
> The gods, not yet well knowne; what Citie wall,
> What temple had not fear'd at Caesar's stroke? (5.527–31)

Several times he breaks off his description of the battle of Pharsalus to reflect on its crucial significance (7. 185ff; 385ff; 638ff; 847ff). We are never allowed to forget the presence of an individual voice, with a particular point of view, and it is the presence of this voice which gives the poem much of its distinctive character and what unity it has.

Even Raphael's didacticism has its parallel. At a feast of extravagant luxury given by Cleopatra in Alexandria, Caesar asks about the causes of the Nile flood and the secret of the river's source, and is answered at length by the Egyptian priest Acoreus (10.172ff). This exchange is usually regarded as irrelevant padding, but Lucan may have had good reasons for including it. The description of the feast and its setting is designed to contrast with the account given earlier in the poem of Cato's austere home and frugal life-style (2.380ff).[34] Caesar's disgraceful liaison with Cleopatra is opposed to Cato's chaste and unconsummated remarriage to Marcia. I think it probable that the poet is also inviting us to compare Caesar's intellectual curiosity (which Ceasar himself calls *virtus* and *amor veri*, 'virtue' and 'love of truth' 188–9) with Cato's genuine concern with moral virtue, the only true *virtus*.

In the 'epic of ideas' as described above it is natural that characterization should to some extent be tailored to theme. It is an assumption of much modern criticism that the freer characterization that we associate above all with Shakespeare and certain novelists is superior to such 'controlled' characterization. But restrictive dogmas of any sort are undesirable, and it seems reasonable to argue that different types of characterization suit different types of work. It has already been observed that Lucan treats the Civil War as a struggle of cosmic significance. Milton, of course, is dealing directly with a cosmic event. This is reflected in the characterization. In both poems there is a triad of principle characters, two of them representing the polarities of good and evil, God and Satan, Cato and Caesar, and caught between them, much more ordinary and recognizable, 'like us' as Aristotle says, Adam and Pompey. Lucan's Pompey is in fact a plausible enough portrait of the historical figure. The same can hardly be said of his Cato or Caesar.[35] Cato is the perfect Stoic saint, whose every word has an almost oracular quality. To him is assigned the task of embodying and enunciating the sacred truths of Stoicism, to which Lucan, like his uncle Seneca, subscribed. For example, in book 9 Cato instructs one of his lieutenants on the omnipresence of deity, a tenet of Stoicism:

> estque dei sedes nisi terra et pontus et aer
> et caelum et virtus? superos quid quaerimus ultra?
> Iuppiter est quodcumque vides, quodcumque moveris. (578–80)

Is there a seat of god, save earth, and sea,
Aire, heaven, and virtue? Why for gods should we
Seeke further? What ere moves, what ere is seen
Is Iove.

Milton imitated these impressive lines in *Paradise Lost* 11, but hardly improved on them (Milton's 'virtual' was presumably suggested by Lucan's *virtus*):

Adam, thou know'st heaven his, and all the earth,
Not this rock only; his omnipresence fills
Land, sea and air, and every kind that lives,
Fomented by his virtual power and warmed. (335–8)

Caesar is Cato's complete antithesis, a tyrant in the sway of his every passion, the perfectly bad man. This is in accordance with Stoic theory: 'a wicked man does not lack any vice', Seneca observes (*De beneficiis* 4.27.2), *dicimus...malum ac stultum nullo vitio vacare.*[36] Caesar rejoices in every act of violence and political chicanery. He has no religious scruples: after the battle of Pharsalus he forbids the burial of the senatorial dead, electing to feast in a place where he can view the piles of already putrefying corpses (7.792–4). He is a hypocrite who weeps crocodile tears over the head of the decapitated Pompey (9.1035ff). Though so totally evil, Caesar nevertheless has a kind of perverted greatness. A man of huge vigour, he is prompt in action, restless, energetic, 'thinking nought done, whilst ought undone remain'd' (2.657), in contrast to Pompey who is content to rest on his laurels:

but in *Caesar* now
Remaines not onely a great Generalls name,
But restlesse valour, and in warre a shame
Not to be Conquerour; fierce, not curb'd at all,
Ready to fight, where hope, or anger call
His forward Sword; confident of successe,
And bold the favour of the gods to presse:
Orethrowing all that his ambition stay,
And loves that ruine should enforce his way. (1.143–50)

He has qualities which, if his purposes were not depraved, might be considered virtues. In particular he is in a sense courageous, though Lucan clearly regards such misdirected courage as mere recklessness (this was the usual Stoic view).[37]

W. Blissett in an article entitled 'Caesar and Satan'[38] argues convincingly that Lucan's Caesar is one of Milton's sources of inspiration for his characterization of Satan. Blissett describes the similarity thus:

> The Satanic in Lucan's Caesar is plain to see: the continual restlessness and demonic impatience are stressed over and over again; the unhesitating leadership in evil, the impulse of the gambler and allied to that the fascination of the idea of total ruin; the moments of hesitation, remorse and magnanimity which serve only to make more horrifying the defiant impenitence. The Caesarian in Milton's Satan is as plain. Satan is the enemy, as Caesar had been, of quiet and custom and accepted right: he is a tyrant, a sultan, more than a king.

Both Caesar and Satan, it should be added, are tyrants who pose as democrats, exerting an almost hypnotic control over their followers. Thus both obtain silent attention with a mere gesture of the hand: 'who with hand/Silence, and with these words attention won' (10.458–9) is another of Milton's explicit imitations of Lucan (*B.C.* 1.298). More particularly Blissett shows how Satan's journey through the abyss is to some extent modelled on the episode in the *De bello civili* where Caesar by night and alone but for a single companion, the fisherman Amyclas, tries to cross the stormy Adriatic in a little boat, an episode which illustrates, as we have seen, Caesar's superhuman arrogance. In each case we have 'a lone heroic voyage through chaos by the antagonist', and this general resemblance is re-inforced by verbal echoes. It may be (a point not observed by Blissett) that the simile with which Milton ends his account of Satan's journey, comparing Satan to 'a weather-beaten vessel', is meant formally to signal the debt (although we may also think of the voyages of Jason and Odysseus referred to in lines 1016–20):

> here nature first begins
> Her farthest verge, and Chaos to retire
> As from her outmost works a broken foe
> With tumult less and with less hostile din,
> That Satan with less toil, and now with ease
> Wafts on the calmer wave by dubious light
> And like a weather-beaten vessel holds
> Gladly the port, though shrouds and tackle torn. (2.1037–44)

The protagonists of both episodes display a grotesque heroism. Like Satan, Caesar remains outwardly unbowed, scorning the storm which threatens to destroy him:

> Are the Gods troubled so to ruine me,
> Whom sitting here in a small barke (quoth he)
> They have assaulted with a storme so lowd?
> If on the seas, not warres, they have bestow'd

The glory of my death, fearlesse I come
Ye gods, to any death that ye can doome:
Though this too hasty fate great acts breake off,
I have already done things great enough. (5.654–60)

His bravado has a heroic ring, until we remember the wickedness of his overall ambitions. In both respects the analogy with Satan is exact.

The similarity between Milton's Satan and Lucan's Caesar is interesting when we recall the parallelism between Cromwell and Caesar implied in Marvell's *Horatian Ode*. The point may even be of some relevance to the long-standing debate about Satan. It is a familiar paradox that Milton, a Republican on earth, should be a Royalist in heaven. A Satan who poses as a democrat and has the energy of Lucan's Caesar may have made some readers think of contemporary politics. Milton's attitude to his earthly chief can hardly have been free from ambiguity, and mixed feelings about his Republican colleagues may well be reflected in his portrayal of Satan and the fallen angels. Or to put the point another way, when Milton puts Republican sentiments into Satan's mouth, that is because he wants the reader to have sympathy with the arguments, if not their proponent: Satan should be plausible.

Both Caesar and Satan are marked by a tremendous energy which is to some extent denied their opponents, a fact that has seduced some critics into regarding them as the 'true' heroes of the poems. In fact the search for a hero has in both cases led to much bad criticism. In the case of the *De bello civili* a surprising number of candidates have been fielded over the years, including Pompey, Cato, Caesar, the Senate, the Roman People, Lucan himself.[39] Likewise disagreement about who is really the hero of *Paradise Lost* began early with the neo-classical critics. Addison shows awareness of the true nature of the problem, but just fails to have the courage of his convictions:

There is another Objection against *Milton*'s Fable...namely, That the Hero in the *Paradise Lost* is unsuccessful, and by no Means a Match for his Enemies. This gave Occasion to Mr. *Dryden*'s Reflection, that the Devil was in reality *Milton*'s Hero. I think I have obviated this Objection in my first Paper. The *Paradise Lost* is an Epic, or a Narrative Poem, and he that looks for an Hero in it, searches for that which *Milton* never intended; but if he will needs fix the Name of an Hero upon any Person in it, 'tis certainly the *Messiah* who is the Hero, both in the Principal Action, and in the chief Episodes.[40]

In fact Addison could have pointed out that Aristotle, whose 'rules' were so often invoked, was opposed to the idea that real organic unity could be achieved in an epic merely by having a single hero, and that the much admired *Iliad* has in fact not one hero but two. At all events we have here another important difference between the *De bello civili* and *Paradise Lost* on the one hand and on the other Virgil's *Aeneid*, which, like Homer's *Odyssey*, owes part of its unity to the presence throughout of a single hero. In the former cases, by contrast, the search for a hero is at best irrelevant, at worst positively misleading.

It is a truth that cannot be too often stated that style should not be considered *in vacuo*: style is not an absolute, it is relative to the job to be done. As we have seen, in the 'epic of ideas' the job to be done is in part an intellectual one. Jonathan Richardson's judgement on Milton's language is well known, but will bear repetition: 'A Reader of Milton must be Always upon Duty; he is Surrounded with Sense, it rises in every Line, every Word is to the Purpose; There are no Lazy Intervals, All has been Consider'd, and Demands, and Merits Observation.'[41] The *De bello civili* too makes heavy demands on the reader. Both poets make extensive use of puns, paradoxes, word plays, pointed collocations of words, *figurae etymologicae*. In each case the style helps to create that tremendous 'argumentative drive' which J. Carey has noted as 'a factor which activates the whole framework of *Paradise Lost*'.[42] Phrases like 'darkness visible', 'this windy sea of land', 'the fiend/Saw undelighted all delight', 'kindly rupture', 'stupidly good' can be related to the Horatian oxymoron, as in *lene tormentum*, 'gentle torture' or *splendide mendax*, 'magnificently false'.[43] It was Lucan, however, who first demonstrated the effectiveness of such stylistic devices *in epic* (Virgil does not write in this way).[44]

It will be helpful to give a few examples of 'pointed' writing of various kinds in the *De bello civili*. A typical example occurs near the beginning of the poem. Of the first triumvirate Lucan writes:

> tu causa malorum
> facta tribus dominis communis, Roma, nec umquam
> in turbam missi feralia foedera regni (1.84–6)
>
> you, Rome, are the cause of woe, made common
> to three masters, and the fatal compact of
> power never before sent among a crowd

In turbam applied to three men is a touch of wit. One might say that for Lucan two consuls are company, three triumvirs a crowd.[45] Three further examples of this style of writing all come from the sixth book. In 513 Lucan tells us how the witch Erictho was able 'to listen to the assemblies of the silent dead': *coetus audire silentum*. *Silentes* is regularly used to mean no more than 'the dead', but Lucan glances at its literal meaning 'the silent'. The idea of 'hearing the silent' is characteristically piquant. Later (640–1) we learn of the cave which 'grim Erictho had damned to witness her sacred rites': *quem tristis Erictho damnarat sacris*. There is a deliberate clash here between the verb *damnare* ('to doom') and the noun *sacra* (literally 'sacred rites' and hence any rites). Again the witch talks about Hades 'hearing her magic herbs': *licet has exaudiat herbas* (715). To translate *exaudire* as 'obey'[46] glosses over the tension in the words: strictly speaking one cannot 'hear' herbs, only spells, but Lucan would be rightly hurt by one editor's uncomprehending comment 'an absurd collocation'.[47]

Milton too required a style that appealed to the mind, forcing the reader to think, as well as to the emotions. He, too, frequently exploits the tensions obtainable by pointed collocations of words. Documentation is superfluous, for the matter has been treated at length by C. Ricks[48] (the similarity of some of his examples to the passages quoted above is striking). Suffice it to say that the spendidly ponderous pun in the lines describing the bridge-building activities of Sin and Death may not be to the taste of some of Milton's modern critics, but would have undoubtedly delighted Lucan:

> Now had they brought the work by wondrous art
> Pontifical, a ridge of pendent rock
> Over the vexed abyss, following the track
> Of Satan (10.312–15).

It is interesting to observe how both poets suffered from the attentions of Bentley, greatest of classical textual critics. Bentley had a brilliant but slightly prosaic mind. His notorious 'emendations' of *Paradise Lost* are an attempt to remove some of the 'faults' that offended classic taste in what Johnson, adopting a phrase of Samuel Butler, called Milton's 'Babylonish dialect'.[49] One of the most valuable features of Ricks' book is the way that he shows how the twentieth-century battles about Milton's style had to a large extent already been fought in the eighteenth. It was a shrewd and not merely polemical stroke to cast Leavis in the role of a modern Bentley. Housman, in the preface to his edition of the *De bello civili*, makes the following observations on Bentley's work on the text of Lucan:

> The characteristic which Napoleon so much admired in Turenne, that he grew bolder as he grew older, was not for Bentley a fortunate endowment. His judgment ripened early and reached perfection before he was forty: from that time onward the vices of his temper began to invade his intellect, and confidence usurped the place of consideration...by the time he came to Lucan he had acquired the worst habits of deity.[50]

One revealing example of this over-confidence concerns another passage from the sixth book. Erictho is described as being 'weighed down by pallor': *pallore gravatur* (517). The metaphor is a striking one in Latin without exact parallel. Bentley proposed emending *pallore* into the more commonplace *squalore* ('filth'), commenting 'is there any weight in pallor?'[51] This is, of course, precisely the point: there is a deliberate tension between the noun and the verb. Bentley's procedure here and in many of the emendations of *Paradise Lost* discussed by Ricks is strikingly similar. In both cases he should at least be given the credit of having read the text attentively. With both poets 'a Reader must be alway upon Duty'.

Particularly close to Lucan in spirit and style is Milton's account of the war in Heaven. This is full of passages in which the poet pulls out all the stops, and which have been censured as bombastic or even absurd. (Carey's comments are typical: 'the slapstick war in Heaven can be debited to the classical tradition: epics were meant to have battles'.[52]) The war in Heaven is an obvious target for those who regard Milton's 'grand style' as mere pomposity. Its grandeur is in fact a debased grandeur.

> Part hidden veins digged up (nor hath this earth
> Entrails unlike) of mineral and stone,
> Whereof to found their engines and their balls
> Of missive ruin; part incentive reed
> Provide, pernicious with one touch to fire. (6.516–20)

Lines like these, as Fowler points out in his note, are marked by ponderous wit and the sort of inflated diction that the rhetoricians call bomphiologia. It would be tempting to regard the war in Heaven merely as a parody of an epic battle, particularly in view of Milton's later attack on traditional heroism in the prologue of the ninth book (13ff) and in book 11 (689ff; cf. 12.386ff), but the episode is structurally too important to be a kind of farce, though some have taken it as such.[53]

R. M. Frye has recently done well to remind us that physical battles between anthropoid angels in armour are a commonplace of the visual art both of Milton's day and of previous centuries.[54] Seen in its full European context Milton's work can often seem less eccentric than when viewed against an exclusively English literary background. It was thus not without significance that one of the main charges of the anti-Miltonists was that Milton's writing was 'un-English'. Nevertheless I cannot accept Frye's view that, seen in its context, there is *nothing* peculiar or incongruous about the war (after all the Father in Raphael's narrative talks about 'wild work in heaven' 6.698 and 'perverse commotion' 706), any more than I can accept the other extreme that the description is meant to be pure comedy or farce. Rather, once again Milton is putting the epic form and the epic style under deliberate pressure.

The charge of absurdity is an old one. Johnson's often quoted criticism that 'the confusion of spirit and matter which pervades the whole narration of the war in heaven fills it with incongruity'[55] is in fact very much to the point, so long as 'confusion' is not taken to imply that the poet himself was confused. The whole description is a tour de force in which Milton pushes the basic idea of spiritual beings fighting a very physical battle to its extreme, deliberately skirting absurdity. One might describe the result as a species of surrealism. It is not really simple bombast that repels many readers of the sixth book but rather the combination of exaggeration and particularity. It is not bombast but something more disturbing when Satan and Belial exchange schoolboy jokes after first firing their cannon. There is no vague 'grandeur' about the moment when the good angels pick up and hurl hills at their opponents. Instead Milton describes with literal-minded precision the appurtenances of the hills:

> From their foundations loosening to and fro
> They plucked the seated hills with all their load,
> Rocks, waters, woods, and by the shaggy tops
> Up lifting bore them in their hands. (643–6)

The result in such cases is hardly 'sublimity' as Dennis thought,[56] nor is it simple parody, but a kind of virtuoso extremism which is a form of abstraction and which cannot be judged by the criterion of naturalness. This extremism has become interesting for its own sake (and to that extent is likely to remain a minority taste), but it should be noticed that there is a kind of decorum at work as well. As usual Milton is adapting his style to suit his subject matter. The unusual stylistic inflation of the war in Heaven is a reflection of the sheer enormity of rebellion against God. In the brilliant passage in which Satan first fires his newly invented cannon (571ff), the incongruous juxtaposition of low language ('belched', 'entrails', 'glut' and so on) with deliberately inflated diction (like 'with hideous orifice', 'portending hollow truce', 'deep throated engines')[57] is purposely grotesque, mirroring the grotesqueness of Satan's attempt to overthrow God. The war in Heaven is thus part of the process by which the brightest of the angels is gradually stripped of his glamour. One of the remarkable features of the style of *Paradise Lost* is its flexibility: it is not Milton, but his critics who want to turn it into a blunt instrument. Even the comparative flatness of parts of books 11 and 12 which many critics have censured is probably designed to convey the wearisomeness of the fallen world.[58]

Such stylistic extremism is notoriously characteristic of the *De bello civili*. A particularly striking example is the description of what might be called the 'Compleat Storm',[59] the storm which prevents Caesar from crossing the Adriatic in Amyclas' boat.[60] Here Lucan pretends to take completely seriously what to other poets had been merely tropes. His treatment of the 'battle of the winds' (conventional in epic storms), in which the four winds struggle for the possession of the sea, is typical. The reader is wittily shown what the necessary consequences would be if such a battle really took place in nature:

> the barke upright mainteines
> Her course, supported by all winds (5.649).

The contrary winds simply neutralize each other! No less extreme is Lucan's account of the sea battle at Massilia (3.509ff). 'The episode of the siege of Massalia', writes Heitland, 'is one mass of absurd hyperbole: it is meant to be very impressive and grand, but its effect is grotesque and unreal.'[61] *De gustibus non est disputandum*, but it is important to understand exactly what Lucan is doing and why he is doing it. In the description paradoxes abound. Some of these are merely verbal tricks, although they help to enliven the poetic texture. For example the phrase *sanguis/emicuit lentus* (638–9) is a paradoxical way of saying 'the blood trickled out', since the literal meaning of *emicare* ('to appear quickly') is contradicted by the adjective *lentus* ('slow'). More commonly the situations themselves breed paradox. A land battle is fought on the sea (566); it is not the enemy who break up the ships, but rather their own crews in search of weapons (671ff); fire puts out water (680ff). Lucan also lays stress on the horror and abnormality of the fighting. The words *multaque ponto/praebuit ille dies varii miracula fati* (633–4), 'that day provided many strange forms of varied deaths on the sea', introduce a virtuoso series of grotesque and bizarre deaths. As with Milton's war in Heaven this display of stylistic fireworks is no doubt meant to be enjoyed (if that is the right word) to some extent for its own sake, but we also need to remember Lucan's attitude to his subject. The Civil War to him is something unnatural and monstrous. It has its origin in the superhuman wickedness of Caesar, and leads to the disastrous overthrow of political liberty. It produces every form of bizarre and perverted behaviour. Style then reflects situation. As the war involves the collapse of all moral restraints, so Lucan breaks all stylistic bounds. Thus decorum is maintained.

Such are the general similarities between the two epics. How much Milton owed directly to Lucan's example is harder to determine. We have seen that in the seventeenth century Lucan was a highly esteemed and influential poet. Milton, who clearly knew the *De bello civili* well, must surely have responded warmly to Lucan's ardent Republicanism and fierce hatred of tyranny. Aubrey interestingly reports that May, originally a Royalist, was first attracted to Republicanism through study of Lucan (the cynical attributed this volte-face to his failure to gain the laureateship),[62] and Milton presumably knew the man as well as his translation. All this is surely significant. It is true, of course, that there are relatively few explicit allusions to the *De bello civili* in *Paradise Lost*, but it is worth remembering that *Samson Agonistes* contains few enough *direct* borrowings from the Greek tragedians, and yet conveys the essential manner and style of Greek tragedy far better than any modern translation known to me. It is precisely in manner and, to a lesser extent, in verbal style that *Paradise Lost* resembles the *De bello civili*. All in all it seems reasonable to conclude that the *De bello civili* was an important direct influence on *Paradise Lost*, and that Lucan, as well as Homer, Virgil and the rest, deserves some of the credit for the success of Milton's greatest poem.

More interesting than the question of literary influence is the overall similarity between the two epics which has been the main subject of this essay and which in conclusion may be briefly sketched again. During antiquity and in the Renaissance epic was regarded (at least after tragedy)[63] as the 'highest' poetic genre. The problem, at least for serious poets, was quite simply how to write epic, a 'naive' narrative form, in a sophisticated age. Virgil, for example, attempted to solve the problem without radical alterations to the Homeric form, which he reverenced, and it can be argued that the results involved compromises that prevent the *Aeneid* from being a complete success.[64] The 'epic of ideas' was a natural late development, a development at once post-classical and, in a sense, anti-classical. The classical epic form was retained (as it was not, for example, by Spenser), but personalized and made a vehicle for the explicit expression of, in Lucan's case, Stoic ideas and, in Milton's, Christian ones. Further, both the *De bello civili* and *Paradise Lost* could be regarded as much as anti-epics as epics. Lucan parodies Virgilian episodes and polemicizes against Virgil in his main theme.[65] Thus, while Virgil praises Augustus as Rome's second founder and restorer of the

Golden Age, Lucan castigates the Caesars as the subverters of political liberty and Rome's true greatness. In *Paradise Lost* Milton attacks the traditional subject matter of epic. He found epic values morally reprehensible and their literary expression, to use his own word, 'tedious' (*P.L.* 9.30). Both Lucan and Milton make sophisticated 'modernist' use of the tired epic machinery. In *Paradise Lost* episodes like the war in Heaven show how the poet is no longer prepared to use conventional epic ingredients, in particular the fights (which Spenser had still been able to take seriously) in the old way. The heroic endeavours of Satan must be seen to be a mere sham when compared with 'the better fortitude of patience and heroic martyrdom' (9.31–2). Lucan, struck down by Nero in his twenties, was too young and inexperienced, and perhaps insufficiently gifted, to make a complete success of his brave and exciting experiment. Rather, like Dante's Virgil, he was

> come quei che va di notte,
> che porta il lume dietro e sè non giova,
> ma dopo sè fa le persone dotte.[66]

NOTES

An earlier draft of this paper was read to the Renaissance Society of the University of Sussex. I am particularly grateful to Professor A. D. Nuttall who suggested a number of valuable improvements. I have also learned much from discussion with Dr J. H. Martindale and my wife Miss M. A. Levy.

1 See *The Works of John Milton*, edited by F. A. Patterson et al., 18 vols. and 2 index vols. (New York, 1931–40), index vol. II, 1182–3.

2 See also O. A. W. Dilke, 'Lucan and English Literature', in *Neronians and Flavians*, edited by D. R. Dudley (London, 1972), pp. 100–1. Convincing allusions are *P.L.* 2.938–40 = *B.C.* 9.303–4; *P.L.* 10.458–9 = *B.C.* 1.298; *P.L.* 10.524ff = *B.C.* 9.700ff (the whole section from 607 is in fact relevant, though Milton had other sources besides Lucan for the snakes: see Fowler's note *ad loc.* in *The Poems of John Milton*, edited by J. Carey and A. Fowler (London and Harlow, 1968)); *P.L.* 11.335–8 = *B.C.* 9.578–80. The simile *P.L.* 10.273–8 could well have been suggested by *B.C.* 7 (not 8 as in the Columbia edition) 831ff, and the phrasing of *P.L.* 10.1008–9 may have been influenced by *B.C.* 7.129–30. *B.C.* 3.280–1 is obviously not the source for the story about the Arimaspian *P.L.* 2.943–7, since Lucan says nothing about the gryphon. The mention of the sands of Mount Casius in *B.C.* 8.539 does not make the passage the source for *P.L.* 2.592–3, while *B.C.* 6.696 seems remote from the phrasing of *P.L.* 2.1009. The naming of the Demogorgon in *P.L.* 2.965 has a complex ancestry, in which Lucan plays only a subsidiary role. (In *B.C.* 6.744ff the witch Erictho invokes, without naming, a higher power to force the gods of the Underworld to comply with her demands. The passage was imitated by Statius in *Thebaid* 4.516–17,

where Teiresias calls on a supreme power, *triplicis mundi summum, quem scire nefastum,/illum – sed taceo.* In his note the scholiast known as 'Lactantius Placidus' identifies this *summum* with the Δημιουργός who featured in some philosophical systems (e.g. Plato's *Timaeus*): *dicit autem deum* δημιουργόν, *cuius scire nomen non licet. infiniti autem philosophorum, magorum, Persae etiam confirmant re vera esse praeter hos deos cognitos, qui coluntur in templis, alium principem et maxime dominum, ceterum numinum ordinatorem...sed dire sentiunt, qui eum interesse nefandis artibus actibusque magicis arbitrantur* (see D. Vessey, *Statius and the Thebaid* (Cambridge, 1973), p. 255). In some MSS of the 'Lactantius' scholium the name of Teiresias' *summum* appears as Demogorgon, which probably arose simply as a corruption of δημιουργόν. Dilke, however, 'Lucan and English Literature', p. 100, sees a possible allusion to the name Demogorgon in Erictho's words *qui Gorgona cernit apertam* (746): the supreme power can look with impunity on the head of the Gorgon. At all events the Demogorgon, whether the product of genuine occult lore or textual corruption, enjoyed an extensive subsequent history: see C. S. Lewis, *The Discarded Image* (Cambridge, 1964), pp. 39–40.) On the other hand the Columbia edition ignores the probable allusions to Lucan in the account of Satan's journey through the abyss (see above p. 144), and fails to note that 'admantine chains' (*P.L.* 1.48) comes from *B.C.* 6.801 by way of May's translation. It is interesting that the genuine allusions to Lucan are clustered in books 2 and 10 of *Paradise Lost*, mainly in passages dealing with Satan.

3 He also had his critics, particularly after the Restoration. Dryden is tepid (*Of Dramatic Poesy and other Critical Essays*, edited by G. Watson, 2 vols. (London, 1962), I, 95, 201; II, 22, 82, 118–19, 204). In *An Essay upon Unnatural Flights in Poetry* (1701) George Granville, Lord Lansdowne, criticizes the famous line *victrix causa deis placuit sed victa Catoni* (1.127); see *Critical Essays of the Seventeenth Century*, edited by J. E. Spingarn, 3 vols. (Oxford, 1909), III, 294, 296f. For Addison see above p. 141.

4 See a letter of Horace Walpole to the Rev. H. Zouch dated 9 December 1758, in the Yale edition of *Horace Walpole's Correspondence*, edited by W. S. Lewis, 39 vols. (London and New Haven, 1937–74), XVI, 22–3.

5 *Lucan: Pharsalia*, translated by Robert Graves with the subtitle *Dramatic Episodes of the Civil War* (Harmondsworth, 1956), introduction pp. 23–4.

6 See Dilke, 'Lucan and English Literature', for a useful survey.

7 Ben Jonson, *The Poems, The Prose Works*, edited by C. H. Herford, P. and E. Simpson (Oxford, 1947), p. 395. Cf. *Conversations with William Drummond of Hawthornden*, now available in *Ben Jonson: The Complete Poems*, edited by G. Parfitt (Harmondsworth, 1975), p. 478.

8 A. L. Rowse, *Christopher Marlowe: A Biography* (London, 1964), p. 42.

9 Abraham Cowley, *The Civil War*, edited by A. Pritchard (Toronto, 1973). My brief remarks owe a great deal to the introduction, especially pp. 40ff. To his list of parallels add 1.181ff, which recalls *B.C.* 1.231ff.

10 For Lucan's style see above pp. 146ff.

11 Pritchard compares rather *B.C.* 6.262.

12 All quotations are from the third edition corrected (1635). All subsequent verse translations are from this version, which, as we have seen, was known to Milton.

13 Especially 143ff (the source of Marvell's lightning simile), 225ff, 239ff. See also H. M. Margoliouth's commentary (3rd edition, Oxford, 1972).

14 R. H. Syfret, 'Marvell's *Horatian Ode*', *Review of English Studies*, n.s. 12 (1961), 160ff especially 171f.

15 See Dante, *Inferno* 25 especially 94ff; Shelley, *Prometheus Unbound*, 3.1.40f, 3.4.18f (see Dilke, 'Lucan and English Literature', p. 104).

16 For the sources of this passage and some analogues see Fowler *ad loc.* in *Poems of John Milton* (all my quotations from *P.L.* are taken from this edition). Dante, *Inferno* 25 (partly inspired by Lucan, as lines 94–6 show) was obviously in Milton's mind when describing the metamorphosis. That Lucan was a direct source for Milton's snakes is shown by the reference in lines 526–7 to the story that snakes were formed from the blood of the Medusa (clearly from *B.C.* 9.619ff).

17 I follow the text of A. E. Housman's edition of Lucan (Oxford, 1926). All the prose translations are my own.

18 See F. M. Ahl, *Lucan: An Introduction* (Ithaca and London, 1976), p. 261; M. P. O. Morford, 'The Purpose of Lucan's Ninth Book', *Latomus*, 26 (1967), 123ff.

19 Graves, *Lucan: Pharsalia*, introduction, p. 22.

20 W. A. Camps, *An Introduction to Virgil's Aeneid* (Oxford, 1969), p. 110.

21 A. J. A. Waldock, *Paradise Lost and its Critics* (Cambridge, 1947), passim.

22 See E. M. Sanford, 'Lucan and his Roman Critics', *Classical Philology*, 26 (1931), 233ff.

23 Petronius' own attitude is disputed: see J. P. Sullivan, *The Satyricon of Petronius* (London, 1968), pp. 165ff; P. G. Walsh, *The Roman Novel* (Cambridge, 1970), pp. 48ff (both with bibliographies).

24 See B. Marti, 'The Meaning of the *Pharsalia*', *American Journal of Philology*, 66 (1945), 354.

25 See my article 'Lucan's Nekuia', Studies in Latin Literature and Roman History II, edited by C. Deroux, *Latomus*, 168 (1980), 367ff.

26 See M. P. O. Morford, *The Poet Lucan* (Oxford, 1967), pp. 37ff.

27 It would of course be wrong to exaggerate the anonymity of ancient epic: see e.g. Virgil's promise to Nisus and Euryalus *Aen.* 9.446–9. It is simply a matter of degree. For a useful discussion (but without mention of Lucan) see F. C. Blessington, *Paradise Lost and the Classical Epic* (Boston and London, 1979), pp. 90ff.

28 *Lives of the English Poets*, edited by G. B. Hill, 3 vols. (Oxford, 1905), I, 175.

29 L. Martz, *The Paradise Within* (New Haven and London, 1964), p. 106.

30 Waldock, *Paradise Lost and its Critics*, p. 83. Waldock's criticisms have been ably met by S. Fish, 'The Harassed Reader in *Paradise Lost*', *Critical Quarterly*, 7 (1965), 162ff, 279ff; and *Surprised by Sin: The Reader in Paradise Lost* (London and New York, 1967), passim.

31 Martz, *The Paradise Within*, p. 107.

32 *Notes Upon the Twelve Books of Paradise Lost*, 1719, reprinted in *Milton: The Critical Heritage*, edited by J. T. Shawcross (London, 1970), p. 167. Professor Nuttall points out to me how 'this gambit of expressing disapprobation followed by indulgent affection becomes as it were a trope in its own right in eighteenth-century criticism'.

33 Introduction to C. E. Haskins' edition of Lucan (London, 1887), p. lxxi.

34 See Marti, 'The Meaning of the *Pharsalia*', pp. 366–7.

35 My remarks on characterization in Lucan owe a great deal to Marti's discussion, *ibid.*, pp. 358ff (Cato); 361ff (Caesar). Cf. Ahl, *Lucan*, chs. 5–7.
36 Quoted in Marti, 'The Meaning of the *Pharsalia*', p. 364.
37 Cf. Cicero, *Off.* 1.62–3 where *fortitudo* and *audacia* are distinguished.
38 W. Blissett, 'Caesar and Satan', *Journal of the History of Ideas*, 18 (1957), 221ff. The quotations are from page 231.
39 See Marti, 'The Meaning of the *Pharsalia*', pp. 352–4.
40 Shawcross, *Milton: The Critical Heritage*, p. 166.
41 J. Richardson, Father and Son, *Explanatory Notes and Remarks on Milton's Paradise Lost* (London, 1734), p. cxliv.
42 J. Carey, *Milton* (Literature in Perspective) (London, 1969), p. 121.
43 *P.L.* 1.63; 3.440; 4.285–6; 7.419; 9.465: Horace, *Odes* 3.11.35; 21.13. I owe these examples to Dr J. H. Martindale.
44 The style of *Paradise Lost* cannot of course be tied to any one model. Lucan would be only one among a number of influences classical, Elizabethan, Metaphysical and Italian. For the last see F. T. Prince, *The Italian Element in Milton's Verse* (Oxford, 1954) – for good remarks on word play see pp. 123ff.
45 For this and other examples of conscious paradox see my article 'Paradox, Hyperbole and Literary Novelty in Lucan's *De Bello Civili*', *Bulletin of the Institute of Classical Studies*, 23 (1976), 45ff. I owe the epigram to Professor Nuttall.
46 So J. D. Duff, Loeb translation (London, 1928).
47 C. M. Francken in his edition, 2 vols. (Leiden, 1896–7), note *ad loc.*
48 C. Ricks, *Milton's Grand Style* (Oxford, 1963); cf. W. Empsom, *Some Versions of Pastoral* (London, 1935), ch. 5. There are good remarks on style in Carey, *Milton*, pp. 113ff.
49 *Life of Milton*, p. 191.
50 Housman, Introduction, p. xxxii.
51 *An in pallore est aliquid ponderis?* Bentley's notes were published by Horace Walpole at Strawberry Hill in 1760.
52 Carey, *Milton*, p. 120.
53 So A. Stein, *Answerable Style: Essays on 'Paradise Lost'* (Minneapolis 1953), p. 22. For another approach see M. Roston, *Milton and the Baroque* (London, 1980), especially pp. 116ff.
54 R. M. Frye, *Milton's Imagery and the Visual Arts* (Princeton, 1978), pp. 43ff.
55 *Life of Milton*, p. 185.
56 See Shawcross, *Milton: The Critical Heritage*, pp. 237ff. Carey's brief remarks are to the point, *Milton*, p. 118.
57 See Fowler's note on 6.578ff in *Poems of John Milton.*
58 Cf. H. Gardner, *A Reading of Paradise Lost* (Oxford, 1965), pp. 94–6.
59 I borrow this phrase from G. K. Galinsky, *Ovid's Metamorphoses* (Oxford, 1975), p. 145, where it is used to describe the storm in the Ceyx/Alcyone epyllion.
60 For a fuller analysis see my 'Paradox, Hyperbole', pp. 48–50.
61 Haskins' edition, introduction, p. lxxvii.
62 *Aubrey's Brief Lives*, edited by A. Clark, 2 vols. (Oxford, 1898), II, 56. See Blissett, 'Caesar and Satan', pp. 228–9.
63 Aristotle in the *Poetics* eventually indicates his preference for tragedy over epic. The

Renaissance *cursus generum* sometimes culminated in tragedy, and this is the sequence that Milton seems to have followed (unless *S.A.* is really earlier than *P.L.*), calling tragedy 'the gravest, moralest, and most profitable of all other poems' ('Of that Sort of Dramatic Poem which is called Tragedy', prefixed to *S.A.*). Both in Rome and Renaissance England, however, tragedy was to some extent tainted by association with the popular stage.

64 Cf. Sullivan, *The Satyricon of Petronius*, pp. 183–6.

65 See my 'Paradox, Hyperbole', p. 52 (with bibliography).

66 *Purgatorio* 22.67–9: 'like him that goes by night and carries the light behind him and does not help himself but makes wise those that follow' (text and translation from J. D. Sinclair, *The Divine Comedy of Dante Alighieri*, 3 vols. (reprinted London, 1971), II, 284–7).

Foundations of oriental and comparative studies: The correspondence of Sir William Jones

GARLAND CANNON

After a century-long decline in Sir William Jones' once phenomenal reputation in literature and philology, a decline initiated by the utilitarians' attack on the defenders of a supposedly dead language and culture and then hastened by changes of taste and method, the tide has turned. A. J. Arberry's lamentably brief *Asiatic Jones: The Life and Influence of Sir William Jones* (London, 1946) did much to restore Jones' reputation and to depict objectively his many contributions to scholarship, in contrast with Lord Teignmouth's prejudiced 'official' biography.[1] Then there were noteworthy published doctoral dissertations: Fatma Moussa-Mahmoud's *Sir William Jones and the Romantics* (Cairo, 1962) and S. N. Mukherjee's *Sir William Jones: A Study in Eighteenth-Century British Attitudes to India* (Cambridge, 1968). Other biographical studies were my *Oriental Jones* (Bombay, 1964) and the excellent chapters in Hans Aarsleff's *The Study of Language in England, 1780–1860* (Princeton, 1967, pp. 115–61) and in Peter Brown's *The Chathamites* (London, 1967, pp. 339–420), besides dozens of specialized articles in literary and linguistic journals.

My edition of *The Letters of Sir William Jones* (Oxford, 1970) made available 304 previously unpublished letters, along with another 292 letters usually transcribed from the original, which not only corrected Teignmouth's religious and political alterations in the texts, but also showed Jones to be an incisive scholar, as well as a letter-writer worthy of the century of Chesterfield and Walpole. Agam Prakashan started reprinting Jones' 1807 edition of *Works* in Delhi in 1976. My *Sir William Jones: A Bibliography of Primary and Secondary Sources* (Amsterdam, 1979) annotated 497 works by or about him that throw further light on his life and scholarship. In fact, the sheer quantity of new materials required a complete rewriting and updating of my *Oriental Jones*, which

Asia Publishing House will publish in 1981. There will undoubtedly be a major new scholarship in 1984, when the Royal Asiatic Society and other London groups will sponsor the International Symposium on the Bicentenary of the Asiatic Society, and various journals will devote space to the bicentenary. This article, which presents five newly discovered letters by Jones and a few letters to him as a complement to my Clarendon edition of his *Letters*, initiates the bicentennial celebrations for the famous society that Jones founded and then inspired with his genius. We hope thereby to elicit more letters from Jones's world-wide correspondents, in order to establish the full range of his influence.

THE CORRESPONDENCE IN GENERAL

Besides his 596 letters in *Letters*, others were edited in my 'Five New Letters by Sir William Jones',[2] which added William Scott and John Symonds to the previously known 126 people represented in the total traced correspondence. His British and American correspondents are so important that virtually all are treated in *The Dictionary of National Biography* or *Dictionary of American Biography*. Three revealing epigraphic letters from Lieutenant William Steuart to Jones will shortly appear in my 'Early Indian Epigraphy and Sir William Jones', in the *Journal of the Asiatic Society of Bengal*. The present article adds Henry Savile Starck and his wife (Madame de Vaucluse) to the previously known ninety-eight people to whom Jones wrote in his 608 traced letters.

The 106 traced letters to him were from fifty-six people, and there were at least another eighteen correspondents for whom no letters to or by him have been found. These include the Dutch scholars David Ruhnkenius and Everardus Scheidius, the French scholars Louis-Mathieu Langlès and Jean-Baptiste Le Roy, the Irish philological theorist Charles Vallancey, the Scottish geologist John Playfair, and twelve Englishmen, of whom only the critic Joseph Warton and the botanist William Roxburgh were not philologically inclined. Besides the Sanskritist Henry Thomas Colebrooke and the geographer James Rennell, there were six students of Persian and/or Arabic – William Davy, William Francklin, John Richardson, John Swinton, John Uri, and Joseph White – and the major philological theorists Jacob Bryant and Bishop Robert Lowth. Jones probably also corresponded with the poet William Haley, who composed the eulogy *An Elegy on the Death of the Honourable Sir William Jones* (London, 1795).

Of Jones' 608 traced letters, 146 were to Viscount Althorp, his pupil, who became the second Earl Spencer. Though these are some of his fascinating letters, especially those from India, they do not deal with scholarly topics. Certain major figures of the day do not figure among his correspondents. For example, no exchange with Dr Johnson has been found. As Jones later wrote in Letter 559:

> a similarity of political principles has ever been considered as the strongest cement of friendship; and I feel its attractive power so strongly, that, were I to hear of a man at the extremity of the globe, who maintained those principles and carried them into action, I should instantly find my heart struggling to unite itself with his; while opposite principles have a power so repulsive, that I never by my own choice associate with such as profess them. (II, 886–7)

As he was not in sympathy with Dr Johnson's Tory views, despite his admiration for the lexicographer's mind, there was probably little or no correspondence between the two. It is also disappointing that he evidently did not correspond directly with Goethe, whose great interest in the *Śakuntalā* was initiated by Georg Forster's 1791 retranslation of Jones' pioneering English version of 1789, and whose diary and correspondence laud Jones. Nor does he seem to have corresponded with Herder, whose writings were an important intermediary in the German reception and acceptance of Jones' works. Of his correspondence with major figures, his nine letters to Benjamin Franklin and Franklin's single traced answer are lively, personal, and politically revealing, but not on the subject of Jones' scholarly pursuits. Neither is his generally personal, political letter to Gibbon, though he may have exchanged letters with the historian that were more concerned with the Oriental past. His eleven letters to Burke are of considerable interest for their scholarly approach to law. His eight letters to Joseph Banks display incisive insights and the exchange and advancement of ideas, especially in botany, and are his most scientific letters.

His correspondence did not cause contemporary scholars immediately to turn to the study of Oriental languages and literature, with the eventual goal of editing and translating that literature. For example, his rapturous description of Nizámí's *Khamsa* to James Bate did not stimulate that Cantabrigian to arrange for its translation, nor did his suggestion that Bate's colleagues edit Nizámí's works have any effect. Similarly unfruitful in the first instance was his argument in several works that the staleness of European poetry caused by the constant repetition of the same images and allusions could be corrected 'if the principal writings of the *Asiaticks*, which are reposited in our publick libraries, were printed with the usual advantage of notes and illustrations, and if the languages of the *Eastern* nations were studied in our great seminaries of learning'.[3] His frequent public calls for an English rendition of Firdausi's *Sháhnáma* had to await Arnold's partial version, just as his call for a version of Omar Khayyám had to await FitzGerald. His formal proposal to the Bodleian to publish Uri's projected English translation of Sa'dí's *Bústán*, to accompany Uri's earlier printing of the original Persian text, was also fruitless. His appeals to Whang Atong and others to translate the Chinese *Shih Ching* were unsuccessful, just as his long-term efforts toward a new national epic that he titled 'Britain Discovered' and slowly projected into an Anglo-Indian *Aeneid* incorporating the Hindu pantheon never inspired Thomas Caldecott or any other literary friends whom he consulted about this planned epic.

However, his *Poems* and translations introduced new subjects, themes, and styles that were to stimulate much of the Oriental current in the Romantics, even though posterity has judged that his own poetry is, at best, only good minor eighteenth-century verse. *Poems* was translated into Portuguese by Francisco Manoel de Oliveira in 1793.[4] The appended 'An Essay on the Poetry of the Eastern Nations', which uses a rich comparative perspective to assert, shockingly for the time, the greatness of Arabic and Persian literature, was reprinted and rendered into Spanish by the Conde de Noroña early in the nineteenth century.[5]

Among the members of Dr Johnson's Club,[6] in which Jones was a well-liked participant, Joseph Warton obligingly offered criticism, which Jones originally planned to include as emendations in *Poems*, on the model of Pope. Reynolds also made comments on the circulated draft, as did Bishop Shipley and Thomas Percy. His old friend Samuel Parr and William Hawkins, a former professor of poetry at Oxford who had translated part of the *Aeneid*, made further suggestions. Jones' high standards of revision and his optimistic estimate of his talents are reflected in his gratitude expressed to Hawkins in Letter 55: 'Had Dryden and other poets met with such a friend, their poems would have been more polished, and consequently more fit to see the light' (I, 101).

Since much of his correspondence has not been found, a study of his association with Continental scholars would be inconclusive. The letters of his two known French correspondents and of two of his Dutch correspondents have not been found, and most of Schultens' answers are untraced. No Scandinavian correspondents are known. Of Jones' German correspondence, only one letter to the Orientalist Johann David Michaelis has been found; but the presence in Halle of 'A Hymn to Narayena' in Jones' holograph may suggest a second German correspondent.[7] Two of Jones' letters to the Spanish philologist Francisco Pérez Bayer are available, as are four of the letters exchanged with the Polish general and prince, Adam Czartoryski. Jones' rather well-preserved correspondence with Reviczky and Schultens best reveals how he exchanged artistic and scholarly ideas with contemporary Continentals, at a time preceding the development of international congresses and learned journals in adequate numbers. The present article will concentrate on the scholars represented in Jones' correspondence as we have it, particularly Banks and various philologists interested in certain languages.

His Advertisement in the Asiatic Society's *Asiatick Researches* II (Calcutta, 1790) was an ambitious and pioneering effort to foster international exchanges between learned societies that might transcend correspondence between individual scholars or even between his new Society and the Royal Society:

It may greatly conduce to the advancement of useful knowledge, if the learned Societies established in *Europe* will transmit to the Secretary of the Society in *Bengal* a Collection of short and precise Queries on every Branch of *Asiatic* History, Natural and Civil, on the Philosophy, Mathematics, Antiquities, and Polite Literature of *Asia*, and on Eastern Arts, both Liberal and Mechanic; since it is hoped that accurate Answers may in due time be procured to any Questions that can be proposed on those subjects; which must in all events be curious and interesting, and may prove in the highest degree beneficial to mankind.

The response was better than even his native optimism might have anticipated. Sir George Yonge and the Bishop of Llandaff had not waited for an invitation, but had submitted lists of wide-ranging questions centred on India but extending into general intellectual matters. As Jones and Banks were old friends, a connection with the Royal Society was already established by the botanical commissions that its president was sending Jones. William Shipley had already initiated exchanges with his Kentish Society for Promoting Useful Knowledge. Jones' long-standing friendship with Franklin would surely have led to exchanges with the American Philosophical Society, had it not been for the old man's death.

The major response came from John Playfair, whose article in the *Transactions of the Royal Society of Edinburgh* on Brahmanic astronomy prompted 'Questions and Remarks on the Astronomy of the Hindus', which Jones proudly printed in *Asiatick Researches* (IV, 159–62), along with Playfair's apology for making the queries: 'they will, perhaps, be forgiven to one who feels himself deeply interested in the subject to which they relate, and who would not lose even the feeblest ray of a light, which, without the exertions of the *Asiatic* Society, must perish for ever'. Jones briefly answered some of the crucial questions, and he promised to describe Indian astronomy in his next discourse, which his sudden death in 1794 prevented his composing. He and two botanical colleagues were elected to membership in the Scottish society.

From America came three responses that were important in their own right and that might have had far-reaching results, but Jones died before they arrived. Ezra Stiles, the president of Yale College, submitted a voluminous inquiry on 18 January 1794.[8] On 7 February 1795 James Sullivan reported Jones' election to membership in his Massachusetts Historical Society, enclosed books to initiate 'an intercourse of true philanthropy... to support that harmony in the great family of mankind, on which the happiness of the world so much depends', and requested facts about the natural history of America or other parts of the world (*Works*, II, 314–16). The most evocative of the three responses was Eliphalet Pearson's involved biblical query from his American Academy of Arts and Sciences, which is reproduced for the first time below.

Jones' Advertisement further encouraged Europeans in India to collect artefacts, drawings, and data for the Asiatic Society's Archives, which are now so rich; but the numerous letters transmitting such contributions were primarily elicited by his personal request and general scholarly enthusiasm. A letter by James Anderson shows the variety of materials submitted and approaches used by Jones' colleagues. Other examples are the physician Francis Balfour's submission of his 'On the Introduction of Arabic into Persian', Lieutenant Colonel James Browne's elaborate letter enclosing his translation of a Persian history of India, the trader Francis Light's gift of a rare Balinese religious document on tree bark, and a translation done by Henry Vansittart (son of the Governor of Bombay) of a Persian abridgement of a Pashto history. The tone of such submissions is perhaps typified by Lieutenant Alexander Macleod's sending of 'a copy, written with a stylus on five palmyra-leaves, of the engraving on copper-plates preserved in the great pagoda of *Conjeveram*'; he described himself as 'the slave, who digs from a mine the rough diamond, which others, of superior skill and capacity, cut and polish into its full lustre and value' (*Asiatick Researches*, III, 38). Indian scholars were also encouraged to submit their work, the best of which Jones translated, read to the Society, and published in *Asiatick Researches*. Almost certainly he wrote to them in Arabic, Persian or Sanskrit; but this correspondence is untraced. His letters to Nathaniel Brassey Halhed, Reviczky, and Schultens were usually in Latin and occasionally in French.

His letters are of intellectual value in themsevles, representing the best answers available at the time to queries sent by scholars who considered him a kind of Oriental encyclopaedia. His scholarly correspondence sheds light on his role in the development of comparative studies in general and especially comparative linguistics, the encouragement of translation of fundamental texts, and on the eighteenth-century use of correspondence as a means to the advancement of ideas. His enthusiasm for Oriental studies was to give impetus to the development and advancement of new disciplines in Europe.

THE CORRESPONDENCE IN DETAIL

Jones' scholarly correspondence chiefly deals with politics, law, history, botany, astronomy, and language and philology, subjects which are richly interlaced with literary comparisons. His political letters reveal an advanced or even radical Whiggism. To Americans like Arthur Lee and Franklin he expressed a strong sympathy for America. This partly motivated his three somewhat mysterious trips to Paris to see Franklin in war-time and led him to contemplate migration. His 'A Fragment of Polybius', a naive proposal for a compromise nine-point commercial treaty that was intended to eventuate in America's independence, was a thinly disguised literary allegory based on Polybius' history. But this imaginative use of classical history to try to solve contemporary problems was gently rejected by Franklin, as America had already rejected the official, more advanced proposals of the Carlisle Commission, and as the British defeat at Saratoga had marked the turning point of the war.[9] Jones also expressed such views to the radical Whigs, who attempted to canvass for him in his unsuccessful parliamentary candidacy. These included John Wilkes, the Lord Mayor of London, who sought his legal help in an important impressment case; the Nonconformist minister Richard Price; Bishop Shipley; the inventor Edmund Cartwright, who wrote a sonnet extolling the candidacy; and Major Cartwright, the founder of the Society for Constitutional Information and a political reformer whose democratic positions Jones espoused in various speeches and whose Society published some of his political works. Jones' letters to Burke, Lloyd Kenyon, and Samuel Parr also evinced Whiggish views.

He furnished legal scholarship to Major Cartwright to underpin legislative reforms that the Society was advocating. He exchanged views on bailments with the legal antiquarian Francis Hargrave, preparatory to publishing his immediately famous *An Essay on the Law of Bailments* (London, 1781). He provided much-appreciated legal aid to help the successive Governors-General to govern Bengal according to Indian religious laws and customs. To Sir John Macpherson, who had no legal training, Jones acted as informal legal tutor in various letters. In letters and personal discussions Jones provided the Marquis of Cornwallis with principles and detailed provisions for the innovative Cornwallis Code, which founded the Indian Civil Service and became the basis for laws for new territorial acquisitions. This association gave Jones' legal philosophy an empirical reference and reality. Potentially as important was 'The Best Practicable System of Judicature for India', which he prepared for Burke. Although Jones optimistically sent it in accordance with the two men's informal plan for co-operation devised before he left England, this excellent recommendation was never utilized in Burke's Indian speeches, because of the rift occasioned by Jones' friendship with Hastings. Jones then restated these suggestions to William Pitt, the prime minister, again with no results. Yet the democratic principles of his 'System' might have done much to reform colonial governmental practices that were to have deleterious effects. However, his letters reveal legal help to Burke for Indian legislation in 1781, in a close association that partly inspired Jones' translation *The Mahomedan Law of Succession to the Property of Intestates.*[10]

His best letters to a professional historian were to Robert Orme, whose *A History of the Military Transactions of the British Nation in Indostan from the Year 1745* (London, 1763; 1778) received Jones' laudation and literary suggestions and later drew high praise from Macaulay for its authenticity and style. The Scottish historian Gilbert Stuart also approached Jones. His books strongly attacked William Robertson, whose generalizing from massive detail appealed to Jones, in contrast with Stuart's occasional shallowness. Jones and Stuart shared the view that philosophy and especially law should underpin history, and their correspondence was mutually instructive. Their acquaintance may have been one reason why Jones apparently never corresponded with Robertson, whose *History of America* (London, 1777) influenced him more than any of the three histories that Stuart gave him.

Jones' greatest historical assistance went to Thomas Maurice, whose projections for *The History of Hindostan* (London, 1795–9) recognized that classical sources must be buttressed by primary data from Sanskrit, which Jones was asked to supply; Jones was further asked to provide a critique of Maurice's projected outline of the multi-volume work. His seven-volume *Indian Antiquities* (London, 1800–1) likewise extensively used Jones' scholarship. His finest literary acknowledgement was *An*

Elegiac Poem, Sacred to the Memory and Virtues of the Honourable Sir William Jones (London, 1795), honouring the man who had much to do with starting him on his distinguished career in Orientalism.

The historian John Bruce initiated his brief correspondence very near to Jones' death. In 1794 he acknowledged that Jones' Indian essays had led him to revise part of the draft of his history. As has been said, no serious correspondence between Jones and Gibbon about Oriental history has yet been found, though Gibbon's admiration for and use of Jones' scholarship is acknowledged in six gracious footnotes in his great history. Such associations with historians may have moved Jones to plan an objective study of the American Revolution and to collect information for years from primary sources like Franklin, Shelburne, and Vergennes, a study that he never had time to compose. In India he did other historical research and was stimulated by historically oriented queries from men like Yonge and the Bishop of Llandaff.

His botanical correspondence began in India, primarily with European physicians there. Jones probably corresponded with John Gerard Koenig, a Lithuanian botanist-naturalist for the East India Company in the Carnatic, and was disappointed when Koenig's papers were forwarded at his death to Banks instead of going to the Asiatic Society. Another botanist-member of the Society was James Anderson, the Company's Physician-General at Madras, who sent Jones specimens and introduced Roxburgh. That surgeon, who was the pioneer exponent of Indian flora and was already part of Banks' informal network of collectors in India, became an active member of the Society and contributed five papers, usually sent by mail and read by Jones at the weekly meeting. Roxburgh participated in Jones' unsuccessful search for the biblical spikenard and commemoratively named the famous Saraca tree the *Jonesia asoca*, 'Consecrated to the remembrance of our late President, the most justly celebrated SIR WILLIAM JONES, whose great knowledge of this science, independent of his other incomparable qualifications, justly entitles his memory to this mark of regard.'[11] Jones' most active botanical correspondent in India was the physician Patrick Russell, whom Jones encouraged in his making large collections of specimens and drawings and then in publishing the preliminary version of his later *Account of Indian Serpents Collected on the Coast of Coromandel* (London, 1796–1809). Unlike other Fellows of the Royal Society, such as Roxburgh and Charles Wilkins, Russell unaccountably sent his articles to Banks instead of to Jones.

Jones' correspondence and close friendship with Robert Kyd, who was a lieutenant colonel in the Bengal infantry before founding the Botanical Gardens of Calcutta, may have been originally stimulated by the commissions from Banks and especially Yonge for the Botanic Garden of St Vincent. Kyd submitted his 'Remarks on the Soil and Vegetation of the Western Side of the River Hooghly' and wrote at least four letters to Jones.[12] Jones enthusiastically sought to add Arabian, Persian, and Chinese plants to Kyd's Gardens, which were to supply many useful and ornamental tropical plants to the world. He had some *Pandanus leram* transplanted there from Nicobar in an attempt to improve the Bengalese variety, in an early effort toward the production of fertile stable hybrids by crossing members of the same genus. This wish to develop a new food source in India that might end the frequent famines exemplifies the humanitarianism in his correspondence.

When Banks' botanical requests became too time-consuming, even requiring the packing for and arranging of a conveyance to St Vincent or Kew, Jones firmly responded that he would continue his own collecting and even the organizing of others' collecting in India, but that Kyd and Roxburgh must handle the shipping, since his Sanskrit research took precedence. Scientifically, his correspondence with Banks was his most important. That explorer-collector had made the Royal Society a leading scientific centre partly by enlisting the help of scholars like Jones around the world; but Jones was building a unique, geographically specialized society which soon was publishing articles that might otherwise not have been written or that might have appeared in *Philosophical Transactions*. Ironically, it was partly Jones' association with collector-scholars in India, which was sometimes inspired by Banks' expanding commissions to Jones, that thus reduced the number of 'Oriental' articles in *Philosophical Transactions*. Jones even solicited Governors-General from Hastings through John Shore to release Company servants' reports from throughout India. The commissions for Banks' personal herbarium and for Kew and St Vincent impelled Jones into a more comprehensive collection and description and advanced his botanical study, which ultimately projected a complete Indian taxonomy that would supplement Linnaeus when needed.[13] Utilizing extensive correspondence, this study gave Jones important experience in comparative taxonomy that helped to make his linguistic studies more scientific.

Banks may have inspired Sir John Sinclair's request that Jones help in the innovational scheme to cross merino sheep with British sheep so as to produce finer British wool, which gave rise to England's modern wool industry. Jones' devotion to Sanskrit studies made him relay the commission to Kyd and others, but he embraced this plan for improved animal breeding even though he did not transport Oriental sheep and goats to England. He delightedly acted as an intermediary for Sinclair, whose special committee of the Highland Society was investigating the merits of various wools, especially Shetland.

Banks' commissions also had a role in starting Jones on elaborate astronomical investigations, which potentially added a Sanskrit component to Banks' well-known interest in astronomy. The pair exchanged and circulated articles on the subject; Jones even had some sceptical Brahmans react to Sir William Herschel's speculative 'Account of Three Volcanos in the Moon', from *Philosophical Transactions* for 1787. The astronomical aspect of his Sanskrit research helped him widen his comparative formulations about the Indian past, which contributed to his identifying the Maurya emperor Chandragupta as the Sandrocottus of Greek sources. Later historians could work back and forth around this important identification to correlate Indian dates and events with known classical ones and thus eventually construct a unified Asian–European history. Playfair further stimulated Jones' astronomical interest. Jones' most extensive correspondent on the subject was Samuel Davis, a district judge and the Governor-General's agent at Banaras, where Davis had an observatory and helped Jones identify astronomical allusions in Sanskrit writings. Jones' thirty-seven traced letters to Davis exemplify his best collaboration in the broad humanistic sense of systematic co-operative research that he had envisioned when founding the Asiatic Society. But though the pair made good use of the Sanskrit manuscripts which he was systematically collecting, a final indication of his esteem for Banks may be seen in the fact that he sent him eighty-one Persian, thirty-seven Arabic, and sixty-nine Sanskrit manuscripts for safekeeping at the Royal Society. These irreplaceable manuscripts were eventually given to the India Office Library for preservation, unlike the several which he retained for final legal work in Calcutta and which were sold along with his books at auction and thereby perhaps lost forever.[14]

When we turn to the subject of language and philology in his correspondence, we might first ask whether any of three or four scholars may have helped him construct his well-known explanation of the similarities among certain languages on the basis of their earlier descent from the same single language. Though he and Wilkins worked together fairly closely for two years, the texts of his eleven letters to Wilkins up to February 1786, when he delivered that pregnant formulation in his Third Discourse, demonstrate that Wilkins was not a direct source. The only allusion to derivation is Jones' brief speculation about the Etruscans' origin, and his answer to Wilkins' untraced response indicates that the speculation did not elicit a reaction.[15]

A second obvious candidate is Jones' old Oxford colleague Halhed, whose *A Grammar of the Bengal Language* (Hooghly, 1778) described some Bengali forms in terms of their Sanskrit kinship, in a kind of overview of North Indic languages that compared several Sanskrit items with Greek and Latin ones. Though the Third Discourse did not mention Halhed or Bengali, Jones annotated his copy of Halhed's *Grammar*, according to Nicol's auction catalogue. As a forthcoming biography indicates that Halhed only indirectly influenced Jones,[16] it is especially interesting that a newly found letter of Jones to Richard Johnson, which is reproduced for the first time below, contains the only known evidence that the pair met during Halhed's few weeks in Calcutta in 1785 on his second stay in India. However, Jones' mystifying, somewhat negative statement about Halhed's tearing up by the roots everything that he touched would suggest that this renewed association produced no contribution to Jones' celebrated formulation about language derivation eleven months later.

A third obvious candidate is Jones' acquaintance Lord Monboddo, a major language theorist of the day. But as one of his untraced letters elicited Letter 499 in 1788, which stated that Jones had no time to answer Monboddo's questions about India and enclosed in response a copy of the still unpublished Third Discourse, Monboddo could not have provided any direct assistance. Although his and Halhed's comparative bent may have stimulated Jones, he almost certainly arrived at his conclusion independently.

We cannot seriously consider Jacob Bryant as an influence, not simply because the pair's correspondence is untraced, but because Jones was so sceptical of Bryant's wild etymologies that he finally felt compelled in his Ninth Discourse of 1792 to point out their conjectural quality and to remark that Bryant was a classical scholar who knew no Oriental language except possibly Hebrew. Since Bryant was so angered by this moderately phrased appraisal that he would not even send Jones his rebuttal, Jones' usually constructive suggestions were of no avail to this creative but highly speculative philologist.[17]

Jones' correspondence discusses six languages and occasionally Greek and English, often in a comparative vein: the Semitic tongues Hebrew and Arabic, Persian, Sanskrit, Latin, and Irish. Except for Irish, Hebrew is the least revealingly treated. Somewhat resisting the Hebrew-oriented tradition of the day, Jones did not accede to the urging of scholars like Thomas Hunt, the Regius Professor of Hebrew at Oxford, that he pursue 'that venerable channel, through which the sacred compositions of the divinely inspired poets have been conveyed down to us' (*Works*, I, 210). Hunt's influence may have contributed to the quantity of biblical literary comparisons in Jones' remarkable *Poeseos Asiaticæ commentariorum libri sex* (London, 1774), which mainly described Arabic and Persian poetry.

The influence of Lowth, the Bishop of Oxford, was greater in that respect, inasmuch as Jones modelled his 542-page *Commentariorum* on Lowth's *De sacra poesi Hebræorum prælectiones* (Oxford, 1753) and perceptively compared Hebrew passages and Arabic and Persian poetry in terms of form, imagery, subject matter, and diction. Perhaps indicative of Lowth's influence is the fact that when Jones received a Hebrew problem from Michaelis, who had already published a Hebrew grammar, Jones replied that he would soon go to Oxford to consult his books and 'His Excellency'. In Letter 96 he demurred politely when the famous Göttingen Orientalist sent him several books and evidently asked for his reaction. His Latin response can be translated as 'I do not flatly disagree with what you say about Hebraic legends, nor do I accept what you say at every point. Therefore, since I have not sufficiently examined and thought about the subject, I am not inclined to diverge from the general opinion' (I, 172).

Except for some Hebrew questions that he answered for Joseph White in Letter 255, Letter 86 is the best instance of biblical scholarship in his traced correspondence. There he intriguingly interwove Hebrew and Arabic semantics and religion to answer a series of questions that his fellow-barrister John Alleyne asked before completing *The Legal Degrees of Marriage Stated and Considered* (London, 1774). Alleyne publicly thanked Jones in the Advertisement to the second edition (1775) for the 'able and critical exposition of the text in Leviticus'. Letter 86 illustrates Jones' seeming preference for correspondence, rather than face-to-face discussions, to transmit and extend scholarship. To answer the questions he had to do further work with his copy of John Parkhurst's *An Hebrew and English Lexicon, without Points* (London, 1762),[18] adding Arabic and Latin annotations and making a Roman transliteration of the Hebrew letters. This work later helped him classify Ethiopic and some other languages into a clearly defined Semitic family.

It was partly Hebrew that led to his study of Arabic, culminating in his fine prose translation of the very difficult *The Moallakát, or Seven*

Arabian Poems, Which Were Suspended on the Temple at Mecca (London, 1782), which introduced Europe to the *qasidah* and the concept of kismet. His untraced exchanges with John Richardson, who prepared the index for the second edition of Jones' famous *Grammar of the Persian Language* (London, 1775), evidently considerably benefited Richardson, whose *A Grammar of the Arabic Language* (London, 1776) was modelled on Jones' *Grammar* and who was assisted in other ways as well.

By far Jones' best correspondent about Arabic was Schultens, who, like Gibbon and other friends, urged him not to abandon his career in Orientalism in order to concentrate on studies at the Middle Temple. But he had discovered, to his dismay, that the writing of scholarly books, despite the praise accorded by fellow-scholars and reviewers, produced little income, though he shared Schultens' deep love of literature and encouraged the Arabist to pursue Persian also. They shared the pleasure of studying language, which they considered to be a necessary tool that could uncover literature and culture unknown to Europe. Even in that early period they agreed, as Schultens said in 1774, that a translator needs 'a competent knowledge, not only of the language of the East, but of Oriental history, ceremonies, and manners'. Schultens' letters introduced Jones to Dutch scholars like the Arabist Scheidius and the Latinist Ruhnkenius and summarized their research. The pair assisted each other, as in Jones' *Moallakát* and Schultens' three volumes of a long-projected edition of Al-Maidání in Arabic and Latin, which began with *Specimen proverbiorum Meidanii* (London, 1773). Albert Schultens, the Arabist's grandfather, had translated and partly annotated Al-Harírí's linguistically rich *Maqámát*. Jones vainly urges his friend to complete and publish that complex work; De Sacy finally edited it in 1822. Aesthetically, Jones' eleven traced letters and Schulten's four traced answers are some of the richest of all Jones' correspondence. His Letters 93 and 271 are among his most sensitive and urbane; Letter 253 tersely lists questions vital to Arabic work that he was pursuing, exemplifying the pair's interdependence.

His correspondence with Reviczky has been better preserved – eleven letters by and twelve to him in 1768–89. His initial letter and Reviczky's answer set the comparative tone characterizing much of their association, which was conducted entirely by post except for the thirty-minute meeting that introduced them. The Hungarian-born diplomat encouraged Jones' projected 'Un traité sur la poësie orientale', predicting that it would satisfyingly mortify 'all our European poets, who must blush at the poverty of their prosaic language, when they find that the Oriental dialects (independently of rhyme, which is of their invention) have true syllabic qualities as well as the Greek, and a greater variety of feet, and consequently the true science of metre and prosody'. Reviczky enclosed his own prose version and his verse paraphrase of an ode by Háfiz, on which he marginally copied several Greek and Latin poetic passages expressing the same sentiments, thus deepening the comparative vein on which Jones was already working. After unsuccessfully urging him to translate the six hundred odes in Háfiz's *Divan* into French, Jones made French prose translations of ten odes for the 'Traité', including two that Reviczky had rendered into Latin. Jones constructively criticized Reviczky's Latin version of these and fourteen others, which appeared in the Persian edition *Specimen poeseos Persicæ* (Vienna, 1771); no doubt Jones' influence was at work when John Richardson rendered them and some others into English and added a commentary, in *A Specimen of Persian Poetry* (London, 1774). When Reviczky published *Traité de la tactique, ou méthode artificielle pour l'ordonnance des troupes* (Vienna, 1769), his French version of Efendi Ibrahim Muteferriqa's Turkish treatise, Jones vainly tried to find someone who would translate it into English.

Meanwhile, Reviczky provided astute criticism of Jones' Greek and Latin translations, imitations, and compositions, and versions from the Arabic and Persian. He also elaborated on Jones' 1768 observation that the numerous cognates and very similar verb inflections show a linguistic relationship between Hebrew and Arabic. After Reviczky interpreted the first couplet of Háfiz's 'Shírazí Turk', Jones began working on a version that finally appeared as 'A Persian Song of Hafiz', a fine poem that has taken its place in English literature. His greatest help came in the form of enthusiasm for and translations of Persian literature, which were to be of lifelong service to Jones. Humanistically, his letters are perhaps the most interesting of all the letters to Jones that have been found. Their correspondence perceptively embraces tenets vital to the later development of comparative literature and makes an innovatively favourable comparison of Persian to classical literature.

Jones' other correspondence makes only scattered references to Persian except for his extended exchange with the Orientalist Thomas Hunt. This throws historical light on Jones' queries to certain Oxford philologists about Avestan and Anquetil-Duperron; his pamphlet mistakenly concluding that the Frenchman had translated a modern forgery of Zoroaster was to retard the development of Avestan studies for some fifty years. As Prince Czartoryski was the highest-ranking person ever to write him, Jones especially appreciated the prince's provocative question in 1778 of 'by what chance so many words from other European languages, or at least used in our European languages, are got into the Persian'. His answering generalization was a forerunner of his famous 1786 formulation. Jones' correspondence with Langlès has not been found, a considerable loss, as that Continental scholar first introduced the Asiatic Society to France and became a professor of Persian in the school for Oriental languages that he established.

The Orientalist Harford Jones presented a rare manuscript of Wahshí of Báfq's *Farhád u Shírín* and, after Jones delightedly circulated copies of it among pundits in Calcutta, wrote at least three other unpublished letters to Jones. One letter introduced the traveller William Francklin, who was so gratified by the association that he dedicated his translation *The Loves of Camarúpa and Cámalatà, an Ancient Indian Tale* (London, 1793) to Jones and joined the Asiatic Society. John Herbert Harington was another Persian scholar, whose only traced letter to Jones is an unpublished 1792 one resigning from the secretaryship of the Society and thanking Jones for 'liberal assistance'. In view of Jones' love for Sa'dí, it is likely that he helped in the preparation of Harington's two-volume Arabic and Persian edition (Calcutta, 1791–4), just as he probably gave assistance to the translations and grammars done by Francis Gladwin, to whose periodical, *Asiatick Miscellany*, he contributed.

His most pleasurable correspondence in India about Persian literature was with John Shore and Richard Johnson. His sixteen traced letters in 1787–93 to Shore, a member of the Supreme Council who succeeded Cornwallis as Governor-General, reflect the pair's aesthetic sharing of Persian poems, the texts of which were often carried by a servant who brought back the other's response. That Shore became president of the Society upon Jones' death is further evidence of Jones' dynamism and that capacity to stimulate others which he demonstrated throughout his relatively short career. Jones was also close friends with Johnson, a supernumerary member of the Board of Revenue, to whom he wrote at least ten letters in 1783–9 and whom he urged to publish Johnson's rare manuscript of Háfiz. Johnson supplied helpful information about Persian for Jones' hymns to Hindu divinities that drew primarily on Sanskrit manuscripts; his literary and linguistic assistance was considerable.

Jones always advised his correspondents to use primary rather than secondary sources when possible. Thus he advised Maurice to study the

Persian historian Ferishtah. Such encouragement partly inspired a major blunder, when Lieutenant Francis Wilford sought to document one of Jones' comparative hopes – to locate Judaic references in Sanskrit – without knowing Sanskrit. In 1787 Wilford wrote to him: 'you will find I am not conversant with the *Hindu* antiquities: indeed, I have no time to study languages' (*Letters*, II, 785). So when Wilford's over-stimulated pundit secretly forged and inserted sheets in the *Purāṇas* that mentioned Noah and Noah's three sons, the unsuspecting Jones and Europe were startled but delighted. Though Jones gradually become more dubious about the stunning references, the damage was done. Thus John Bruce's request for help from the Asiatic Society particularly specified Wilford. After Wilford later acknowledged his gullibility, the scholarly record was corrected; but the uncritical acceptance of the forged sheets during Jones' final years helped to confirm the utilitarians' later suspicion that the crafty Hindus had duped their European rulers, thereby providing Macaulay with ammunition against Jones and the other early Orientalists. Nonetheless, Wilford's 'discoveries' furthered the comparative spirit in Europe.

Jones' correspondence with other Britons interested in Sanskrit culture was more salutary. The most provocative exchange was with Monboddo, who in several passages in his important six-volume *Of the Origin and Progress of Language* (Edinburgh, 1774–92) echoes his letters to Jones but does not mention Jones (VI, 96–7, 142–3). Monboddo's several references to Wilkins there, along with other evidence, suggest that Wilkins rather than Jones was a primary source for his speculations about Sanskrit in the book. Unmoved by Jones' urging of caution, this early anthropologist expanded his linguistic speculations in his letters, still without real evidence. After he theorized from erroneous, second-hand data that the ancient Egyptians, who supposedly spoke Sanskrit, went to Japan or that at least their religion and arts and sciences went there, Jones enthusiastically procured a small statue of Buddha for him and promised to send information about it. Though Monboddo's comparative generalizations came too late to influence Jones' famous 1786 formulation, Jones' belief in the essential unity among the large ethnic groups of Asia and ultimately of the world apparently drew on Monboddo's conclusion that the world's languages derived from one primitive language. Thus Jones stated in 1792:

> If the human race then be, as we may confidently assume, of one natural species, they must all have proceeded from one pair... They must people in time the region where they first were established, and their numerous descendants must necessarily seek new

countries, as inclination might prompt, or accident lead, them; they would of course migrate in separate families and clans, which, forgetting by degrees the language of the common progenitor, would form new dialects to convey new ideas, both simple and complex.[19]

His fourteen traced letters to Wilkins reveal his indebtedness for Sanskrit epithets and other materials about the divinities celebrated in his poetic hymns, as well as for information needed to devise an oath that would compel Hindu witnesses to tell the truth in court. As Wilkins evidently encouraged him to study Sanskrit, their association was potentially the richest collaboration within the Society, with these two early Sanskritists co-operatively uncovering ancient India for the world. Because Wilkins' letters to him have not been found, we do not know why the collaboration never really took place, but the enthusiasm and tone of Jones' letters indicate that he expected and received help. His realization that Wilkins was not going to do the needed English translations, especially of the legal works on which his law digest would depend, was a major reason why he undertook the comprehensive study of Sanskrit. He paid Wilkins public tributes for Sanskrit discoveries and general literary stimulation, although Wilkins soon left India and made no contribution to Jones' *Śakuntalā*, his greatest translation and a landmark in comparative literature that successfully bridged the cultural, linguistic, and chronological gulf. Wilkins strongly supported the Society, contributing five essays, primarily translations of inscriptions that heightened Jones' keen interest in epigraphy. Jones encouraged Wilkins' epochal translation of the *Bhagavad-Gita*, which the British press ignored or attacked, and urged Wilkins to translate the rest of the *Mahābhārata*. His friend reciprocated the admiration, later preparing an annotated catalogue of the manuscripts that Jones had sent Banks for safekeeping.

Jones' letters to Davis discussed Sanskrit extensively, but the pair's astronomical and historical aim precluded any real linguistic discoveries. Jones' one known letter to Colebrooke was evidently a polite, flattering acknowledgements of a submitted paper, which Jones read to the Society at his last meeting. When Colebrooke was asked to finish the law digest after Jones' death, the intensive two-year study and revision gave him the command of Sanskrit that was to distinguish him. *A Digest of Hindu Law on Contracts and Successions, with a Commentary* (Calcutta, 1797–8) was a major event in the history of Indian administration. Then in 1808 Colebrooke published an English interpretation of Amarasiṃha's

Amarakósa, a 12,608-word lexicon that Jones had translated in 1788 to aid his own study of Sanskrit.

Jones similarly inspired Lieutenant Steuart, who organized reliable copying of the inscriptions in the Delhi area to advance Jones' pioneering desire to copy all the inscriptions in India and thus initiate the study of Indian epigraphy, which would eventually provide a key to unlock the Sanskrit past. Steuart's three recently discovered letters reflect the scholarly zeal with which Jones imbued the members of the Society. Indeed, in 1789 Steuart wrote Jones that the inscription on the Jantar Mantar contains 'many characters exactly similar to those on Firoze Shah's Lat', vainly suggesting the very clue which permitted James Prinsep to decipher the Pālī inscription on that lat in 1838. Other collectors sent Jones copies of inscriptions from the Budal pillar, a Vellore cave, and elsewhere. General John Carnac sent six copper plates from Salsette Island, Bombay, containing verse inscriptions which the Gujarati Brahmans could not explain, but which Jones was able to decipher.[20]

Jones' devotion to Sanskrit and antique Oriental learning left him little time for vernacular languages like Bengali and Hindi. Thus when the assistant surgeon John Gilchrist cogently questioned the East India Company's policy of having their servants gain some command of Persian (the language of the courts and government but not of the people), studied Hindi, and later inspired that study, Jones never collaborated in the project. He may not have corresponded with this fine philologist who did a two-part English–Hindi dictionary in 1787–90, though he proudly seconded the nomination of Gilchrist for membership in his Society. Had he assisted Gilchrist, conceivably Macaulay's shrill Minute of 1835 and the decision to use English rather than an Indic language in the Indian schools might have been forestalled.

Jones' correspondence about the classical languages was mainly carried on in England, especially with the classicist Samuel Parr, whom Jones assisted throughout his career. They criticized each other's Latin and Greek imitations, besides their translations and creative compositions. Jones notably made the requested corrections of Parr's Latin epitaph to Robert Sumner that was finally inscribed in Harrow Church, as well as of various sermons that Parr then published as books. The corrections sent in Parr's usually untraced letters were also valuable, beginning with suggestions for Jones' curious appendix of Latin and Greek Poems attached to *Commentariorum*, and reaching a peak with

Jones' translation *The Speeches of Isæus in Causes Concerning the Law of Succession to Property at Athens* (London, 1779), which Burke warmly complimented. In Letter 152 Jones complained good-naturedly about Parr's penmanship: 'Your Greek is wholly illegible – it is perfect algebra; and your strictures on my Isæus, excellent and valuable as they are, have given more fatigue to my head and eyes than the whole translation' (I, 260). Even when Jones was indulging in his love for Arabic and Persian, the pair's correspondence reflects the kind of adulation of the classics that dominated British literature and that Jones' Oriental researches would do much to alter.

Except in Jones' letters to Parr, his correspondence contains only scattered references to Latin and Latin writings. When sent Pérez Bayer's Spanish and Latin treatise on Phoenician (Madrid, 1772), he reciprocated with a copy of *Commentariorum.* He also received the Prince Infante Don Gabriel's elegant Spanish translation of Sallust, which inspired his eloquent comparative criticism in Letter 92. He always praised classical literature. His Latin Letter 445 thoughtfully likened Orme's style to that of Xenophon, in a rich consideration of translation and classical poetry. He concluded: 'As to the works of the Greeks I perfectly agree with you, and think every line of them to be a gem of exquisite beauty; but I consider the Romans as bright only with borrowed rays' (II, 716).

Little of his correspondence about Celtic has been found. He wrote to the antiquarian Joseph Cooper Walker at least twice, praising Walker's *Historical Memoirs of the Irish Bards* (London, 1786), which was sent him. Walker also transmitted other Irish scholars' books and may have stimulated Jones's correspondence with Colonel Charles Vallancey, the founder of the school of writers who theorized about Irish history, literaure, and language without studying the original texts or even knowing the languages. When Vallancey sent Jones some names from druid mythology, he misunderstood Jones' suggestions and wrote in a major essay: 'Sir W. Jones encouraged my pursuit, and was convinced, as I am, that the first Eastern Colonists that settled in Ireland, were the Indian Scythæ, whom Berosus says settled on the Indus and Ganges, in the fortieth year of Belus, the Nimrod of the Scriptures.'[21] Though Jones' Third Discourse did propose linguistic affinity between Celtic and Scythian, in Letter 467 he privately criticized Vallancey's deriving Irish from Persian, Arabic, and Sanskrit: 'According to him, when silly people gave me the surname of *Persian*, they in fact called me *Irishman.* Do you wish to laugh? Skim the book over' (II, 769). But apparently undisturbed by the speculative philologist's use of his name in *A Vindication of the Ancient History of Ireland* (Dublin, 1786), which Vallancey subtitled *Proved from the Sanscrit Books*, Jones instructed Earl Spencer never to repeat this private criticism so as not to hurt an honest man. Walker also sent Jones proposals for the publication of Charlotte Brooke's *Reliques of Irish Poetry* (Dublin, 1789) by subscription. Jones dutifully distributed these to his friends in Calcutta and praised her poetry. Evidently carefully choosing the word *faithful*, he told Walker in Letter 468: 'We shall soon I hope see faithful translations of Irish histories and poems. I shall be happy in comparing them with the Sanscrit, with which the ancient language of Ireland had certainly an affinity' (II, 771).

But he had no time to make Celtic comparisons in these last years, as he was frantically labouring to complete his monumental translation of the *Mānava-Dharmaśāstra* (Calcutta, 1794) and his law digest. When Richard Morris Jr proposed to edit Lewis Morris' 'Celtic Remains', a dictionary of Welsh place-names, Jones had time only to circulate the proposals and express his warm interest as a Cymmrodorion in British antiquities and literature. Perhaps partly because he could not indulge in his natural interest in Welsh, his father's language, only the first part of the dictionary was every published (London, 1878). The request for his aid further illustrates his stature in comparative studies, which he had a central role in founding.

NOTES

1 *Memoirs of the Life, Writings and Correspondence of Sir William Jones* (London, 1804), which was reprinted as the first two volumes of the thirteen-volume *The Works of Sir William Jones* (London, 1807). For the role of the Utilitarians, see Eric Stokes, *The English Utilitarians and India* (Oxford, 1959).

2 *Philological Quarterly*, 51 (1972), 951–5. Bishop Jonathan Shipley's only traced letter to Jones was also first published there.

3 Preface to *Poems, Consisting Chiefly of Translations from the Asiatick Languages* (Oxford, 1772).

4 *Escolha das poesias orientaes, qui Guilherme Jones traduzio daquelles idiomas em verso Inglez, e ornada agora em Portuguez, seguidas de outras varias rimas* (Lisbon, 1793).

5 *Poesias Asiáticas puestas en verso Castellano* (Paris, 1833), pp. 1–79.

6 See my 'Sir William Jones and Dr Johnson's Literary Club', *Modern Philology*, 62 (1965), 20–37.

7 Universitäts- und Landesbibliothek Sachsen-Anhalt, Francke-Archiv I C 58: 7.

8 The 148-page manuscript copy in the Cambridge University Library (Oo.1.6) was made from the original, which was received in Calcutta.

9 See my 'Sir William Jones and Anglo-American Relations during the American

Revolution', *Modern Philology*, 76 (1978), 29–45; and my 'Sir William Jones and Benjamin Franklin', Oxford University *College Record*, 4 (1961), 27–45. 'A Fragment of Polybius' is in *Letters*, I, 291–6.

10 London, 1782. See my 'Sir William Jones and Edmund Burke', *Modern Philology*, 54 (1957), 165–86, which includes the text of 'Best Practicable System'.

11 'A Description of the Jonesia', *Asiatick Researches*, 4 (1794), 355.

12 In India Office Library, MSS. Eur. F. 95.

13 See my 'Sir William Jones, Sir Joseph Banks, and the Royal Society', *Notes and Records of the Royal Society of London*, 29 (1975), 205–30.

14 See W. Nicol's *Catalogue of the Library of the Late Sir William Jones* (London, 1831), which prints some of Jones' annotations.

15 None of Wilkins' letters to Jones has been found. The manuscripts of Jones' thirteen letters to him, which were first published in the *Journal of the American Oriental Society* in 1880 and then were lost for almost a century, have turned up in the India Office Library.

16 Rosane Rocher's *Orientalism, Poetry, and the Millennium: The Checkered Life of Nathaniel Brassey Halhed* (Princeton University Press, forthcoming).

17 To Thomas Maurice on 8 July 1794: 'As to Sir W. Jones, he is by many thought to shew great duplicity, and to be very unfair in his allegations. I have written my opinion of his behaviour for my own private amusement: for I shall hardly send it into the world: especially while he is abroad. When he returns, I may probably let him see it. A writer more inconsistent and so often in opposition to himself, I never encountered.' In Maurice's *Memoirs of the Author of 'Indian Antiquities'*, second edition (London, 1820–2), Part II, p. 36.

18 In the British Museum, No. 12904, f. 23.

19 Ninth Discourse, *Works*, III, 188. See my 'The Correspondence between Lord Monboddo and Sir William Jones', *American Anthropologist*, 70 (1968), 559–61.

20 'An Indian Grant of Land in Y.C. 1018', *Works*, IV, 334–47.

21 'On the Oriental Emigration of the Ancient Inhabitants of Britain and Ireland', in *The Oriental Collections*, edited by William Ousely (London, 1799), III, 31.

Letters of Sir William Jones and his correspondents

The texts of Jones' newly discovered letters follow.[1] Separate contextual headnotes will introduce his letter to Richard Johnson, the two letters to Sir John Macpherson (the third was unavailable for printing), and the single ones to Thomas Maurice and to the Henry Savile Starcks. Because of limitations of space, these texts will be followed by a few of the extant letters to Jones. We solicit information about any untraced letters by and to Jones, in view of the increasing interest in this great eighteenth-century scholar.

LETTERS FROM JONES

To Richard Johnson (d. 1807)

Jones wrote Johnson numerous letters, including Letter 391 which contains no addressee's name and was mistakenly ascribed to Wilkins. Johnson had collected intriguing materials on Indian music, which significantly deepened Jones' interest in that subject. This new letter is important because it (1) reviews the state of the Asiatic Society, (2) is Jones' only known comment on Sir Robert Chambers' dilatoriness, (3) documents his association with Halhed in Calcutta in 1785, and (4) provides the earliest known date of Jones' mastery of Devanagari and of his determination to start studying Sanskrit, which was to produce his greatest scholarly achievements.

CALCUTTA
2 MARCH 1785.

MY DEAR SIR,

I should reproach myself for the long suspension of a correspondence so instructive and flattering to me, if the real cause of my silence had not been a series of disorders, which twice brought me nearly to the point of death. Your letter enclosing the very *ingenious*, but *too artificial*, Poem of the Asiatick Laureat, I received at the house of Mr Speke,[2] our common friend, whose conversation on every subject, political as well as literary, made me regret extremely the necessity of leaving Jengipore after a visit of two days: He favours me to-day with his company at dinner, and we shall drink your health, in conformity to the rule of *Hháfiz*[3]

چو با حبیب نشینی رباده پیماي بیاد دار حزیفان بادیه پیمارا

although this would have been more applicable to your expedition through Bezoara. After a confinement for two months at Boglipore, where botany was my only amusement,[4] I found it impossible to discharge my duty on the bench, and, having spent a week at Patna, went by land to Gya and thence to Benares: on my return I had the pleasure of visiting Gour and Pendua, and of seeing the Sunderbunds in all their beauty. The business of the term, which began yesterday, and the hurry of sending letters to Europe by the few ships that remain, occupy all my time, and will interrupt both my corrrespondence and my literary pursuits till the middle of April; especially as my recovery is by no means complete, and I am apprehensive of a relapse, if I suffer my spirits to be much agitated. You will pardon, therefore, the brevity and dryness of this letter, and, if you receive soon *a Discourse to the Asiatick Society*, and a little *Jeu d'Esprit*, called *The Enchanted Fruit*, *an Antediluvian Tale*, you will know from whom they come, even if I should not be able to enclose letters in the same covers. Many thanks for your ideas on the advancement of the Society: it is in a thriving way, and its archives begin to be full. I will take steps to secure the assistance of Col. Pearse.[5] Halhed has left us: he is, indeed, one of those genius's, who, like the *Bráh Outár*, penetrate all as they pass and tear up by the roots whatever they touch; but my brother Chambers, like the *Coorm Outár*, moves very slowly, and I wish his tardy motions were not as unpleasant in the administration of justice, as they are in the promotion of learning: he sits in court a little before twelve, and rises a little after one; so that you will agree with me, that his arms should be supported by two tortoises.[6] You and I take a middle course, and I have only to lament, that we are destined to labour at such a distance. Burrow has just left me: he has nearly finished the survey of your grounds; and promises two or three papers for the Society.[7] What a dreadful picture you give of *Hyderabad!* A punster would say that you are *a bad hider* of its defects and miseries; but lord Verulam, who was no wit, but a great Philosopher, pronounces, that *Truth is majestick and must prevail.* As I do not, therefore, suspect you of colouring too highly, I most heartily deplore your residence in a city, where your talents have not room for *their full expression*; though I am informed by many that you have acquired great honour already by your negotiations. Rest assured, that I will miss no opportunity of expressing my opinion of the great service that you may do us at Poona, whenever I converse in private with our rulers; but I have not often that pleasure; since they are much engaged, and the Sun, whom I adore only that he may not injure me, though I should otherwise *tell him how I hate his beams*, confines me to my house as long as he appears in the heavens. Mr Croftes and I regret the departure of Mr Hastings, Shore, and Anderson:[8] indeed, I am grieved to find in India, what I found a great evil at Oxford, that my friendships, which are formed on the surest foundation, *a similarity of pursuits and sentiments*, are constantly liable to interruption, at the very time when they are advancing to maturity. Lady Jones desires me to present you her best compliments: pray give mine to your Philosopher and Poet; I may add, to your Pundit, as I have learned the Deo Nagry characters and will set about Shanscrit in earnest, if I have six months longer.[9] Your books are, I believe, perfectly safe: that you may enjoy their *quiet and stability*, as well as their fame, is the hearty wish of, my dear Sir,

Your faithful friend
and obedt. Servt.

W. JONES.

Original: Staatsbibliothek Preussischer Kulturbesitz, Berlin (Dokumentensammlung Darmstaedter 2b 1771)

To Sir John Macpherson (1745–1821) and the Bengal Supreme Council

When Jones arrived in Calcutta in 1783 as the junior member of the Bengal Supreme Court of Judicature, relations between the Court and the Supreme Ccouncil were so bad that at times there was virtual war between the two governing bodies, partly because the Regulating Act of 1773 had not specified the division of authority between them. One of Jones' lesser purposes in establishing the Asiatic Society was to bring about a rapprochement as a means to a just government based on the Indians' religions and laws. He was immediately successful in part when his two fellow-judges became charter members, and Hastings and the Council accepted his invitation to become Patrons. When Hastings sailed, Macpherson, as the senior member of the Council, became the Acting Governor-General. Jones persuaded him to join the Society, discreetly instructed him in the ways of government based on law, and led him to rely on the Court in judicial matters. Two recently discovered letters from the Court to the Council illustrate this reliance, which was perhaps requested by a letter like the following:

FROM THE BENGAL SUPREME COUNCIL TO THE BENGAL SUPREME COURT

FORT WILLIAM,
19 JULY 1786.

HONORABLE SIRS,

We have received a Letter from the President and Council of Fort St George, expressive of their own Doubts upon the underwritten legal Question, and their anxiety to be furnished as soon as possible with your Opinions thereon: And as the Public in general are interested in the Decision we request an early communication of your Sentiments, viz. Whether the Commander in Chief as second in Council, or whether the third in Council, and eventual Successor to the Government, is, in the case of the Governor's Absence through Sickness, to preside at the Quarter Sessions.

Original Copy: Commonwealth Relations Office (Home Misc. Series, vol. 418, pp. 157, 159)

The judges' ruling in favour of the Commander in Chief is Letter 435. Jones continued the same practice with Cornwallis, the next Governor-General, as exemplified in the ruling in Letter 493.

TO THE HONBLE JOHN MACPHERSON
GOVERNOR GENERAL, & THE GENTLEMEN OF THE
COUNCIL AT FORT WILLIAM IN BENGAL,

HONBLE SIRS,

Enclosed in yours of the 21st of last month, we had the honor to receive a Copy of a letter addressed to you by the President & Council of Fort St George, wherein they desire that you will apply to us for our opinion on the 44th Section of the late Statute, 24 Geo: III. Cap: 25, and particularly on this question: Whether by Virtue of that section any crime which was committed in India by a British Subject, before the first of January 1785, and which at the time of its being committed was not cognizable by any of the Courts of Justice established by Charter at Madras, be now cognizable and can be tried by the said Courts?

Having perused the above mentioned Statute and fully considered the question proposed to us, we are of opinion that any crime committed in India, by a British Subject, even before the first of January 1785, in any of the Lands or territories of any native prince or State, is now cognizable by the Court of Oyer and Terminer at Madras, provided that it do not amount to Treason or Felony: But it is clear and the general words in the 44th Section of the abovementioned Statute are not intended to include High Treason, which the Court of Oyer and Terminer at Madras is not empowered in any case to try; and we think also that they do not extend to Murder, or any other Felony, because it is an established rule, with regard to the construction of Acts of Parliament that a statute which speaks of things of an inferior nature cannot, by any *general words*, be extended to those which are of a higher degree.—

In delivering our opinion, we have varied the terms of the question, by adding these words 'in any of the lands or territories of any native prince or state', because they are the words of the statute itself; in which those lands and territories seem to be contradistinguished and opposed to the '*territories directly subject to and under the British Government in India*'. With regard to these last mentioned Territories, we do not conceive that the statute has at all altered the local Jurisdication, and we therefore incline to think that the Court of Oyer and Terminer at Madras, ought not to take cognizance of any offence committed within the Territorial acquistions of the East India Company in Bengal Bahar or Orissa; neither would the Supreme Court of Judicature here take cognizance of an offence charged to have been committed at any place that is clearly within the ordinary Jurisdiction of the Court of Oyer and Terminer at Madras.

Fort William
April 16. 1785.
A true Copy
W. BRUERE
Secry.

We have the honor to be,
Honble Sirs,
Your most obedient
Humble Servants
ROBT. CHAMBERS
JOHN HYDE
W. JONES.

Original copy: Bodleian Library (MS. Eng. hist. c. 80, pp. 20–1)

TO THE HONBLE JOHN MACPHERSON
GOVERNOR GENERAL AND THE GENTLEMEN OF THE COUNCIL.—

HONBLE SIRS,

We are of Opinion, that Lord William Murray cannot, *in the Circumstances stated to us*, be tried either by a Court Martial or by the Court of Oyer and Terminer at Madras; but we think that he may be tried, under a Special Commission of Oyer and Terminer, in England, by Virtue of the Statute of 33 Hen: 8: c 23.—

Fort William
July 29. 1785.

We have the honor to be
Sirs,
ROBERT CHAMBERS
JOHN HYDE
W. JONES.

Original copy: Bodleian Library (MS. Eng. hist. c. 81, p. 41)

To Thomas Maurice (1754–1824)

This letter contains important advice that Jones gave his long-standing friend – the necessity of relying on primary sources like Persian and Sanskrit if Maurice wanted to compose a reliable history of India. Maurice publicly acknowledged Jones' help: 'Sir William Jones afforded the clue which has directed my path through this dark and intricate labyrinth. I have cautiously adhered to the outline which his pencil drew, and have in no instance deviated from my honoured guide' (Preface, *History of Hindostan*, II, v). The candid remarks that Maurice deleted in printing Jones' letter were probably about Bryant, whose methodology and speculative etymologies were soon to be publicly criticized by Jones as ultimately permitting almost any word to be derived from any other word.

CRISHNA-NAGAR,
10TH OCTOBER, 1790.

DEAR SIR,

It is not possible for me to forget the pleasure which I have received from your conversation, and the opinion which I always entertained of your parts and industry. The arduous undertaking, of which I have just perused the plan, fully justifies my opinion; but I am so oppressed with a heavy arrear of business, that I cannot write at large on the subject of it. I will desire my agent in London to subscribe for me, and will do all I can to promote the subscription here. Such is the expense of printing at Calcutta, that it would cost thirty pounds sterling to reprint the pamphlet; but the proposals shall be reprinted, and carefully circulated.

I am confident that you might learn Persian in six months, (if you have not learned it already,) so well at least as to read the original text of Ferishtah, whose work, with submission, is very *highly esteemed* by all learned Indians and Indian scholars. To an historian I must express every truth, even though friendship might induce me to conceal it; * * * * * * * * * * * * * * *. Let me, at the same time, exhort you not wholly to rely on *my* authority; for, though I have diligently avoided errors, yet I have made many: for instance, *Por*, a word which I found for *Porus* in the Shah-Nameh, is, I now find, pronounced *Pur*, or *Poor*, by the native Persians; and I have reason to believe from Sanscrit authorities, that the true name of that prince was PAURAVA. If you read Persian, Mr Boughton Rouse will, I dare say, lend you the *Modern History of India*, by Gholam Husain. Farewel, my Dear Sir, and believe me to be, with great regard,

Your ever faithful humble servant,
WILLIAM JONES.

Printed: Maurice, *History Hindostan*, second edition (London, 1801), III, vi

To Anne Marie La Cépèdes de Fauques (de Vaucluse) Starck (1720–1804) and Henry Savile Starck

According to a 1768 letter from Reviczky, Jones had written 'letters' to the French Oriental romancer; but the following letter to her and her husband is the only traced holograph from this apparently sizeable correspondence. Some details of her romantic, shadowy life are provided in Fatma Moussa-Mahmoud's 'Mme Vaucluse: Author & Femme Philosophe of the 18th Century', in the Cairo University *Bulletin of the Faculty of Arts* (1978), pp. 155–80. Other, somewhat tenuous details of her supposed assistance to Jones, as well as of Jones' literary help to her, are to be found in Starck's embroidered, unpublished 'Memoirs of the Life and Character...of the Late Madame de Vaucluse', which Starck evidently composed with the hope of capitalizing on her long literary career and which survives in the William Beckford archive. In it Starck credits Jones with introducing the couple and quotes from Jones' untraced letter to him in 1779, a year before he married the ageing writer and amanuensis of Beckford:

> 'You do right,' says Sir William, at that time Mr Jones, 'to cultivate the acquaintance of Madame de Vaucluse; and you cannot too frequently visit her. She possesses, what is very rarely found joined with transcendent abilities, much affability and a most engaging complacency of manner. The more you know her, the more you will perceive, by the depth and variety of her erudition, how far superior she is to any idea we can form, by their works, of the Maintenons, the Sevignés, &c—'

This extract appears in Fatma Moussa-Mahmoud's 'Sir William Jones and Mme Vaucluse', in *Revue de littérature comparée.*

CRISHNA-NAGAR
15 OCT 1791.

MY GOOD FRIENDS,

I have sent you several letters, short in themselves, but long for me; and have not received a line in return. If you are gone to France to enjoy freedom under the new constitution, send me at least some account of it: if you are well, le me have the pleasure of knowing it, if ill, let me at least express my hope of your recovery. I live in health but in constant occupation, and the glare of the sun so dazzles my weak eyes, that I write nothing, which I can avoid, and would not write these few lines for any other purpose than to assure you that I am, my good friends,

very constantly yours

W. JONES.

Original: The Beckford archive, Blackwell's, Oxford
Printed: Fatma Moussa-Mahmoud, 'The Republican Ideas of Sir William Jones (1746–1794)', Cairo University *Bulletin of the Faculty of Arts*, 29 (1972), 120
Text: Original

LETTERS TO JONES

Whang Atong (d. 1796)

This very able Cantonese, whom Reynolds had befriended and painted in London, represented Jones' last, unsuccessful effort to have the *Shih Ching* translated, in order that Western readers might benefit from that superb poetical collection. Jones urged him to bring a colony of Chinese artists to Bengal if the Company would support this pioneering scheme for a government-financed emigration; the Company would not.

[CANTON?], DEC. 10, 1784.

SIR,

I received the favour of your letter dated 28th March 1784, by Mr Cox. I remember the pleasure of dining with you in company with Capt. Blake and Sir Joshua Reynolds; and I shall always remember the kindness of my friends in *England*.

The *Chinese* book, Shí King, that contains three hundred Poems, with remarks thereon, and the work of *Con-fu-tsu*, and his grandson, the *Tai Ho*, [I] beg you will accept; but to translate the work into *English* will require a great deal of time; perhaps three to four years; and I am so much engaged in business, that I hope you will excuse my not undertaking it.

If you wish for any books or other things from *Canton*, be so good as to let me know, and I will take particular care to obey your orders.

Wishing you health, I am, Sir,

Your most obedient humble Servant,

WHANG ATONG.

Printed: Asiatick Researches, II, 204

James Burnett, Lord Monboddo (1714–99)

Monboddo's untraced inquiry of about 1788 relative to the Brahmans' philosophy led Jones to hypothesize that 'the doctrines of the Vidanti school are Platonic' (II, 818) and to send Monboddo his Third Discourse, which gave rise to Monboddo's elaborate query about the country from which the nations named in that Discourse derived their language, manners, and arts. Ingenious argument and inaccurate data underpinned his conclusion that Sanskrit was the ancient language of Egypt, where the Greeks supposedly learned it. As the universalism in this wild speculation appealed to Jones but led him to advise caution in his untraced answer, Monboddo again argued that the Egyptians anciently visited India, concluding that all languages came from one primitive language in Egypt, which gave arts and sciences to the world. In 1792 Jones corrected one of Monboddo's mistakes without naming him: the Arabs, Hindus, and Tatars did not use even one word in common.

Jones's exuberant exchange of speculations about such broad comparative relationships illustrates both the tone of erudition in his day and his capacity to make pioneering corrections of contemporary mistakes.

EDINBURGH,
JUNE 20, 1789.

DEAR SIR,

I had the honour of your very polite letter and with it a discourse pronounced by you in that noble Society which you have erected in India, and from which I expect information concerning many curious things relating to the history of *Man*, and of Arts and Sciences. In this discourse you propose to open a wonderful field of enquiry: and if you can discover that central country from which all those nations, which you have named, have derived their affinity in language, manners and arts, which you observe, it will be a most wonderful discovery in the history of man. Of the three things I have named, by which the connection and relation of one nation to another is discovered, I hold Language to be the principal. It is the first art that was invented among men: and it is the foundation of civil society, and of all other arts. And as it is the first of arts, so it is the most lasting, and one that travels the farthest, and is propagated to the most distant regions. The substance of this has been lately discovered by a Prussian gentleman, who was sometime in Lapland, and learned the language there: he had also learned the language of Hungary. Upon the subject of these two languages he has written a treatise, in which I think he has proved demonstratively that the two are the same.

Now we know with great certainty that the Hungarians are originally of a country lying betwixt the Euxine and the Caspian Seas. They call themselves not Hungarians, but *Magars*: and the Russians not long ago discovered a people of that name, in the country I have mentioned, betwixt the two Seas. This joined with the testimony of Ammianus Marcellinus, who says that the Huns came from that country, puts the matter beyond all doubt. So here we have a language that has travelled all the way from betwixt the Euxine and Caspian Seas and Lapland, and I am persuaded that the language of a country still further north, I mean Greenland – of which I have seen a grammar, and find it to be a language of more art than the Latin – must have also come with the people from the East, as it is impossible it could have been formed among a people living the savage life that the Greenlanders live in that country.

From what I have been able to learn of the history of Man, which I have studied for several years, I have formed an opinion that not only all arts and sciences have come from the East, but even the race of man. For I hold that man is not originally of all countries, any more than the horse, the ox, and many other animals, but that his native country is the East, from whence he has spread over all the rest of the earth. And this migration is to be traced chiefly by language: and I believe that the same language you mention – the Sanscrit – is the original of many other languages. I made a kind of study of it this last spring when I was in London, under a man you speak of in the end of your paper, but do not name – I mean Mr Wilkins – who appears to be perfectly master of it, having studied it for years under two Brahmins. I entirely agree with you that it is a more perfect language than the Greek, and in three great arts of language, viz. derivation, composition, and flection it excells, I am persuaded, all the languages that ever existed. And its rules of analogy are so complete that it has no heteroclites: and I am persuaded it is true, what a Jesuit says of it – Du Pont I think is his name – that if a man have learned the roots of this language, which are not many in number, and has learned the rules of its derivations, compositions and flections, he may make a language himself which will be very well understood by those who have learned Sanscrit; whereas, in other languages, though we know the grammatical art of them never so well, we must learn the words of them, otherwise we never can speak or write in them so as to be understood. But the most curious thing concerning this language, and which appears to me to decide a most important point in the history of *man*, is its affinity with the Greek, and the most ancient dialect of Greek, the Latin. This affinity is so great that either the Greek is a dialect of the Sanscrit, or they are both dialects of the same parent language.

He has collected about seventy words, in which the two languages agree, with such variations as must be in different dialects of the same language: and many of these are words that must have been original in all languages, such as the names of numbers, the names of relations – such as that of father, mother, and brother – and the names of members of the human body, and particularly the foot, the name for which is precisely the same with the Greek word. Not only so, but there is a compound of it, with the number *three*, (viz. tripod), denoting precisely the same thing that it does in Greek. Now the question is this where, or whence, did the Greeks learn this language? They certainly did not go to India to learn it, nor did the Indians come to them. And if so, I can find no other place where they could have learned it except Egypt, where we know they learned all their arts and sciences, and – as it appears – language among other arts. So that here we have discovered that the ancient language of Egypt was Sanscrit, and it is not to be wondered that the Greeks learned it from Egypt; when we consider that they got not only their arts and sciences thence, and also their religion, and even their people. For the most ancient people in Greece, the Arcadians, were from Egypt; and the Athenians were also an Egyptian colony: And Herodotus tells us that all the chief men or leaders of the Dorians – the most ancient people in Greece – were from Egypt.

The only question then that remains to be considered, is one in which I expect to get great light from your Society; the question is, whether the Egyptians learned the language from the Indians, or the Indians from the Egyptians, or both from some other nation. That the Indians did not come to Egypt is I think certain. But, if we can give any credit to the Sacred Books of the Egyptians, or to the Indian traditions in the days of Alexander, the Egyptians were in India. There they may have found this Sanscrit language in use, and so have learnt it. And then the only remaining question will be, whether the Indians were self-taught, or learnt this language from any other nation. And all I shall say further upon the subject is that there is such a wonderful conformity betwixt the religion, policy, customs, manners, and (as it now appears) language of the two countries, that it is impossible but that the one must have copied from the other, or both from some third nation.

I present my best respects to my Lady Jones...

[J. BUR.]

Original copy: National Library of Scotland, MS. Acc. 5738
Printed: William Knight, *Lord Monboddo and Some of His Contemporaries* (London, 1900), pp. 267–71
Text: Original copy

EDIN. 20 JUNE 1791.

I had the favour of your letter of the 12th of October 1790. And a very great favour I think it is from a man so much occupied as you are. I am glad to find that you agree with me in most of the things, which I mentioned in my last letter. You say you incline to believe that not only the Egyptians, but the Indians came from Chaldaea. If you can make out this, it will be a great discovery at least to me, who have not so much as a conjecture about the origin of either of these two nations; and I should be glad to be informed by you whether you think that not only these two great nations came from the small country of Chaldaea, but also their Arts and Sciences. At present I have formed an opinion that from whatever country the Egyptians derived their Arts and Sciences, they imported these Arts and Sciences into India. That the Egyptians were in India in very antient times, all must believe otherwise we must reject the testimony of Diodorus Siculus and Arrian and I may say all the antient authors who have treated of India and Egypt. And besides their testimony, there are Monuments yet to be seen, as I am informed, not only in India but even in Jappan, which I think prove demonstratively not only that the Egyptians were in India, but that they or at least their Religion and their Arts and Sciences went as far as Jappan. For in both these countries there are Idols to be seen, of black men with woolly hair, flat noses and thick lips. This is a fact attested by a Frenchman, one Bailly in his Letters upon the origin of Sciences, and of the people of Asia: and also by Bryant in his Mythology Vol. 5, who in the quotations he gives us from a French Book upon the subject of the Dutch Embassys to Jappan, puts it out of all doubt that there are several Idols of the kind I have described, that are worshipped by the Jappanese in their temples, and which as he observes is at least Proof, that those men whom they had deified came from a foreign country, the Jappanese being white men, and woolly hair not being found any where in the East: whereas it is well known that the antient Egyptians were black men with woolly hair.

Now this proves to me that the Egyptians not only were in India and even in Jappan, and that they did not come to these countries to learn Arts but to teach them, for which reason they were deified by the Indians and Jappanese. Now I should be glad you would take the trouble to let me know whether you have seen or heard of any of those Idols with woolly hair in India – There is another proof of the Egyptians, or at least their Religion, having gone as far as Jappan, which you may perhaps never have heard of, as it is known to very few. But it is a fact that I have from good information. It is this, that the Jappanese give the name of Typhon (the name you know of the wicked Egyptian God) to a violent hurricane that is frequent in the seas betwixt China and Jappan. And the Greeks and Romans have borrowed the same word from the Egyptians to express the same thing. And there is a German whose name I cannot recollect, that has made a Collection of other words that the Jappanese have in common with the Greek – In short there are so many words which are common to all the Languages we know, of which M. Buller in his Celtic Dictionary has made a great Collection that I am persuaded there was one primitive Language from which all other Languages are descended; and that this Language was the Language of Egypt, the parent country in my opinion of all Arts and Sciences.

I present my best respects to Lady Jones, and ever am with great regard and esteem, obliged Sir,

Your most faithfull

J. BUR.

Original copy: National Library of Scotland, MS. Acc. 5738
Printed: Garland Cannon, 'The Correspondence between Lord Monboddo and Sir William Jones', *American Anthropologist*, 70 (1968), 560–1
Text: Original copy

Eliphalet Pearson (1752–1826)

Asiatick Researches reached Harvard College and stimulated the Hancock Professor of Hebrew and Oriental Languages to invite exchanges with his American society, which was Jones' general purpose. Though Jones was dead even before this searching query was composed, we can only speculate as to what might have happened had he lived to receive Pearson's innovative appeal for Oriental manuscripts to be housed 'in each quarter of the globe' and especially at Harvard, considering that only he and Chambers were seriously collecting manuscripts in India, that he sent most of his own collection to the Royal Society, and that Chambers' huge collection was ultimately scattered when sold at auction.

CAMBRIDGE, NEAR BOSTON,
2 FEBY. 1795

SIR,

I have it in charge from the American Academy of Arts & Sciences, to request the honor of your presenting its Memoirs, herewith transmitted, to the Asiatic Society. Tho' these infantile essays have no claim to merit; it is hoped they will be candidly accepted, as evidence of the respect, which a young & distant institution feels for a society, from whose situation, character, & learned President, the world has been justly led to indulge the highest expectations. That your laborious researches & learned diligence may be crowned with merited success, must be the united, fervent wish of the Literati in all parts of the globe. Be so good, sir, as to excuse the trouble of this address; which would have been avoided, had the Secretary's name been known to us. But, having thus intruded on your goodness, I frankly confess that, from the wellknown character of Sir William Jones, I feel myself irresistibly impelled to commit a still greater trespass. Pardon therefore, good sir, my embracing this oppty. of seeking to gratify, with the best prospect of success, a curiosity, which for some time past has possessed my mind.

Reflecting on the early transplantation of the ten tribes of Israel by the Assyrian monarch; the long captivity of the Jews at Babylon; the extent of the Persian empire subsequent upon it; the diffusion of the Jews thro' many parts of Asia in our Savior's time; & their universal dispersion thro' the world, upon the destruction of their city; it has appeared to me probable, in connexion with their extreme veneration for their sacred writings, that they carried with them copies of the same to every place, where they made considerable settlement; & that in every such place, copies of their sacred books must have been preserved in writing till the introduction of the art of printing; tho', since that period, they may have passed into general disuse. This idea has been strengthened by reading a dissertation [by] Dr Kennicott; who, among other places, speaks particularly of a Jewish settlement on the Malabar coast. Excuse my transcribing his quotation from Wolfius. Present *Moses Peneyra* se invenisse M.S.S. exemplaria (Heb. textus) Malabarica. Tradit Judæos, a Sito fuguntes, per Persiam se ad oran Malabaricas contulisse, ibique cum 80 animabus salvos advenisse. Also another quotation from Hamilton's account of the E. Indies. 'At *Cochin* (a little south of Cranganore) there are now about 4000 Jews, who have a synagogue; in which are carefully kept their records, engraven on copper plates; so that they can shew their history from Nebuchadnezzar to the present time.'

Some geographers also tell us that formerly there were 80,000 Jewish families at Cochin, tho' now exceedingly reduced; & that like discoveries of Jews & of their records have been made in China & other parts of Asia.

What credit, if any, ought to be given to such accounts, it is impossible at this distance to determine. Perhaps none. Still it would be a satisfaction to know this. – But if on the other hand, there be at Cochin & many other places in India & Asia considerable settlements of Jews; it seems highly probable that there may be still in existence some Heb. & perhaps other M.S. copies of the O. Test., which, whenever printing is adopted, may be of little use, & consequently of little real value to the present possessors, & therefore procurable on some terms or other.

Situated in the midst of the antient world & having been much engaged in exploring the religion, learning, language & antiquities of the Gentoos; it may possibly have fallen in your way, Sir, to ascertain the truth relative to the present subject of inquiry. Presuming this to be the case, may I be permitted to beg the honor of a line determining the point in question; acquainting me, if any there be, what & where such M.S.S. are, & in what way & upon what terms some of them may be procured. This request is made, not merely for my own gratification, but principally for ye. sake of the University in this place, with which I have the honor to be connected. I am sensible, that England has the first claim to discoveries of this kind. But, when it is considered, that she already possesses more M.S.S. than any other country in Europe; that the addition of more might be in some instances an addition of duplicates; that this large portion of the globe has not been blessed with a single ant. M.S. of this kind; & that, perhaps, it may ultimately bc most for the benefit of mankind, that these antient records of truth should be deposited in each quarter of the globe; your benevolence will doubtless pardon the wish, that our College library, which is at present 14,000 volumes, a good collection, may be enriched by the venerable addition of some ant. M.S.S. – I shall request Capn. Chapman, the bearer of this, to wait upon you, sir, to take your commands, previously to his return to America. Should a compliance with my request be attended with trouble, I beg it may be dismissed.

With all possible respect for your character, permit me the honor to subscribe myself, Sir,

Your most obed. & very humble servant,
ELIPHALET PEARSON
corres. Secy.

Original copy: Asiatic Society of Bengal (MS. Proceedings)
Pearson's rough draft: Yale University Library (Hist. MSS. Park)
Text: Original copy

Sir George Yonge, Baronet (1731–1821)

The European need for the Asiatic Society is further evinced by the astute Heads of Inquiry that the Secretary for War enclosed in his elegant letter. While he did not mention botany here, soon he was submitting detailed commissions to Jones for seeds and plants to be cultivated in the Botanic Garden on St Vincent for commercial and military-medicinal purposes, in which the king took a personal interest. Yonge later eulogized Jones' scholarship in a four-part review of *Asiatick Researches* I (Calcutta, 1788) in the *Monthly Review* (Appendix 1789, pp. 648–53; March, April, Appendix 1790, pp. 317–29, 431–45, 559–68, respectively).

OXFORD STREET—
DECR. 20TH 1784.—

SIR,

Though I have not the honour to be particularly known to you, yet I flatter myself, I need little apology in addressing myself to you, as a Lover of Science; on any points of Importance to Literature and to Mankind. I have therefore ventured, being desirous of obtaining Information on these points, to make my application to you, and trouble you with the enclosed Paper, containing Heads of Enquiry, which myself and Others in this part of the world, think of Importance to be made in India as well as in Europe, in order to obtain, and diffuse, if possible a more extensive knowledge of Antiquity the most remote, and thereby to reconcile the various opinions of Mankind, or at least to discover the truth – Reports in this part of the world say that a most useful Society is already established in India for this valuable purpose, of which Society it is also said you are a Member. If so, I find a propriety in addressing this to you – If not, I know not to whom I can with more propriety address it than to one so well qualified to gratify every wish on the subject. If therefore other most important avocations do not interfere to render this address impertinent, I flatter myself the Object of it is of a nature which will hold me excused in making it. I will only add, that if, exclusive of your pardon, you will favor me with your compliance with my wish to obtain satisfactory and authentick answers to the several heads of Inquiry here enclosed, I beg leave to assure you I shall not be the only one, who will think himself obliged by it—

I am, Sir,
GEO: YONGE.

Original copy: Asiatic Society of Bengal (MS. Proceedings)

Heads of Inquiry (abridged from the original copy)

1. Ancient religion, mythology, history, customs, traditions of original inhabitants of India
2. Changes in the people since then & the original inhabitants
3. Any inscriptions relative to the origin of man or the first principles of religion
4. Origin of worship of fire & water, including the Ganges
5. Ancient religion & foundation of mythology of Tibet
6. Worship of water related to the Flood, origin of man after the Flood, & identity of those who taught him agriculture
7. Origin of worship of fire of the Parsis
8. Buildings, temples, inscriptions; drawings, translations, etymologies
9. Emigrations & their descent
10. Original names of the most ancient cities, towns, promontories, rivers, etc.
11. Worship of a Sumatran god
12. Original languages of India – from an original one or a dialect or derivative of
13. Indian chronology, solar & lunar years
14. Ancient names of the most important 'Objects in Religion and Nature' – words such as *God*, *Time*, *Space*, *Heaven*, *Hell*, *Fire*, *Water*; pronouns such as *I*, *thou*, *he*; etc.

NOTES

1 I am grateful for permission to publish copies of letters by Whang Atong, Eliphalet Pearson, and Sir George Yonge, in the Asiatic Society, Calcutta; Jones' letter to the Starcks, and a copied extract from Jones' letter to Starck, in Blackwell's Rare Books, Oxford; copies of the Bengal Supreme Court's two letters to the Governor-General in Council, in the Department of Western Manuscripts, Bodleian Library, Oxford; Unpublished Crown Copyright material in the India Office Records reproduced in this article by permission of the Controller of Her Majesty's Stationery Office; and copies of James Burnett's two letters, by permission of the Trustees of the National Library of Scotland, Edinburgh.

2 Mir Muhammad Husain, who had been with Johnson at Lucknow and was now with him at Hyderabad, had composed an Arabic elegiac poem, which Johson printed and then gave the plates to the Society. Peter Speke eventually took a seat on the Supreme Council in 1789.

3 'When you sit with the beloved and you are drinking wine, keep in mind those companions who are travelling in the desert', from Ghazal 4 in Háfiz's *Díván* as edited by Mírzá Muhammad Qazvíní and Qásim Ghaní. Háfiz's last line is usually

something like 'keep in mind the true lovers, those loudmouthed vagabonds'. Jones' version fits his context, but does not quite fit Háfiz's metre. Mr. M. I. Waley, Assistant Keeper of the Department of Oriental Manuscripts and Printed Books of the British Library, kindly supplied this information.

4 Even during his near-fatal illness on his Ganges odyssey, Jones did not abandon his Indian studies. He had John Fleming, his surgeon and a good botanist, bring flowers to his bed for him to examine and describe or revise Linnaeus' description, a taxonomic experience that indirectly contributed to his famous linguistic formulation in 1786 and that started his botanical studies.

5 Colonel Thomas Deane Pearse, Commandant of the Artillery, thereupon attended almost every meeting of the Society and contributed two papers, besides keeping a comprehensive meteorological journal.

6 *Bráh Outar* and *Coorm Outár* are Hindi/Urdu versions of two of Vishnu's incarnations: '(2) The Tortoise (*Kurma*)...(3) The Boar (*Varaha*)' (A. L. Basham, *The Wonder That Was India* [New York, 1954], p. 302), where there is a *b/v* variation in *buraha* or *baraha*, and where the eighteenth-century *uvutar* or *uotar* varies from the Sanskrit *avatara* 'incarnation'. Just why Jones made such a strong reference to Halhed is unknown, but his term *genius* shows his estimation of his friend. Sir Robert Chambers' inactivity as the Acting Chief Justice of the Supreme Court was continuing to dampen the two men's long-standing friendship. He never composed a paper for the Society, but he attended about four meetings a year.

7 Reuben Burrow was a mathematician and charter member of the Society, contributing several short papers and astronomical lists.

8 Charles Croftes, Jones' financial agent in Calcutta and a member of the Society, was the Accountant-General. When Hastings left for his long impeachment trial, Shore accompanied him. David Anderson, a charter member of the Society, had had the chief responsibility for concluding the Treaty of Salbai with Mahadaji Sindhia. Characteristically, Jones had gravitated toward these very able members of Hastings' administration.

9 Jones had been so intrigued by the *Mānava-Dharmaśāstra*, which he had seen in Banaras in December, that he had decided to begin studying Sanskrit on his autumn vacation, in order to translate that celebrated law book.

PART II

Translations

‘Pentecost’ and other poems

ALESSANDRO MANZONI

TRANSLATED BY KENELM FOSTER

THE FIRST CHORUS FROM ‘ADELCHI’[1]

From the moss-grown courtyards and the ruined forums, from 1
the woods, from the din of the flaming smithies, from ploughlands wet with the sweat of slaves, a scattered people is suddenly awake, and raises the head and listens as strange sounds, growing ever louder, strike on the ear.

In their wondering looks and frightened faces, like a ray of 2
sunlight through thick clouds, glimmers the proud spirit of their fathers: in those eyes and faces mingle, in a confused, uncertain medley, humiliations endured and a hopeless pride in times gone by.

Eagerly they gather and then, in fear, disperse; with unsure 3
steps, by winding paths, half fearing, half desiring, they advance and then halt; and looking, they see and gaze at the scattered crowd of their pitiless masters, now a frightened rabble that flees unceasingly from the sword;

see them in breathless flight like terrified wild beasts, their tawny 4
manes abristle with fear, that seek the safety of hidden familiar dens; where the proud womenfolk of those lords, all their usual arrogance forgotten, stare, pale with anxiety, into the anxious faces of their children;

and then see, pressing on these fugitives with eager swords, 5
warriors in pursuit, running like hounds on the scent, unleashed, now here, now there. All this they see and, seized by a joy never

felt before and with rapid hope anticipating the event, they dream that now their harsh servitude is ending.

Listen! These strong men who now hold the field and cut off 6
your oppressors' retreat, they have come from afar, following rough ways; they've deferred the joys of feasting, risen in haste from soft couches at the sudden summons of the war-trumpet.

In their homes they've left their sad womenfolk turning to 7
repeat farewells with prayers and advice cut short by tears; they have burdened their brows with heavy helmets, saddled the dark horses, ridden out thundering over the drawbridge.

In squadrons they've passed from land to land, singing gay 8
warsongs, but in their hearts still thinking of the castles they love: along rocky valleys and precipitous mountain slopes they have kept armed watch through the freezing nights with their memories still on the heart to heart speech of love.

Obscure perils of irksome encampments, exhausting marches 9
along pathless hillsides, the stern commands, the hunger, all this they have endured; have seen lances pointed at their breasts, grazing their shields and helmets, have heard the whistle of arrows in flight.

And the reward hoped for and promised to such men, is it to 10
bring about, fools, a reversal of your fate, to end the sufferings of a foreign rabble? Get back to your grand ruins, to your arts of peace at the workshop fires, to the ploughlands wet with the sweat of slaves.

The victor joins hands with your vanquished enemy, the old lords 11
remain with the new, both nations tread you underfoot. They share out the slaves, they share the cattle, they settle down on the blood-stained lands of a people scattered and nameless.

IL CINQUE MAGGIO[2]

He is dead. As the corpse, after he had breathed his last, lay 1
still, all memory gone, void of so great a spirit, so the world stands
still in wonder, stunned by the news,

silently thinking of the last hours of the man of destiny; nor does 2
it know when a like print of mortal foot will come to tread earth's
bloodstained dust.

My genius saw him enthroned in glory and kept silent; when, 3
with rapid changes of fortune, he fell, rose again and fell finally,
it never joined its voice to the sound of a thousand others:

innocent of servile praise and of cowardly abuse, it rises now, 4
stirred by the sudden extinction of a light so dazzling, and sings
out to the funeral-urn a song which may perhaps live on.

From the Alps to the Pyramids, from the Manzanare to the Rhine,
the thunderbolts of that master of decision followed hard upon 5
the lightning; thundering from Scilla to the Don, from sea to
sea.

Was it true glory? The difficult judgement remains for posterity:
enough for us to bow before the Supreme Maker who chose 6
to impress on him so large a trace of the creative Mind.

The turbulent, eager joy of a great conception, the restless-
ness of a heart that unwillingly submits while it dreams of power; 7
and then grasps it and holds a prize it was madness to hope
for;

he knew it all – glory, the greater for following hard on peril; 8
flight and victory; kingly state and sad exile: twice in the dust,
twice raised to the altars.

He spoke his name: two centuries, each armed against the other, 9
turned in submission to him as if awaiting his verdict; he called
for silence and sat down as judge between them.

And then was lost to sight, and closed his days in idleness, shut 10
in such narrow bounds, object of immense envy and deep pity,
of relentless hatred and unconquerable love.

As over the head of one shipwrecked, when a wave has arched 11
up and hung – the wave across which, a moment before, the poor
wretch, lifted up by the swell and gazing ahead, had just
discerned, in vain, a far-off shore –

so did the weight of memories pour down upon that soul! O how 12
often he began to tell his story for posterity, and the tired hand
fell on the eternal pages!

O how often, at the silent end of a dull day, as he stood with 13
flashing eyes lowered and folded arms, the remembrance of days
past took him by storm!

And he thought again of the tents always in movement, and lines 14
of defence under attack, and the flash of the moving squadrons,
and the waves of cavalry, and the eager words of command and
the prompt obedience.

Ah, in such torment perhaps the spirit, gasping, broke down and 15
despaired; but a strong hand came from heaven and bore him
mercifully into more breathable air;

and turned his steps along the flowery paths of hope, to fields 16
eternal, to the prize that exceeds desires, where the glory that
has passed away is silence and darkness.

Lovely Immortal! Faith abounding in gifts, faith so accustomed 17
to triumphs, record this one too and rejoice; for no prouder
greatness has ever bowed to the ignominy of Golgotha.

Drive away from those tired ashes every evil word: the God who 18
humbles and lifts up, who afflicts and consoles, came to that
deserted bed and sat down by him.

PENTECOST[3]

Mother of the Saints; image of the heavenly city; perpetual guardian of the ever-living Blood; you that for so many centuries have suffered, fought and prayed; that set up your tents from sea to sea;

realm of those who hope; Church of the living God; where were 2
you? what dark corner received you at your birth, when your King, drawn by villains up the hill to die, encrimsoned the clods of his sublime altar?

And then, the sacred body now issued from the dark, when he 3
breathed in the power of the new life; and when, the price of our pardon in his hands, he rose from this dust to the Father's throne;

you, who suffering had watched him suffer, aware of the 4
mysteries of his being, you, deathless daughter of his victory, where were you? Awake to nothing but your fears, safe alone in being forgotten, you stayed in seclusion and secrecy until that sacred day,[4]

when upon you the renewing Spirit descended, and kindled in 5
your right hand the ever-burning torch; when as a beacon for the nations he placed you on the mountain,[5] and on your lips set flowing the fountain of speech.

As swift light pours down from one thing to another, bringing 6
out diverse colours wherever it rests, such was the multiple echo of the Spirit's voice: Arabians, Parthians, Syrians heard it, each in his own tongue.

O worshippers of idols, scattered on every shore, turn your eyes 7
to Jerusalem, hear that holy cry: weary of its vile abasement, let the earth return to HIM: and you who are starting the course of happier times,

wives whom the sudden throb of a hidden burden rouses; you 8
now nearing the release from childbirth's pains; to the lying

goddess of maternity[6] raise no song: sacred to the Holy One is that which grows within you.

Why does the slave still sigh as she kisses her little ones? and look with envy at the breast that suckles the free-born? Does she not know that to his kingdom the Lord raises the wretched whose lot he shared? that in his agony he had all Eve's children in mind? 9

A new freedom the heavens announce, and new peoples; new conquests and a glory won through nobler trials; a new peace, firm against terrors, firm against sly flattery; a peace the world scoffs at, but cannot take away. 10

O Spirit! We – whether suppliants at your high altars, or lonely travellers through wild forests, or roaming the open seas; from the freezing Andes to Lebanon, from Ireland to rocky Haiti, scattered on every shore, in heart at one in You – 11

we implore You! Come down again, gentle Spirit; gracious to your worshippers, gracious to him who knows you not; come down and remake us; revive the hearts grown faint with doubt; and may the victor be a divine recompense to the vanquished. 12

Come down, Love; calm in our souls all anger born of pride; inspire thoughts which the hour of our death will leave unchanged, when the past comes back in memory; and may your gifts be nourished by your kindly strength; as the sun draws out from the torpid seed the flower, 13

that will droop and die on the common grass, nor rise with the coloured splendour of its unfolded petals, unless, poured down through the air, that soft light return to it, giver of life, untiring nourisher. 14

We implore You! Into the weary thoughts of the unhappy come down as a breath of joy, as a soft consoling breeze; come down as a whirlwind on the tumid thoughts of the violent; inspire them with a fear that may teach them pity. 15

Through You may the poor man lift his gaze to the heaven that is his, turning lament into songs of joy as he thinks of the Man he resembles; and let him to whom much has been given give in his turn, with that friendly glance and shy reserve which commends the gift to You. 16

Breathe through the marvellous smiles of our children; shed on the cheeks of girls the crimson of modesty; to the cloistered virgins send your pure, secret joys; consecrate the chaste love of wives. 17

Discipline the eager intelligence of ardent youth; guide unfaltering to a sure end the aim of men in their prime; shed on the aged the beauty of happy, holy desires; shine in the wandering gaze of him who dies hopeful. 18

NOTES

1 Written in 1822. Manzoni intended the chorus in his verse-dramas to be the comments of the poet himself, or of the 'ideal spectator', on the action of the play. He got the idea from A. W. Schlegel; see the Preface to *Il Conte di Carmagnola* (1819). His second tragedy, *Adelchi* (1822), has two choruses; the one given here coming immediately after the turning point of the action, at the end of Act III. The play depicts the moral effects on the principal protagonists of the victory of Charlemagne (Carlo) in 773–4 over the Lombards under their king Desiderio and his heroic son Adelchi. The Lombards themselves, two centuries before, had conquered and enslaved the people of Northern Italy (the 'latini'). The chorus represents and confutes the illusory hopes of these 'latini' when, seeing their oppressors routed, they dream that their own liberation is at hand. Indirectly it also expresses the poet's reflections on the history of Italy in his own time – a prey to successive foreign overlords (the Austrians, then Napoleon, then the Austrians again).

2 'The fifth of May', written 1821, on the death of Napoleon.

3 Written 1817–22.

4 Acts 2:1–4.

5 Matthew 5:14; Isaiah 2:1–3.

6 Juno Lucina, patroness of childbirth; cf. Virgil, *Aeneid* IV, 166.

Manzoni's poetry and the witnessing of events

MICHAEL CAESAR

In *I promessi sposi*, the historical novel with which Manzoni's name is most closely associated,[1] the perspectives of narrator (speaker), characters, and reader are made mobile and their roles confused in a way which would be inconceivable in Manzoni's earlier work. Such 'confusion' is of course entirely appropriate in a form (the novel) which is denounced by its detractors as 'formless', a monstrous hybrid of the genres, and which is elaborated by Manzoni precisely as the vehicle of a middle style which allows the combination of the socially elevated and the humble, the tragic and the comic, 'history' and 'invention'. It also allows him for the first time to exploit the possibilities of a protagonist (Renzo) who, in a morally distorted and misleading world, gathers experience, learns from his mistakes, sees himself as others see him, and changes; 'Renzo' in the novel means simultaneously experience, judgement on that experience, action on that judgement; he is a moral agent. At the same time, the reader is not limited to the role of moral judge: rather, it is in the space between the judgements to which he is assisted by the author and the imaginative complicity which he must bring to his understanding of the plot, the characters, and so on, that the possibilities of irony lie. In both these respects, in the characterization of both protagonist and reader, the novel offers an alternative, though one that Manzoni will himself reject as unsatisfactory,[2] to a tendency that is apparent in his earlier work and which the present essay attempts to make explicit: the tendency towards a rigid division of labour between protagonist and reader, precisely as witnesses of the events represented.

Each of the poems translated here[3] proceeds as if it were telling a story, that is, from an opening that is confused, oblique or incomplete, it advances through the accumulation of detail to that point, a reversal or a resolution, at which the thread is unravelled and leads directly to a conclusion. This is true even of *Pentecost*, where the resolution comes very early in the poem, with the words 'quel sacro dì' (that sacred day) in the fourth stanza. Confusion, or more precisely fear and self-effacement, dominate the experience of the Church as described in the four stanzas leading up to that line, and we shall see that in the other two poems as well, the narrative starts from the registering of psychological dislocation or disturbance. But an effect of confusion is created also in the mind of the reader simply by the fact that a Church which enters militant and triumphant upon the stage of the poem is unexpectedly transformed into a question and an absence: 'Dov'eri mai? (where were you?; second stanza). Nor is it easy for the reader to grasp in the opening stanzas precisely what time-scale the poem is operating on. What begins as a long retrospective from the writer's present – 'da tanti secoli' (for so many centuries; first stanza) – gives way to an accelerating future in the past, where the successive moments of the Church's 'oblivion' (crucifixion, resurrection, ascension) are matched by an augmentation of its spiritual attributes, attributes that precisely stress its timelessness: 'nascente', 'seconda vita', 'immortal' (at your birth; new life; deathless; second, third and fourth stanzas respectively). All of this is resolved by the 'sacred day', the Pentecost, the renewal of the Spirit. The identity of the Church is established, and the tense of the poem settles, through the almost imperceptible transition from the earliest to modern unbelievers (stanzas six and seven), into an eternal present, what might best be described as an 'after Pentecost', spiritual as well as chronological, a condition enabling prayer.

This 'settling' in no way corresponds to a state of spiritual or moral inertia; it is the fixing of a firm object of prayer and hope for the Christian community, for the 'wandering gaze' of the dying at the end of *Pentecost* as for the restless spirit of the exiled Napoleon at the end of *Il cinque maggio*. In both these poems, divine love is shown as the only source of assurance, the only way forward from the perplexity that otherwise governs the world and man's perception of his place in it. In the first chorus of *Adelchi*, a rather different kind of authority, but one performing an analogous function, is entrusted to the retrospective voice of the poet, that which utters the imperative 'Udite!' (Listen!) in the sixth stanza, and corrects the misapprehensions and delusions of the subject race. We are, in fact, at a stage in Manzoni's writing at which the actors themselves in the human drama are not vouchsafed insight into their own condition, only acute moral anxiety and spiritual unhappiness arising from it. While

Manzoni's novel will be structured in such a way as to allow, and to expect, the hero to learn from his experience, the protagonists of the plays, but also of a poem such as *Il cinque maggio*, are understood as fulfilling a destiny whose meaning is as obscure to themselves as to their contemporaries, and will be clarified only outside the limits of their mortal perception – at the moment of death, or in the eyes of God, or history, or the reader. They embody that aspect of man that Manzoni calls his 'weakness'[4], and indeed fear, anxiety, uncertainty, spiritual exhaustion, melancholy are the elements in which these figures move till lifted by the salving hand of providence. Whether brutish (the 'latini' or Latins of the chorus) or exalted (Napoleon, Adelchi), their lack of insight is the intended object of our moral consideration.

It is the confusion, however, not of the protagonist but of the world at large, the public, that is Manzoni's starting-point in *Il cinque maggio*. The death of the hero, the 'man of destiny' ('l'uom fatale'; second stanza), raises for his contemporaries the question of the 'meaning' of his life, and it is the bewilderment of the world when faced with this question that Manzoni stresses in the opening stanzas of the poem. There are obvious and conventional reasons for which the meaning of Napoleon cannot be vouchsafed to his contemporaries: primarily, the lack of temporal perspective (sixth stanza), and the distortion of public events by private and political interest: the 'servo encomio' and 'codardo oltraggio', servile praise and cowardly abuse, of the fourth stanza. The poet's claim to freedom from the latter disability in the third and fourth stanzas, while it allows the initial amazement of the reader to be resolved into insight (the bald 'He' of the opening line becoming in due course the hero's soul), does not substantially alter the relationship between the hero and the world within the poem. The hero appears to the world as an event ('Ei fu', He is dead, but also, literally, He was), and the world's perception is limited to and by the event. That is why the poem begins not merely with the news of a death, but with the corpselike stillness with which the world greets that news, one unconsciousness assimilated to the other.

This interdependence between the event and its perception is, however, the necessary condition of the world's view of Napoleon in life and the source of the perplexity with which Manzoni shows his figure to be surrounded. Napoleon indeed is portrayed as so dominant and omnipresent a figure as to escape all definition, largely because, as 'l'uom fatale', he both realizes his own time to the fullest and is filled by it; he is at once the figure of constant attention and always protean, out of reach, undefined. He experienced everything (seventh and eighth stanzas), which is to say that everything was experienced in him and through him as the 'orma' (trace; sixth stanza) of the creative Mind: filled with life for himself, he was the sign of life for others. In defeat and exile, Napoleon will be the 'segno' (object; tenth stanza) of the most divergent and contradictory emotions, and he will reach that state having been 'lost to sight' at the very moment when he most fully occupied the attention of his contemporaries, exalted as the central figure straddling two centuries (ninth and beginning of tenth stanzas). The man of destiny is the most ambiguous of historical figures: in his very representativeness he is exceptional; by giving his name, he becomes anonymous; the moment of judgement, of discrimination, signals his disappearance from our view.

The first chorus of *Adelchi* provides the author with the opportunity to comment on the political and military events of his tragedy by means of a device – the 'eye-witness' description of a battle in progress – to which Manzoni has recourse on two other occasions at this period[5]. Here, as in *Il cinque maggio*, the observer is depicted as subordinate to the event, and the same verb, 'percuotere', to strike, is used to describe the effect of its announcement on the receiver of the news in the opening stanza of both pieces. But what in the ode might be explained in purely psychological terms is given here in the chorus sharp political point by the fact that the blindness and ignorance of the 'volgo disperso' (scattered people; and again in the last stanza) is not only a quality of their being contemporary to the events being described, but also of their being a subject and oppressed nation. And indeed, the first and principal intention of this chorus must be to bring out that fact: Manzoni himself described the chorus as 'indispensable pour porter l'attention sur ce qu'il y a de plus sérieux et de plus poétique dans le sujet que j'ai maltraité: ce qui ne pouvait se développer dans l'action, ni par les discours des personnages' (indispensable in order to focus attention on what is most serious and poetic in the subject I have treated so badly: and which could not be developed in the action or through the speeches of the characters).[6] The chorus does indeed bring to the fore the plight of the Latin (or Italian) people, reduced to serfdom, and upon whose lands the Lombards and Franks conduct their domestic and dynastic battles. The Latins have not been entirely absent from the play up to this point: they have been alluded to in passing by the Pope's messenger Martino,[7] and they have begun to occupy the thoughts of Adelchi (Act III, scene I, lines 66ff): their plight is a part, the most substantial part, of the injustice for which he feels helplessly responsible as the king's son and co-ruler. At the same time, as Manzoni indicates in the letter to Fauriel quoted above, there is no way in which they can take the central place in a historical tragedy, centred as it necessarily is on the single hero. The Latins are thus seen in two perspectives. Morally, they might be considered as central, inasmuch as their fate constitutes the fundamental issue of justice and injustice on this earth, from the point of view of Manzoni, and, to some extent, of his hero. But at the same time, they are marginal: they take no part in the events of history, they have no independent voice, they are merely passive onlookers, bystanders, degenerate and capable of only the most confused perceptions. They are utterly subordinate, dependent on what others do.

Yet, while the Latins suffer this particular political subjection, an enslavement of the mind as much as of the body if it generates delusions only, none of the actors in this chorus sees very much more clearly than they. All three peoples have a limited and particular perspective on events. The Lombards, for example, are momentarily, in the initial confusion, identified with the Latins whom they oppress – while the latter are described as 'confuso ed incerto' (confused, uncertain; second stanza), the former are 'scorata e confusa' (frightened rabble; third stanza); and the 'turba diffusa' of the Longobards (scattered crowd; third stanza) echoes the 'volgo disperso' of the Latins (a scattered people; first stanza). The Franks are certainly more knowledgeable politically than either of the other two groups – or, to put it more accurately, if they win, their expectations will be realized, while the hopes of the Latins at least have no possibility of realization, and the fears of the Lombards are perhaps exaggerated if they can look forward to some kind of accommodation with the victors. But, though the Franks may be greedy, their actual grasp of events does not extend beyond the comfortable memory of what they have just left behind them and the immediate and fragmentary contact with present reality which is emphasized by the synecdochic technique of stanzas 6–9. All three groups in the chorus then, the mass of humanity for once seen without its leaders speaking for it, are in their different ways dominated by their immediate, particular interests, and in their own ways deluded. The political delusion of the Latins is exposed by Manzoni in the chorus itself; that of the Franks will be given voice at the very end of the play when Adelchi in his dying speech will remind his captive father that Charlemagne, the symbol of Frankish power, is 'un uom che morrà' (a man who will die; Act V, scene 8, line 364). Thus, in the chorus, it is not that the Franks 'see' more into the reality of their time, simply that they are more powerful (and the theme of the blind arrogance of power is one that will develop from its initial treatment in the figure of Charlemagne in this play to fuller treatment in the 'villains' of *The Betrothed*).

The confusion or perplexity which surrounds events in the minds of those who witness them or may indeed be part of them is prolonged in the subjectivity of the protagonists. This at least would seem to be the lesson of Napoleon in *Il cinque maggio*, to whose 'inner self' we are allowed apparently privileged access (enabled by the 'innocence' of the poet established in stanzas 3–4) only to discover that in one crucial area at least its mechanisms are defective: the memory, though infested with recollections of command and control, cannot itself impose order – Napoleon tries in vain to 'narrar se stesso' (tell his story; twelfth stanza). If the meaning of his life cannot be fixed with certainty as it is being lived, neither can it be given shape by memory. But it is important to notice the reasons that Manzoni gives for this, which are not primarily psychological (to do with the defectiveness and distortions of memory), but moral. Manzoni will not allow his man of destiny the *comfort* of memory which might consist in the possibility of integrating his experience and personality in time – integration can only occur in an eternal future and another life. For this reason, memory is a 'torment', as it is also to Adelchi's sister Ermengarda whose death is a final release from the memory of happier times, after months of prayer in vain for 'oblio', forgetfulness.[8]

Two conditions, finally, characterize the fate of Manzoni's two tragic heroes, Adelchi and the Count of Carmagnola: their anachronism, and the fact that they are preoccupied with thoughts of treachery, either other people's betrayal of them, or other people's suspicion of their loyalty. By anachronism, I mean the gap between the hero and his times, which Manzoni consciously exploits and opens up into a central concern, particularly in the first play, *Il conte di Carmagnola*. Here the gap is both explicitly formulated by Manzoni – 'Un uomo di animo forte ed elevato e desideroso di grandi imprese, che si dibatte colla debolezza e colla perfidia de' suoi tempi', a 'dissonanza' which he specifies as 'quella che io ho voluto rappresentare' (it was this dissonance that I wished to represent)[9] – and is at the same time given precise historical contours in the theme of the 'code of honour' to which Manzoni had devoted some considerable thought outside the confines of the play itself.[10] In *Adelchi*, the gap is less explicable in strictly historical or cultural terms, and Manzoni himself felt doubts, almost despair, about the historicity of his principal character.[11] But it is strongly felt in psychological and moral terms, and it is this gap, the distance between the hero and his times, which in both plays leads into our second condition, the ubiquity of treachery. It is the possibility and reality of treachery which makes the world in which the heroes move an uncertain and dangerous place: it is, more precisely, the name by which the uncertainty of the world is known, and the struggle of the hero, especially Adelchi, to achieve integrity takes the form precisely of the struggle to overcome his divided loyalties, to suppress his doubts, and to demonstrate his unswerving loyalty (in this case, to his father), even at the cost of committing an impiety, and beset though he may be by mental reservations.

Perceptual confusion and moral uncertainty are the point of departure for Manzoni's protagonists, who are caught up in the midst of events for which they either have no responsibility, or (perhaps this is the case of Adelchi) the responsibility which they do bear is assumed unwillingly and without real control over the consequences. The meaning, of both events and their doers, is concealed and unclear to actors and audience alike. This uncertainty is the fundamental attribute of the moral suffering ('patimento') whose depiction, in a page of the 'Materiali estetici' that was to remain unpublished during Manzoni's lifetime, he regarded as far more suitable to tragic poetry than that of desire (love, ambition, etc.) with its more definite and particular reference:

> Il desiderio eccita minor simpatia, perchè per desiderare bisogna trovarsi nelle circostanze particolari, e per esser commosso e atterrito basta esser uomo. La rappresentazione dei dolori profondi e dei terrori indeterminati è sostanzialmente morale, perchè lascia impressioni che ci avvicinano alla virtù. Quando l'uomo esce coll'immaginazione dal campo battuto delle cose note e degli accidenti coi quali è avvezzo a combattere e si trova alla regione infinita dei possibili mali, egli sente la sua debolezza, le idee ilari di vigore e di difesa lo abbandonano, e pensa che in quello stato, la sola virtù e la retta coscienza, e l'aiuto di Dio, ponno dar qualche soccorso alla mente.

> [The reader or spectator] is less sympathetic to desire, because in order to desire one has to be in that particular situation, while to be moved and terrified it is enough to be a man. The representation of deep sorrow and indeterminate fears is essentially moral, leaving as it does impressions that direct our steps to virtue. But when in his imagination a man departs the beaten track of familiar things and the problems he is accustomed to dealing with and comes upon the boundless territory of possible evils, then he feels his weakness, cheerful thoughts of his own strength and power to resist abandon him, and he thinks that in such a state only virtue and a clear conscience, and the help of God, can give some succour to the mind.[12]

In the same spirit of abandonment and acceptance, the unhappy minds of Napoleon and Adelchi will at the end of their respective stories find succour and consolation from the only source capable of providing them: 'Il Dio.../Che affanna e che consola' (the God... who afflicts and consoles; *Il cinque maggio*, last stanza); 'Il Dio/ Che di tutto consola' (the God who consoles for all things; *Adelchi*, Act v, scene 8, lines 365–6).

At the same time that in the plays, first and foremost, and then also in the poems written in 1821 and 1822 Manzoni was elaborating the world of moral indeterminacy and resolution described above, he was laying emphasis in his theoretical writings on the rationality, perceptiveness and critical judgement of the reader. The reader, in fact, at this period of Manzoni's work, is the counterpart to the fictional protagonist in so far as he embodies virtues which the latter cannot 'realistically' have: clarity (in that events present themselves to the reader in a certain shape), analytical curiosity, distance. The reader is the 'knowledge' to the protagonists' 'action'; he represents, in abstract, the possibility in all men of attaining a point from which to survey and judge experience, a point deemed superior to the experience itself. What is striking is the way in which these two dimensions, experience and reflection on experience, are kept rigorously apart at this stage in Manzoni's work, with the protagonist rendered unhappy or ill-at-ease with the indeterminacy or inappropriateness of his experience, and the role of ordering consciousness delegated to the reader.

The reader, in the first place, is presented with an action, a cluster of events, which is, as Manzoni puts it, 'detached' from the chain of history, and which can be apprehended as having internal unity and coherence:

> Que fait donc le poëte? Il choisit, dans l'histoire, des événemens intéressans et dramatiques, qui soient liés si fortement l'un à l'autre, et si faiblement avec ce qui les a précédés et suivis, que l'esprit, vivement frappé du rapport qu'ils ont entre eux, se complaise à s'en former un spectacle unique, et s'applique avidement à saisir toute l'étendue, toute la profondeur de ce rapport qui les unit, à démêler aussi nettement que possible ces lois de cause et d'effet qui les gouvernent.

> What then does the poet do? He selects interesting and dramatic events in history which are so strongly linked with each other and so weakly with what happened before and after that the mind, being forcibly struck by the relationship between them, is happy to consider them as one spectacle, and eagerly sets about grasping the whole breadth and depth of this relationship by which they are united, and to unravelling as clearly as possible the laws of cause and effect by which they are governed.[13]

The eagerness of the mind to see clearly into the tangle of events is the second distinguishing feature of the reader (as against the protagonist) which is emphasized by the letter to Chauvet and elsewhere in Manzoni's theoretical writings. This keenness to know is taken by Manzoni to be the very basis of the 'intellectual attraction' of tragedy (as it also underlies, he maintains, the child's insistence on knowing whether a story is 'true'):

car quel est l'attrait intellectuel pour cette sorte de composition? Celui que l'on trouve à connaître l'homme, à découvrir ce qu'il y a dans sa nature de réel et d'intime, à voir l'effet des phénomènes extérieurs sur son âme, le fond des pensées par lesquelles il se détermine à agir; à voir, dans un autre homme, des sentimens qui puissent exciter en nous une véritable sympathie.

for what is the intellectual attraction for this sort of composition [tragedy]? It is what helps one to know man, to discover the real and inmost side of his nature, to see how external phenomena affect his soul, and the grounds on which he decides the action he will take; and to see feelings in another man which can arouse true sympathy in us.[14]

Thus, not only is the reader, or Manzoni's ideal reader, presented with a coherent body of events to scrutinize, but he is motivated by a prior desire to *know*, to know man and human nature, and to know them as accurately and fully as possible. It is of course in view of such a reader, and only such a reader, that Manzoni will argue the superiority of the Romantic drama in general (against the distorting, anti-realistic, effect of the unities), and the historical drama in particular. History, in Manzoni's account of things, provides the guarantee of the authenticity of the events depicted – not only their practical, but their moral, authenticity: for this reason, poets should not invent facts even when the real facts are not widely known.[15] But history is also incomplete, and it is the job of the poet specifically to 'fill in' those parts of history that are 'missing' (on the basis of, and not in contradiction with, the known facts) in order to satisfy more completely the reader's thirst for knowledge than a mere chronicle could ever do. Thus, history acts as the warranty of the truth and as that which has to be interpreted if the full truth (of a given, recorded, human experience) is to be arrived at:

Car enfin que nous donne l'histoire? des événemens qui ne sont, pour ainsi dire, connus que par leur dehors; ce que les hommes ont exécuté: mais ce qu'ils ont pensé, les sentimens qui ont accompagné leurs délibérations et leurs projets, leurs succès et leurs infortunes; les discours par lesquels ils ont fait ou essayé de faire prévaloir leurs passions et leurs volontés sur d'autres passions et d'autres volontés, par lesquels ils ont exprimé leur colère, épanché leur tristesse, par lesquels, en un mot, ils ont révélé leur individualité: tout cela, à peu de chose près, est passé sous silence par l'histoire; et tout cela est le domaine de la poésie.

For in the end what does history give us? A certain number of events which are known only, so to speak, from the outside; what men did: but what they thought, the feelings that accompanied their plans and deliberations, their successes and their failures; what they said in order to make, or try to make, their wills and passions prevail over the wills and passions of others, or the words with which they expressed their anger, or gave vent to their sorrow, with which, in short, they revealed their individuality: all of this, practically speaking, is ignored by history, and all of it is the domain of poetry.[16]

Yet, if there is any suggestion here that history is merely a pretext for poetry, Manzoni is at pains to correct it, insisting as he does on the 'positive' force of history as a record of what actually happened (and indicating therefore the *necessity* of that particular combination of events,[17] and 'son caractère le plus grave et le plus poétique, l'impartialité' (its gravest and most poetic feature, its impartiality).[18]

The historical drama, then, is presented as a way of knowing ourselves as fully as possible. This is a kind of 'interest' that is sharply differentiated from other kinds of interest that may engage, or historically have engaged audiences in the theatre: the 'admirative interest', for example, which audiences feel for the perfect hero,[19] or the kind of identification with the vicissitudes and passions of the characters on-stage which Manzoni dismisses in the succinct formula 'la platea non entra nel dramma' (the auditorium is not part of the play).[20] The latter sort of interest, identification with the characters, is close to what Manzoni calls more generally the 'romanesque', a term denoting the fact that the 'roman' generally speaking is built round an invented plot and is always liable to slip into 'falsehood'. This danger is increased the more the poet wanders from whatever 'real' information he has available into the realms of the invented or the purely fantastic. There, he is likely to have recourse to unlikely coincidences or sudden changes of fortune to make his story work out, conventional solutions that his audience can accept without thinking. And it is this danger that Manzoni is most alert to. His attack on the 'romanesque', like his attack on the unities with which it is closely associated, is focused on its (and their) tendency to create a false sensibility that it is all too easy for the public to accept. Two demands dominate his argument in favour of the historical drama: firstly, that the events depicted should be 'real' or 'verisimilar', historical or based on and compatible with known history; and secondly, that the audience should be detached from the events depicted, not 'swept along' by them.

The latter point brings us to the firm moral conviction underlying Manzoni's theory of the drama, and of literature in general. In some notes on the question precisely of the morality of tragedy, he reaches the heart of the problem of the audience:

> Le obbjezioni contro il dramma si risolvono in questa:
> Che si eccitano le passioni – e che non si può esser poeta drammatico altrimenti.
> Questo giudizio è nato dal non esaminare che drammatici francesi.
> Essi sono tali, ma si può e si deve interessare altrimenti.
> Essi fanno simpatizzare il lettore colle passioni dei personaggi, e lo fanno complice.
> Si può farlo sentire separatamente dai personaggi e dei personaggi, e farlo giudice.
> Esempio insigne Shakespeare.

The objections to the theatre come down to this: that the passions are aroused – and there is no other way of being a dramatic poet. The origin of this judgement lies in considering only French dramatists. They are like that, but one can and should interest in other ways. They make the reader sympathize with the passions of the characters, and turn him into an accomplice. One can make him feel separately from the characters, and turn him into a judge. Supreme example Shakespeare).[21]

What is demanded of the reader or spectator is a degree of moral alertness which cannot be expected of him if the playwright himself encourages that kind of complicity or 'sympathy' with the characters on-stage which we are all too ready to afford, almost, Manzoni seems to argue, as a compensation for our experience in real life of the illusoriness and unreliability of promised goods. The danger of art is that it will make us believe in the possibility of complete satisfaction on this earth even though our experience constantly reminds us that such hopes are illusory (it always has to remind us, since we are always inclined to imagine otherwise). Manzoni concludes his notes on the topic:

Opinione ricantata e falsa: che il poeta per interessare deve movere le passioni. Se fosse così sarebbe da proscriversi la poesia. – Ma non è così. La rappresentazione delle passioni che non eccitano simpatia, ma *riflessione sentita*, è più poetica d'ogni altra.

A false and oft-repeated opinion: that in order to interest, the poet must move the passions. If that were so, poetry would have to be forbidden. But it is not so. The representation of passions which arouse not sympathy, but *felt reflection*, is more poetic than any other.[22]

The reader emerges from Manzoni's theoretical writings as one who surveys and judges human actions and passions on the evidence of what men have actually done or are likely to have done in the circumstances. He assumes an attitude of 'contemplation désintéressée' (disinterested contemplation), as Manzoni puts it at the conclusion of the letter to M. Chauvet, above the 'souffrances inutiles' and 'vaines jouissances' (the useless sufferings and vain enjoyments) of men.[23] He is, in short, a man of experience, or who gains experience, concerned with the truth-content of his experience, who stands at some distance from the 'suffering' hero (individual or collective) of the poems and plays. The hero is pathetic, the reader reflective. Their fates are separate and distinct, and it is only through the form of the novel[24] and the development of a hero (Renzo and, to a lesser degree, Lucia) who grows, matures and learns from his experiences within the bounds of the fiction – in short, the emergence of a hero who is also a reader of his own experiences – that the sharp separation between the two is to any extent attenuated.

NOTES

1 Translated into English as *The Betrothed*, the novel was published first in 1827, and in its definitive version in 1840–2. Alessandro Manzoni was born in 1785 and spent almost all his long life in or near his native Milan, where he died in May 1873. By the time he came to write the novel, he was already an established poet (particularly as the author of a series of 'sacred hymns', of which four were published in 1815, the fifth being *La pentecoste*) and playwright (his first historical tragedy, *Il conte di Carmagnola*, written between 1816 and 1819, was published in 1820), and the most respected member of those intellectual circles in Milan arguing in favour of a modern, historically conscious and tendentially Christian literature which since 1816 had gone under the general heading of 'Romanticism'.

2 In his essay on the historical novel (*Del romanzo storico*) written around 1830, after the publication of *I promessi sposi*, Manzoni argues that it is impossible for the reader of a 'mixed genre' such as this one to combine both a 'poetic' and a 'historical' assent to the events represented.

3 The three texts were written within fifteen months of each other, at one of the most productive moments of Manzoni's literary career. *Il cinque maggio* was begun almost as soon as news of Napoleon's death reached the Manzonis' villa at Brusuglio on 16 or 17 July 1821, and was completed between the 20th and 26th of the same month. The first chorus of *Adelchi* was written 15–19 January 1822 (the second chorus had been drafted during the preceding four weeks, and the tragedy itself had been completed towards the end of September 1821). Manzoni had made previous attempts at a poem on the theme of *La pentecoste* in June 1817 and again in April–June 1819, but this final version was written between 26 September and 2 October 1822.

The year 1821 had also seen the drafting of the first two chapters and the introduction of the first version, entitled *Fermo e Lucia*, of the novel that was later to become *I promessi sposi*, and of all or part of the political ode *Marzo 1821*. The creative period of 1821–2 was bracketed chronologically by no less intensive moments of theoretical reflection, represented by the *Lettre à M. Chauvet* on the unities of time and place in tragedy (first half of 1820, published 1823), and the so-called *Lettera sul romanticismo* of September 1823.

4 The expression is taken from Manzoni's unpublished notes of the late 1810s known by the title of 'Materiali estetici'. See Alessandro Manzoni, *Tutte le opere*, edited under the direction of Bruno Cagli (Rome, 1965), p. 1168. This edition will be referred to henceforth as Cagli.

5 The description of the battle of Maclodio which is the subject of the one chorus in

the earlier tragedy *Il conte di Carmagnola*, at the end of the second act; the crossing of the Ticino in *Marzo 1821*.

6 Letter to Claude Fauriel of 6 March 1822, no. 158 in Alessandro Manzoni, *Tutte le opere*, edited by Alberto Chiari and Fausto Ghisalberti (Milan, 1957–), vol VII, part 1, pp. 258–9. This edition will be referred to henceforth as Chiari–Ghisalberti.

7 Act II, scene 3, lines 136–43. It was part of the political intention of the play to revise the common opinion of eighteenth-century historians that the actions of the Papacy in opposing the Lombards had been motivated by material and territorial considerations; it is in this connection that the Popes are exalted as the only defenders of the hapless Latins in the historical reflections that Manzoni wrote to illustrate his tragedy. See his 'Discorso sur alcuni punti della storia longobardica in Italia', in Chiari–Ghisalberti, vol. IV, pp. 236–9, 244–6.

8 See the second chorus of *Adelchi*, in Act IV. It is precisely the consoling and integrating potential of memory that Leopardi is beginning to explore at about this time.

9 'A man of forceful and elevated spirit, desirous of great enterprises, who does battle against the weakness and perfidy of his times': letter to Gaetano Giudici of 7 February 1820, no. 128 in Chiari–Ghisalberti, vol. VII, part 1, p. 193. See also the detailed account given of this 'dissonance' in the letter to M. Chauvet: 'Lettre à M. C*** sur l'unité de temps et de lieu dans la tragédie', in Cagli, p. 1102.

10 In particular, to its role in encouraging the desire for vengeance, and the conflict between this and Catholic morality; cf. the second part of Manzoni's *Osservazioni sulla morale cattolica* (1819–20), in Cagli, pp. 885–6.

11 Cf. letter to Fauriel of 3 November 1821, in Chiari–Ghisalberti, vol. VII, part 1, pp. 247–8.

12 'Materiali estertici', in Cagli, p. 1168.

13 Letter to Chauvet, in Cagli, p. 1065.

14 Letter to Chauvet, in Cagli, p. 1099.

15 Letter to Chauvet, in Cagli, p. 1100.

16 Letter to Chauvet, in Cagli, pp. 1097–8.

17 'Nous découvrons, dans une série donnée de faits, une partie de notre nature et de notre destinée; nous finissons par dire en nous-mêmes: Dans de telles circonstances, à l'aide de tels moyens, avec de tels hommes, les choses devaient arriver ainsi' (In a given series of facts we discover a part of our nature and our destiny; and we conclude by saying to ourselves: in such circumstances, given those means and those men, that is the way things had to turn out). Letter to Chauvet, in Cagli, p. 1105.

18 Letter to Chauvet, in Cagli, p. 1125.

19 Cf. letter to Giudici, in Chiari–Ghisalberti, vol. VII, part 1, p. 194.

20 'Prefazione a *Il conte di Carmagnola*' (1820), in Chiari–Ghisalberti, vol. I, p. 283.

21 'Della moralità delle opere tragiche', written in the second half of the 1810s but first published posthumously; in Cagli, pp. 1183–4.

22 Cagli, p. 1184.

23 Letter to Chauvet, in Cagli, p. 1125.

24 The first draft of the novel was completed in September 1823, when Manzoni immediately began revising it for publication.

Allegories of trivialization: Strindberg's view of history

GÖRAN PRINTZ-PÅHLSON

I

In his account of the ill-fated wedding trip to London of 1893, Strindberg describes his dismay at having to share a room in Pimlico with his second wife, the German journalist Frida Uhl (called Maria in the story, like the woman in *Le Plaidoyer d'un fou*, which depicts his first marriage: an almost disdainful consistency). He is, in particular, distraught at the thought of not being able to use and work on the manuscripts contained in the famous 'green sack', which was, at the time, a constant companion in all his travels. He describes its contents thus:

> During the past two years he had systematically subjected the fundamental principles of chemistry and physics in particular to a critical investigation and had come to the conclusion that no further progress would be made in these two sciences unless a new method was devised. He believed that he had discovered this method and proved by experiment that it would produce results. As he could neither write nor remain idle he was now filling up his time by theorizing and making calculations. As he always had a feeling that out of his green sack something fateful would emerge, which would affect his life either to his advantage or to his disadvantage, he kept the matter a secret from his wife.

This is the original version of the story, as it is told in *The Cloister*,[1] a novel written after *Inferno* and *Legends*, but never published in this form, and in fact never completed during the author's lifetime. But when Strindberg revised part of his manuscript for publication as 'The Quarantine Officer's Second Story', the description of the contents of that fateful sack is quite different: 'It was the project known to his friends as the Last Judgement. It was a work of historical exegesis in which he from a new and daring point of view treated universal history as a science. A planned folio which would never be printed, perhaps; at least never earn any money.'[2] This was written in the spring of 1902 during the first period of his marriage to Harriet Bosse. In the nine years since his visit to London, Strindberg had gone through experiences which would be more than enough to fill a normal lifespan: he had lived through the 'Inferno' crises, first in Paris and then, returning to his native land, in Lund; he had in a sustained spasm of creativity written most of his important post-Inferno plays, including the Damascus plays, *The Dance of Death* and *A Dreamplay*; and perhaps more important in this context, he had returned to his earliest preoccupation with historical drama and completed the first series of great dramatic works with themes on Swedish history, including, at the tail end, the two important psychological plays *Charles XII* and *Gustav III*. Obviously, he wanted to distance himself from his experiences in 1893 and to establish evidence of his present emphases and preoccupations partly, but not wholly or primarily, in order to conceal the autobiographical nature of his work.[3] As the autobiographical fragment is presented here, in the collection of poetry and prose called *Fair Haven and Foul Strand* (*Fagervik och Skamsund*), it serves as an exemplum in a slightly detached world, closely associated with the moral universe of *A Dreamplay*, not only through its title but even more so through its social and ethical texture. The Quarantine Officer is, as every reader of *A Dreamplay* will know, the character with blackened face who runs around gleefully torturing the rich summer tourists in Fair Haven.

The articles that make up 'The Mysticism of World History' were published from 20 February to 30 May 1903 in *Svenska Dagbladet*, a daily newspaper closely associated with policies Strindberg did not normally approve of. These articles are clearly a result of a life-long struggle with themes and ideas which come to fruition in this very period. Strindberg wrote in his letter of 12 December 1902 to Schering, his German translator:

> After Fagervik I understood that there had to be a pause in my writing and as a means of killing time I read right through world history. This strange story, which has always seemed like a picaresque novel, revealed itself as a creation of a Conscious Will, and I discovered logic in its antinomies, a result of its conflicting components. Thus I found at the very beginning the world spirit revealed itself concurrently in several places on the earth without these places having any contact with each other. For example: at the very time the Mosaic Law was handed down on Sinai (1300 B.C.) India got Rigveda, Greece Orpheus... and China Schi-King. This is not chance!... My investigations were continued synchronically and the 'Conscious Will' in history was proved.[4]

In an earlier letter to Schering (13 May 1902) he referred to the period of inactivity which had come into his life and concluded: 'Now I am idle and think I am finished – as in 1892.'

The reflections on history in the articles in *Svenska Dagbladet* are clearly the outcome of this new period of introversion and stock-taking which was to culminate in the last instalment of his 'autobiography', *Ensam* (Alone), in the following autumn, where he in fact projected and predicted the solitary existence he was to lead for the rest of his life after the final collapse of his third marriage. They are, of course, of enormous importance to the understanding of the historical plays written in this period – and because of Strindberg's stature as a dramatist his series of dramatic presentations of Swedish history include some of the most remarkable historical plays of our time (and as a continuous dramatic sequence it has no counterpart but Shakespeare) which obviously served as inspiration for the development of the historical play in the twentieth century, from Shaw to Peter Weiss. The essay on history has been used to interpret the historical plays to great advantage by Walter Johnson in his masterly monograph on *Strindberg and the Historical Drama*.[5] However, as Johnson quite reasonably points out, it represents just one instance of a life-long preoccupation with history which has not yet had its full due of attention in Strindberg criticism.[6]

Strindberg himself no doubt regarded his essay as an important step in his further development, pointing to a new liberation and canalization of inner powers derived from the period of his youth. He noted in a characteristically desultory way in his *Occult Diary* for 1 March 1903: 'My articles on the "Mysticism of World History" in *Svenska Dagbladet* continue. I feel that with them I have regained the role I assumed in *Master Olof*.'[7] He then went on to describe an act of bibliomancy which he often resorted to in this later period. The passage he turned up is in fact the same quotation from the first chapter of Jeremiah which he had used to such great effect in the first scene of his first major drama, his first major *historical* drama, where the young preacher Olaus Petri denies his vocation, but still is chosen by the voice of the prophet inside him:

6 Then said I, Ah, Lord God! behold, I cannot speak: for I am a child.
7 But the Lord said unto me, Say not, I am a child: for thou shall go to all that I shall send thee, and whatsoever I command thee thou shalt speak.
10 See I have this day set thee over the nations and over the kingdoms, to root out, and to pull down, and to destroy, and to throw down, to build and to plant.

It was with apparent conviction that Strindberg copied out these verses in his diary. The striking portentousness of the various contexts in which 'The Mysticism of World History' is referred to in Strindberg's notes and works points towards a much greater importance or momentum than these quite relaxed musings on historical coincidences warrant in themselves. Is there a secret doctrine concealed in these various observations – they play in Strindberg's later *oeuvre* very convincingly the same role as the more ostentatiously arcane theories on history of the later Yeats put forward in *A Vision* – or are they just scraps from the desk of the working dramatist, material collected for a projected series of 'world history' plays, of which only one, *The Nightingale of Wittenberg*, was published during his lifetime? Such a mystification would not be foreign to Strindberg's capacious character which included the confidence trickster and showman – and never more so than in private moments – as much as the prophet and self-flagellant. The question is intriguing but cannot be answered unless some more light is shed on his views of history from the point of view of nineteenth-century historiography and metahistory. Nor is it in any way clear how it relates to the wider question of Strindberg's later parafictional writings, be they on science, on history, or on linguistics, and the illumination they can provide for the very methods used in the major fictional and dramatic works of his last period. The direct bearing these notes on history have on the major *historical* plays which rely to such a large extent on forceful character presentation and dramatic technique of quite traditional, although admittedly astutely modernized design, is quite oblique and of a very general nature compared with the relevance of, say, Shaw's prefaces, or Brecht's miscellaneous writings on history and dialectics, for their respective plays.

II

The attempt to make sense of the whole of world history or at least the whole 'world process' in an essay of some fifty pages is an undertaking of awe-inspiring dimensions. The great model for this kind of synoptic treatment of history in the nineteenth century is, of course, Hegel's *Lectures on the Philosophy of History*, which, as has been pointed out many times, most recently by Hayden White,[8] does not contain his philosophy of history in its purest form, but is rather to be regarded as an essay on universal history, in which the historical imagination at work displays its Enlightenment roots, and its ironical character (or, as White might say, 'comic emplotment') is dominant. Strindberg is following Hegel in conceiving the 'plot' of world history as a drama, employing a mode of description which is in turn tragic and comic – and here White's observations on the rhetorical modes in Hegel become increasingly pertinent. In fact, they become so pertinent that they incur the danger of being self-evident. Hegel, on this view, regarded history as a drama or tragedy of his time, in which its very form as a teleological or goal-directed process counteracts or is plotted against the minor tragic conflicts and incidents of individual and national history, to form a variegated and intensely structured pattern. Strindberg's view of the same 'emplotment', although basically agreeing on its form and final destination, i.e. the presenting of a 'True Theodicaea, the justification of God in History',[9] tends towards a much looser structure of constant flux and conflict, whose 'emplotment' itself mirrors a much looser conception of drama as tragicomedy. In Strindberg's conception of tragicomedy, a subgenre of drama which he had as a playwright been instrumental in shaping and defining, the interaction on all levels of events, many of them exceedingly trivial, brings the plot to fruition. In short, what intervenes between these two so similar conceptions of world history is the whole nineteenth-century ideology of 'realism'.

This is a very tempting way of explaining the differences and similarities involved in an assessment of Strindberg's debt to Hegel. Unfortunately, it is also rather simple-minded and question-begging, and hardly does justice to the subtle dialectics of either mind.

Strindberg was very much aware of his debt to Hegel in a generalized methodological way: he constantly stressed the dialectical pattern of events and also once used these favourite pseudo-Hegelian tags, relating them to the logical system of their origin: 'Perhaps in its limitations mankind establishes false oppositions such as Catholic and Protestant, which are not purely contradictory even if they appear to be so? Perhaps the forces of history operate like the laws of thought, through thesis and antithesis forward to synthesis, which is creation' (*SS*, LIV, 366; not included in the translation in this volume).

What is further apparent is the strong stress on civilizations outside Europe, and particularly the Far East, where Hegel's insistence, in his *Lectures*, served as an important model for any future attempt at universal history. In Strindberg's case, his early interest in Far Eastern history and historiography, which he had developed during his years as a librarian at the Royal Library in Stockholm and which had resulted in several articles and monographs,[10] was undoubtedly a further inducement for him to include the now very newsworthy countries of China and Japan in his picture of world history. He might not have remembered Kierkegaard's caustic comments on this undertaking in his section on the subject in his major criticism of Hegel:[11]

It is not yet quite clear where China finds its place in the world-historical process, where every *Privatdocent* from the day before yesterday finds clearly and definitely an ample space. All *Privatdocents* are in fact included... The Method has room for one Chinese thinker... But of course, the System is not yet complete; perhaps it anticipates being able soon to appropriate the toilsome labour of some genuine scientist... by having one or two additional Chinamen presented to it.

If he did, he could claim with some satisfaction that he had added more than *one* 'Chinaman'. However important the example of Hegel's *Lectures* may have been to Strindberg, there is very little in his account that can be ultimately and indubitably derived from them. Strindberg's mind is following very different tracks from Hegel's, and his examples, although partaking of the same preconceived plan, are much racier and often disposed of almost gleefully. 'It is strange, but in the same year as Christ was born, the young Hiao P'ing Ti came to power. In the Annals he is called "the humble and peaceful" and he was soon poisoned' (below, p. 240).

Strindberg's instinctive populist bias is always noticeable, as is his innate optimism: 'History can appear grim, but it isn't, we know that now, we who have seen the beginning of a happy end' (below, p. 253).

The young Strindberg, student of Spencer, Taine, Buckle, the author of works like the two-volume *Svenska folket* (The Swedish People) and the many, often quite delicately placed short stories with historical themes from *Svenska öden och äventyr* (Swedish Fortunes and Adventures), is in fact never very far away in this essay, for example when he disposes, with remarkable equanimity, of '9000 superfluous noblemen, counts, princes and dukes at Agincourt'. Even darwinist ideas, otherwise in this period passionately denounced, reappear, and one is often reminded of the somewhat callous remarks, in the preface to *Miss Julie*, on the relief of seeing representatives of 'inferior races' expire, 'as when somebody sick is allowed to die'. There is, in the whole of this curious piece, a strand of brisk empiricism which sometimes becomes more brusque than brisk. This is in marked contrast to the Hegelian concepts openly invoked: Strindberg is, as insistently as Kierkegaard but apparently for quite different reasons, suspicious of any systematic presentation of his material.

III

As an offshoot of a long tradition of speculations on universal history, including Kant's *Idee zu einer allgemeinen Geschichte in weltbürgerlicher Absicht*, Hegel's *Lectures* and Nietzsche's *Vom Nutzen und Nachteil der Historie für das Leben*, 'The Mysticism of World History' is hardly in itself worthy of much attention. The arguments are sloppy and perfunctory, often self-contradictory, the style repetitious and sometimes quaint, the examples adduced frequently trite. The two main ideas expressed can hardly lay claim to originality: the notion of a 'conscious will' governing the details of world history unbeknownst to the vying participants is a Christian commonplace of long standing, and the complementary one of simultaneous expression of similar ideas in different parts of the world is of even longer pedigree (see below and note 15). There are, as always in Strindberg, occasional glimpses of lively, sinuous strength of argumentation. Much of what Paul de Man has been maintaining about Nietzsche's rhetoric of argumentation in his important recent book *Allegories of Reading*[12] – the importance of exclamations, rhetorical questions, the *style* of argument – is also *mutatis mutandis* applicable to Strindberg, a kindred spirit to Nietzsche if ever there was one. But the deconstruction of the historical consciousness with Strindberg is largely a deconstruction by default: a certain impatience with the whole slow process.

Although sharing the moment of the late-nineteenth-century confluence of scientism and nihilism, Strindberg and Nietzsche differ in their premises. Strindberg's concept of history is ultimately not the scientific one but the figural or homilectic ones of Christian tradition: he was not, as Nietzsche was, interested in a vindication of reason at all costs, even involving a destruction of reason itself. Although Strindberg could agree with Nietzsche (and Kierkegaard) that the final court of appeal would be within the consciousness of the individual – to organize one's own chaos: 'das Chaos in sich organisieren'[13] – he was not willing to destroy the traditional forces that offer help in these undertakings. He can be, as de Man says of Nietzsche, 'epistemologically destructive', and even more he quite definitely considered his whole work as 'a narrative moving from false to true, from blindness to insight. But the question remains historical, i.e. revelatory of a teleological meaning, or "allegorical", i.e. repetitious of a potential confusion between figural and referential statement.'[14]

But this is exactly the confusion that Strindberg is not willing to admit, or will admit only on the individual, ethical level, as resulting from innate tendencies to deceit and falsehood in mankind. Of the two main ideas in Christian historical thought, the theory of figural or allegorical meaning in history[15] (so that, for example, in the paradigmatic instance, New Testament events are prefigured in the Old Testament) is in itself destructive of any positing of a literal, mundane meaning, that is, of any semiotic interpretation in terms of sign and referent (as both Testaments are to an equal degree canonical): the hermeneutic situation itself destroys the possibility of an allegoric reading of an exemplar theory of history[16]. In the same way this second idea – of much greater antiquity than the Christian era – precludes the heuristic value of examples of history. In other words, there is no reason to believe that the preaching of historical example will induce the main participants in history to change their behaviour, as this is governed by 'laws', 'Conscious Will' or 'The Powers'. This is an antinomy of traditional mould which is far from being resolved in 'The Mysticism of World History'. 'The study of the past ought to teach us, first a certain consideration for the future, once we see how it nevertheless proceeds onwards towards a definite goal, and then tolerance...' (below, p. 253). Strinberg is quite open in this insistence on the instructional value of history. At the same time, he is insisting on a personal or at least an anthropomorphic will behind the forces of history. 'The great synthesis which unites the opposites, resolves the contradictions, maintains the balance, is no human being and can be no other than the invisible legislator who alters the laws in freedom according to changed circumstances: the creator, the dissolver and preserver he may then be called – what you will' (below, p. 256). If there is a question of deconstruction of past stances and statements here rather than plain carelessness, it must be seen as a very subjective and personal allegory which is closely tied up with his general scheme of his life-story or 'autobiographical pact'.[17]

IV

Dilthey, who devoted his life to the study of these problems and those of 'the hermeneutic circle', shows himself in his late writings (almost contemporary with 'The Mysticism of World History') fully aware of this interconnection of the private and the universal. 'In autobiography we encounter the highest and most instructive form of the understanding of life',[18] and further on in the same passage: 'Constantly changing connections have been formed from different standpoints within life itself, so that the task of historical presentation is already half-performed by life.' And in another context, referring to Goethe: 'In *Dichtung und Wahrheit* a man looks at his own existence from the standpoint of universal history.' This could as well have been said of Strindberg.

In order fully to appreciate the significance of 'The Mysticism of World History', one is forced once again to consider it in its genetic context, wedged into the vast scheme of autobiographical writings that occupied Strindberg's time and energy during such a considerable period of his life. It is prefigured in *The Cloister*, inserted into its revision, 'The Quarantine Officer's Second Story', and written in close conjunction with the crowning last instalment of that series, *Alone*. Furthermore, and perhaps even more importantly, its arguments closely connect (and much more so than with the more superficially related history plays) with the third and final part of the dramatic spiritual 'autobiography', *The Road to Damascus*, a play which has been shamefully neglected by the Strindberg critics in comparison with its two more famous predecessors.

In *Damascus III*, which was completed in 1902 and first collected in the volume of the three plays, Strindberg set out again to tell the story of his second marriage and the breakdown of coherence of his personal life system which is known, on his own instigation, as the Inferno crisis. But while the first part tells the story in terms of psychological and mythological/folkloristic parallels, much along the same lines as Freud was investigating at that time, and the second employs traditional religious models of conversion psychology, the third is, perhaps more ambitiously and with less regard for theatrical efficacity, relating the life story to the problems of universal history. At the end of the play, the protagonist, the Stranger (Den Okände), is confronted with a succession of quickly sketched figures from world history, in a series of portraits shown by Father Melcher, 'most of them with two heads'. This represents a *tableau vivant* technique which prefigures Brecht at his most didactic epic theatre, as in *Die Tage der Kommune* or *Das Verhör des Lucullus*. Among these figures appear Boccaccio, Luther, Schiller, Goethe, Napoleon, Victor Hugo and Bismarck, who are all and sundry revealed as being 'dimorphous', two-faced, renegade. They obviously serve as homiletic exemplars, presented by Father Melcher for the instruction and mortification of the Stranger. But another authority than the highest is also invoked, i.e. Hegel's, in terms very reminiscent of 'The Mysticism of World History':

> It is the Powers themselves who promulgate contemporary opinion as they develop in *apparent* circles. Hegel, the philosopher of the present, himself dimorphous, for both a 'left'-minded and a 'right'-minded Hegel can always be quoted, has best explained the contradictions of life, of history and of the spirit, with his own magic formula. Thesis: affirmation; Antithesis: negation; Synthesis: comprehension![19]

Although not included in the numbered panopticon of the play, Hegel is here reduced to an exemplar among others, and, together with Kierkegaard (who is perhaps surprisingly but characteristically paired with Napoleon!)[20] and the mysterious Uriel d'Acosta whose life span is, somewhat like Ahasuerus' in the Sue novel, much admired by Strindberg, extended to the nineteenth century in order to encompass Strindberg's own foibles and fears:

In 1830 our friend became an Hegelian, though, to be sure, rather late in the day. Then he rediscovered God, a God who was immanent in nature and in man, and found he was a little god himself. Now, as ill-luck would have it, there were two Hegels, just as there were two Voltaires... I'll shorten the whole sad story for Father Uriel's sake. In 1850 he again became a materialist and an enemy of Christianity. In 1870 he became a hypnotist, in 1890 he wanted to shoot himself![21]

These exemplars of the dead are in fact no less living than any of the characters of the play: the Lady revealing herself as the Mother of the Stranger says: 'the dead aren't dead and maternal love can conquer death'. Death is, however, the Master- or Mother-metaphor of the play (as anagnorisis, or recognizing, had been in the first Damascus play and exorcism in the second) and the Stranger has to go through a feigned death ceremony to be allowed to enter the monastery which in its both arcane and worldly organization shows affinities with the secular order, in pursuit of Truth and a new Science, which Strindberg was describing already in *The Cloister* (a dream which is almost exactly synchronic with that in Henry James' 'Great Good Place').[22] Here at the end of the Damascus trilogy, Strindberg is slowly defusing his characters of their elemental charges: they are being named and classified as examples in the *tableau* life of history by the dramatist who deconstructs his dramatic technique in the direction of the epic and didactic. History has entered into biography, autobiography has invaded the closed panopticon of history.

This is fully in accordance with the incisive criticism of Hegel and universal history launched by Kierkegaard in 'Becoming Subjective' in *Concluding Unscientific Postscript:* 'If world-history is the history of the human race, it follows, as a matter of course, that it does not show forth the ethical. What it lets us see must be something that corresponds to the abstraction which the race is, and therefore to something equally abstract.'[23]

In his observations of details Strindberg is willing to follow Kierkegaard's criticism of world history: as a defiant searcher for truth and salvation he is acutely aware of what Kierkegaard considers the crucial point: 'the possibility-relationship [*Muligheds-Forhold*] which every individual has to God. This is entirely ignored world-historically, because everything is understood in retrospect, and *so it is forgotten that the dead were once alive.*'[24] As an historical dramatist it is his *métier* to do exactly this, bringing the dead back to life, and as autobiographer he is constantly made aware of the impossibility of his task. If 'world history is simply the history of the individuals', there is, as Kierkegaard was quick to point out, no difference between the king and the hermit. It is something of the same honesty that compelled Strindberg in his remaining works – the important late novels, the *Chamber Plays*, the extensive miscellaneous prose, collected in the *Blue Books* and elsewhere – to renounce the dramatic in favour of the homiletic.

If, as I have suggested above, the ideology of nineteenth-century 'realism' (which is, of course, to be taken in both its philosophical and technical sense) is what intervenes between the conception of world history in Hegel (and negatively in Kierkegaard) and in Strindberg, then this is not an explanation, but in fact the very problem to be faced. Strindberg was in nineteenth-century drama the great master of the trivial, of the detail which is not symbolic of anything but its own lack of significance, and it is fitting that Freud should quote him, if only once, in the third edition of *The Psychopathology of Everyday Life*. He saw specificness as in itself the innermost core of realism, and the truth-value of literature as a technique of intensional logic.[25] When the boundaries of discourse are broken down in such a radical fashion, it is not only the conventional genres that have to go, but any graduation of experience according to significance. In *Damascus III* the Stranger's fate is in the balance between the whole of world history on the one hand, and a torn copy of *The Swiss Family Robinson*, surreptitiously hidden in a wardrobe, on the other. 'The wardrobe was painted in oak graining, and clothes hung in its upper part, whilst shoes stood below.'[26] The trivialization of existence is no longer the plight of modern men (as in Tocqueville or Kierkegaard), but in fact a deliberate technique to be pursued with passion. The quest has come to an end, the autobiographical pact has been dissolved: Strindberg can devote his remaining years to collecting and processing the curious coincidences and often ludicrous pieces of information which make up the main part of the late *oeuvre*. One can deplore the lack of tension that inevitably damages his dramatic work after this period, but the strange world it presents has a translucent beauty of its own. 'The Mysticism of World History' is a crucial document in the process of deconstruction of 'realism'.

V

It is important to remember that there are two main traditions in which 'The Mysticism of World History' can make itself at home.

One is the tradition of occultism with which it is associated mainly by its title. The strength of this tradition for the whole background of French Symbolism is well researched.[27] Strindberg did not need many sources, outside his long acquaintance with Swedenborg and Balzac, although his interest in Eliphas Levy and Sar Peladan is well known.[28] The more vulgar aspects of spiritualism and popular thaumaturgy were evidently abhorrent to him,[29] as they had been in his positivist days when he wrote the strange novella *Scheidewege*.[30] There is, on the whole, very little of ordinary occultism in Strindberg: even the name he gave to his secret diary. *Ockulta Dagboken*, seems to refer mainly, in spite of the somewhat sensational accounts of telepathic 'intercourse' with Harriet Bosse, to his avowed intention never to have it published. Compared with, for instance, Yeats' *Vision* with all its diagrams and tables, cones and gyres,[31] 'The Mysticism of World History' is very tame and conventional indeed.[32] Only in one respect does it belong to a strand of occultism which seems to have gained in importance after Strindberg's time. This is in its insistence on synchronicity in history, a concept which has become extremely fashionable in our time through the writings of Jung and Koestler. It is useful to be reminded by no less an authority than Arnaldo Momigliano that synchronism has a long and respectable ancestry in historiography:

> Chronographers and historians collaborated in the production of synchronisms. Synchronisms had long been known to the historians of Mesopotamia and Israel but they played a special part in Greek historiography. The wide range of interest and explanations of the Greek historians would never have been possible without synchronisms. They represented the bridges between the stories of different cities, nations and civilizations. The very story of Herodotus hangs upon a chain of synchronisms, which is no less robust for being hardly visible to the casual observer.[33]

As a matter of fact, even the work of modern cult-figures like Velikovsky is, at least in its later, less sensational phase, mainly concerned with the question of synchronisms of Middle Eastern history,[34] exactly as Strindberg is, in the opening of his essay: much of the literature of the arcane is in spirit no less rational than other kinds, but perhaps more single-minded in its use of rationality. This is the case at least with Strindberg's famous *Blue Books*,[35] where a sometimes delightfully zany rationality is allowed to reign supreme. Many of his observations there, like the famous debunking of the findings of assyriology – 'impressions of chaff in clay' is his reductive explanation of cuneiform – or the denial of the corporeal existence of the corncrake, are absurdities only in view of their exaggerated scepticism. Trivialization has become, for Strindberg, a continuation of literature 'by other means'.

'The Mysticism of World History' can and, as I see it, must also be placed in the context of the strategies of 'deconstruction' which link Nietzsche with the current grouping of Heidegger, Blanchot, Derrida and their American followers. This has become, suddenly and somewhat unexpectedly, a fashionable subject[36], and much could be said against the rhetorical bias of its present adherents. If one is willing to look at more wide-ranging strategies, rather than at the rhetorical or linguistic deconstruction tactics of individual writers, one will be able to observe, from the end of the nineteenth century well into the twentieth, a wide variety of attempts at dismantling received ideas, ideological sacred cows, and kindred denizens of the ill-defined fields between history, philosophy and politics. I do not find it advisable to limit the range of these activities to the province of philosophical idealism. They are as noticeable in the positivist and empiricist camp: Remy de Gourmont's series of articles from 1891 in *Mercure de France* which resulted in his technique of 'dissociation des idées'[37] (which Strindberg cannot possibly have been unaware of, although he never refers to it), Samuel Butler's various polemics in England, Henry Adams' *Mont St Michel and Chartres*, all partake of this tendency. Strindberg, as 'dimorphous' as his historical exemplars, has one foot in each camp. No doubt the important studies of Hegel and Nietzsche by Jacques Derrida,[38] and the chapters on Nietzsche and Rousseau in the book referred to above by Paul de Man, must also shed considerable light on Strindberg, and not only because of the proximity of the subjects to his thought. Nevertheless, one should remind oneself that 'deconstruction' is part and parcel of the method of these thinkers and efficient not as a mechanical critical tool, but only to the extent that it can be brought to the surface from the subject itself. The method could as well be called construction as deconstruction, and I think this is how these fellow construction-workers of the turn of the century would like to regard it, not least Strindberg. One has to remember that his vocation, as a present-day Jeremiah, ordered him not only 'to root out, and to pull down', but also 'to build and to plant'. If he saw himself as a destroyer of ideals, an iconoclastic revealer of the hidden emptiness behind locked doors, he also saw himself as, in his rage for reduction, united with bonds of loyalty to the simple and the meek.

He preferred in this late period to find solace in the mild debunkings of Maeterlinck in his *Trésor des humbles* and similar later writings, or in Balzac's simple tales, rather than in the titanic wrestlings with logic and society in Nietzsche. There is a moral urgency in his strategies of trivialization which is the result of an identification with the suffering and oppressed: without taking this into account, it is impossible to understand Strindberg's last phase, neither the apparent sentimentality of, say, *Svarta handsken* (The Black Glove), or the violence and sarcasm of his polemics against the establishment during the 'Strindberg Feud'. He may have resigned himself to the view of history as an 'enormous game of chess played by a single player', as in the most often quoted simile in the essay, who 'has only one aim: to maintain balance and justice, while ending the match as a draw'. But there is still room for manoeuvre for the individual if he keeps his aim low enough. The trivial has its allegories, which are read as nature can be read, as signature. One might remind oneself that 'trivial' is derived from *trivia*, the crossways where idle gossip is gathered. But it is also connected with 'trivium': the medieval lower tier of the seven liberal arts, consisting of logic, grammar, arithmetic: the purveyors of simple and incontestable truths. Derived from it is 'trifle', the small morsels or shavings from the crossroads or the curriculum. This is the favourite form of independent thinkers: the *Philosophiske Smuler* of Kierkegaard, the *krísmata* and *peritémata* of Hippias Major[39] from which the Kierkegaard book derived its title. This fragmented form conserves the *skepsis*. On the road to Damascus there is always another crossroads where the Tempter may catch up with you.

NOTES

In the text and notes, the abbreviation *SS* is used to denote August Strindberg, *Samlade skrifter*, edited by John Landquist, 55 vols. (1912–18).

1 *The Cloister*, edited by C. G. Bjurström, translated and with a commentary and notes by Mary Sandbach (London, 1969), p. 67 f. Swedish edition first published 1966 (p. 74).

2 *SS*, XXXVII, 146.

3 Mary Sandbach points this out in her thoughtful commentary to *The Cloister* (p. 147).

4 Walter Johnson, *Strindberg and the Historical Drama* (Seattle, 1963), p. 3.

5 *Ibid.*, *passim.*

6 The only existing monograph seems to be Harry V. E. Palmblad, *Strindberg's Conception of History* (New York, 1927).

7 The facsimile edition of the complete diary was published by Gidlunds, Stockholm,

in 1977. The reference is to p. 166, not included in *From an Occult Diary*, edited by Torsten Eklund, translated with additional notes by Mary Sandbach (London, 1965).

8 *Metahistory: The Historical Imagination in Nineteenth-Century Europe* (Baltimore, 1973), p. 85.

9 Hegel, *Philosophy of History*, translated by J. Sibree (Dover reprint, 1956), p. 457.

10 From *Relations de la Suède avec la Chine et les Pays Tartares. Mémoire lu à l'Académie des Inscriptions et Belles Lettres, à Paris 1879* to *Kina och Japan* (Stockholm, 1911) and *Kinesiska språkets härkomst* (Stockholm 1912).

11 Kierkegaard's *Concluding Unscientific Postscript*, translated by David Swenson and Walter Lowrie (Princeton, 1974), p. 134n.

12 Paul de Man, *Allegories of Reading. Figural Language in Rousseau, Nietzsche, Rilke and Proust* (New Haven, 1979).

13 *Vom Nutzen und Nachteil*, last paragraph.

14 De Man, *Allegories of Reading*, p. 116.

15 The seminal investigation of this idea is without doubt Erich Auerbach, '*Figura*' in *Neue Dantestudien* (Istanbul, 1944). For the application of this idea to literature, see, among many others, C. A. Patrides, *The Grand Design of God* (London, 1972) with very full bibliographical notes.

16 Cf, *inter alia*, George H. Nadel, 'Philosophy of History before Historicism', in *The Critical Approach: Essays in Honor of Karl R. Popper* (New York, 1964).

17 Cf. Philippe Lejeune, *Le Pacte autobiographique* (Paris, 1975).

18 Dilthey, *Selected Writings* (Cambridge, 1976), p. 214.

19 *The Road to Damascus, a Trilogy*, translated by Graham Rawson (Grove Press repr. New York, 1960), p. 283.

20 See article by Nils Norman, 'Strindberg och Napoleon', *Svensk Litteraturtidskrift*, 4 (1959), 151–70, and the very perspicacious discussion of this theme with reference to *The Scapegoat* and *Damascus III* in Eric O. Johanneson, *The Novels of August Strindberg* (Berkeley, 1968), pp. 290 f.

21 *Road to Damascus*, pp. 274 f. The historical Uriel d'Acosta lived 1591–1640.

22 James' short story first appeared in *Scribner's Magazine* (January 1900), when Strindberg first started to entertain ideas about a retreat of a worldly order.

23 Kierkegaard, *Concluding Unscientific Postscript*, p. 138.

24 *Ibid.*, p. 139.

25 See the early article 'Om realism', *SS*, XVII, 191–200, and my discussion in 'Realism as Negation', in *Literature and Reality – Creatio versus Mimesis*, edited by Alex Bolckmans (Ghent, 1977).

26 *The Road to Damascus*, p. 272.

27 See Alain Mercier, *Les Sources ésotériques et occultes de la poésie symboliste* I (Paris, 1969).

28 See *inter alia*, article on the sources of *Inferno* in *SS*, LIV, 332f.

29 *Ibid.*

30 First published in German in Vienna *Neue Freie Presse* (August–September 1887). As Gunnar Brandell has pointed out, it seems probable that Freud noticed this short story which depicts a hysterical 'case study' not dissimilar to the ones that were to occupy him and Breuer in the next few years. *Freud – A Man of his Time*, trans. by Iain White (Portsmouth, 1979), p. 14.

31 For Yeats' philosophy of history see, e.g., T. R. Henn, *The Lonely Tower* (London, 1965), ch. 12, '*A Vision* and the Interpretation of History'.

32 The only reference to the conventional canon of occult sources is, at the very end, to Piazzi Smyth and his work on the great pyramid (*SS*, LIV, 401).

33 Momigliano, 'Time in Ancient Historiography', in *Essays in Ancient and Modern Historiography* (Oxford, 1977), p. 192.

34 See, e.g. *Ages in Chaos* (1952, many reprints).

35 A selection from the *Blue Books*, in English translation by C. Field with a theosophical introduction by Arthur Babillotte, entitled *Zones of the Spirit* was published in New York in 1913. This is a period when similarly empirical-minded occultism is being presented in, for instance the collections of curious 'facts' by Charles Fort (*Book of the Damned*, 1920). See Louis Pawels and Jacques Bergier, *Le Matin des magiciens* (Paris, 1960) for examples. It is worth noticing that many of the examples adduced by Pauwels and Bergier, in their investigation of the occult interests among the early Nazis, are to some extent shared by Strindberg, in particular in Austrian 'natural philosophers' like Hörbiger and Lanz-Lieberfels. See article on Lanz by Peter Cornell, *Expressen* (13 August 1980).

36 See the recent collection of essays by Harold Bloom e.a. *Deconstruction and Criticism* (London, 1979).

37 Later collected in *La Culture des idées* (Paris, 1900).

38 Derrida, 'Le puits et la pyramide' in *Marges de la philosophie* (Paris, 1972) and *Éperons: les styles de Nietzsche*, (Paris, 1978).

39 304a.

The mysticism of world history

AUGUST STRINDBERG

TRANSLATED BY MICHAEL ROBINSON

When the people of Israel departed from Egypt the country was ruled by a pharaoh of the eighteenth dynasty. The founding of Palestine, the small state from which Europe would receive its culture once Graeco-Roman civilization had ceased to flourish, faded away, and become the fertile mulch beneath the newly sown seed, dates from this exodus. The obscure myths relate that in the same year a mighty expedition from Greece was fitted out to seek unknown lands to the north and north-east. This coincidence is of course truly remarkable in itself. But at the same moment, like an insatiable earthquake which spreads in a particular direction with no known cause, the legendary Assyrian queen, Semiramis, is supposed to have crossed into India, where an enormous movement was already under way. The Hindus were also migrating to the east, and the two races encountered one another in the mighty conflicts depicted in the Mahabharata. The movement extends still further eastwards, to China under the Yen dynasty, which was the scene of great strife. Races from the south pressed northwards, struggles raged over the succession, and the regent once more transferred the capital from Shensi to Honan and then back again, just as Moses moves Israel's camp in the desert. Now the question is: is it the same disturbance which is transmitted from

* In Strindberg's title, *Världshistoriens mystik*, 'mystik' carries the sense of the English 'mysteries' as well as 'mysticism'. The essay was originally published in *Svenska Dagbladet* in 1903 and reprinted in volume 54 of John Landquist's edition of Strindberg's works. This translation offers somewhat more than half of Strindberg's text, enough to illuminate his associative way of thinking, the rapidity with which he moves between recurring preoccupations, and the brevity of his style. One section (IX), which contains an excursus on physiognomy and Greek and Roman sculpture in the manner of Strindberg's essayistic general work, *En blå bok*, has been omitted in its entirety, and excisions have been made elsewhere where material is repeated. This is especially the case in the passages dealing with Luther and with the Thirty Years' War, in which the accumulation of detail is in part a result of Strindberg's exhaustive and exhausting research into the historical and social background of his huge play, *Gustav Adolf* (1900). All these cuts are indicated by the convention [...].

the Nile delta to the deltas of the Danube, Euphrates, Punjab and the Yangtse? (It is a question of deltas, too!) Or did these upheavals arise simultaneously in several isolated places, issuing from the same unknown source of energy?If we suppose that these earthquake-like movements of peoples could arise in a so-called natural fashion by an initial movement from the Nile, it becomes still more difficult to explain the great upheavals in spiritual life which occurred simultaneously within the then known world.

When Moses wandered in the desert for forty years instead of taking the direct caravan route to Palestine in fourteen days, he had, as we know, a definite purpose. And he initiates his – conscious or unconscious – world historical epic by climbing Mount Sinai (which was occupied by Egyptian temples and possessed working copper mines). On Sinai he exchanges the Noachian laws for the Ten Commandments. Correctly interpreted, the first of these commandments expresses the great secret of monotheism, the doctrine of unity, monism – one God, the father of all, in whose name every people will one day be united.

Tradition has placed the departure of Cecrops, bearing the seeds of culture from Egypt to Greece, to about the same time. The learned have dismissed Cecrops as apocryphal, but he can certainly be retained as the complement to the voyage of the Argonauts, and it is expedient to have him play this role here.

On the other hand it is certain that at precisely the same time as the Mosaic law was published, the Indians received their Vedic books, particularly the Rig Veda. In this collection of laws monotheism is also proclaimed, for the Indians consider their many gods to be only symbols: 'There is only one God', the Veda declares, on many occasions, 'the highest spirit, the Lord of the world.'

And this moment in the history of the Indian people is also the moment of transition from nature worship (Indra) to intellectual religion (Brahma). (In contrast to the Mosaic doctrine of exclusivity, the Veda has explained 'that all religions must be equally pleasing to God, since he would otherwise have founded only one religion!') This occurred thirteen centuries before Christ, at the same moment that the people of Kashmir situate the birth of Buddha, whereas the Chinese and the Japanese assign his birth to 1000 and others to 600 or 650. If the former is true, then it is all the more remarkable since Buddhism, in advance of Christianity, teaches atonement through suffering and self-denial as well as ordaining love for one's neighbour. This love for all, which people have wanted to make a uniquely Christian commandment, is to be found in all religions and even in the Israel of the Old Testament. For in Leviticus 19: 17ff it is explicitly stated: 'Thou shalt not hate thy brother... Thou shalt not avenge... Thou shalt love thy neighbour as thyself.'

What happened then in the Far East, in China? In 1324, that is, when Moses is in the twenty-fifth year of his wandering in the desert, Wu-ting reigns there. He appears in the midst of general disorder to reform morals and institute laws. [...] And if one wishes to locate Zoroaster's advent at this time, which according to the experts occurred between 1700 and 1200 B.C., it would seem as if the entire civilized world had simultaneously awakened to a consciousness of mankind's great common aim and mission, or as if the world soul had forced its way down into the consciousness of the masses at the same moment, revealed itself, and been transformed according to the capacity of each people to understand and express it. How this came about is not known, but thinkers have sought to explain it in two different ways. Some believe that the will and the movement are innate and implanted in human souls from the outset (immanence), others that this soul is influenced from without and fashioned as an instrument for a will that exists outside us (transcendence), which leads the destinies of peoples and individuals from above towards a conscious goal which only the guide has complete knowledge of. The present author would subscribe to this second view, since he has found it confirmed by his excursions through world history. [...]

II

Now many people have no doubt asked themselves what is meant by gods. Who was Zeus, who Jehovah? Have these gods existed as objective personalities or are they the creations of mankind's ideas or fantasies? The latter is surely the general opinion nowadays, and we are able to see how fantasies can develop into enormous generators, from which nations draw strength, powers which, having once been conjured up, finally establish themselves in control of and judgement over their own creators. If one assumes that 'the gods' have existed – and all people have believed as much as long as a certain form of religion prevailed – in what relation did they stand to each other? [...]

In the century before Christ Europe possessed only one culture, the Greek, for Roman culture was mainly a copy, a translation and an echo. But four hundred years earlier poets and thinkers had already begun to doubt in the gods, and in his tragedies Euripides rebelled against them as depraved oppressors whom it was unworthy to serve. He even permits one of his heroes to say that men are better than the gods. Socrates took poison on this account, and with that the decline of Olympus begins. But Greece was not suited for the role of missionary, for the nation was also depraved. Thus its culture was laid fallow while the Romans accomplished their task of christianizing Europe.

The Romans occupied Greece but they also sacked it. Mithridates and Sulla ravaged and destroyed temples. And when they grew tired, the mysterious pirates, of whose origin nothing is known, continued the great work of destruction. They plundered the largest temples of their treasures, altars and consecrated gifts. Then the oracle fell silent, the tragedies ceased to be performed and farces, bullfights and gladiatorial games were put on in the amphitheatres.

Eventually Caesar cleared a way through Gaul, Germany and Britain, where the spadework was done for the western culture of the future. This is Germanic and Christian grafted on to the Graeco-Roman wild shoot.

But the period around Christ's birth is also characterized by important movements, both of nations and in spiritual life. India was invaded by warriers who killed all the native princes. The land was subsequently liberated in order to embark on a new period called the Saka era. This movement seems to give a thrust to the east, for with the birth of Christ Buddhism penetrates into China. It is true that Christianity did not arrive, but the doctrine of atonement and asceticism of the mild Buddha came instead. It is strange but in the same year as Christ was born, the young Hiao P'ing Ti came to power. In the Annals he is called 'the humble and peaceful' and he was soon poisoned. During the rule of his successor, Wang Mang, a comet was seen (A.D. 16), and the people of the west rose up in revolt. His son, Ming Ti, dreamed of a gold-coloured man whose head and throat shone. He consulted his ministers who informed him: 'In the west there is a genie or supernatural being whose name is Fo.' This was Buddha, who had died five hundred years earlier and whose teachings were now adopted by the emperor. [...] A Messiah is also announced in the Zend-Avesta. Called Sosiosch, the saviour and redeemer, he will awaken the dead. The Veda, too, proclaims its Krishna who will be born of a virgin in Kali-juga, the present epoch, and the world will be saved by a god who becomes a man. In any case the spirit of Christianity existed in India when Christ was born, and we have recently heard it confirmed on the European stage in the drama, *The Little Clay Cart*, which dates from the year of Christ's birth. [...]

What ought one to believe of these coincidences which regularly appear on every major historical occasion? Is the power of thought so enormous that it defies time and place and immediately transmits itself, setting kindred spirits in comparable movement even at a distance? Or is the world soul the sum of all souls, and does mankind comprise only a single being which responds in all its parts when a movement occurs in any one of them? Or does the conscious world will stand above everything, ordering and controlling? The latter seems most probable when one observes a well arranged campaign such as the christianization of Europe, where every troop movement seems to have been decided at headquarters, and the field commanders carry out their orders without knowing the purpose behind the whole plan. The heathen, Caesar, believes he is romanizing North Europe when he is in fact baptizing it for Christ. The migratory hordes move from east to west without knowing why, and they lay waste the rotten cultures of Rome and Greece in the belief that they are conquering nations and amassing treasures. [...]

The highly knowledgeable sinologist, M. G. Pauthier, who has discovered the regulated movement of mankind's destiny particularly in the history of China, has in the course of a discussion on Chinese philosophy, made the following remarkable observation:

> Mencius was born in the fourth century before Christ and he was active in the period when Socrates, Xenophon and Aristotle taught in Greece, just as Lao-Tzu and Confucius flourished at the same time as Thales and Pythagoras. This contemporaneousness of great men who were to enlighten the world leads one to reflect on the existence of secret links, unknown means of communication between the most widely separated peoples, or else one must suppose that – just as they are governed by the same sun – all these peoples are ruled by the same intelligence.

III

The next great event of world importance after Christianity and the great migrations is probably the appearance of Mohammed. That he, like Attila, was a man sent by providence the Christians did not doubt. Christianity was in fact so degenerate that it was worse than heathendom. The bishops of the various Churches excommunicated one another after having spent two hundred years quarrelling over Christ's divinity and the place of the Holy Ghost in his genealogy, and even the official record, or the Apostolic Creed (*Symbolum*), was falsified (and remains so today, when every Christian denomination has a different version). The worship of images had developed to such an extent that the heathens believed the Christians were worshippers of idols.

Then Mohammed, the Arab, came and sounded his war cry: there is only one God! This antichrist, who nevertheless loved and worshipped Christ, assumed Israel's mantle and raised the banner of monotheism again [...] It was a terrible moment for Christians when they saw themselves abandoned by their God, and many probably asked themselves if they had lived and believed in a chimera. [...]

The Lord of Hosts appeared to stand on the side of the Mohammedans against the Christians and his only begotten son! What was one to believe? What couldn't one believe? Neither Attila nor Alaric had founded a religion or created a culture but Mohammed did both and more, for his pupils possessed learning and scientific knowledge that had not existed since the time of Aristotle and Pliny.

The age of Christianity appeared to be over and Rome trembled. Then, to speak in the style of the Old Testament, the Lord aroused a man in Rome itself who became a mighty bulwark against the christianized heathens and it was Gregory the Great. [...]

Yet does it not appear as if the 'Conscious Will' in history was as prepared to make use of its friend, Mohammed, as of Gregory in order to carry out an intention that is incomprehensible to man? And that the same will set up targets for both of them? Italy, Gaul, Britain and Germany were protected from Mohammed's assault, but Spain was relinquished, albeit one hundred years later. The preparatory work was performed in Mohammed's time, however, for the Visigoth, Leovigild, destroyed the power of the Suevi in Galicia, Reccared I merged Goths and Romans, and the Arian Goths became Catholics. It is rather as if a statesman sat and planned the political events of the future a century in advance.

In Greece at the same period matters are also arranged for the arrival of Islam when new semi-savages pressed into the country. It is the Slavs who arrive, eight years after Mohammed's birth.

Great events occur in the east. Islam achieved what Christianity had not been capable of, namely to root out heathen idolatry among the Arabs, Persians and their neighbours. Mohammed was what would nowadays be termed a syncretist and unitarian. In the Koran he achieves a compromise between Judaism, Christianity and eastern monotheism, and he therefore succeeded in creating a kingdom so great that Alexander had not conceived a greater.

But while the Arabs founded the Caliphate, another empire with fresh powers was already being planned for the future, far away in the east, by another unused nation that would, in the fullness of time, succeed the somewhat worn out Bedouin. It is the Turks who can be espied upon the horizon, where the sun rises. When these semi-savages step out of their dark hiding places at Altai, in the time of Mohammed, they first come into contact with the Chinese. At this time China experienced a renaissance under one of its greatest emperors, T'ai Tsung. A vague fear of some indefinite pressure in the west aroused the nation, and the somewhat down-at-heel commonsense religion derived from Confucius received new life. People collected and revised the canonical books again, set the university and schools in order; in a word they armed themselves against Islam without knowing it, and it seems as if Islam was not permitted to enter China but only India. In the same period China comes into contact with the west. Its chronicles mention, perhaps for the first time, the Christian religion, which is found worthy of admiration but unnecessary, 'since all religions are good'. Ambassadors from Byzantium are received in China, which hears of the enormous triumphs of the Arabs. The Turks also send emissaries after they have attempted to force a way eastwards, where they are checked, and they later turn about slowly towards the west, where they are finally to come to rest, maintaining the balance of Asia against Europe.

Just as Greece planted an offshoot in the Roman empire, China will now graft a branch onto healthy wild stock – Japan! Here Chinese culture, writing and Buddhism is introduced in Mohammed's life-time, evidently as a buttress against the pressure from Islam.

It is exactly like an enormous game of chess played by a single player who moves both black and white, is completely impartial, takes when he ought to, makes plans for both sides, is for himself and against himself, thinks everything out in advance, and has only one aim: to maintain balance and justice, while ending the match in a draw!

Another milestone in history is the year A.D. 1000. The Christian part of mankind also had a presentiment that something new and important would take place, for during the whole of the previous century people had awaited the end of the world and the arrival of the millennium. Of course the fear increased the nearer the appointed day approached. People gave away their possessions, ceased to work, and resorted to prayer. The emperor himself became fearful, undertook a pilgrimage to Adelbert's grave in Gnesen, opened Charlemagne's grave in Aachen and took out the gold cross. Then the legendary emperor awakes and it is as if his spirit resumes its arrested activity. An immense new kingdom is incorporated into Christianity with the conversion of Russia under Vladimir. And in almost the same year Europe stretches itself and extends to the north where the king of Sweden enters into relations with Rome as a Christian. Hungary, the border post against Islam, receives an apostolic crown from Pope Sylvester II. France is already civilized and the Capets transform Lutetia into Paris. Germany acquires the imperial crown and the German, Otto III, settles in Rome. The Margravate called Austria begins to train for the great role it will play later on. The Scandinavians become Europeans and settle in France, Spain and Italy, after they have founded the kingdom of Russia.

Iceland embraces Christianity and plants the cross on the other side of the Atlantic, in America, but here the 'conscious will' seems to have changed its mind! More preparations were necessary before America could be discovered in earnest, or perhaps the outlet to the west was not yet required. Before the new Israel was allowed to march in, Leif Eriksen should only glimpse the new land of Canaan, confirm it existed and hide the secret until the chosen man appeared. Meanwhile, in the Far East, it appears that even without the book of Revelations and its chiliasm, people had become full of unease towards the end of the century, for the emperor, Shen Tsung, warned by a comet, settled matters with his conscience precisely as Otto had done. He published an edict, implored people to tell him his faults, subjected himself to a penance, freed three thousand prisoners and lowered taxes. [...]

IV

What the Romans were able to accomplish by means of the Punic war against a Carthage that embodied the threat of Asia, the newly fashioned Europe could not achieve against the Caliphs, who had taken the shores of the Mediterranean in the east, south and west and surrounded the new Roman empire with a whole series of Carthages. The Crusades had helped form a closer acquaintance with these new Cathaginians, who were not heathens and yet not Christians either. The Arabs, this paradoxical people, who were nevertheless fired by the spirit of Christendom, possessed superior learning, could display all the virtues of chivalry, courage, magnanimity, generosity, compassion, which were finely displayed in the character of Saladin, and they taught the Europeans that their faith was not the only one. And when the Christians saw that the Lord of Hosts did not side with his first-born, but shared his favours equally, a faint scepticism began to arise in the minds of the westerners. An epoch of reflection, which goes under the names of humanism and renaissance, commenced and people began to read the ancient pagan authors in whom they discovered many things worthy of consideration. Thus, after one thousand years of penitence, with their gaze upon heaven, men turned their eyes to the earth and resumed their concern with everyday life. [...]

Christianity, which had fled to Byzantium during the era of the Germanic invasions, had there degenerated into a theology. Every sin flourished, but the Lord wanted to spare this Sodom until Rome reached maturity. Certainly the Arabs had attempted to conquer Byzantium, but they were not permitted to. When the forces of Islam had taken Sicily for a second time, and were intending to attack Rome, under Otto II, the Byzantine emperor, Basil II, was unchristian enough to aid the Muslims, although unsuccessfully. Nevertheless, the Alexander idea had emerged quite unexpectedly in another part of the world. Between Siberia and China, where a secret self-generation of peoples seems to have taken place, in a distant region which was vaguely named Tartary, a mighty man of providence was born, whom we know as Genghis Khan. Inspired by a prophet, he decided to conquer the world. He was a strict monotheist but did not adhere to any creed or faith and so bound himself neither to Islam nor Buddhism. He therefore permitted all kinds of religion to flourish about him. Anyhow, he conquered China, which was no small thing, and since he only had a single goal, the conquest of the world, he intended to murder all China's farmers and peasants as useless, since they were not fit to be warriors and the cultivated land could best be used for pasture and so did not need to be tilled. This illustrates the man's grandiose conception of his task. What the crusaders had not managed in the east, he achieved both to east and west. His kingdom stretched from China all the way to Poland, from India to Siberia. He was an uprooter and an incendiary, and he destroyed the empire of the Caliphs in Baghdad and paved the way for the Turks. Europe was now pushed westwards, and the Mongols, who controlled Russia, pressed ever onwards. At that moment the Turks suddenly captured the capital of the eastern empire, Byzantium. Europe anticipated its fall and no longer looked to the east, for now they would be destroyed or forced westwards, into the ocean, to drown as if in a new Flood. Then another Noah appeared and begged together an ark which would save the Europeans. It was Columbus, on the caravel Santa Maria. [...]

Constantinople was bound to be captured before America could be discovered, but something else also had to occur. We know that Columbus was forced to wait a long time for his ship and that this is blamed on the war against the Arabs who still held Granada. Granada fell – and Columbus got his ship! When the Turks entered from the east, the Arabs, like the Mongols, had to leave the west. But the Mongols, who had accomplished their task in Russia, were now dispatched eastwards to found the kingdom of the Great Mogul in India. This mission was carried out by a descendant of Genghis Khan. He was called Babur and was born the same year that Louis XI died, the year Luther and Raphael were born. He has left some memoirs behind in which, among other things, he writes about his arrival in Hindustan, which occurred at approximately the same time as Balboa's discovery of the Pacific and Cortes' conquest of Mexico: 'I had never seen Hindustan before, nor any other so southern land. It was a new world!' One can thus say the East Indies, which Columbus believed he was seeking when he found the West Indies, were discovered. Columbus died without knowing what he had done, another example of how people do not know what they are doing when they are sent with sealed orders on the missions of the 'conscious will'.

In the same move as the great discoveries were made in the west, the Portuguese settled in China, in Ningpo and Macao, and the old walled-in kingdom was literally shaken to its foundations when an earthquake carried off half a million people, probably of the same type as the children of Korah.

However, the cargo was trimmed, the old earth had been given new centers of gravity apportioned according to the needs of the state of equilibrium, and the news of the existence of the antipodes was spread around the world with undreamt of speed by the newly invented printing presses. The new land, a new world which had lain in reserve for future needs, had no conception of its purpose, the real nature of which has only been revealed in our own times: to gather and mix all peoples, to tolerate all religions and languages in a single nation, all kinds of manners and customs, and where all remember the words of the apostle: 'Ye are bought with a price; be not ye the servants of men.' [...)

All in all the current of civilization moved westwards and to the east, but also northwards as far up as the polar circle. But *always north of the equator*. 'And the strong went out and desired to go forth over the earth. And he said: Go and travel over the earth. And he called me and spoke to me and said: See, they who go to the land in the north, they shall spread my spirit over the land in the north.'

Why does 'the spirit of the Lord dwell in the lands of the north', or all lands in the northern half of the globe? Why are prophets, heroes and lawmakers not born in the southern half, why did the tree of knowledge not grow beneath the equator and south of the meridian?

Perhaps north and south have a real existence after all, although the existence of this dimension is denied by present-day science. It is certain that there is a Zenith, just as there is a Nadir! [...]

V

It was a doctor of theology in Wittenberg, who wanted to reform the articles of faith, and who died in the belief that he had done so, who became the cause of the fall of Roman power, spiritual and temporal. This was Luther's task. Just as the whole art of chemical separation can be traced back to two basic procedures, to dissolve and to precipitate, so in the whole progress of peoples two courses of action prevail, namely to divide and to unify. The task of the divider is probably the most difficult and thankless but at the same time the most effective. The chemist is well aware how difficult it is to obtain a clear solution, while precipitation most frequently takes place on its own.

Luther was a man of discord who began with denial and ended with affirmation, and it is quite unbearable to follow him in all his self contradictions. He maintained to the end, and at all times, that his life's task was to combat papism. But both Julius II and Leo X were humanists and men of the renaissance, who represented the emancipating tendency of the time, and Luther therefore finds himself in conflict with its spirit at the same moment as he is borne up by its undercurrent. [...]

A man of Providence, a common soldier who proceeds blindly without knowing the commander's intentions, a great instrument, a token of contradictions and a rock of offence, a man full of pride and humility, of clear thoughts and unclear purposes, this was Luther. A warrior of the spirit who hated war and armed violence, he did not live to see the religious war, but it broke out the year he died, in 1546. [...]

VI

The whole of North Europe was thoroughly tired of Rome, no longer had need of it, and wished to emancipate itself. It was found to be out of place that only Spaniards and South Germans should occupy the imperial throne, in a distant country which had seen its best days and really belonged to heathendom and antiquity, its christianization notwithstanding. And when the emperor began to stretch out his hand over Poland, the heritage of the Vasas, when Spaniards, Italians and South Germans stood on the shores of the Baltic, then the Swedes under Gustavus Adolphus took the field, fully conscious that it was a question of north against south, the Germans against the Romans. [...]

It is curious that during its first hundred years the new period was preoccupied by petty doctrinal disputes, discussions of religion, and exchanges of opinion. It is probably the case that once someone has an idea or opinion, it is as it were incorporated in his person and becomes his property, which first requires defending and then prompts him to go onto the attack in order to increase its domain, as with any other kind of property. To relinquish one's belief or opinion for another's is rather like being defeated and becoming another man's subject, and no one wants that to happen. Hence intolerance arises, which is nothing but the self-defence of the personality and the striving of the individual to grow and expand by planting the seed of his thought in another's life cycle, to be present and in control in the realm of the spirit. And so a great deal of natural struggle and pressure arises, and these conflicts on a higher spiritual plane become of course more violent than quarrels about mere earthly possessions. Luther probably enjoyed a more intense sense of power when he defeated an opponent in a public dispute than Tilly when he won a battle. [...]

The religious wars cease with the first half of the seventeenth century, and in the later part of this century men's minds were preoccupied with more mundane matters. [...] By its close all parts of the world may be thought of as having been placed on the map. Communications were maintained by sea and over land; post and transport now existed; and in the Thirty Years' War, newspapers began to appear. Ideas now had material means of conveyance, and from this time on all people may be considered as living and working together for a common but unknown end.

But now the portioning out of the earth between the kingdoms of the old world begins. America is divided according to the latitudes, so that the northern Englishmen take North America and the southern Spaniards confine themselves to the south. The Dutch, pressed by their importunate sea, set off on the billows and are found almost everywhere, least of all at home. The little coastal land, Portugal, does the same, and becomes a nation. New worlds were reserved for new peoples, and one hears no more of Romans and Greeks as colonists. They had gone to rest. The Jews are without land but dispersed throughout all of them, following a belief in their mission to extend and maintain the faith in the one true God. But they were also to disseminate western science and philosophy and appear as the masters of the art of trading and finance.

The first half of the eighteenth century is taken up by numerous rearrangements in the shape of the old world. New kingdoms arise and old ones are dissolved, all with the purpose of retaining an equilibrium, and it is with this century that one begins to speak of diplomacy and a balance of power.

The great wars of succession which follow one another reveal a number of circumstances which were already well known but whose consequences had not yet been estimated. The European royal families had, in defiance of nationality and patriotism, intermarried so that they all finally found themselves to be related to one another, and consequently put themselves forward as each other's successor on every demise. [...] But even the common people had been rendered kin by the enlisted armies, which comprised all peoples. They were truly cosmopolitan, not least because of the frequent changes of nationality that arose from the continual to and fro of conquest. In parts of the north the French were Englishmen one minute and Spaniards the next. Certain of the Dutch had been alternately French, German and Spanish. And what hadn't the Italians been, not to mention the Greeks, who for the moment were Turks!

Anyway, the states of Europe were now not even races but abstract ideas, amalgamations of peoples of different religions, different languages, differing customs and traditions, and so long as the sovereigns regarded the lands and people as their private property, disputes over the inheritance would of course arise. But altered circumstances and new ideas of natural law and good manners soon brought these to an end.

VII

The map of Europe, completed in the north and west, now begins to take shape in the east, where two new states are formed and an old one erased. Russia, which is said to have received its first culture from the Scandinavians, takes its Christianity from Byzantium, its influx of peoples from the Mongols, and finally its civilization from Peter the Great. Thus Europe obtains a mighty ally against the Turks and a dependable border guard against the hordes of Asia. One can imagine what a lack of sense Charles XII reveals when he tries to prevent the rise of Russia, and what an unchristian disposition he betrays when he enters into an alliance with the Asians in Constantinople against Europe's common friend, Tsar Peter. The Swedish warrior king is still more short-sighted when he attempts to retain Poland, which is now historically superfluous and must fall away like an unused limb. Poland, a provisional country, an improvised territory, had extended itself here and there like a several-celled amoeba, lacking a centre because it possessed three, Gnesen-Posen, Warsaw, and Cracow. An open land of passage without natural frontiers, always sedentary, never sending out hordes, never conquering, never colonizing, it had grown up as a pendant to Austria and become a stronghold of the Roman empire and of Catholicism. For a long time it was a thorn in the side of the Swedes, who called it an inheritance of Vasa, although the hereditary kingdom ceased with Sigismund II, when Poland became an elected monarchy. Playing around with foreign princes – a Swede, a Saxon, a Frenchman – and always occupied with civil war, it first lost its importance when the young Prussia arose, and later fell apart in three segments, precisely as if from the beginning it had been perforated in order to be torn into just so many pieces.

Europe required a powerful Russia, but not too powerful. Therefore Prussia was needed as a counterweight. But Prussia also had another mission: to become the core of a nordic Germany as opposed to the romanized southern Germany. The Scandinavians had dreamt of this role during the Thirty Years' War, but Charles XII's incompetence and political stupidity prevented it. The honour of having given Prussia a start remains, however, with Sweden and Gustavus Adolphus and Charles X. A conglomeration of pieces from Denmark, Sweden, Poland and Austria, Prussia later became Germany, and from the half-Roman Vienna, government was transferred to the harsh, serious, half-nordic Berlin as culture moved northwards. Berlin is not the Prussian capital, nor Brandenburg's, nor Germany's, but it is one of Europe's capital cities, in which all cultures have been intermingled and where all races soon will be too.

The newly drawn boundaries were ready and people began to devote their attention to the inner life of nations. They discovered that many things were out of date and backward, that the new had to be made and the old remade. The second half of the eighteenth century bears the stamp of something very light. It was light of heart and it appeared as if mankind had been given a school holiday. The austere era of penitence was at an end and the carnival followed upon the fast. The teachings of Christianity, with their contempt for the world, began to be taken less seriously, and the sovereign's rod felt less sharp. The people of Europe had had a hard upbringing and entered upon their majority, and the rulers felt called upon to grant their subjects their rights. The fact that the monarchs began the process of reform and thereby served the revolution is the most distinctive feature of the period. Fredrik II, Joseph II, Catherine II, and Gustav III in their different ways did what Danton and Mirabeau would do. Yes, one saw the Emperor Joseph act more democratically than his people and come to see his reforms founder on their conservatism. It was a spectacle never witnessed before, this topsy-turvy world, and ought to have taught the more sensible that kings and their subjects were not entirely hostile adversaries. But the sovereigns served high ends without knowing it. Catherine II did not know what she was doing when she supported the publication of the Encyclopedia, and neither did Gustav III when he granted freedom of the press. Louis XVI is blind when he supports the American war of independence and assists the rebels against their legal ruler. The spirit of the age, the all-pervasive, penetrated everyone's mind, harmonized all thoughts, and mankind awoke again. In France, where conditions had been worst, the effect was correspondingly serious. But this people, who no longer wished to have a king, found itself with an emperor, and then with kings again, before finishing up a republic.

The nineteenth century begins with reaction, a counter-movement against the process just begun. In times of reaction a closing of ranks takes place, in which the vanguard halts to await the rearguard. The impatient suffer and complain until the forward march begins again.

The nineteenth century is probably the greatest of all centuries – the great age of discovery and invention, of constitutions, parliament and social revolution.

Life gathers speed, becomes richer and more intense. Peoples move closer to one another. Japan is Europeanized, China opened up, Africa colonized. And the century ends with religious congresses at which people of all confessions talk to one another in concord about insoluble riddles. The peace congress, summoned by a good-willed autocrat, begins slowly and carefully to discuss the question whether or not peace can exist on earth.

The socialist congress had laboured far earlier with the aim of being able to share the bread more evenly among all!

A quick reading of world history gives one the impression of a picaresque novel with glaring surprises and violent leaps, proceeding relentlessly and with a certain lack of feeling for man's suffering. A hasty consideration of world events makes one more inclined to regard their course as somewhat in keeping with nature's insensitive method of employing thousands of years to form a geological strata, only to break up and recast what it has made. Here, for example, a small state with peaceful citizens grows up, cultivating its soil, fulfilling its duties and thinking no evil. Then along comes a conqueror who sets fire to their houses, tramples their fields, and drives out the meek and law-abiding to wander the wide world, homeless, desperate, doubting in providence and bereft of their faith in the good. Either one assumes that change is part of the design of the world, and sedentariness incompatible with the development of the higher forms of organic life (only plants remain fixed, sleep without awareness and die on the spot), or one takes consolation in the thought that this uprooting from an old, sullied dwelling on undrained land is an act of charity, and when the fire takes hold of the ramshackle houses it is a hygienic measure. Perhaps the expelled feel a secret pleasure in being able to see new lands and leave the patch of earth on which they had lived a torpid existence like oysters. A little pain for a great pleasure! Who knows if the pain even existed? Those who leave home and friends in our time to go to the colonies without really knowing why are probably driven by an unconscious purpose in their own life and in the lives of others, and although it hurts to abandon something old, the new and unknown has the enticement of an enormous approaching pleasure.

It is also possible that history in outline shows events as too close to one another, foreshortened, so that extremes appear too rapidly, unfolding in an altogether insufficiently worked out form, as in a bad play. [...] If one thinks of how the revolution appears in one's memory, then the blazing Bastille surges up as the culmination. And yet it is only the point of departure, for on July 14 and the following days the king sat in Versailles quite calmly, without lifting a finger, although troops were on hand. Louis XVI seems to have taken the matter fairly good-naturedly, for it is now that he reconciles himself with the National Assembly and recalls Necker. No idea of a dethronement or republic existed yet, and it was only in the third year after the fall of the Bastille that the king was executed. Portioned out over three years, with long pauses, with great and beautiful deeds, brilliant victories against foreign enemies, legislative reforms, the revolution forms a picture both beautiful and ugly, but mostly beautiful, and finally of such overwhelming sublimity that seen from a distance it could leave Goethe with a feeling of tranquillity. Either he did not really understand the scope of events or he felt that something was taking place which ought to happen and which could not be prevented.

VIII

History can appear grim, but it isn't, we know that now, we who have seen the beginning of a happy end. [...] The study of the past ought to teach us first a certain consideration for the future, once we see how it proceeds onwards towards a definite goal, and then tolerance, since we have seen how many mansions there are in the house of the Lord, how one child is not rejected for another, or – what amounts to the same thing – how just it is when no nation and no religion can be said to have the advocacy of the great teacher. Unlimited tolerance like that of the freethinker Frederick the Great, who opened a sanctuary even to the Jesuits when they were persecuted, but with the proviso: 'as long as you leave others in peace. If not, the rod will follow.' This was in a Protestant country, however, and since Protestantism was only a negation from the beginning it worked then. But Protestantism has now ceased to negate, and already it has had time to make doubt a precondition, without creating anything other than Pietism, which has become north Europe's 'Only saving faith'. The reproach that has been directed against Protestantism, that it produced nothing, neither a religion nor a religious style of art, is no reproach, for the removal of excessive and cumbersome limbs, pruning, cutting, and thinning out is an important part of the art of gardening. But that two bodies of Christian people with the same religion could oppose one another so stubbornly as complete opposites amazes both heathen and Christian alike.

Each of the states of Europe has had its period of flowering. Some have bloomed again like certain roses in the autumn; others have the prospect of doing so. Palestine stood highest about 1000 B.C. under King David and Solomon. Greece flourished between 500 and 400 B.C., with the successful conclusion of the wars against Persia and under the wise government of Pericles. Rome was mightiest immediately before Christ, under Caesar and Augustus, but Italy in our day is better equipped as a state and probably happier. France was united under Philip Augustus II and Louis XI, became greater under Louis XIV, terrible under Napoleon I, went downhill but rose again under Napoleon III only to sink once more in the war of 1870–1. Something strange happens here: with the political decline of France after 1870 the old Roman country not only retains its spiritual ascendency but, hardened by misfortune, immediately raises itself and takes precedence in literature, art and science, which of course all require an economic foundation. Liberated from the political management of Europe, the Third Republic reorganizes its administration, legislation, education and defence, and at the same time is able to take part in the great division of the glove outside Europe. Thus it seems that states can prosper under very circumstance and the trappings of external power do not always provide Augustan periods. Israel had its greatest prophets in the days of misfortune and exile. The German nation ruled the spirit through its great thinkers, who grew numerous and fruitful during the hard times when Napoleon went backwards and forwards like a steam roller over Germany's fields.

England was outwardly powerful from 1500 onwards, but at its most brilliant about 1600 when it was most threatened and hated.

Conquered Greece subdues Rome through its culture, and with the fall of Byzantium, Byzantine learning spread out into the world to govern the spirit. Never was the North German spirit so glad and full of the courage of life as when the Nightingale of Wittenberg sang, when pyre and axe awaited the victor and civil war laid waste the land.

World history perhaps appears more cruel than it is, and the ruler of this world is probably not the prince of darkness referred to in the Bible. [...]

X. SUMMARY

If in the beginning of this rapid journey through world history we could see no goal, but only made out dark purposes, the goal and intention began to be discerned at the beginning of the last century. All the lands of the earth entered into a closer relationship with one another, people drew together in great common interests, and dissimilarities in education, custom and habit were evened out. In short, there was a great striving for homogeneity, and uniformity became apparent in every sphere. This is of course the way in which Herbert Spencer has described the movement and goal of development: from the heterogeneous to the homogeneous, and this is the aspiration which socialism has discovered and which it consciously seeks to follow.

But development and movement forward can only follow upon the internal interaction of conflicting forces, and we have seen that the entire conscious striving of mankind to achieve this homogeneity has foundered. It seems as if the spirit of history hated the universal monarchies and religions formulated by mortals, and yet the goal of development was precisely that. It was thus not the goal but the means which disunited people.

One wonders with justification: why, when the whole of Europe, excluding Russia, once comprised a Christian society under a single spiritual leader, the pope in Rome, should the split with the Protestant churches occur. The power of the papacy was of course at one time an excellent counterweight to the imperial power and therefore possessed a beautiful *raison d'être*. But it nevertheless disappeared from the history of the North Germans. Charles V was in the process of building a universal monarchy for the whole of Europe, and so was Henry IV. Napoleon had almost realized the idea, yet on each occasion the work disintegrated. The one unites, the other divides, and vice versa, but with every return to the old, something new has been added. This undertaking bears a strong resemblance to the chemical analysis in which one precipitates a solution and then dissolves the solution in order to precipitate again, and in both cases one remains in ignorance as to how it has happened, for only the result is visible. But this secretive aspect of the world process which we cannot explain, this unconscious aspiration of mankind which lacks knowledge of the goal but acts in the service of the conscious will, is what I have called mysticism, which is of course the name of everything which is for the moment, or perpetually, inexplicable. It has been inexplicable to us that two contrary meanings are both correct, for it was our limited intelligence that set up the false assumptions. It was inexplicable to us that so many religions exist when there is only one God, for we could not give a precise definition, either of religion or of God. It is still incomprehensible to us why the people of the Mediterranean should be allotted the role of civilizing and dividing up the world. We do not understand why Christ should make an end of Zeus and why Christianity succeeds antiquity in Europe. But we cannot deny the fact that it was the cathedral, and not the synagogue or the mosque, that was built upon the Greek temple.

We saw states arise, develop with difficulty and in conflict, and then very rapidly be laid waste without our being able to fathom the purpose. We saw great spirits step forward with the call to preach new truths. After struggles and in adversity the truth conquered, only for a later generation to refute it and cast it on the scrap heap. The human race wandered in the desert among ruins without knowing where the path was to be found. The signposts were many, but no one knew the destination. One believed he had discovered the east when he journeyed to the west; others thought they fostered their own power when they were undermining it. A man of the spirit was convinced he founded a new religion when he in fact established a new state. In short, human beings acted unconsciously in ignorance of the end, but a conscious will made use of all the conflicting forces, the upward flight of the spirit and the earthly striving of matter, the good and the evil, selfishness and sacrifice, division and unity. And sometimes the goal allowed itself to be glimpsed at the limit of the horizon in order to disappear again and then once more to show itself. That people do not know what they do is their excuse, but it should also teach them to see that they are tools in someone's hand, someone whose intentions are incomprehensible to them, but who looks after their best interests.

It has long been believed that the course of history has been governed by certain laws similar to those which prevail in the kingdom of nature. Traces of the law of the state of equilibrium have been observed in history (the European balance of power), the power of attraction (the inclination of larger states to assimilate smaller), elective affinity, substitution, and so on. And from the organic world men have adopted the ideas of the splitting of cells, segmentation, struggle and selection and the like. But the course of history shows such a combination of freedom and necessity that on the one hand one must to some degree recognize the freedom of the will, while on the other concede the existence of a necessity which restricts the efforts of the individual according to prevailing circumstances and brings about the synthesis. The great synthesist who unites the opposites, resolves the contradictions, maintains the balance, is no human being and can be no other than the invisible legislator who alters the laws in freedom according to altered circumstances: the creator, the dissolver and preserver, he may then be called – what you will.

CONCLUSION

These articles published here are the sketch of a book and therefore were thrown off in haste in order that the context and the outline should not be lost in the course of detailed research. It is naturally full of faults, but they will be corrected at a future date.

PART III

Essay reviews

The rhetoric of history and the history of rhetoric: On Hayden White's tropes

ARNALDO MOMIGLIANO

I

I may start by saying that the basic reason for my disagreement with Hayden White (a friend whom I admire and from whom I constantly learn) is about the future rather than about the past. I fear the consequences of his approach to historiography because he has eliminated the research for truth as the main task of the historian. He treats historians, like any other narrators, as rhetoricians to be characterized by their modes of speech. We must recognize, says Hayden White, that history-writing like any other form of literature constructs reality by choosing specific modes of discourse, each of which implies a different conceptualization of the relation between the individual and society. With the support of Giambattista Vico on the right side and of Kenneth Burke on the left side – and perhaps with the general blessing of R. Jakobson – White reduces the modes of discourse to four: metaphor, metonymy, synecdoche and irony. Though he gives no precise explanation of the circumstances in which each of the four modes tends to prevail in chronological sequence, it would appear from the essay on 'Foucault decoded', reprinted in *Tropics of Discourse* (pp. 231–60), that in the sixteenth and seventeenth centuries metaphor prevailed, only to yield to metonymy in the eighteenth century and to synecdoche in the nineteenth century, while we are or should be in the ironic age, or rather in that late period of the ironic age which is characterized by irony about irony. This, however, can only be a vague approximation, because *Metahistory* makes it abundantly clear that all four modes are very vital and competitive in the nineteenth century, when Michelet stands for metaphor, Ranke for synecdoche, Tocqueville for metonymy and

* Hayden White, *Metahistory* (Johns Hopkins University Press, Baltimore, 1973). Hayden White, *Tropics of Discourse. Essays in Cultural Criticism* (Johns Hopkins University Press, Baltimore, 1978). Peter Munz, *The Shape of Time. A New Look at the Philosophy of History* (Wesleyan University Press, Middletown, Conn., 1977). Karl Büchner (ed), *Latein und Europa* (Reclam, Stuttgart, 1978).

Burckhardt for irony: in fact irony prevails in the late nineteenth century.

Four basic figures may seem to be too few for the variety of attitudes of nineteenth-century historians. But White enriches, and in a sense complicates, his analysis of the four modes by combining them with literary genres, such as comedy or epic. Furthermore, he admits something like 'mixing of metaphors'. Thus metonymy, as an emphasis on cause–effect relationships, can lead to irony: 'he who approaches history as a field of cause–effect relationships is driven, by the logic of the linguistic operation itself, to the comprehension of that field in ironic terms' (*Metahistory*, p. 67). That helps to keep Tocqueville near to Burckhardt and the other liberal-conservative to whom White attributes an ironic turn of mind, Benedetto Croce. As one could expect from this sample of allegedly ironic historians, straight irony is no longer the suitable mode for our time. White therefore favours irony about irony for a 'history that will educate us to discontinuity more than ever before; for discontinuity, disruption, and chaos is our lot' (*Tropics of Discourse*, p. 50).

I shall not test how White develops his classification and connects it with the social attitudes of individual historians because I feel in no mood to controvert the use of rhetorical categories in the analysis of story-tellers. Why should I worry if a historian prefers presenting the part for the whole rather than the whole for the part? After all, I never worried if a historian chose to write in epic style or to introduce speeches into his account. I have no reason to prefer synecdochic to ironic historians or vice versa. But I have good reason to distrust any historian who has nothing new to say or who produces novelties, either in facts or in interpretation, which I discover to be unreliable. Historians are supposed to be discoverers of truths. No doubt they must turn their research into some sort of story before being called historians. But their stories must be true stories.

I advisedly use the term 'historical research' because historians (it seems necessary to state) do research, as the word *historia* has implied since the days of Herodotus. Nor has any of the historians so far renounced that ancient and indispensable weapon which was used even before Herodotus by his master Hecataeus of Miletus when he declared the discourses of the Greeks to be 'many and ridiculous'. Every story produced by a historian implies the elimination of alternative stories. The process of creating a new story by critical elimination of other stories meant at the beginning of the fifth century B.C. what it still means at the end of the twentieth century A.D., that the true story has to be shown to be in agreement with the evidence while the false stories are shown to be in conflict with the evidence. Two of the oldest and still valid tests for the choice between two stories are what Herodotus called autopsy (being present at the events instead of reporting what other people said) and what Polybius called experience (knowing war at first hand or having travelled in the country the story of which you are telling). Since the sixteenth century an arsenal of new, increasingly sophisticated tests for the evidence has been put together – from palaeography to stratigraphy, from carbon dating to psychoanalysis. We historians of course quarrel about the validity or at least the limits of effectiveness of the various instruments at our disposal. But what has come to distinguish historical writing from any other type of literature is its being submitted as a whole to the control of evidence. History is no epic, history is no novel, history is not propaganda because in these literary genres control of the evidence is optional, not compulsory.

Hayden White olympically brushes aside all these questions about evidence, or rather treats them as specific aspects of his rhetorical positions which do not deserve independent treatment. This is how he deals with Ranke's basic concern with evidence:

> So Ranke prefigured the historical field in the mode of Metaphor, which sanctioned a primary interest in events in their peculiarity and uniqueness, their vividness, color and variety, and then suggested the Synecdochic comprehension of it as a field of formal coherences, the ultimate or final unity of which could be suggested by analogy to the nature of the parts... The comic mythos served as the plot structure for most of Ranke's historical works and as the framework within which each of these works can be envisaged as an individual act of macrocosmic drama. This mythos permitted Ranke to concentrate on the individual details of the scenes that he narrated, but to proceed with unwavering self-confidence through the flood of documents to the sure selection of those that were significant and those that were insignificant as evidence. (*Metahistory*, p. 167)

In this account of Ranke I do not find the two facts which seem to me characteristic of his attitude to evidence: (1) he went into the archives because the archives told him facts he did not know before, and we have no reason to believe that he was wrong on this point; (2) he went into the archives because there he found evidence he could trust, and we have no reason to believe that he was wrong on this point either. In other words, Ranke was concerned, as every historian has always been, with new and safe evidence: the prefaces to his major works insist on this.

II

That historians are concerned with new and safe evidence is one of those indispensable platitudes of historical method which not only White but many other theoreticians of history tend nowadays to underrate, while they were duly appreciated by nineteenth-century theoreticians such as J. G. Droysen who is therefore, to my mind, misunderstood by White. While I was re-reading White's books in the last months I was also involved in ordinary pieces of historical research in my own field. The contrast between what I was doing and what White supposed I was doing was really too much. It is perhaps worth while exemplifying, by the two questions with which I was concerned, what I believe to be the difference between the History we historians practise and the Metahistory the theoreticians attribute to us.

1. Like many other students of archaic Roman history, I have been giving due attention to an inscription of the old town of Satricum in Latium which was discovered by the Dutch School of Rome in 1978 and after preliminary publications has been splendidly edited and commented on in a collective volume *Lapis Satricanus* in 1980. The text of the inscription says:

]iei steterai Popliosio Valesiosio
suodales Mamartei

The date of the inscription seems to be fixed by archaeological, rather than epigraphical, criteria to between 550 and 480 B.C. The text does not separate words, and therefore the transcription I give is already an interpretation. The text is incomplete and various criteria seem to converge into suggesting a lacuna at the beginning of no more than one or two words. We can take the language as Latin and translate it into English if we accept that 'steterai', a word not otherwise attested in that precise form, means 'placed'; that Popliosio Valesiosio are names in the genitive according to an ending in *osio* which appears in words of the Faliscan dialect at the border of ancient Latium; and finally that 'suodales' and 'Mamartei', though so far unattested in Latin, are the equivalents of ordinary Latin 'sodales' and 'Marti'. Interestingly enough, all these assumptions do not bother us very much, though at any moment they can be challenged. They are supported by a great many corroborative considerations. The real problems develop when we accept the translation 'The companions of Publius Valerius placed... in honour of the god Mars'. Leaving aside the question of what they placed, which presumably will be answered only by finding the missing words, we want to know who Publius Valerius was, what sort of companions he had, what he was doing in Satricum, and why his companions decided to make a dedication to the god Mars. If we were able to answer these elementary questions convincingly we would know much more than we do now about the social and political life of Latium in the sixth century. The *new* fact is that a Publius Valerius was active with his companions in Satricum about 550–480 B.C. But can he be identical with the Publius Valerius whom tradition gives as a consul of Rome in the first year of the Republic (c. 509 B.C.)? And was his band a band of warriors? And was Mars therefore already a god of war in the sixth century B.C. – which has been doubted? If it were possible to conclude that Publius Valerius was really an aristocrat of Rome who was active with his private band in another city we would have a confirmation of what some of us have been suspecting for a long time from less good evidence, namely that in the sixth century B.C. 'ordinary' civic institutions were challenged by bands of adventurers passing from city to city in Latium and Southern Etruria.

We are interested in this sort of problem because social history attracts us especially when aristocracies are involved and real power appears in conflict with formal institutions. But whatever may be the impulse to turn to this text, the text engages us in historical research because it is new and raises questions of its own. Novelty is indeed such an important feature of historical research that there are categories of perfectly respectable historians (who call themselves archaeologists, epigraphists, papyrologists, 'chartists', etc.) who devote their life to searching for and illustrating new evidence.

2. In the other research in which I happen to be involved – the characterization of so-called Jewish Hellenism – the element of novelty is less apparent and, at least to me, less important. I am a Jew myself and I know from my own experience what price Jews had and have to pay to be Jews. I am not collecting facts for academic purposes when I try to understand what moved the Jews to refuse assimilation to surrounding civilizations. But I could choose to give an answer to this question in religious and moral terms. If instead I choose to clarify my ideas on this matter in historical terms and I make the Greco-Roman period the central point of reference for my quest, I subordinate myself *ipso facto* to what the specific evidence (the Books of Maccabees, Philo, the Gospels, Flavius Josephus, the *Mishnah*, etc.) will tell me. Of course I am not bound to confine myself to what the evidence tells me. I may

add whatever other considerations I like. But I shall have to be careful to keep my private thoughts separate from the evidence I use. Whatever ideological considerations guide my research, I shall be judged by my use of the evidence.

What is true about me is true about any other historian, past or present. As history of historiography is basically a study of individual historians, no student of the history of historiography does his work properly unless he is capable of telling me whether the historian or historians he has studied used the evidence in a satisfactory way. This is enough to dispose of most of the present over-production in the history of historiography: all these dear little dissertations on Baronio, Gibbon, Renan and Grote by people who would not be able to translate any of the texts which those historians controlled. The result is even more contemptible if the examination is extended to whole schools of historical research. What can one expect from people who write about the history of Oriental studies in the nineteenth century without any personal experience of Oriental studies? Hayden White is not, of course, to be confused with this *inutile genus*. His elimination of the evidence is a deliberate act of interpretation. But can we really believe that Ranke and Tocqueville would be the same if we discovered that they misunderstood the evidence they used or worked on forgeries without recognizing them?

We must not confuse the position of Croce in relation to evidence with that of White, though the comparison may throw some light on the difficulties both have in coming to terms with the requirements of evidence. Ignoring the evidence was not characteristic of Croce. He was by instinct a student of evidence. To save the evidence against *a priori* philosophies of history was his main effort both in his theory and in his practice of historiography. That led him to identify philosophy and history – a step he took, admittedly under the influence of Gentile's criticisms, between the first and the second editions of his *Logic* (that is, in approximately 1907). But having removed the barrier between philosophy and history, Croce found himself provided with a theory of the mind which seemed to assure him that at any given moment any human mind possessed all the evidence it needed. For there is no difference, according to Croce, between the Mind which is the universal Spirit and the mind of a mortal individual. I do not think that for most of the time Croce's own historical research was much affected by this pose. His great trilogy on counter-reformation Italy, his own Southern Italy and Italy after 1870 – the trilogy in which he tried to oppose his own version to the Nationalistic-Fascist version of Italian history – is based on the solid rock of facts. But facts became rather thin in his more ambitious attempt at a philosophical history of European liberalism in the nineteenth century. And what is more, his own theory of historiography, both in the version of 1915 and in the re-elaboration of 1938, did not account for the limitations which evidence imposes on historical knowledge. When one reads the pages devoted to evidence in the book on history of 1938 (pp. 105–12), one discovers that they are limited to the question of forgeries. Croce tries to console himself in the face of forgeries by the consideration that forgers can only imitate the authentic and therefore do not add anything to or detract anything from what we know. The self-sufficiency of the Spirit is left untouched. Croce, in other words, underrated the value of evidence because he never felt he would be without it when he needed it. But White is no believer in the omnipresence of an absolute Spirit producing from itself all the evidence it needs. White, like us, is not certain of the rationality of reality – he envisages chaos. Chaos makes the use of evidence even more indispensable, if one has to *know* chaos. Where does White find the evidence he will need either to live in chaos or to save himself from chaos?

III

It is a sign of the prestige Hayden White's *Metahistory* has immediately acquired that Professor Peter Munz – one of the most learned, thoughtful and rigorous historians and theoreticians of history of our time – describes his recent book on *The Shape of Time* as 'nothing more than a complement to Hayden V. White's superb *Metahistory*' (p. 20). At first sight the complementarity is not evident, but further reflection makes me inclined to accept this claim at its face value.

Remarkably enough, Munz starts from a presupposition which seems extremely distant from White's basic assumption. He sides with the angels in emphasizing that all history is about evidence. Evidence can be explained or interpreted. Explaining the evidence means recognizing as authentic the motives the actors give for their own actions, whereas interpreting means replacing the explanations provided by the actors with our own explanations (for instance, seeing economic motives where the actors provide moral ones). In their turn both explanations and interpretations depend on covering laws which provide the principles of selection according to which we understand the transition from one event to another. In practice, any generalization of experience can become a covering law. There is apparently one interesting exception to the need for covering laws in history: it is when the story is a myth, because the myth provides its own meaning and therefore is 'a story that exists without recourse to general laws' (p. 117).

It turns out, however, that Munz envisages covering laws as necessary for any narration, with the exception of myths. He says on p. 218: 'some stories are true in the sense that all the particular events they contain can be said to have actually happened. Such stories are histories, are non-fictitious.' I have been unable to discover the criteria whereby Munz decides that the events can be said to have really happened. He elaborates at a certain point two criteria – of sufficient variety and sufficient specification – for deciding which interpretation is more persuasive; but these criteria are equally applicable to fictitious events and do not help to establish whether facts are facts.

Munz is therefore correct in claiming that he supplements White because he provides in the covering-law procedure a supplement to White's thesis that there is no basic difference between a true and a fictitious story. I am therefore left with my initial conviction that neither White nor Munz can tell me the difference between Stendhal's *Chartreuse de Parme* and Renan's *Vie de Jésus* (I am putting my case in the most favourable terms for White and Munz!). I must consequently also reiterate my point that the question whether Stendhal relates something which happened is optional – and perhaps irrelevant – whereas the question whether Renan relates something which happened is compulsory and decisive.

To put it in a different way, any question any historian asks about something which happened implies the possibility that what he thinks happened did not happen: therefore the historian not only has to make sense of the event but also has to make sure that it was an event. Unlike Munz, I am not disgusted by the comparison this suggests with the daily work of a policeman (or of a judge). Both have to make sense of certain events after having ascertained that the events happened. But their activities are confined to a few categories of events within defined chronological limits and seldom have any interest for the outsider. Historians are paid by society to inquire about events of general interest, the reality and the meaning of which cannot be established without complex knowledge. Policemen are not supposed to understand, still less to publish, medieval charters. Even judges nowadays seldom have to deal with them: when they do, they are welcome to the historians' table.

IV

It remains to account for the fascination that the rediscovery of rhetoric is exercising on the students of history of historiography at present. After the perennial effort of the historians to extricate themselves from the embrace of the rhetoricians it is perhaps not surprising that somebody should remember with nostalgia that history used to be claimed by the orators in the good old days. It is not my purpose here to follow up the revival of the relationship between rhetoric and historiography, except for mentioning the obvious interest in the rhetorical side of history for any believer in history as ideology. But there is a point in the ancient connection between historiography and rhetoric which is too often overlooked and seems to me to be decisive for any correct evaluation of the import of rhetoric for historiography. A self-conscious interference of rhetoricians with the field of historiography is perhaps not earlier than Isocrates in the fourth century B.C. But it was later generally recognized, to put it with Dionysius of Halicarnassus (*De Thucydide* 5), that Herodotus 'invested his style with all the virtues which previous historians had neglected'. For Isocrates and his school (which seems to have included three historians of the rank of Ephorus, Theopompus and Philistus) rhetoric was the instrument best suited to produce those effects of praise and blame which the historians were expected to impart. As such, rhetoric might be absolutely welcome to the historian. Some historians, however, sensed a danger to the honesty of their profession in the means rhetoric offered of distorting facts. Polybius attacked those historians whose works more resembled panegyrics than histories (8, 8, 4–8). And a non-historian who had reflected seriously on the historian's task, Lucian, added the more subtle remark that the historian's concern is different from that of the orators in so far as he has to relate what has already happened (*De historia conscrib.* 50). In other words, rhetorical devices played an ambivalent role in ancient historiography both by reinforcing the effectiveness of historical discourse and by endangering its moral integrity. Polybius' distrust of rhetoric (and of poetry) in history and Cicero's attempt to make the 'orator' the best man to write history stem from this ambivalence.

I am not aware that this situation changed radically when the humanists took over from Cicero. Readers of Nancy Struever's *The Language of History in the Renaissance* (1970) may think differently, but Professor Struever did not include Flavio Biondo in her horizon. Ambiguity made rhetoric an art which could improve the historian's task and render it easier but which could also cripple it by distorting the truth. The situation changed when historians claimed to be able to carry on without rhetoric. For those of us who want to consider the situation of history historically the first task is, therefore, to establish the exact relationship of history to rhetoric as long as it was accepted – and feared. The second task is to ascertain the conditions under which the separation happened. In what terms the relationship can be re-established is no longer a question of history but of theory. Here White and Munz are welcome. But I would suggest that the second edition of their books should reckon with the historical fact that rhetoric has long been for the historian an effective (never essential) device to be used with caution.

I wish I could say that recent students of the function of rhetoric in the classical tradition have been adequately aware of this element of ambiguity in the relation between history and eloquence. Yet the foundations for such research were laid in 1947 by Fritz Wehrli in less than twenty pages ('Die Geschichtsschreibung im Lichte der antiken Theorie', *Eumusia. Festgabe für Ernst Howald*, pp. 54–71). A whole volume appeared in 1978 on *Latein und Europa*. It contains a chapter by an eminent specialist, Alfons Weische, 'Zur Bedeutung der römischen Rhetorik', and adds the pleasing surprise of another chapter by Golo Mann on 'Römische Historiker – Tacitus als Beispiel'. Though Tacitus has come to us with a Dialogue *de oratoribus*, the authenticity of which is hardly to be suspected, neither Weische nor Mann whispers a word about the pleasures and troubles which rhetoricians gave to historians and their readers throughout the centuries, before history became scientific.

New rhetorics for old

PETER FRANCE

If this yearbook had existed twenty years ago, it is unlikely that it would have devoted a volume to rhetoric. Now this seems quite normal, inevitable even. Why this revival of a subject which not long ago looked virtually defunct?

It does not seem enough to say that it was simply a neglected area in the history of literature which was due for exploration. Clearly the return to rhetoric, in Europe at least, is also connected with the set of attitudes to literature (or more generally, to writing) which flourish under the names of structuralism, formalism and semiotics. More broadly still, rhetoric is congenial to what Roland Barthes would call 'notre modernité'. The modernist consciousness that sets itself against widely held views of literature often takes a provocative pleasure in linking the new with the old. It is satisfying to be able to suggest that certain apparently self-evident features of literature (such as the importance of the author's vision or message or the realistic rendering of the world) are perhaps only a passing phenomenon, or at any rate not as central as they seemed. Not of course that there can be any simple return to the old, any more than Pierre Menard could reproduce the old *Don Quixote*. Rhetoric revived is a very different thing from rhetoric in its heyday.[1]

Once, and for more than two thousand years,[2] it was a vocational art: it taught you how to *do* something, to make speeches, defend clients, sway audiences, or at one remove to write letters or even compose poems. The way to this mastery led through a good deal of practice in reading, so that the rhetoric student did in fact learn what we might now call

* Michel Charles, *Rhétorique de la lecture* (Editions du Seuil, Paris, 1977). Edwin Black, *Rhetorical Criticism, a Study in Method*, 2nd edition (University of Wisconsin Press, 1978). *Rhetorik. Kritische Positionen zum Stand der Forschung*, edited by Heinrich F. Plett (Wilhelm Verlag, Munich, 1977).

reading codes, but this was by the way. The point was to *produce*, and what we now call literature was only tangentially concerned in this.

This practical art still exists (how could it not exist?) and it is still sometimes called rhetoric, especially in America, where a version of the old tradition is kept alive in university departments and in periodicals such as the *Quarterly Journal of Speech*. In such contexts one often meets a distinction between so-called 'rhetorical' (or persuasive) and 'imaginative' (or poetic) discourse – rhetoric is concerned with the former, poetics or literary criticism with the latter. In his recently reissued book *Rhetorical Criticism*, Edwin Black makes it clear that this is not to be thought of as a clearcut division (rhetorical discourse can be poetic, poems can be rhetorical); even so, the bulk of his argument is concerned with the traditional objects of classical rhetoric, the analysis and appraisal of persuasive discourse, by which one should understand such things as sermons or political speeches.

The collection of articles edited by H. F. Plett shows that in Germany too the discipline is not thought of in purely literary terms, and indeed that it can be the subject of vigorous ideological debate involving the reform of the schools and the politics of advanced industrial societies. The volume consists for the most part of rather abstract theoretical papers given at a conference held in Essen in 1974. It is a very interesting publication, which makes clear once again what different things can be meant by rhetoric, even in one country and at one time. The editor's view is that there can be no single view of the subject, and indeed his contributors are often in complete disagreement about the nature and function of the discipline.

The first three pieces discuss the usefulness of rhetoric for modern literary theory, literary history and textual interpretation. Then there is a group concerned with rhetoric from a more linguistic point of view; here the theory of the figures is at the centre of interest. Most of the second half of the book is not so much literary or linguistic as sociological and ideological in emphasis, and here we move from the study of literary texts to the problems and possibilities of rhetoric in society, particularly in schooling. This involves an energetic critique of existing rhetoric, inspired largely it seems by the positions of the Frankfurt School (particularly the work of Habermas) and an ideal of communication which is indicated by these words of Adorno: 'Mündig ist der, der für sich selbst spricht, weil er für sich selbst gedacht hat und nicht bloss nachredet; der nicht bevormundet wird' (p. 294).

Just as churchmen in seventeenth-century France attacked existing rhetoric as a frivolous and/or immoral discipline, so Joseph Kopperschmidt and Hellmut Geissner here accuse modern rhetoricians of excessive concern with technique (whether it be literary style or the techniques of mass persuasion) and call for a new, critical or emancipatory rhetoric. This would aim to increase the student's – and thus the citizen's – capacity for two-way, rational communication (a somewhat similar notion is found, though much less radical in tone, in the last chapter of Black's *Rhetorical Criticism*, 'The Genre of Argumentation'). Other contributors to the Plett volume see such aspirations as utopian and divorced from the historical reality of rhetoric. The debate remains open; it shows in any case the possibility of transforming rhetoric to fit the needs of modern society, and it is a welcome reminder that literary rhetoric is only a small part of the subject.

For readers of this yearbook, however, for better or worse, rhetoric is likely now to be concerned above all with the *reading of literature*. Few of us are in the habit of consciously putting into practice the old lessons of *inventio*, *dispositio* and *elocutio*, let alone *pronuntiatio* and *memoria*. Even the analysis of other people's persuasive speech is not necessarily what comes first to mind when one talks of rhetoric in European universities now. Perhaps to see modern literary rhetoric as an art of reading is unduly limiting – it may also be regarded as a contribution to a 'science' of literature,[3] or perhaps as a guide to understanding the composition of literary works. But in the end the justification of both these is to be found in the process of reading.

The least controversial use of this kind of rhetoric is as an aid to the reading of old texts, texts written when most writers and many readers were exposed to some version of classical rhetorical training. They knew the parts of an oration, they had learnt to recognize tropes and figures, and we may suppose that we shall read their writings with a fuller historical understanding – and perhaps a greater pleasure – if we can revive in ourselves something of this rhetorical awareness. So we have work on the rhetoric of Chaucer, Montaigne, Milton, Racine, Pope and many others.

In such readings the critic will usually try to adopt something of the values which he or she attributes to the contemporaries of the writer in question. This is what Edwin Black calls 'recreative criticism'. In the Plett volume there is an interesting programmatic account of this process by Dieter Breuer, who posits four stages in the understanding of texts written in earlier times. The first is the direct emotional reaction, the second brings a conscious knowledge of the linguistic means by which this seems to be brought about, the third involves understanding the historic specificity of the writing and its rhetoric, and the fourth is the awareness of the relativity of the reader's own literary presuppositions. It will be seen that this process takes the reader ever further from the anachronistic direct response. For the modern reader it may mean a considerable shift of perspective, a revaluation of qualities previously despised. Such has been the case for much sixteenth-century literature, for which we are invited to relearn a love of copiousness and display. More provocatively, Paul Zumthor has recently tried to rehabilitate the poems of the much despised 'Grands Rhétoriqueurs', using the criteria of fifteenth-century rhetoric strongly reinforced by an appeal to modern textual practice.[4]

In such critical revaluation old rhetoric can serve as a powerful corrective to the apparently more natural values of romanticism or realism. Against expressive or mimetic views it sets an awareness of the necessary artifice and obliqueness of writing, an interest in the working – or the play – of literary language. One can see how easily such an approach will join hands with the enterprise of the Russian Formalists, for instance with Boris Eikhenbaum's demonstration of the complex and pleasurable working of a short story which had usually been given a sentimental or tendentious reading.[5] The Formalists, however, chose to place their literary analysis under the banner of poetics and, like the American rhetoricians, reserved the term rhetoric for the science or art of public speaking.[6]

It is as a propaedeutic to the complexities of modern literary reading that Michel Charles invokes rhetoric in his interesting, though sometimes obscure, set of essays. Much of his book concerns work written long ago, but he writes entirely and unashamedly from the standpoint of 'notre modernité', and his work is much more personal and less scientific in tone than that of the contributors to Plett's *Rhetorik.*

His hope is that rhetoric will provide the starting point for a theory of reading which will allow for, or indeed produce, the pleasures of the text, pleasures which are generally those of diversity, contradiction and ambiguity. At the same time he insists that he does not want to open a door on total subjectivity of reading. In his view rhetoric, as an art of communication, should enable one to define 'les lieux où le texte permet la dérive, les lieux où il contraint, les lectures qu'il propose, celles qu'il refuse, celles qu'il laisse indéterminées ou incertaines, "mésurer" alors cette indétermination ou cette incertitude'. In practice this means principally concentrating, as so much modern criticism does, on the reflexivity of texts, which are seen as containing their own 'mode d'emploi'. Thus the opening pages of Lautréamont's *Chants de Maldoror* suggest contradictory notions of the reader's activity, and Rabelais, in such passages as the prologue to *Gargantua* or the 'frozen words' episode, dwells on the very problems of fixed or free interpretation which confront his reader.

In themselves these readings are not always particularly new (much of the point of the Rabelais essays is anticipated elsewhere in a more telling form, for instance in Gabriel Josipovici's *The World and the Book*) or particularly illuminating (the piece on *Adolphe* pursues a fairly obvious argument amid a welter of diagrams). What is more interesting in Michel Charles' book (to me at least) is the more theoretical attempt to suggest the possibilities of a new rhetoric appropriate to literary modernism and yet still related to the old tradition. This is done almost entirely in relation to French literature, principally in a chapter entitled 'Propositions' and in a central section devoted to two neo-rhetoricians, Jean Paulhan and Gérard Genette and three paleo-rhetoricians, Bernard Lamy, Pierre Fontanier and Claude Fleury.[7] The dominant idea of literary rhetoric here is that it provides the theory of what Roman Jakobson called the 'poetic function', but with the addition of a 'conative' element. In other words, it is the theory of the 'effect littéraire' or the 'mise en condition' of the reader. Whereas many of the old rhetoricians were (or thought they were) concerned with practical effectiveness, generally achieved through an art that conceals art, the modern literary rhetorician is attentive above all to the production of the peculiar pleasures of literature, pleasures which depend greatly on splintering the apparent coherence or naturalness of discourse and revealing the space for the play of writing and reading: 'La rhétorique comme art de lire et, plus généralement, comme théorie de la réception du discours, artificialise, dénaturalise le discours... c'est-à-dire, en bref, fait du discours oral un "discours" écrit' (p. 189).

This opposition of speech and writing has a ring of Derrida about it, but it is also a proper reminder that rhetoric did indeed evolve away from speech and towards writing, so that by the time of Paulhan or Genette it can quite fairly be seen as a literary art. The discussions of these two writers bring out very clearly the modernist possibilities of rhetoric. In both cases it is seen as a productive art of reading. Thus Paulhan wrote that 'les figures ont pour seule caractéristique les réflexions et l'enquête que poursuivent à leur propos les rhétoriqueurs'; rhetorical analysis actually brings the figure into active existence. Similarly, and most tellingly, Genette, who is of course one of the most brilliant modern writers on rhetoric, is quoted as saying: 'Mon intérêt pour la "rhetorique" est né le jour où j'ai compris que telle "image" poétique ("l'or tombe sous le fer") *gagnait* à l'analyse: c'est-à-dire la saveur d'une dissonance (entre la métaphore *or* et la métonymie *fer*).' Rhetoric is here an initiation; its function is to liberate the centrifugal possibilities latent in a written text, to reactivate figures that have lost their force, to introduce the complexity which a more message-oriented reading will disregard or suppress. And it is of course essentially a rhetoric of *elocutio* and the figure, the 'rhétorique restreinte' of which Genette has written.

What would the old rhetoricians have thought of all this? It would be absurd to generalize about an art which flourished in so many places for so many centuries, but if one takes the three French rhetoricians discussed by Michel Charles, the answer would have to be that this was not what they were after at all. He knows this very well – indeed, he sees his book as a 'relecture de la rhétorique... à partir de l'expérience du texte, de l'écriture', a deliberate distortion. For the old theoreticians, being teachers of a practical public art, held for the most part to a functional doctrine of persuasion which allowed little play to the centrifugal forces which he is trying to set free. Pierre Fontanier, in a passage of his *Figures du discours* not discussed here, declares that communication (of ideas, feelings etc.) is the be-all and end-all of speech and writing and castigates the abuse of figurative language with the vehemence of a Victorian father condemining self-abuse: 'Que cet abus existe, et voilà infailliblement le style recherché, précieux, incohérent, inintelligible, absurde, ridiculement outré, emphatique, et n'offrant partout qu'un horrible amas de sottises, d'extravagances.'[8]

It is the same with both Lamy and Fleury, the latter indeed being one of the most vigorous proponents of a functional view of rhetoric. In spite of this, Michel Charles manages in his witty essay on Fleury to show how the harlequin figure of playful speech peeps out from behind the screen of good persuasive intentions. And one may well ask whether the vehemence of a Fontanier is not to be explained partly by the awareness of the conventional, normative rhetorician that his art did lead easily into profitless but pleasurable ways?

There is a nice passage in Dryden's dedication to *The Spanish Friar*, where he speaks of his youthful enthusiasm for some lines in Sylvester's translation of Du Bartas:

> Now, when the Winter's keener breath began
> To chrystallize the Baltick Océan,
> To glaze the Lakes, to bridle up the Floods,
> And periwig with Snow the bald-pate Woods

and concludes sensibly, 'I am much deceived if this be not abominable Fustian.'[9] So it was with many of the classical rhetoricians; adult good sense struggled with childish sophistry. The epideictic side of rhetoric led naturally away from meaningful discourse to literary play. And if one reads the Latin rhetoric textbooks studied in Jesuit colleges in the heyday of classicism, one wonders how those who learnt their lesson ever managed to talk straight again.[10] In earlier periods, moreover, rhetoric had been less tightly held in. There was a rhetoric of display, that of Erasmus' *De Duplici Copia*,[11] that of the *acumen* teaching discussed in recent article by Renate Lachmann,[12] or that of the *pointe* described by Jeanne Goldin.[13] Michel Charles could have chosen more congenial precursors than Lamy or Fleury.

In any case, whatever the conscious aims of rhetoric teachers, their discipline must at all times have encouraged a feeling of distance from one's own language, the more so as in modern Europe it was often a training in a foreign tongue, Latin. It is not surprising that those who want unmediated communication in words have always attacked rhetoric or felt it as a threat. At its most extreme, rhetorical consciousness could lead to the vertiginous perils of which Michel Foucault speaks in the afterword to the second edition of his *Histoire de la folie*, where the 'auto-implication' of language is seen as a modern taboo area, more worrying than sexuality, madness or death.[14]

Rather less dramatically, rhetoric has obvious uses as a negative or critical tool, a demystifier. We dissect to murder. Thus Roland Barthes in his description of the nauseating 'code de référence' in Balzac's *Sarrazine*. Nor need the rhetorician's intention be destructive for this to happen. I recall listening to a paper which analysed the rhetorical strategies of Locke and Hume; the analysis was by no means hostile, but it was regarded by some members of the audience as an attempt to belittle two great philosophers. In the same way students resist the pressure to 'take (or tear) a poem to pieces'.

Against such romantic preconceptions, Genette and Charles stress the potential liberating effect of rhetoric. A similar programme (theoretical only) is to be found in the Plett volume in a most interesting article by Renate Lachmann, which discusses the possibility of freeing rhetoric from its time-honoured normative role. Instead of encouraging conventional admiration for tried and tested verbal strategies (and this is after all the purpose of most literary 'appreciation'), the rhetorician would aim to introduce movement and contradiction into texts. Instead of being a pillar of the established order, he or she would become a subversive:

'hier sind neue Ergebnisse zu erwarten, in denen die Rhetorik eine systemstörende, innovierende Aufgabe übernimmt, das eingeschränkte dialogische Prinzip zur Entfaltung bringt und damit eine Dynamisierung und Umschichtung im Bereich der habitualisierten Kommunikationsordnung ermöglicht' (p. 182). This is the rhetorician's Bakhtinian utopia, the 'liberation of the signifier' performed by the discipline which might have seemed the least libertarian.

There is clearly something in common between the disruptive approach outlined here and in *Rhétorique de la lecture* and the emancipatory programme proposed by such writers as Kopperschmidt and Geissman. Both in the field of literary rhetoric and in that of practical rhetoric there is a potential conflict between approaches that one can broadly describe as conservative and critical. Most readers of this journal are likely to encounter this question professionally in debates about the reading of literary texts, but in a wider perspective the debate about practical rhetoric is clearly more important. What matters most is how people become accustomed (in school, among other places) to receive and transmit spoken and written messages – or to put it less technologically, to talk together. Nor is this unconnected with the narrower business of literary reading; we bring to reading the communicative habits we have learnt elsewhere.

What emerges finally from all this is the centrifugal development of a discipline which for all its variations remained unified over two millennia. Old rhetoric held together – with difficulty perhaps – many different impulses. Having the stability of a central element in the curriculum, it found room for speaking, writing, listening and reading, for persuasive communication and the sort of play which we today associate with the word literature. In the last twenty years or so rhetoric has perhaps risen from its ashes, but it is hard to see a common purpose in the functional rhetoric of the public relations expert, the critical rhetoric of Kopperschmidt, Edwin Black's academic rhetorical criticism, the literary-historical endeavour of Dieter Breuer (and of many English and American critics of similar persuasion), the taxonomies of the linguistic rhetoricians, and the Parisian modernism of Michel Charles. We could do with a book on the uses of rhetoric.

NOTES

1 For a more extended discussion see my article 'Rhetoric and Modern Literary Analysis', *Essays in Poetics*, 5:1 (1980), 1–14.

2 A welcome attempt to trace the vast and varied history of the discipline is George A. Kennedy's *Classical Rhetoric and its Christian and Secular Tradition from Ancient to Modern Times* (Chapel Hill, North Carolina, 1980). This book came to hand too late to be reviewed in detail here. It is very much the work of a classical scholar in the American rhetorical tradition; from a European point of view this involves some odd emphases and omissions in the treatment of post-Renaissance rhetoric, but for the classical period in particular it gives a very helpful conspectus.

3 See for instance the publications of the group μ led by J. Dubois, *Rhétorique générale* (Paris, 1970) and *Rhétorique de la poésie* (Paris, 1977).

4 P. Zumthor, *Le Masque et la lumière : la poétique des Grands Rhétoriquers* (Paris, 1978).

5 Boris Eikhenbaum, 'How Gogol's *The Overcoat* is Made', *Russian Review* 20 (1963), 377–99 (in Russian in *Poetika*, Petrograd, 1919).

5 See *LEF* 5 (1924), which contains articles by leading Formalists on the language of Lenin, particularly in his speeches.

7 The main works discussed are G. Genette, *Figures* and *Mimologiques*; J. Paulhan, *Oeuvres complètes*, P. Fontanier, *Les Figures du discours*; C. C. Dumarsais, *Des Tropes*; B. Lamy, *De l'art de parler* and *C. Fleury*, *Dialogues sur l'eloquence judiciaire*.

P. Fontanier, *Les Figures du discours*, edited with an introduction by Gérard Genette (Paris, 1968), p. 189.

9 See A. D. Nuttall, 'Fishes in the Trees', *Essays in Criticism*, 24 (1974), 20–38.

10 See P. France, *Rhetoric and Truth in France: Descartes to Diderot* (Oxford, 1972), pp. 20–3.

11 See T. C. Cave, *The Cornucopian Muse* (Oxford, 1979).

12 R. Lachmann, 'Rhetorik und Acumen-lehre als Beschreibung poetischer Verfahren', in *Slavistische Studien zum VII. Int. Slavistenkongress in Warschau 1973* (Munich, 1973), pp. 331–55.

13 J. Goldin, 'Jeux de l'esprit et de la parole, d'une rhétorique à un art de la pointe', in *Critique et création littéraire en France au XVIIe siècle* (Paris, 1977), pp. 129–37.

14 Compare Paul de Man's statement: 'rhetoric radically suspends logic and opens up vertiginous possibilities of referential aberration' in his recent book, *Allegories of Reading* (New Haven, Conn., 1979), p. 10. This challenging work came to me too late to be properly discussed here. Of particular interest for my present purpose are the chapters on Nietzsche, who is quoted as declaring that 'no such thing as an unrhetorical "natural" language exists that could be used as a point of reference' (p. 110). See also J. Preston, 'The Rhetoric of Reading', *Yearbook of English Studies* 10 (1980), 150–9, a discussion of G. D. Josipovici (ed.), *The Modern English Novel* (London, 1976) and W. Iser, *The Act of Reading* (London, 1978) and *The Implied Reader* (Baltimore, 1974).

Translating the humanists: Erasmus and Rabelais

TERENCE CAVE

In the last fifteen years, the writings of Erasmus and Rabelais have been the object of an immensely painstaking and thorough job of literary restoration. The text of Erasmus' complete works is at last appearing in a proper critical edition (the Amsterdam *Opera omnia*, known as 'ASD') which will itself be sufficient to generate a great deal of new discussion: a striking example is provided by the recent ASD *Encomium Moriae*, edited by Clarence Miller, where this deceptively well known text is shown to have important variants.[1] As for Rabelais, the editions of the four authentic books in the *Textes littéraires français* series, two of which were prepared by Professor Screech, have superseded the still unfinished 'Lefranc' edition. In addition, an enormous number of books and articles on both Erasmus and Rabelais have been published.

Erasmian studies were given a powerful impetus by the double quincentenary celebrations of his putative years of birth (1466 and 1469); in addition the image of Erasmus has perhaps benefited from shifts in modern Church ideology which now make him look like a founding father rather than a devious outsider. Rabelais, by contrast, has become fashionable largely because his works respond particularly well to certain of the preoccupations and methods of recent Continental criticism: the translation into English and French in the 1960s of Mikhail Bakhtin's study provided a powerful impetus here. During this period, Erasmian scholarship has been surprisingly free of major disagreements (surprisingly, because he has always been considered since his own day as a controversial figure); Rabelais, on the other hand, has been at the centre

* *Collected Works of Erasmus*, vols. 23 and 24: *Literary and Educational Writings*, edited by Craig R. Thompson (University of Toronto Press, 1978). *Essays on the Works of Erasmus*, edited by Richard L. DeMolen (Yale University Press, New Haven, 1978). M. A. Screech, *Rabelais* (Duckworth, London, 1979). These works are referred to in the text as *CWE*, *Essays*, and *Rabelais* respectively.

of lively and often acrimonious debate between traditional literary historians – of whom Screech is now clearly the most eminent – and the *nouveaux critiques*. Controversy is not always a bad thing, but the extreme polarization of views in this instance has had something of the effect of a Judgement of Solomon: no one seems to be able to put the two halves of Rabelais back together again.

The three publications which will be considered in the present essay all fall firmly within the domain of traditional scholarship. They aim to rediscover and to make accessible the authentic Erasmus and Rabelais, much as Erasmus himself aimed to rediscover and make accessible the authentic New Testament.

CWE 23 and 24 will form, in the end, only a small fraction of the complete translation which is appearing as it were in tandem with ASD; but the fraction is an important one, being the first instalment of the writings of Erasmus on literary education. There is, rightly, no attempt to reduplicate the full scholarly apparatus of ASD. The aim of the editorial committee is to produce an accurate and readable translation for Renaissance scholars who have insufficient Latin to read Erasmus fluently in the original, and to provide enough information in the introductions and notes to guide the reader through unfamiliar literary, intellectual, and historical territory. This double aim is admirably fulfilled. The translations are a model of lucidity and elegance, while following the original with great fidelity, and Professor Thompson and his translators act as efficient but not over-intrusive guides.

Essays is a disguised Festschrift, being dedicated to Craig Thompson on the occasion of his sixty-fifth birthday. Instead of allowing his contributors to produce a random collection of *nugae*, the editor decided to commission 'a collection of essays on the individual works of Erasmus that would attempt to provide an interpretation of each work in terms of a central theme' (p. vii). His own introductory essay traces a common theme (Erasmus' Christian moralizing purpose) in nineteen major works. The result is very much more coherent than the traditional Festschrift. Each essay presents its text in sufficiently general terms for the book as a whole to appear as an informed survey of Erasmus' principal works. It is not an introductory manual; but anyone who knows something about Erasmus already and wants to gain an impression of the variety of his work would do well to consult this volume.

Screech, too, is quite explicitly concerned with accessibility as well as what one might crudely call 'coverage'. He quotes Rabelais in translation (his own), and avoids cumbersome footnotes. His book follows the chronological order of Rabelais' works, book by book and episode by episode, lingering here and there in order to elucidate a broader topic. He includes Rabelais' lesser vernacular works such as the *Almanachs*, but excludes the Fifth Book because of its uncertain authenticity. His prime purpose is the explication of the historical and intellectual dimensions of the text, with the result that he dwells at length on 'bookish' episodes while passing rapidly over others which, it is assumed, the ordinary reader can understand for himself. His style is clear and attractive to read, provided that the non-specialist is prepared to take an interest in the complex and often disconcertingly unfamiliar questions – legal, medical, theological, linguistic – raised by Rabelais' writings.

It might well appear, then, that what we are witnessing here is the establishment of a monumental 'authorized version' of both Erasmus and Rabelais, prepared by scholars who in some cases (I am thinking particularly of Professors Thompson and Screech and of Margaret Mann Phillips) have dedicated their entire scholarly careers to the task. Although willing to concede that some local questions must remain open, they would claim, I think, to have understood their authors, to have become familiar with their habitual gestures and with the precise historical milieu which gives those gestures meaning. When Screech speaks of reading Rabelais with 'that peculiarly satisfying pleasure which comes from understanding' (p. xi), he seems to echo the Erasmian scholars of *CWE* and *Essays*. Moreover, the images of Erasmus and Rabelais which are presented to us in these works are remarkably similar. Both are evangelical humanists, deeply concerned with the spiritual and institutional maladies of the Church, with the possibilities of moderate reform, and with the Christian welfare of the common man. Both are capable of wit, irony, and satire, but always in the interests of a higher aim. Both are, in the last analysis, extraordinarily serene, despite the traces in their writing of the tensions and aggressions of the world they lived in. A wisdom redolent of great learning, together with an evangelical *pietas*, infuses them with a dignity finally embodied in the Pantagruel of Rabelais' Third and Fourth Books. One might indeed, adjusting a celebrated phrase in Erasmus' *Convivium religiosum*, be tempted to say not 'Saint Socrates' but 'St Desiderius and St François Rabelais, pray for us'.

It is not my purpose here to deny the value of these powerful images, which arise from the best of modern empirical scholarship and embody (hardly by accident) some of the essential qualities of the mid-twentieth-century liberal imagination, tinged as it were by an irenic Christianity. What I should like to do is rather to reflect briefly on what one might call the elimination of problems in these three works. By this I mean the way in which they all (with one or two marginal exceptions) seem to presuppose that a single correct reading is possible, and that this reading is reached when no further serious problems are visible. This is indeed one of the founding conventions of empirical interpretative scholarship, a convention which goes together with the use of plain, self-effacing prose. To make it clear that these devices are only a convention, not part of a self-evident, natural method, one need only propose as a counter-convention the equally plausible assumption that literary works – if not all utterances other than sentences in symbolic logic – are fraught with tensions, uncertainties, and ambiguities which are not secondary but primary: that is to say, they cannot be eliminated except by critical sleight of hand, and should be kept in view as the object of study rather than as an obstacle to some ultimate self-evidence.

The translations of *CWE* are, as I have said, quite remarkable in following the letter of the original Latin while preserving the rhythms and idioms of English prose; by contrast, those of the *Essays* which have been translated from French or German are so full of foreign phrasings that they are at times difficult to understand (unless, of course, one is able to reconstruct the original sentence from the translation). The *CWE* team are expert translators, each of whom has established his or her own stylistic level and sustained it throughout.

The problem – and it is one which affects all good translations – is that the text undergoes a process of naturalization which removes many of its stylistic idiosyncrasies and blurs its conceptual particularity. The very subtitle of *CWE* 23 and 24 – 'Literary and Educational Writings' – renders a Latin phrase ('[opera] quae spectant ad institutionem literarum') which would be more literally translated as 'works concerning education in letters'. One could argue that the subtitle is a mistranslation, since it suggests that these volumes will contain all those writings which may be termed literary as well as all the educational writings: few indeed of Erasmus' works do not fall into one or the other category. Any such misunderstanding would, however, rapidly be cleared up by a glance at the editor's Introduction. A more insidious problem arises from the assumption that *literae* (elsewhere *literatura*) may confidently be rendered as 'literature'. In any individual instance the difference is slight, but the cumulative effect is to tempt a modern reader to assimilate Erasmus' reflections on 'letters' into the context of twentieth-century views of literature as a mode of discourse and as a branch of education. In the same semantic area one might cite the words *disciplina(e)* (translated as 'systems of knowledge' in *CWE* 23.59; 'learning', 23.61; 'disciplines', 23.62; and 'liberal arts', 23.65), and *eruditio* (sometimes translated as 'erudition', sometimes as 'learning' in *CWE* 23.61–6). The notorious problem of how to render *res*, *verba*, and *copia* is nowhere mentioned by Betty Knott in her translation of the *De copia*, although she is most scrupulous in supplying in parenthesis the Latin or Greek rhetorical and grammatical terminology used by Erasmus. A brief note on the conceptual background of *res* and *verba* is provided by Brian McGregor, the translator of the *De ratione studii* (24.666). To take one example from a different area, that of ethics, one wonders whether the overtones of romantic sensibility in the phrases 'emotional impulses' and 'emotive life' do not distort the Stoic notion of the *affectus* which they are supposed to render (23.65 and 99).

In such instances, I would have preferred a more systematic indication of the problems concerned by the translators, whether in their introductions or their footnotes. At a broader level, and particularly in the domain of 'letters', Thompson's general introduction might well have considered this terminological problem more precisely in relation to the history of education. Thompson makes many remarks on the similarities and differences between Renaissance and modern educational thought, but avoids the (admittedly difficult) task of suggesting ways in which humanist educational programmes, together with their characteristic terminology, founded later categories of educational thought; or the extent to which these categories have slipped and shifted under new social and ideological pressures. At the very least one might pose questions such as: how did the category 'literature' come into educational theory? what kind of distinctions and oppositions did it presuppose in Erasmus's day? The history of such words is central to (if not coterminous with) the history of our intellectual frames of reference.

The tendency to erase the difference between Erasmus' discourse and our own affects many aspects of the *CWE* translations and their presentation. One particularly striking one is the disappearance in some of the translations of Erasmus' allusive use of Greek words and phrases. Another, which goes beyond translation as such, is the reduction of the gnomic similes of the *Parabolae* to the level of a quaint and outmoded lore: 'A modern reader who lingers longer over the curiosities of natural history in *Parabolae* than over Erasmus' moralizings of them does injustice to the order of emphasis intended, but he can hardly be blamed' (23.xlix). But the order of emphasis is not so self-evident. The force of the *parabola* derives in part from the metaphysical assumption that truths lie hidden in the phenomena of nature and, by extension, in the authoritative writings of the ancients. The simile may not be simply an illustration, but a 'sign' granting access, for those who know how to read such signs, to a privileged insight. This aspect of the *Parabolae* is apparent in the extent to which it draws on the lore of bestiaries, herbiaries, and lapidaries: it is perhaps significant that Erasmus refers to his own similes as 'jewels' (23.130). Of course, one might argue that in Erasmus one is witnessing the reduction of a semi-occult gnomic tradition to the status of rhetorical ornament; but the point must at least be argued in order to measure and maintain the correct historical distance.

A final example of the way in which apparently innocent scholarly procedures may contain implied assumptions is provided by the ordering of Erasmus' works. Erasmus' own ideas on the subject are carefully (even repetitiously) set out by the editors of *CWE*. But in practice, the order adopted is rather different. The reasons for change arise in part from the problems of organizing such a complex scholarly project, and from the exigencies of modern publishing and librarianship. But there are also positive decisions motivated by methodological conventions. Most striking among these is the precedence given to the *Epistolae* in the collection as a whole and to the *Antibarbari* in the 'Literary and Educational Writings' (Erasmus himself placed the latter work among his controversial writings). The editors have, it appears, abandoned with some regret the idea of a chronological order; after all, for historians a chronological sequence is also a 'rational' one (see 23.xii). The Correspondence, which can be presented in strict chronological order, is seen not only as the 'perfect introduction' but even as the 'key' to the works (23.xvi). It is asserted that 'the modern reader tends to regard [the works] from a different point of view from that of the aging humanist as he looked back over his life's work' (23.xv). But the assumption that the conventions of the modern intellectual historian are universally 'rational', 'logical', and 'natural' may strike one at this point as slightly odd. If Erasmus' works are read in the context of the recorded historical events and controversies in which he was engaged, certain of their features will predominate; others – among them, perhaps, ones valued by 'the aging humanist' – may risk being submerged. Furthermore, there is no doubt a more fundamental assumption lurking here: namely, that Erasmus' writing may be explicated and, in the end, thoroughly understood by exhaustive historical glossing. The techniques of empirical scholarship will allow us to reconstruct what Erasmus really thought, which is itself assumed to constitute a coherent, if no doubt constantly evolving, structure; and when we have discovered this structure, all the protean variety of Erasmus' writing will have been mastered and naturalized. Translation into a comfortable modern English prose is but the most natural and logical consequence of such a method.

It is not possible, within the limits of this discussion, to give a proper account of the many good things in *Essays*. There are outstanding contributions by Margaret Mann Phillips and Clarence Miller, as well as a number of useful discussions of texts such as the *Apologiae*, the New Testament paraphrases and annotations, the *De libero arbitrio*, and the *De civilitate*. Jean-Claude Margolin departs somewhat from the guidelines of the volume to compare Erasmus' *De pueris* with a seventeenth-century work of educational theory; he does, however, recognize and grapple with the conceptual difficulties arising from the opposition between 'words' and 'things'. Although the presuppositions of the contributors are necessarily various, the norm is provided by DeMolen, with his systematic reduction of Erasmus' major works to the proportions of a single didactic intention. Most of the contributors assume that a careful examination of the conceptual structures underlying Erasmus' writings will reveal their ultimate coherence and will thus provide a key to the corpus as a whole.

Robert G. Kleinhans, for example, argues that the *Ecclesiastes* 'may provide an interpretive tool for elucidating remarks on theology and the church which appear in previously written works, for at the time of their composition Erasmus was already intermittently engaged in the composition of the *Ecclesiastes* and his basic perspective was presumably being formulated, though less clearly stated' (p. 255). Like many of his colleagues, Kleinhans has little difficulty in constructing a conceptual framework which, it is to be assumed, represents the 'basic perspective' (and states it, perhaps, more clearly than ever Erasmus did?). A rather more extreme example is provided by Ernst W. Kohls, who repeatedly emphasizes the systematic character of Erasmus' theological thought. One might well argue that it is Kohls himself, not Erasmus, who likes the systematic. Moreover, the conclusion of the piece reveals a motivation of an apparently different kind: 'The more we recognize the important theological concepts of Erasmus, the more we must grasp the entire truth of the sixteenth century, which was soundly debated by Luther and Erasmus. We must make a decision about this dispute... This decision cannot be reached through human means. Only God can grant this unto our hearts, through his Holy Scripture' (p. 79). I say 'an *apparently* different kind' because the desire to systematize and the overtly personal commitment of the commentator to the presumed meaning of the text are in reality aspects of a single principle. The commentator, like the translator, seeks to eliminate the problems of a text and to reduce its distance from the discursive world of the reader (guaranteed in this instance by no less a personage than God himself).

All readings, no doubt, move in that direction: to preserve the distance with full rigour would be to make an alien text incomprehensible. But it is possible at least to recognize the problem, and to allow it to become a theme of one's own analytic discourse. One can insist at every point on the idiosyncrasies and discontinuities of texts from the past, even as one attempts to find a frame of reference within which they may be accommodated. The most systematic of thinkers have their discontinuities and idiosyncrasies; in non-systematic writers like Erasmus they abound. To insist on them in this way is not to suggest that they are simply mistakes or failures of intellectual or aesthetic purpose. Quite the reverse: they are symptoms of the desire that drives a major writer beyond the limits of bland uniformity; and they provide an important indicator of the possibilities and limitations inherent in the sensibility of a given moment in history.

To illustrate this point more precisely, one may compare two attempts, in *Essays*, to deal with disconcerting shifts or tensions in Erasmus' writing. In discussing the variants of Erasmus' New Testament paraphrases, Albert Rabil, Jr, asks why Erasmus made certain changes while leaving other passages untouched: 'Previous generations of interpreters might have found in these examples instances of Erasmus' fundamental ambivalence. It seems much more plausible to me that he was trying to find – haltingly but seriously – a middle path between opposites that would not be reconciled' (pp. 151–2). Clarence Miller, in his account of proverbs in the *Praise of Folly*, makes a similar point from a different angle: 'Erasmus, who experienced and propounded extreme views but who knew better than to love them exclusively and wholeheartedly, managed Folly's presentation of extremities in such a way as to leave his audience intensely aware of the need for some *tertium quid*' (p. 94). Rabil adds up the two extremes, divides by two, and comes up – inevitably – with the golden mean. Miller, while suggesting that

Erasmus is suspicious of extremes, more cogently finds a way of allowing the suspicion to coexist with the movement towards, and fascination for, those extremes (as well as stressing the fundamentally heuristic nature of much of Erasmus' writing). If one accepts Miller's approach, writing will be seen to lead Erasmus into paradox and provocation; it is never simply the serene instrument of a well organized mind. The overt configurations of his evangelical humanism, his moral intention, conduct a ceaseless dialogue with what one might call his rhetorical impulses. In Rabil's defence, it should be said that he is discussing a different kind of work, and that he is countering an outmoded partisan view of Erasmus as a perpetual vacillator, always taking refuge in ambivalence. But to eliminate altogether Erasmus' 'deviousness', the characteristically shifting patterns of his language, is to deprive him of life, interest, and historical *vraisemblance*. The reputation he achieved during his lifetime, however subject to polemical pressures, was not that of a mild advocate of the golden mean. He was, in a sense, one of the greatest of moderates in an age of extremes; but he was also a writer who stirred up controversy, flew in the face of received opinion, and explored an extraordinarily wide area of the intellectual imagination of his period.

Screech makes it clear from the outset that Rabelais is a difficult and complex writer: 'everyone soon finds', he says, 'that Rabelais will not fit into easy categories' (p. xii). In order to help the reader 'to pass from easy and trivial popular conceptions to an understanding of the text itself' (*ibid.*), he adopts the method of historical elucidation practised at the Warburg Institute, which, as he puts it, 'consists in trying to place a work of art back into its fullest intellectual, historical and aesthetic context' (p.xv). Thus he insists on commenting on Rabelais' works in their strict chronological sequence, this being the only way to understand 'the development of Rabelais' art and thought' (p.xvi). Each episode which poses problems of elucidation at the level of intellectual history is explicated in detail, so that the reader gains a powerful grasp of the kind of issues to which Rabelais' text refers and of the angle from which it refers to them. Full account is taken of possible changes of outlook and manner, from the relatively straightforward humanist comedy of the earlier books to the delicate imaginative probings, in the 1552 Fourth Book, into the possibility of supernatural knowledge. In order to achieve his goal of authenticity, Screech has steeped himself for many years in the intellectual and literary writings of the Renaissance, always preferring to read them in Renaissance rather than modern editions. Although he is certainly familiar with modern scholarly work, he gives it low priority in his own writing: there are hardly any references to secondary sources in the footnotes, and the critical bibliography is astonishingly selective given the comprehensive character of the study. Except in matters of detail, Screech manifestly feels that he has discovered the right path to the authentic meaning of Rabelais, and that it is consequently better not to point out deviant routes and blind alleys any more than is strictly necessary.

This, then, is a careful and patient commentary on Rabelais' vernacular writings as an episode in the history of Renaissance thought. Screech pinpoints with extreme accuracy the range of religious, moral, and learned themes which may be discovered in the text; carefully elucidates their theological, medical, legal, and linguistic frame of reference; and demonstrates beyond reasonable doubt that the work has a constant axis, and that much of its comedy is weighted in specific directions. Rabelais' angle of vision is shown to be consonant with, and no doubt in part determined by, the milieu to which he belonged and the ideology of the patrons for whom he worked. In the light of this study, it is no longer possible to argue that *everything* is placed in question by Rabelaisian comedy; nor that he was a pre-Voltairean anti-clerical satirist; nor that he was a proto-marxist, using the medium of proletarian carnival comedy to subvert every kind of repressive authority. It should perhaps be said that it wasn't really possible to argue any of these theses convincingly even before Screech's book came out, and that many of the fundamental arguments in favour of an 'evangelical humanist' Rabelais were outlined long ago by Lucien Febvre. But there is no doubt that *Rabelais* will act as a formidable bulwark against any recurrence of heterodoxy.

My account, up to this point, might give the impression that Screech ignores the role of comedy in determining the nature of Rabelais' work. This is not so. The opening chapter, 'Humanist Comedy', reviews the ways in which the comedy may be understood in relation to the serious humanist and evangelical preoccupations attributed to the author. Space is given to the comic spirit of the twelfth-night revel or pre-Lenten carnival, and to the tradition of farce as reflected in Rabelais' Chronicles, as well as to the influence of Lucian. Screech rightly points out that 'English readers who know their Chaucer and their Shakespeare are not normally puzzled by Rabelais' juxtaposition of the serious and the comic; the exalted and the trivial; the erudite and the obvious' (p. 3); and he admits that 'when emphasising the high humanist and evangelical aspect of Rabelais' comedy there is a risk that other aspects may be underplayed' (p. 6). His view of the comic is not limited to satire; beside 'the kind of laughter which leads to mocking rejection' he places 'the attractive indulgent laughter we reserve, in moments of relaxation, for our innermost beliefs or for objects of awe and veneration' (pp. 5–6). Throughout the study, reference is made to the comic techniques and effects exploited by Rabelais, and to the blending of laughter and seriousness.

It is at this point, nevertheless, that I would begin to take issue with Screech and with his powerfully delineated portrait of Rabelais. The opening chapter is, I believe, rather a concession to the comic – and indeed the literary – perspective than an admission that it should dominate any reading of Rabelais. The following chapter reverts at once to biographical and historical evidence concerning 'Rabelais before *Pantagruel*'. Moreover, in 'Humanist Comedy' itself, broad assertions are made from the start about Rabelais' beliefs: 'Rabelais... is a "syncretist"'; 'Rabelais is a Christian'; 'Rabelais was a humanist' (p. 2). Rabelaisian comedy is seen as part of a 'philosophy'; or again, 'within the dusty encyclopaedic erudition of the Renaissance can be found a *system* of comic wisdom and moral insight which cannot be lightly dismissed as being of only historical interest' (p. 3, my italics). That Lucian is given pride of place as the model for Rabelais' use of comic form is symptomatic, too, of the desire to enclose comedy as far as possible within the realm of humanist learning and of clearly formulated intellectual intentions. The spirit of carnival emerges in this context as the momentary relaxation of a learned man. The laughter which Screech admits to be at the centre of Rabelais' world is a laughter which endorses his seriousness at every point: it is expressly said to be part of a coherent system, blended with the seriousness but never at odds with it. In this way, the possibility that the comic might in some sense pose a threat to the recovery of Rabelais' consciously intended meaning is eliminated – one might even say repressed – *ab initio*.

This taming of the comic is, I think, an error in that it pre-empts or inhibits the discussion of certain central issues. From a literary point of view, the conventions of scholarly discourse as practised by Screech would seem to presuppose that there is a place – a stable, serene, and uncontaminated place – from which the scholar can survey the comic (together with its suspect companions, the bodily functions) and assign to it its limits. This is also the place occupied by the 'real' Rabelais, who knows when to laugh and when to stop, and whose consciousness is responsible for every nuance of the text. One might begin to counter this view by saying that the discourse of *Rabelais* is the inverse of Rabelais' discourse as the reader encounters it: whereas the scholar confidently affirms his own seriousness as a necessary medium for understanding, allowing comedy a major but well supervised role, Rabelais' writing gives *droit de cité* to laughter. Screech passes rapidly over imaginative episodes such as the narrator's exploration of the world in Pantagruel's mouth, whereas in the Chronicles instances of serious discourse appear from time to time amid the comic continuum, disrupting but also nourishing it. For Screech, the confrontation between Pantagruel and Panurge in the Third Book 'guides our laughter authoritatively into desired philosophical channels' (p. 224); in Rabelais, one might argue, the discourses of mastery and of authority are represented by the text only to be outwitted – however utopian they may be – by its deviations.

This point could be taken further and argued in greater detail as part of a defence of the literary imagination against the over-encroachment of intellectual history. But of course that would mean the adoption of a quite different set of analytic conventions. My purpose here is primarily to reveal *as* conventional (rather than necessary) some of Screech's central vantage points. If *Rabelais* is one day rewritten (whether by its author or another), it will remain essentially a historical study, an exercise in literary archaeology. My remaining remarks will be limited to this domain.

The first question which requires attention, one which has already been indicated by another reviewer (D. P. Walker in *The New York Review of Books*), is the psychological and historical problem of the nature and function of laughter. There is, it is true, a passage in which Screech tentatively suggests a connection between comedy and cruelty, and cites Laurent Joubert as a sixteenth-century proponent of this theory (pp. 173–4). But the allusion is a gloss designed merely to counter the view that an inhumanly aggressive Rabelais is visible in certain scenes of *Gargantua* and the Fourth Book. Elsewhere it is assumed that the limits of laughter (what we find funny, what we do not) are broadly similar in all ages, and reflect fixed attitudes towards bodily functions. Screech accepts what he takes to be Rabelais' view according to which laughter is a 'natural sign', common to all men (see p. 409). But it takes little reflection to find evidence against this hypothesis. Literary comedy (and its equivalents in theatre, cinema, and the like) is notoriously dependent on convention. From a social viewpoint, to regard a particular gesture as funny is to respond to a complex set of constraints inherent in a particular society. Belching may provoke laughter in some social groups and be regarded as wholly neutral, or as a gesture of courtesy, in others. Still more delicate conventions govern the distinction between behaviour considered as offensive and similar behaviour considered as funny. In Rabelais' case, it would be instructive not so much to give an account of Renaissance theories of laughter as to examine the rapid shifts in social conventions which took place in the sixteenth century (and of which Erasmus' *De civilitate* provides an example). Perhaps the very possibility of Rabelaisian comedy, and the prominence it gives to bodily functions, is governed by the uncertainties inherent in contemporary attempts to elaborate new systems of convention. Similarly, in contrasting the diet of Gargantua during his education by the 'sophists' and his more moderate regime under the rule of Ponocrates (or indeed in considering the Rabelaisian theme of moderation in general), one would do better to ask how far the ethic of moderation can be related to the evolution of courtly manners or to changes in medical dietetics than to assume that one regime is necessarily gross and the other necessarily enlightened. As Screech himself points out, the comedy of bodily functions appears to have been appreciated at court and among Rabelais' patrons, and should not be associated automatically with a popularist intention. But this is only the beginning of an intricate problem, one which still remains to be properly examined in relation to Molière as well as to Rabelais.

At a broader level, the historical method needs to be adjusted to accommodate those elements which exceed or run counter to the elaboration of coherent intellectual systems. History is not ruled only by the superstructures of intended meaning, whether retailed by monarchs, politicians, or thinkers; and the writing of history is not always best served by the attempt to recover from texts a unitary authentic sense. The works of Rabelais and Erasmus are manifestly unstable. They bring into play most of the imaginative and intellectual possibilities available to their writers, not in the form of a coherent underlying structure, but rather of a constantly shifting pattern of certainties and uncertainties, of conscious intentions and deep-rooted impulses. Their discourse is at least partly mythical; and here myth is not merely a colourful fable to be reduced by explication to a moral quotient. Just as Erasmus' *Parabolae* draw on reserves of imagination which are partly learned, partly grounded in a particular inherited response to the physical world; so the Prologue of Rabelais' Fourth book juxtaposes Lucian, Aesop, and the Bible to create a strangely composite fable in which the ethic of moderation is reiterated in counterpoint to images of sexual and economic desire. In both writers, the none too coherent group of ideas which for convenience may be designated 'evangelical humanism' represents a desire for order, truth, and authority all the more assertive in that the movement of their discourse makes that desire appear, in the last analysis, as a mirage seen from a fallen world.

In his Preface, Screech refers dismissively to those 'passing fads and fancies' which produce spurious readings of Rabelais by contrast to the authenticity which is the goal of his own method. No doubt too many hastily formed views of Rabelais have been committed to print in recent years, and I am willing to bet on the lasting usefulness of *Rabelais* in comparison with theirs. But it ought to be said, in the first place, that the priority given by Screech in his study to the question of language and sign theory is largely absent from his earlier commentaries, and might even, perhaps, have remained absent but for the interest of modern European and American scholars in such topics. Secondly, the 'Warburg' method cannot lay claim to universal truth and permanence: its allegorizing approach – apparent particularly in the later chapters of *Rabelais* – is no longer as fashionable as it used to be in the domain of art history, and its assumption that 'context' exhaustively determines meaning in a complex work is open to question. Lucien Febvre, who is clearly one of Screech's *maîtres à penser*, and who is rightly respected for his innovations in historical method, has himself been overtaken by the social historians who are his descendents. Lefranc felt as confident and secure in the value of his historical method for decoding Rabelais as Screech feels in his own: 'La constance mesme', as Montaigne would say, 'n'est autre chose qu'un branle plus languissant' (*Essais* III.ii).

The extraordinary clarity of the best, the most patient, and the most enlightened scholarship as represented by the three works considered here may thus be said to obscure certain central issues. An incalculable number of readers interested in the intellectual and religious history of sixteenth-century Europe will draw immense benefit from them. But for those who believe that imagination is history, and that imagination cannot be limited to the formulation of coherent philosophies, the writings of Erasmus and Rabelais still need to be explored by a method which conjoins empirical rigour with a more acute sense of the subterranean forces of language. It will be clear from what I have said that I believe the great lacuna in all these studies (with one or two minor exceptions) to be precisely the unwillingness to take language seriously. Just as, in *Rabelais*, the threat of the comic is neutralized by a careful process of selection, so the power of rhetoric, of language escaping the constraints of logic, is systematically underrated (or assigned to the 'bad' character of Panurge). The fact is the more alarming in that both Erasmus and Rabelais discuss, represent, and dramatize that very power from one end to the other of their works. No doubt they too, as rational men, would have liked to tame it. But I would argue that it is their rhetoric, no less than their evangelical humanism, which makes visible the history in which they are inscribed.

NOTE

1 See also *The Praise of Folly*, translated with an introduction and commentary by Clarence H. Miller (New Haven, Conn., 1979), in which the variants are taken into account. M. A. Screech, in a new book which I only received as this essay was being written (*Ecstasy and the Praise of Folly* (London, 1980)), bases a substantial part of his argument on the evolution of Erasmus' *Folly*, and was clearly aware of the textual problems involved long before the appearance of the ASD edition.

Halliday's linguistic model for criticism

ROGER FOWLER

The input of ideas from linguistics into literary theory during the last twenty years, through semiotics and narratology, has been enormously productive, deeply affecting our thinking about literature over a wide range of topics. This fact needs no documentation. Yet, surprisingly, the relationship of linguistics to literature is for many influential critics still problematic: passionate and articulate dismissals by, for instance, Stanley Fish and Barbara Herrnstein Smith come to mind. It is not my task to explore this paradox here in any detail, except that it is relevant to the context of argument within which I want to introduce the ideas of the linguist M. A. K. Halliday. I shall argue that Halliday's theory and practice of linguistic analysis are promising for direct application to literary discourse. By 'direct' I mean simply this: the model relates to the language of literary writings without needing any enabling adjustments either to our concept of literature (we don't need a particularly formalistic view of literature to justify the application of linguistic method) or to our concept of linguistic theory (no 'poetic function' needs to be invented to allow the linguistics to relate in some way which would be peculiar for linguistics).

Examples of the *indirectness* of other existing connections may be helpful. Barthes in *S/Z* or 'Introduction à l'analyse structurale des récits' analyses texts in depth, or designs such analysis; and his approach is clearly inspired by linguistics. Yet he does not use the technical metalanguage of linguistic description, inventing instead his own fanciful terminology. Todorov, Greimas, Genette, all use linguistic terms ('tense', 'predicate', 'actant') but the objects they apply them to are not

* M. A. K. Halliday, *Language as Social Semiotic*, Edward Arnold, London, 1978; paperback edition 1980). Gunther Kress (ed.), *Halliday: System and Function in Language* (Oxford University Press, 1976). M. A. K. Halliday and Ruqaiya Hasan, *Cohesion in English* (Longman, London, 1976).

the customary objects of linguistic description – an agent is a semantic role of nouns in relation to predicates in the linguistic description of sentences, whereas in narratology it is a function of 'character': the 'narrative sentence' is a sentence only metaphorically, the categories of microanalysis having been transferred to a macro level by an analogic procedure. To refer to another tradition of linguistic criticism, transformational-generative grammarians have generally approached literature (if at all) making a special assumption that literary texts are qualitatively different from 'ordinary language' to the extent of deviance: witness the discussion of metaphor as ungrammaticalness by Levin, or the various proposals to apply illocutionary act theory to literature, most of which assume (because literature is supposedly 'fictional' or because it is not face-to-face communication) that speech acts are parasitic, or are mock, or are subject to suspension of felicity conditions.

The beauty of Halliday's linguistics is that it does not need to resort to these kinds of stratagems. Literary texts come within the normal scope of linguistic description, for Halliday; and because the range of structural features he concerns himself with is much broader than is usually the case in linguistics – for example, he is interested in structure 'above the sentence' – he naturally touches on topics that are already of interest to literary critics. Now I do not want to advertise Hallidayan linguistics as the long-sought Elixir of Stylistics; only to say that it is a compatible and suggestive linguistics for the purposes of literary analysis.

One more general observation. On the whole, English (angloscribe) stylistics has been the work of people who fall into one or other of two categories: either scholars of a predominantly literary background who borrow and explore linguistic techniques eclectically (I would put myself under this heading); or theoretical linguists who, without much commitment to literature, make use of instance sentences from literary texts as extensions of their data, in discussions of the limits of responsibility for grammatical description (e.g. the many articles citing e.e. cummings and Dylan Thomas in the mid-to-late sixties). Halliday has the rare advantage, for our purposes, of being basically a linguistic theorist – therefore committed to working out his model systematically and as a whole – who is also interested in, and fairly well informed about, literature. This cannot be said of linguists trained in the transformational-generative (TG) tradition, for whom literature is part neither of their background nor of their data.

As the title of the Kress anthology, *System and Function*, indicates,

Halliday could be typed as a 'systemic-functional' linguist.[1] The two parts of this label suggest the two intellectual traditions which support his work. 'System' recalls the Saussurean – and basic semiological – notion that the value of a linguistic unit comes from its place in a network of relationships with other units: the meaning of 'plural' in modern English is delimited by its opposition to 'singular' in the number paradigm, and similarly with, say, 'past' within the tense system, or any lexical item within the set of its related terms – Saussure's example is that French *mouton* cannot have the same meaning as English *sheep* (although they will inter-translate in many contexts) because the relevant paradigm in English also contains the word *mutton*, a distinction not present in French. Generalizing this systemic principle across the whole spectrum of linguistic levels – meaning, grammar and sound[2] – Halliday claims that a language can be described as a set of systems of options of potentially meaningful items and oppositions of items. (For a tabulation of the system networks of English, see chapter 9 of *System and Function*.) Actual selections from these systems made in constructing texts produce actual structures with their systemically defined complex meanings available to anyone who knows the same systemic organization and therefore can decode. The major difference from Saussure is that in Halliday there is a plurality of distinct though related systems, rather than one inclusive integrated super-system.

But Halliday's immediate theoretical ancestry is not Saussure but the English linguist, J. R. Firth, and before him the anthropologist Bronislaw Malinowski; and it is this tradition which adds *social* to *semiotic*. Malinowski maintained that the anthropological field-worker could not understand what was *said* by members of an unfamiliar culture unless he took note of what was being *done* in what Malinowski called the 'context of situation'. Firth attempted to formalize this context of situation, suggesting that situations, and their components, were regular and recurrent. Thus the principle of *system* is extended to the relationship between texts and their contexts. Contexts of situation are, in Halliday, systematically related and contrasted options within the overall context of culture (a wedding ceremony is opposed to an informal conversation, etc., as cultural occasions). Important in Halliday's earlier work is the development of a terminology for clarifying the major variables in contexts of situation which bear on the selection of what he calls 'register' – the socially appropriate mode of speech (it is unnecessary to go into the details here, but see *Social Semiotic*, pp. 114–15, 143–5). He suggests that particular types of situation prescribe the articulation of different social meanings, and that difference of register (or 'style') is the response to these contrasts of meaning. So in his recent writings registers are treated not merely as socially differentiated speech varieties, but different 'ranges of meaning potential'. It is fairly obvious that one says different things in the register of gardening than in, say, the register of courtroom interaction; for Halliday, these are not simply differences of *topic* which happen to go with differences of style, but possibly profound semantic variations corresponding to the different communicative needs of different contexts of situation. The stylistic (formal) variations that distinguish registers have developed in response to those varying social/semantic necessities. The elements of the communicative process are presented as in a determining/determined relationship: social structure → context of situation → meanings → linguistic forms. These causal relationships between society and language are reminiscent of those proposed by Basil Bernstein (of 'restricted and elaborated codes' fame), the influence of whose ideas Halliday acknowledges.

The following must be absolutely clear: it is not just register variation which Halliday sees as socially determined; but the basic formal structure of a language, i.e., the shape and contents of the 'system networks'. In an excellent introductory essay not reprinted in the volumes under review, Halliday gives this powerful hypothesis a memorable formulation: 'The particular form taken by the grammatical system of language is closely related to the social and personal needs that language is required to serve.'[3] This claim brings Halliday into head-on conflict with the Chomskyan 'innateness hypothesis', according to which the possible forms for languages are genetically constrained, so that the particular form of the specific language a child acquires is 'given' by the community only in the trivial sense that the child has happened to be born into a community in which one of the possible languages happens to be spoken. In Chomsky's view, the community has not shaped the linguistic form. Of course, Halliday realizes that it would be absurd to hold to one of these doctrines exclusively: he does not deny biological constraints on linguistic form, but places very considerable emphasis on social determination of form within the possibilities afforded by biology.[4]

We come to the 'functional' part of Halliday's theory, according to which 'function determines form', a suggestion which also comes under the scope of the sentence quoted in the last paragraph. The background here is the 'functional sentence perspective' of Prague School linguists (Vachek, Daneš, Firbas, Svoboda and others). The theory is that grammatical structures are not arbitrary but motivated by their communicative functions. To take an obvious example, in 'Linguistics I find especially difficult' the object has been shifted to the front of the sentence to make the emphatic point that the sentence is *about* linguistics; as another example, one function of passives is to allow for the agent in a process to be placed at the end of the sentence when that agent conveys *new* information: 'John was eaten by a lion'; another function of passives is to permit deletion of the agent in various circumstances: 'John has been murdered but we don't know by whom', 'Another experiment was conducted', etc. Functional linguistics requires (unlike TG, for instance, which just reports structural facts) that linguistic structures should be explained in terms of their communicative contexts and purposes. There are copious further examples of functional motivation of structure in the books reviewed here – particularly in *System and Function* – so I shall say no more about this aspect of Halliday's theory at this point.

The volumes under review do not address themselves extensively to literary questions or literary texts, except that many of the examples in *Cohesion* are taken from *Alice in Wonderland*, one chapter of *Social Semiotic* ('The Sociosemantic Nature of Discourse') is devoted to Thurber's 'The Lover and his Lass' and another ('Antilanguages') takes some examples from Elizabethan vagabond literature. Halliday has, however, written on literary texts: see his paper 'The Linguistic Study of Literary Texts' (1964), reprinted in S. Chatman and S. R. Levin (eds.), *Essays on the Language of Literature* (Boston, 1967), pp. 217–23 and, especially, 'Linguistic Function and Literary Style: An Enquiry into the Language of William Golding's *The Inheritors*,' in S. Chatman (ed.), *Literary Style: A Symposium* (New York and London, 1971), pp. 362–400. In these books the reader will find, not an introduction to the linguistic study of literature, but the substance of a linguistic theory which is exceptionally suitable for descriptive and interpretative work with literary texts.

It may come as a surprise to non-linguists, but Halliday's linguistics is unusual in admitting 'text' as a valid object of linguistic description. Recently text-grammar has become an important preoccupation of linguists in Europe;[5] but traditional grammar, and modern generative grammar, work with sentences and even smaller units; and generally the interest in sentences is as instances of, or data for the investigation of, the general and abstract processes involved in 'linguistic competence' and 'linguistic universals'. Halliday makes it clear in many of the papers in *Social Semiotic* that texts and their structure are of the greatest importance as the primary units of linguistic interaction, as complete units, and as units with identifiable communicative functions within social context. ('Text' includes spoken as well as written language, of course.) Halliday and Hasan's *Cohesion* is a detailed exposition of some of the structural devices which link sentences together to form unified, semantically coherent, texts. The authors examine in considerable detail and with copious examples five kinds of cohesive ties between sentences: 'reference' (use of pronouns such as 'he' to refer to some entity mentioned in another sentence); 'substitution' (phrases like 'another one' and 'did so too' to refer to an entity or action of the same type as one referred to elsewhere); 'ellipsis' ('Who ate the cake?' 'Mary.'); 'conjunction' (the various logical, causal and temporal relationships between adjacent sentences) and 'lexical cohesion' (repeated or synonymous lexical items, or lexical items in the same semantic field). Evidently this is a survey of some basic 'nuts and bolts' elements of language, and I cannot pretend that *Cohesion* is exciting reading. However, as Halliday and Hasan insist, these are not merely mechanical linking devices but vital semantic processes ensuring the coherence of meaning of a text, making it relate to its topic consistently and comprehensibly; therefore, for the reader, cohesive ties play a decisive role in his retrieval of the text's meaning. The interest of cohesion for the literary critic is partly that the cohesive ties are among the basics of text-building to provide a set of reference points in textual description. Furthermore, these textual features may readily be promoted to literary devices by flouting and/or foregrounding. For instance, attenuated pronoun reference, with multiplicity or ambiguity of pronouns distantly separated from their antecedents, contributes significantly to the feeling of indirectness of conversations in Henry James' novels, making the reader feel like an outsider who has to be exceptionally alert to follow the thread. Or, the thematic importance of lexical repetition and clustering is well known; Halliday and Hasan's analysis of 'lexical cohesion' provides both a model for description and an explanation of the origin of this device in a natural and necessary feature of language. Ellipsis entails closeness of relationship between sentences, and in the presentation of dialogue it is conventionally used to suggest intimacy, tenseness, etc. between characters.

Besides cohesion there are other aspects of textual structure which I have not space to mention; for some important ones, see chapter 12 of *System and Function*, 'Theme and Information in the English Clause'. And of course the structure of *text* is distinct from that of the *sentence*.

Halliday's linguistics also provides analytic categories for sentence-description, but it is his demonstration of a separate level of text structure which is particularly distinctive, and particularly interesting for the critic.

Strictly speaking, textual structure concerns the coherence and distribution of information in a text, and not what *kind* of a text it is. The latter is admitted to Halliday's linguistic theory under 'discourse' or 'genre'. Halliday does not expand on this concept, nor does he describe any genres, so this part of the theory is available for development. But it is clear that these sociolinguistic genres would be analogous to (and would include) the specific genres of literary forms (sonnet and the like) and would be describable in terms of recurrent linguistic patterns at any level of linguistic form; non-literary genres would include interview, telephone conversation, formal classroom lesson, etc. But as we know, some so-called genres are so various in style that they are not susceptible to clear formal description: the novel is the classic example; and outside literature, face-to-face informal conversation has a looser structure than the theory of genre would accommodate. The problems of classification posed by such texts as novels and conversations include great variation in length, and unpredictable shifts and innovations in style. In this situation the concept of genre is less useful than that of 'register' which Halliday has been developing since the early 1960s and which is discussed in many of the essays reprinted in *Social Semiotic*. A register is a variety of a language with typical structural characteristics adapted to the type and function of the communicative contexts in which it is used: stock examples of registers include advertising, scientific writing, popular journalism, etc. A register is a linguistic resource; one or several may be drawn upon in the construction of a text. Now consideration of a text in terms of the registers deployed in it entails a very different attitude from description of it as a self-contained formal structure. Halliday emphasizes that a register is not just a set of structural patterns but 'a range of semantic potential'; and of course these meanings are derived from the social contexts within which registers are formed. The theory of register, and its application in descriptive studies, thus encourage the social contextualization of literary texts. The text is seen as the product and expression of relevant social forces (and, conversely, as an intervention in social process). In Hallidayan linguistics, this perspective is quite different from parallel causal arguments in sociology of literature or the more simplistic forms of Marxist criticism. The difference is that in the linguistic approach the text remains an objective formal structure which is described minutely in its linguistic details; simultaneously the constructions of language are interpreted, their social motivations (functions) hypothesized. Language is not a neutral medium for the ideas which society requires its texts to express, nor just meaningless decoration. Language structure shapes ideas under the constraints of social necessities; texts, constructed thus, are then discourses which intervene in social process. The task for linguistic criticism is the investigation of the sociolinguistic functions of linguistic structures in real texts.

In this review I have attempted to characterize Halliday's general linguistic theory in broad terms, and to suggest its potential values for literary studies. My general characterization has required a good deal of extrapolation, because there are still gaps in the theory and there is still much descriptive work to be done. The books under review do not write out the theory in a systematic fashion; two of them are collections of diverse articles published over a period of nearly twenty years and written for a variety of readerships. But all together, read with care, these books provide a substantial introduction to many facets of Halliday's thinking, and offer analytic tools which promise to be of greater value to the literary critic than the concepts and methods of other schools of linguistics.[6]

NOTES

1 Gunther Kress provides a helpful introduction to Halliday's theory in *System and Function*. See also C. S. Butler, 'Recent developments in systemic linguistics', *Language Teaching and Linguistics Abstracts*, 12 (1979), 71–89.

2 Halliday is extremely fussy, and at the same time idiosyncratic, about his own technical terminology: one can observe him quibbling scrupulously in the conversation with Herman Parret reprinted as chapter 2 of *Social Semiotic*. There are difficulties in expounding his ideas to a non-Hallidayan readership, and sometimes, as with 'meaning', 'grammar' and 'sound' here, I have preferred to use ordinary terms likely to make roughly the right sense rather than adopting his own terminology and then footnoting it.

3 'Language Structure and Language Function', in John Lyons (ed.), *New Horizons in Linguistics* (Harmondsworth, 1970), p. 142.

4 For a study of language development in one child, see Halliday's *Learning How to Mean* (London, 1975).

5 See Teun A. van Dijk, *Text and Context* (London, 1977); Egon Werlich, *A Text Grammar of English* (Heidelberg, 1976).

6 For a fuller theoretical treatment of a critical model involving Hallidayan linguistics, see my paper 'Linguistic Criticism', *UEA Papers in Linguistics*, 11 (January, 1980), 1–26. The model will receive extensive practical exploration in my book *Linguistic Criticism* (Oxford, forthcoming).

On Hugh MacDiarmid's *Complete Poems 1920–1976*

EDWIN MORGAN

The long-awaited *Complete Poems* of Hugh MacDiarmid is a publishing event of some importance. The *Collected Poems* of 1962 (revised edition 1967) was well known to have a great number of omissions, and was an unsatisfactory book in other ways. The present two-volume edition will therefore be warmly welcomed by admirers of MacDiarmid and also by those who have not yet plunged into his extraordinary poetry. He would be a bold man who would ever claim an edition of MacDiarmid, even this 1400-page one, to be 'complete'. Here, for example, one will find only six of the twelve satirical poems privately printed by Duncan Glen in a booklet of 1965 called *Poet at Play*. Now, however, we have for the first time a real feeling of MacDiarmid's *oeuvre*, made available in a handy and well-printed form, the business of looking at his work as a whole being additionally stimulated by the inclusion of two hundred pages of hitherto uncollected poems from books and periodicals.

A review has also to point out some shortcomings in the two volumes, even if these shortcomings can be readily explained, and in a sense defended. There is a brief preface from the poet himself, explaining that the poems are presented in order of book publication, not of date of composition, but there is absolutely nothing from the two editors, either by way of introduction or in the matter of notes; it is to all intents and purposes a plain text. There is a glossary but it is of very limited usefulness; you will still have to scour dictionaries for scores of words whose meaning cannot be guessed from the context. So what is the reader with no access to the *Scottish National Dictionary* to do – to fall back on incantation, on surmise, on 'verbal magic', on phonic suggestion? Here it seems the editors were very much in the hands of the poet

* Hugh MacDiarmid, *Complete Poems 1920–1976*, edited by Michael Grieve and W. R. Aitken, 2 vols. (Martin Brian & O'Keeffe, London, 1978). *The Socialist Poems of Hugh MacDiarmid*, edited by T. S. Law and Thurso Berwick (Routledge, London, 1978).

himself, although they do not say so in the book. W. R. Aitken explained in a speech in Edinburgh in December 1978 (printed in *Aquarius*, 11 (1979), 11–13) that he and Michael Grieve (the poet's son) had strict instructions from MacDiarmid to produce as plain a text as possible, using only such glossaries as the poet had supplied in the past, and giving 'no additional explanatory annotations and/or elucidations at all'. Under these circumstances, the poet's clearly expressed wishes had to be met, though one may still regret that the editors did not, to avoid misunderstanding, include a prefatory note explaining their position. Anyone who knows the shortcomings of the earlier editions, riddled as they were with errors of every kind, will admire the self-effacing diligence with which the silent correction of so many mistakes has now been made. In volumes so full of allusion and quotation, often in other languages, the labour must have been huge, and the remaining crop of some two dozen small errors I have noticed in a quick run-through is as nothing among so many pages.

But why did the poet insist on a plain text? His poetry is, after all, far from plain, and stands in at least as much need of annotation as that of his contemporaries Pound and Eliot. He did admit that glossaries (of a sort) might be appended, and he did from time to time, and as far as one can see on a purely random basis, include a few footnotes of his own. But such minimal help as is given is vastly outweighed by what is left unexplained. In all this, there is something of the self-educated man's protective distrust of a too academic approach; but there is more to it. If one asked, why not *really* have a plain text, why have the inconsistency of a half-hearted glossary and half-hearted footnotes? MacDiarmid's answer would no doubt relate to his deep feeling that consistency is not to be regarded as one of the cardinal virtues, and that the habit of mind which could put that question in the first place is already off his wavelength. Elements of surprise, of provocation, of the incomplete, of the recycled (both his own and others' material), of the tantalizing and the delphic, abound. And it should be remarked that even although the poet is no longer alive, no longer able to ensure that his veto on annotation is obeyed, he has at least ensured by his idiosyncratic methods of composition that scholars will have a hard time tracking him down; scholarship, indeed, will be at a disadvantage unless it understands that the only way to catch him is by being unscholarly, by not searching through the best editions of writers he refers to, or the best encyclopedias and dictionaries, which may be quite useless, but rather by discovering the actual books, or more often the articles and book-reviews, that chance threw in his way. The curious thing about MacDiarmid is that although he is not a poet for the scholar, and not a poet for the common man, he can and does interest both. He might well be called a poet's poet, interesting above all to those who are interested in language and languages, yet such a judgement would clash with the tribute a working-class intellectual might pay to the brutal directness of some of his poetry on social and political themes. And brutal directness is no more his ruling mode than the extreme deviousness he shows on other occasions, a symbolist or quasi-symbolist philolabyrinthinism which will attract professional critics from a number of disciplines.

Among the many possible approaches to MacDiarmid's complex work, one that took up some of the concerns of comparative literature would be proper and profitable. Although no great practical linguist, he had a lifelong interest in the world's languages and literatures, in different conceptions of poetry and the poet, in the whole range of poetic forms, in the fates of languages (particularly minority languages like Gaelic or Basque), in cultural history, and in the idea of cultural evolution. His poetry shows the strong impression made on him by European writers – Dostoevsky, Spengler, Blok, Solovyov, Shestov, Rilke, Karl Kraus, Gide. He has, for example, a long 'dialogue with Dostoevsky' in *A Drunk Man Looks at the Thistle;* he translates poems by Blok and Rilke; and one of his own often-quoted social poems ('Reflections in a Slum') is in fact almost entirely plagiarized from Gide's *Journal* (entries for 3–4 August 1935). In this last instance, it is almost uncanny how a MacDiarmid tone of voice seems convincingly to emerge from a new line-division of Justin O'Brien's English translation:

> It is good that the voice of the indigent,
> Too long stifled, should manage
> To make itself heard.
> But I cannot consent to listen
> To nothing but that voice.
> Man does not cease to interest me
> When he ceases to be miserable.
> Quite the contrary!
> That it is important to aid him
> In the beginning goes without saying,
> Like a plant it is essential
> To water at first;
> But this is in order to get it to flower
> And *I am concerned with the blossom.*

MacDiarmid does not always use translation (whether his own or someone else's), or try to turn everything into either English or Scots. He deliberately leaves, especially in his later philosophical poems, passages in French or German or Gaelic or Greek or Sanskrit or other languages as examples of the world-mindedness he is anxious to induce in his readers. Both *In Memoriam James Joyce* (1955) and *The Kind of Poetry I Want* (1961) address themselves to culturo-linguistic problems. In so far as one can reduce the poems to anything definably thematic, they deal with the place of languages, arts, and sciences in human evolution, and such 'message' as they have is intended to be demonstratively brought out by the method of the poems themselves. Briefly, he is arguing for the values of multiplicity: if a language disappears, something irreplaceable goes with it; auxiliary international languages, or culturally dominant languages, must never be allowed to hasten the obsolescence of minority cultures; people should be taught to develop 'word-consciousness' across languages, and languages should be constantly quoted, confronted, juxtaposed, compared, praised, in order to keep their distinctive characters and essences current and active – a job which MacDiarmid himself takes on and illustrates in his poetry. He links himself with Joyce – though Joyce, by his *Finnegans Wake* stage, had moved away from, or beyond, the linguistic specificity admired by MacDiarmid and was perhaps concealing rather than preserving the many languages he used – and with such writers as Rabelais, Hopkins, Browning, Rolfe, Doughty, Gongora, and Remizov. Charles Doughty is one of his favourites, Doughty who confronted English with Arabic, Doughty the explorer who also explored language, Doughty the geologist obsessed by precise terminology, and yet Doughty the poet too:

> Writing of ogival arches, traps, and basalt,
> But equally ready when it comes to the pasterns of a horse,
> The tilts of a camel-litter,
> The nombril of a shield,
> The burdon of a pilgrim:
> Knowing the squirrel's *drey* is better than the squirrel's *nest*,
> Making language at once more rich and more precise,
> And passionate for naming particular things
> And particular parts of things...

Particularity is not everything, as MacDiarmid well knew; but his devotion to it, as against the generalizing powers which language must also develop, seems to be connected with the encyclopedic cast of his mind as well as with his desire to establish whatever he saw as distinctive in Scottish, as opposed to English, experience, whether linguistic, cultural, historical, or topographical. He would be Scottish, and he would be international. What he would not be would be 'British' or 'European', because these terms blurred the categories. Although he wrote in English as well as in Scots, he saw his main task, when he began to publish his poetry in the 1920s, as a revival of the use of Scots for serious work, and this early Scots verse, whether the short lyrics of *Sangschaw* and *Penny Wheep* or the long poem *A Drunk Man looks at the Thistle*, is still very generally regarded as one of the peaks of his achievement. He wanted to show the expressive potential of Scots by a bold mix of the surviving remnants of Scottish speech and the vocabulary of rare or obsolete words to be found lurking in Scottish dictionaries. The vocabulary of Scots, as anyone will know who has looked through the *Scottish National Dictionary* and the *Dictionary of the Older Scottish Tongue*, is very extensive and is full of surprises and delights. MacDiarmid's own discovery of its riches was evidently an eye-opener, and a great stimulus to his imagination, quite apart fron the patriotic and political motives which were certainly present. As he said in an interview in 1975, 'It was like a revelation when I wrote my first poems in Scots... I must have tapped some source deep in myself' (*Scottish Marxist*, 10 (Winter 1975), 9). I do not know how far it is an acceptable idea that there may be a racial memory of a language which has become attenuated and under-used but which was once a full medium of communication, both spoken and literary, in prose and in verse, as Scots was before James VI became James I and took his court from Edinburgh to London, but MacDiarmid bears witness to the possibility, in his poetic practice as well as in his comments. In an interesting unfinished poem, 'Gairmscoile' (1926), his implicit argument is that there are in effect no obsolete words, so long as a language has sufficient continuity to be still spoken; and it is always open to a writer to give new currency to forgotten words if he can set them in successful poetic contexts which at one and the same time recommend them for their strangeness and re-naturalize them in an acceptable contemporary matrix. After asking ironically whether Gabriel will use Esperanto in announcing the Last Judgement, he defends his use and development of Scots as a sort of clarion cry to awaken slumbering half-forgotten powers:

> It's soon', no' sense, that faddoms the herts o' men,
> And by my sangs the rouch auld Scots I ken
> E'en herts that ha'e nae Scots'll dirl richt thro'
> As nocht else could – for here's a language rings
> Wi' datchie sesames, and names for nameless things.

It's sound, not sense, that fathoms men's hearts, and by means of my songs the strong (sappy, bristly) old Scots language I know will throb (vibrate, pierce, thrill) right through even those hearts that have no knowledge of Scots, and do it in a unique way – for here's a language that rings with secret (cunning, cryptic) communicative keys, and names for nameless things.

(The passage, important to MacDiarmid, is italicized in the original.) The compressed and striking phrase 'datchie sesames' is a good example of how the poet tries to 'make it new'. 'Datchie', obelized in the *Scottish National Dictionary* as 'obsolete', has attention focused on it by being conjoined not with an English word but with a quasi-naturalized Semitic word; the subtextual phrase 'open sesame' helps to suggest the meaning of 'datchie' while at the same time offering, in the word 'open', its opposite, so that the sense of paradox ('names for nameless things') is retained. The *SND* includes an illustrative quotation from MacDiarmid (not the present passage); the question that remains therefore is whether the *SND* editors shouldn't have de-obelized the word? Is it obsolete any longer?

I have concentrated here on only one or two aspects of MacDiarmid, but let me not conclude without saying that his *Complete Poems* is an enormously impressive collection which enables readers to begin to understand, for the first time now that all the poems are gathered together, the unity of his work. That there are some bad poems and some barren pages goes without saying: it is something he himself never denied; but the overall effect seems to me to be clear, that he is one of the great modern poets.

The other book under review is a spirited and polemical selection of MacDiarmid's more political poems, with a lengthy, enthusiastic, committed, though not always sufficiently discriminating foreword by the two editors. It contains some of his best poetry, and some of his worst. A number of the poems can only be called 'socialist' by a rather indulgent stretching of that term, but without them the volume would lose something of its sparkle. The fact is that MacDiarmid's political concerns, opinions, and beliefs not only underwent many transformations, and within the whole gamut between 'left' and 'right' (the terms become almost meaningless in considering MacDiarmid), but also existed within a rich, provocative, often playful and devious personality, in the interpretation of which the man of simple and settled views will always be at a disadvantage. The present editors do not come under that category; but they do give the impression in their foreword that they are not ready to pause over the more crucial, difficult, problematic, or merely under-investigated nodes of MacDiarmid's thinking and development. On his Marxism of the 1930s they write: 'MacDiarmid, of course, was already a Marxist, albeit a very idiosyncratic one, who was determined not to concede a single point to any stereotype thinking that Communism might produce.' But the history of MacDiarmid's political development has still to be written, and we want to know a great deal more, in particular, about when and how he came by his Marxism, how much of Marx he had actually read, how much (as with other writers he admired) he picked up in more oblique and unorthodox ways. It is the length of the foreword which raises these perhaps unfair questions; the anthologists have very honestly exposed themselves to comment and discussion, when they might have presented us with a bare *fait accompli* of choice poems and extracts. Their survey is what they claim: 'a challenge to Marxist critics everywhere, and especially to those in the Socialist countries, to come to grips with MacDiarmid in all his complexity'.

Books received

(The inclusion of a book in this list does not preclude a review in this or another volume.)

Adler, Jeremy, *Even in April, Ferrara and Liberty* (poems). Lobby Press, 1979

Adler, Jeremy and Cobbing, Bob. *A Short History of London* (poems). Writer's Forum, 1979

Amacher, Richard E., and Lange, Victor, eds. *New Perspectives in German Literary Criticism.* Princeton University Press, 1979.

Arden, Heather. *Fools' Plays: A Study of Satire in the 'Sottie'.* Cambridge University Press, 1980.

Argyle, Gisela. *German Elements in the Fiction of George Eliot, Gissing, and Meredith.* Peter Lang Verlag, 1979.

Arkell, David. *Looking for Laforgue.* Carcanet Press, 1979.

Ashton, Rosemary. *The German Idea: Four English Writers and the Reception of German Thought 1800–1860.* Cambridge University Press, 1980.

Bely, Andrey. *The First Encounter.* Translated and introduced by Gerald Janaček. Princeton University Press, 1979.

Blamires, David. *Herzog Ernst and the Otherworld Voyage: A Comparative Study.* Manchester University Press, 1979.

Burns, Richard. *Avebury.* Translated into Italian by Roberto Sanesi. La Nuova Foglio Editrice, 1976.

Carey, John. *Thackeray: Prodigal Genius.* Faber and Faber, 1979.

Cave, Terence. *The Cornucopian Text: Problems of Writing in the French Renaissance.* Clarendon Press, 1979.

Cooke, Michael G. *Acts of Inclusion: Studies Bearing on an Elementary Theory of Romanticism.* Yale University Press, 1979.

Cox, Richard. *Figures of Transformation: Rilke and the Example of Valéry.* Institute of Germanic Studies, 1979.

Davis, A. R., ed. *Modern Japanese Poetry.* Translated by James Kirkup. Open University Press, 1979.

Detienne, Marcel. *Dionysos Slain.* Translated by Mireille Muellner and Leonard Muellner. Johns Hopkins University Press, 1979.

Eco, Umberto. *The Role of the Reader: Explorations in the Semiotics of Texts.* Indiana University Press, 1979.

Fortini, Franco. *Poems.* Translated by Michael Hamburger. Arc Publications, 1978.

Foucault, Michel. *The History of Sexuality. Volume 1: An Introduction.* Translated by Robert Hurley. Allen Lane, 1979.

Gass, William. *On Being Blue*. Carcanet New Press, 1979.

Genette, Gérard. *Narrative Discourse: An Essay in Method*. Translated by Jane E. Lewin, foreword by Jonathan Culler. Cornell University Press, 1980.

Gless, Darryl J. *'Measure for Measure', the Law, and the Convent*. Princeton University Press, 1979.

Goethe, J. W. von. *Wilhelm Meister*. Translated by H. M. Waidson, 3 vols. John Calder, 1977.

Goethe on Art. Selected, edited and translated by John Gage. Scolar Press, 1980.

Golomb, Harai. *Enjambment in Poetry: Language and Verse in Interaction*. Porter Institute for Poetics and Semiotics, Tel Aviv University, 1979.

Green, André. *The Tragic Effect: The Oedipus Complex in Tragedy*. Translated by Alan Sheridan. Cambridge University Press, 1979.

Griffin, Jonathan. *Outsing the Howling. An Interlude* (poems). Permanent Press, 1979.
Camões: Some Poems. The Menard Press, 1976.

Günther, Horst. *Freiheit, Herrschaft und Geschichte*. Suhrkamp, 1979.

Hatfield, Henry. *From The Magic Mountain: Mann's Later Masterpieces*. Cornell University Press, 1979.

Hofstadter, Douglas R. *Gödel, Escher, Bach: An Eternal Golden Braid*. Harvester Press, 1979.

Horowitz, Michael. *Growing Up: Selected Poems and Pictures 1951–79*. Allison and Busby, 1979.

Jameson, Frederic. *Fables of Aggression: Wyndham Lewis, The Modernist as Fascist*. University of California Press, 1979.

Kermode, Frank. *The Genesis of Secrecy: On the Interpretation of Narrative*. Harvard University Press, 1979.

Kleist, Heinrich von. *The Marquise of O— and Other Stories*. Translated by David Luke and Nigel Reeves. Penguin Classics, 1978.

Korg, Jacob. *Language in Modern Literature: Innovation and Experiment*. Harvester Press, 1980.

Lawler, Justus George. *Celestial Pantomime: Poetic Structures of Transcendence*. Yale University Press, 1979.

Lewalski, Barbara Kiefer. *Protestant Poetics and the Seventeenth-Century Religious Lyric*. Princeton University Press, 1979.

Lindenberger, Herbert. *Saul's Fall: A Critical Fiction*. Johns Hopkins University Press, 1979.

Maclean, Sorley. *Poems to Eimhir*. Translated from the Gaelic by Iain Crichton Smith. Northern House, 1973.

Mambrino, Jean. *The Inner Gold/L'Or intérieur* (poems). Translated by Jonathan Griffin. The Menard Press, 1979.

Matthews, J. H. *Surrealism and American Feature Films*. Twayne Publishers, 1979.

Matthias, John. *Crossing* (poems). The Swallow Press, 1979.

McFarlane, I. D. *Renaissance Latin Poetry*. Manchester University Press, 1980.

Meckel, Christoph, and Middleton, Christopher. *Bilderbücher 1968/1978*. Berliner Kunstlerprogramm of the DAAD, 1979.

Minton, Stephen. *Petrarch and Petrarchism: The English and French Traditions*. Manchester University Press, 1980.

Mulhern, Francis. *Moment of 'Scrutiny'*. New Left Books, 1979.
Nichols, Fred J., ed. *An Anthology of Neo-Latin Poetry*. Yale University Press, 1979.
Nicoll, Allardyce. *The Garrick Stage: Theatres and Audience in the Eighteenth Century*. Manchester University Press, 1980.
Parker, Patricia A. *Inescapable Romance: Studies in the Poetics of a Mode*. Princeton University Press, 1979.
Peck, John. *The Broken Blockhouse Wall* (poems). Carcanet New Press, 1978.
Pierssens, Michael. *The Power of Babel: A Study of Logophilia*. Translated by Carl R. Lovitt. Routledge and Kegan Paul, 1980.
Plett, Heinrich F., ed. *Rhetorik: Kritische Positionen zum Stand der Forschung*. Wilhelm Fink Verlag, 1977.
Popa, Vasko. *The Golden Apple* (poems). Translated by Anne Pennington and Andrew Harvey. Anvil Press Poetry, 1980.
Quilligan, Maureen. *The Language of Allegory: Defining the Genre*. Cornell University Press, 1979.
Radnóti, Miklós. *Forced March* (poems). Translated by Clive Wilmer and George Gömöri. Carcanet Press, 1979.
Rather, L. J. *The Dream of Self-Destruction: Wagner's Ring and the Modern World*. Lousiana State University Press, 1979.
Redmond, James. *Drama and Society*. Cambridge University Press, 1979.
Riffaterre, Michael. *Semiotics of Poetry*. Methuen, 1980.
Ripley, John. *'Julius Caesar' on Stage in England and America 1599–1973*. Cambridge University Press, 1980.
Schiller, Friedrich. *The Robbers. Wallenstein*. Translated with an introduction by F. J. Lamport. Penguin Classics, 1979.
Scott, Clive. *French Verse-Art: A Study*. Cambridge University Press, 1980.
Scruton, Roger. *The Aesthetics of Architecture*. Methuen, 1979.
Searle, John R. *Expression and Meaning: Studies in the Theory of Speech Acts*. Cambridge University Press, 1979.
Seidler, Herbert. *Was ist vergleichende Literaturwissenschaft?* Verlag der Österreichischen Akademie der Wissenschaften, 1973.
Simpson, David. *Irony and Authority in Romantic Poetry*. Macmillan, 1979.
Snyder, Susan. *The Comic Matrix of Shakespeare's Tragedies*. Princeton University Press, 1979.
Stambolian, George, and Marks, Elaine, eds. *Homosexualities and French Literature: Cultural Contexts/Critical Texts*. Cornell University Press, 1979.
Stanford, W. B. *Enemies of Poetry*. Routledge and Kegan Paul, 1980.
Steiner, George. *Antigones*. The Twelfth Jackson Knight Memorial Lecture, University of Exeter, 1979.
Tanner, Tony. *Adultery in the Novel: Contract and Transgression*. Johns Hopkins University Press, 1979.
Tatar, Maria M. *Spellbound: Studies in Mesmerism and Literature*. Princeton University Press, 1978.
Tsur, Reuven. *A Perception-Oriented Theory of Metre*. Porter Institute for Poetics and Semiotics, Tel Aviv University, 1979.
Vaughan, William. *German Romanticism and English Art*. Yale University Press, 1979.

Vickers, Brian, *Francis Bacon*. Writers and their Work. Longman, 1978.

Warner, William Beatty. *Reading 'Clarissa': The Struggles of Interpretation.* Yale University Press, 1979.

Welsh, Andrew. *Roots of Lyric: Primitive Poetry and Modern Poetics.* Princeton University Press, 1978.

Wilkins, Nigel. *Music in the Age of Chaucer.* Chaucer Studies I. Rowman and Littlefield, 1979.

Periodicals received

Books from Finland (Helsinki University Library, Helsinki), 13:2 (1979), 13:3 (1979), 13:4 (1979). Enquiries to Box 312, 00171 Helsinki 17, Finland.

Bulletin de la Société Française de Littérature Générale et Comparée. Enquiries to Jean-Marie Grassin (Université de Limoges), Le Puy de Rignac, 87700 Aixe sur Vienne, France. (March 1979), Supplément sur Relations Extérieures.

Cahiers d'Histoire Littéraire Comparée (Aix-en-Provence), 1 (1976), Des Lumières au Romantisme: Études sur les lettres européennes; 2 (1977), Lumières et Romantisme à l'est de Vienne; 3 (1978), La Fiction en prose des Lumières au Romantisme; 4 (1979), La Poésie en prose des Lumières au Romantisme.

Chronica: Acta Litteraria of the Hungarian Academy of Sciences, 1977.

Dictionnaire International des Termes Littéraires (sous la direction scientifique de Robert Escarpit) (Editions Francke Berne), Fascicule 1 (1979), Académie-autobiographie. Enquires to M. Alain Boisson, Université de Bordeaux III, section de Littérature Comparée, Domaine Universitaire, 33405 Talence, France.

The Eighteenth Century: Theory and Interpretation, 20:3 (Autumn, 1979).

Glyph (Johns Hopkins Textual Studies, Baltimore and London), 5 (1979).

Granta (Autumn 1979), New American Writing; new series, 1: 2 (1980), including an abridged version of George Steiner's novel, *The Portage to San Cristobal of A.H.* Edited by William Buford and Pete de Bolla, King's College, Cambridge.

International Comparative Literature Association Bulletin, 2: 2 (November 1979). Edited by John Boening, University of Toledo, Toledo, Ohio 43606.

The Kenyon Review (Kenyon College, Gambier, Ohio 43022), 1: 2 (Spring 1979), George Steiner, *The Portage to San Cristobal of A.H.* (unabridged).

Komparatistische Hefte (Universität Bayreuth), 1 (1980), Europäischafrikanische Literaturbeziehungen.

Lier en Boog: International Journal of Aesthetics and Philosophy of Culture, 4:1 (n.d.). International editor: Dr J. Harskamp, 59 Chichele Road, Cricklewood, London NW2 3AN.

Linguistic and Literary Studies in Eastern Europe (Amsterdam), 1 (1979), Language, Literature and Meaning I: Problems of Literary Theory. Edited by John Odmark, Zentrales Freiespracheninstitut, Universität Hamburg, D-2000 Hamburg 13.

New Asia Academic Bulletin (The Chinese University of Hong Kong) 1 (1978), special issue of East–West Comparative Literature. Guest edited by the Hong Kong Comparative Literature Association.

PN Review 13, 6: 5 (1979), Crisis for Cranmer and King James. Editorial office: Dept of English, University of Manchester, M13 9PL.

Poetics Today (Porter Institute for Poetics and Semiotics, Tel Aviv University, PO Box

39085, Tel Aviv, Israel) 1: 1/2 (Autumn 1979), Literature, Interpretation, Communication.

Proceedings of the 7th Congress of the International Comparative Literature Association held in Montreal and Ottawa, 1973, (Kunst und Wissen, Erich Bieber, Stuttgart) 1 (1979), Literatures of America: Dependence, Independence, Interdependence; 2 (1979), Comparative Literature Today: Theory and Practice.

Rhetoric Newsletter: The Journal of the International Society for the History of Rhetoric (Zürich and Essen), 2 (March 1979), 3 (March 1980). Edited by Brian Vickers, ETH-Zentrum, Rämistrasse 101, 8092 Zürich, Switzerland.

Scandinavica, 19: 1 (May 1980). (From the issue of November 1980 *Scandinavica* is presenting all Scandinavian material in translation as well as in the original. Much of the material is of general interest to comparatists as well as to specialists in Scandinavian studies.) Edited by James McFarlane, School of Modern Languages and European History, University of East Anglia, Norwich, England.

Stand, 21: 2 (1980). Edited by Jon Silkin, 19 Haldane Terrace, Newcastle upon Tyne, NE2 3AN.

Structuralist Review: A Journal of Theory, Criticism, and Pedagogy, 1: 1 (Spring 1978). Enquiries to W. P. Kelly, Department of English, Queen's College, City University of New York, Flushing, New York 11367.

Swedish Books, 1 (1979), 2 (1979). Enquiries to Box 2387, S-403 16 Göteborg, Sweden.

Synthesis (Bulletin du Comité National de Littérature Comparée de la République Socialiste de Romanie), 6 (1979).

Travaux et Mémoires (Publications de l'U.E.R. des Lettres et Sciences Humaines de Limoges), (May 1973), Littérature française – littérature comparée; (October 1976), Littérature compareé.

Yearbook of Comparative and General Literature (edited by Horst Frenz, Indiana University, Bloomington, Indiana), No 26 (1977), including a List of Translations in Periodicals and Magazines 1971–1975; No 27 (1978), including a List of Translations in Periodicals and Magazines 1976–1977.

Zeitschrift für Semiotik, 1: 4 (1979), Semiotik als philosophische Propädeutik – Die Zeichentheorie der deutschen Aufklärung; 1: 1/2 (1980), Ikonismus in den natürlichen Sprachen. Edited by Roland Posner, Institut für Linguistik, Technische Universität, D-1000 Berlin 10.

Bibliography of rhetoric studies, 1970–1980

Compiled by Brian Vickers

This bibliography is restricted to new books published since 1970, excluding reprints and facsimile editions.

Titles marked with an asterisk contain bibliography of work published before 1970. Place of publication is London unless otherwise stated, or in the case of university presses where place is omitted.

1. GENERAL (INCLUDING STUDIES OF MORE THAN ONE PERIOD)

Badura, B., Badura, Ch. Geissner, H. *et al. Reden und reden lassen. Rhetorische Kommunikation*. Stuttgart, Deutsche Verlags-Anstalt, 1975.

Bitzer, L. F. and Black, E., eds. *The Prospect of Rhetoric*. Englewood Cliffs, N.J., Prentice-Hall 1971.

Bolgar, R. R. ed. *Classical Influences on European Culture, A.D. 500–1500*. Cambridge University Press, 1971

Brown, R. L. and Steinmann, M. *Rhetoric 78. Proceedings of Theory of Rhetoric. An Interdisciplinary Conference*. University of Minnesota Center for Advanced Studies in Language, Style, and Literary Theory, 1979.

Burks, D. M., ed. *Rhetoric, Philosophy, and Literature: An Exploration*. Indiana, Purdue University Press, 1978.

Chaneles, S., and Snyder, J. '*that pestilent cosmetic, rhetoric*'. New York, Grossman, 1972.

Caplan, H. *Of Eloquence. Studies in Ancient and Medieval Rhetoric*. Edited by A. King and H. North. Cornell University Press, 1970.

Charles, M. *Rhétorique de la lecture*. Paris, Seuil, 1977.

Chevallier, R., ed. *Colloque sur la rhétorique*. Paris, Société d'édition Les Belles Lettres, 1979.

*Constable, G. *Letters and Letter-Collections*. Typologie des sources du Moyen Âge Occidental, fasc. 17. Turnhout, Belgium, Brepols, 1976.

Dixon, P. *Rhetoric*. London, Methuen, 1971.

Dubois, J., *et al.* [groupe μ de Liège]. *Rhétorique générale*. Paris, Librairie Larousse, 1970.
Rhétorique de la poésie. Lecture linéaire, lecture tabulaire. Brussels, Presses Universitaires de France, 1977.

Dyck, J., ed. *Rhetorik in der Schule*. Kronberg, Scriptor, 1974.
Athen und Jerusalem. Die Tradition der argumentativen Verknüpfung von Bibel und Poesie im 17. und 18. Jahrhundert. Munich, Beck, 1977.
Fisher, W. R., ed. *Rhetoric: A Tradition in Transition*. Michigan State University Press, 1974.
Florescu, V. *La Retorica nel suo sviluppo storico*. Translated from the Romanian. Bologna, Il Mulino, 1971.
Folena, G., ed. *Attualità della Retorica*. Quaderni del Circolo Filologico-Linguistico Padovano 6. Padua, Liviana, 1975.
Poetica e Stile. Quaderni del Circolo Filologico-Linguistico Padovano 8. Padua, Liviana, 1976.
Retorica e Politica. Quaderni del Circolo Filologico-Linguistico Padovano 9. Padua, Liviana, 1977.
Retorica e Poetica. Quaderni del Circolo Filologico-Linguistico Padovano 10. Padua, Liviana, 1979.
*France, P. *Rhetoric and Truth in France, Descartes to Diderot*. Oxford University Press, 1972.
Geissner, H. ed. *Rhetorik*. Munich, Bayerischer Schulbuch-Verlag, 1973; fourth edition 1978.
Genette, G. *Figures III*. Paris, Seuil, 1972.
Grassi, E. *Macht des Bildes, Ohnmacht der rationalen Sprache. Zur Rettung des Rhetorischen*. Munich, Fink, 1970; second edition 1980.
Rhetoric as Philosophy: The Humanist Tradition. Pennsylvania University Press, 1980.
Gray, B. *The Grammatical Foundations of Rhetoric. Discourse Analysis*. Berlin and New York, de Gruyter, 1977.
Harper, N. L. *Human Communication Theory. The History of a Paradigm*. Rochelle Park, N.J., Hayden, 1979.
*Horner, W. P. *Selected Annotated Bibliography of Rhetoric for the English Scholar*. Boston, G. K. Hall, 1980.
Howell, W. S. *Poetics, Rhetoric, and Logic. Studies in the Basic Disciplines of Criticism*. Cornell University Press, 1975.
IJsseling, S. *Rhetoric and Philosophy in Conflict. An Historical Survey*. The Hague, Marinus Nijhoff, 1976.
*Kennedy, G. A. *Classical Rhetoric and its Christian and Secular Tradition from Ancient to Modern Times*. University of North Carolina Press, 1980.
Kibédi Varga, A. *Rhétorique et Littérature. Études de structures classiques*. Paris, Didier, 1970.
Kopperschmidt, J. *Allgemeine Rhetorik. Einführung in die Theorie der Persuasiven Kommunikation*. Stuttgart, Kohlhammer, 1973.
Kustas, G. L. *Studies in Byzantine Rhetoric*. Thessalonika, Patriarchal Institute for Patristic Studies, 1973.
Matlon, R. J. and I. R., eds. *Index to Journals in Communication Studies through 1974*. Falls Church, Va, Speech Communication Association, 1975.
Mohrmann, G. P. *et al*., eds. *Explorations in Rhetorical Criticism*. Pennsylvania State University Press, 1973.

Michael, I. *English Grammatical Categories and the Tradition to 1800*. Cambridge University Press, 1970.

Ong, W. J. *Rhetoric, Romance, and Technology. Studies in the Interaction of Expression and Culture*. Cornell University Press, 1971.

Plett, H. G. *Einführung in die rhetorische Textanalyse*. Hamburg, Helmut Buske Verlag, 1971.

**Textwissenschaft und Textanalyse*. Heidelberg, Quelle & Meyer, 1975.

*ed. *Rhetorik. Kritische Positionen zum Stand der Forschung*. Munich, Fink, 1977.

*Scaglione, A. *Ars Grammatica. A Bibliographic Survey, Two Essays*... (The Hague and Paris, Mouton, 1970.

The Classical Theory of Composition. From its Origins to the Present. A Historical Survey. University of North Carolina Press, 1972.

*Schanze, H., ed. *Rhetorik. Beiträge zu ihrer Geschichte in Deutschland vom 16.-20. Jahrhundert*. Frankfurt/Main, Athenaion, 1974.

*Ueding, G. *Einführung in die Rhetorik. Geschichte, Technik, Methode*. Stuttgart, Metzler, 1976.

*Vickers, B. *Classical Rhetoric in English Poetry*. Macmillan, 1970.

White, E. E., ed. *Rhetoric in Transition: Studies in the Nature and Uses of Rhetoric*. Pennsylvania State University Press, 1980.

II. CLASSICAL

*Benson, Th.W. and Prosser, M. H. eds. *Readings in Classical Rhetoric*. Indiana University Press, 1972.

*Bonner, S. F. *Education in Ancient Rome. From the Elder Cato to the Younger Pliny*. Methuen, 1977.

Bowen, J. *A History of Education. I. The Ancient World*. Methuen, 1972.

Brooks, E. *Rutilii Lupi 'De Figuris Sententiarum et Elocutionis'*. Leiden, Brill, 1971.

Clarke, M. L. *Higher Education in the Ancient World*. Routledge and Kegan Paul, 1971.

Dionysius of Halicarnassus. *Critical Essays I*. Edited by S. Usher. London and Cambridge, Mass., Loeb Library, 1974.

Dorey, T. A., ed. *Empire and Aftermath. Silver Latin II*. London and Boston, Routledge and Kegan Paul, 1975.

Eisenhut, W. *Einführung in die antike Rhetorik und ihre Geschichte*. Darmstadt, Wissenschaftliche Buchgesellschaft, 1974.

*Erickson, K. V., ed. *Aristotle: The Classical Heritage of Rhetoric*. Metuchen, N. J., Scarecrow Press, 1974.

ed. *Aristotle's Rhetoric: Five Centuries of Philological Research*. Metuchen, N. J., Scarecrow Press, 1975.

Fairweather, J. *Seneca the Elder*. Cambridge University Press, 1980.

Fuhrmann, M. *Einführung in die antike Dichtungstheorie*. Darmstadt, Wissenschaftliche Buchgesellschaft, 1973.

Hadot, P. *Marius Victorinus, Recherches sur sa vie et ses œuvres*. Paris, Études Augustiniennes, 1971.

*Kennedy, G. A. *The Art of Rhetoric in the Roman World*. Princeton University Press, 1972.

Martin, J. *Antike Rhetorik: Technik und Methode*. Munich, Beck, 1974.
Murphy, J. J., ed. *A Synoptic History of Classical Rhetoric*. New York, Random House, 1972.
Patterson, A. M. *Hermogenes and the Renaissance: Seven Ideas of Style*. Princeton University Press, 1970.
Quintilian. *Institutio Oratoria*. Edited by M. Winterbottom, 2 vols. Oxford University Press, 1970.
*Russell, D. A. and Winterbottom, M. eds. *Ancient Literary Criticism*. Oxford University Press, 1972.
Schindel, U. *Die lateinischen Figurenlehren des 5. bis. 7. Jahrhunderts und Donats Vergil-Kommentar*. Göttingen, Vandenhoeck und Ruprecht, 1975.
Seneca the Elder, *Declamations*. Edited and translated by M. Winterbottom, 2 vols. London and Cambridge, Mass., Loeb Library, 1974.
Schmidt, P. L. *Politik und Dichtung in der Panegyrik Claudians*. Konstanz, Universitätsverlag, 1976.
*Sider, R. D. *Ancient Rhetoric and the Art of Tertullian*. Oxford University Press, 1971.
Sprague, R., ed. *The Older Sophists*. University of South Carolina Press, 1972.
Sussman, L. A. *The Elder Seneca*. Leiden, Brill, 1978.
Weische, A. *Ciceros Nachahmung der attischen Redner*. Heidelberg, Winter, 1972.

III. MEDIEVAL

Baxandall, M. *Giotto and the Orators*. Oxford University Press, 1971.
Butterworth, C. E., ed. and tr. *Averroës' Three Short Commentaries on Aristotle's 'Topics', 'Rhetoric', and 'Poetics'*. Albany, State University of New York Press, 1977.
Faulhaber, C. B. *Latin Rhetorical Theory in Thirteenth and Fourteenth Century Castile*. University of California Press, 1972.
Gallo, E. *The Poetria nova and its Sources in Early Rhetorical Doctrine*. The Hague and Paris, Mouton, 1971.
*Jaffe, S. *Nicolaus Dybinus' Declaracio Oracionis De Beata Dorothea. Studies and Documents in the History of Late Medieval Rhetoric*. Wiesbaden, Steiner, 1974.
Kelly, D. *Medieval Imagination; Rhetoric and the Poetry of Courtly Love*. University of Wisconsin Press, 1978.
Knight, S. *rymyng craftily. Meaning in Chaucer's Poetry*. London and Sydney, Angus and Robertson, 1973.
Lanham, C. D. *'Salutatio' Formulas in Latin Letters to 1200: Syntax, Style, and Theory*. Munich, Arbeo-Gesellschaft, 1975.
Lawler, T., ed. and tr. *The 'Parisiana Poetria' of John of Garland*. Yale University Press, 1974.
*Miller, J. M., Prosser, M. H. and Benson, Th.W., eds. *Readings in Medieval Rhetoric*. Indiana University Press, 1973.
Monfasani, J. *George of Trebizond. A Biography and a Study of His Rhetoric and Logic*. Leiden, Brill, 1976.
*Murphy, J. J. *Medieval Rhetoric. A Select Bibliography*. University of Toronto Press, 1971.

Rhetoric in the Middle Ages. A History of Rhetorical Theory from Saint Augustine to the Renaissance. University of California Press, 1974.

ed. *Medieval Eloquence. Studies in the Theory and Practice of Medieval Rhetoric.* University of California Press, 1978.

ed. *Three Medieval Rhetorical Arts.* University of California Press, 1971.

Pastré, J.-M. *Rhétorique et adaptation dans les œuvres allemandes du moyen-âge.* Paris, Presses Universitaires de France, 1979.

Paterson, L. M. *Troubadours and Eloquence.* Oxford University Press, 1975.

Riché, P. *Education and Culture in the Barbarian West, Sixth through Eighth Centuries.* Translated by J. J. Contreni from *Education et culture dans l'Occident barbare, 6e–8e siècles* (Paris, Seuil, 1962). University of South Carolina Press, 1976.

Stahl, W. H., Johnson, R. and Burge, E. L. *Martianus Capella and the Seven Liberal Arts, I: The Quadrivium of Martianus Capella with a Study of the Allegory and the Verbal Disciplines; II: The Marriage of Philology and Mercury.* Columbia University Press, 1971, 1977.

Von Moos, P. *Consolatio. Studien zur mittellateinischen Trostliteratur über den Tod und zum Problem der christlichen Trauer,* 4 vols. Munich, Fink, 1972.

Wieruszowski, H. *Politics and Culture in Medieval Spain and Italy.* Rome, Edizioni di Storia e Letteratura, 1971.

IV. RENAISSANCE AND BAROQUE

Altman, J. B. *The Tudor Play of Mind. Rhetorical Inquiry and the Development of Elizabethan Drama.* University of California Press, 1978.

*Barner, B. *Barockrhetorik.* Tübingen, Max Niemeyer Verlag, 1970.

Bayley, P. *French Pulpit Oratory, 1598–1650. A Study in Themes and Styles with a Descriptive Catalogue of Printed Texts.* Cambridge University Press, 1980.

Bolgar, R. R., ed. *Classical Influences on European Culture, A.D. 1500–1700.* Cambridge University Press, 1976.

Bryans, J. V. *Calderón de la Barca: Imagery, Rhetoric and Drama.* Támesis, 1977.

*Buck, A., Heitmann, K., and Mettman, W., eds. *Dichtungslehre der Romania aus der Zeit der Renaissance.* Frankfurt, Athenäum, 1972.

Cain, Th.H. *Praise in 'The Faerie Queene'.* University of Nebraska Press, 1978.

Camporeale, S. *Lorenzo Valla, Umanesimo e teologia.* Florence, Sansoni, 1972.

Castelvetro, L. *Poetica di' Aristotele volgarizzata e sposta.* Edited by W. Romani, 2 vols. Bari, Laterza, 1978.

Cave, T. *The Cornucopian Text: Problems of Writing in the French Renaissance.* Oxford University Press, 1979.

Chamberlin, J. S. *Increase and Multiply: Arts of Discourse Procedure in the Preaching of Donne.* University of North Carolina Press, 1976.

Critique et Création Littéraires en France au XVIIe Siècle. Colloques internationaux no. 557. Paris, C.N.R.S., 1977.

Drew-Bear, A. *Rhetoric in Ben Jonson's Middle Plays: A Study of Ethos, Character Portrayal, and Persuasion.* Institut für Anglistik und Amerikanistik, Universität Salzburg, 1973.

Erasmus. *De pueris, De ratione studii, De conscribendis epistolis, Dialogus Ciceronianus.* Edited by J. C. Margolin and P. Mesnard. Amsterdam, North-Holland, 1971; *Opera Omnia,* vol. 1-2.

Literary and Educational Writings, vols. 1 and 2. Edited by C. R. Thompson. University of Toronto Press, 1980; *Collected Works of Erasmus*, Vols. 23, 24.

Fumaroli, M. *L'Age de l'Éloquence: rhétorique et 'res literaria' de la Renaissance au seuil de l'époque classique*. Geneva, Droz, 1980.

Gerl, H.-B. *Rhetorik als Philosophie. Lorenzo Valla*. Munich, Fink, 1974.

*Gordon, A. L. *Ronsard et la rhétorique*. Geneva, Droz, 1970.

Griffiths, R. *The Dramatic Technique of Antoine de Montchrestien. Rhetoric and Style in French Renaissance Tragedy*. Oxford University Press, 1970.

Holyoake, S. J. *An Introduction to French Sixteenth Century Poetic Theory. Texts and Commentary*. Manchester University Press, 1972.

Kennedy, W. J. *Rhetorical Norms in Renaissance Literature*. Yale University Press, 1978.

Kristeller, P. O. *Renaissance Thought and Its Sources*. Columbia University Press, 1979.

*Lange, H.-J. *Aemulatio Veterum sive de optimo genere dicendi. Die Entstehung des Barockstils im XVI. Jahrhundert durch eine Geschmacksverschiebung in Richtung der Stile des manieristischen Typs*. Bern, Herbert Lang; Frankfurt/Main, Peter Lang, 1974.

Lanham, R. A. *Literary Rhetoric in the Renaissance*. Yale University Press, 1976.

LeCoat, G. *The Rhetoric of the Arts, 1550–1650*. Bern, Herbert Lang; Frankfurt/Main, Peter Lang, 1975.

*Marti, A. *La Preceptiva Retórica Española en el Siglo de Oro*, Madrid, Editorial Gredos, 1972.

Müller, W. G. *Die politische Rede bei Shakespeare*. Tübingen, Gunter Narr Verlag, 1979.

*Murphy, J. J. *Renaissance Rhetoric: A Short-Title Catalogue and A Select Bibliography*. New York, Garland, 1980.

ed. *Renaissance Eloquence: Studies in the Theory and Practice of Renaissance Rhetoric*. University of California Press, forthcoming.

O'Malley, J. W. *Praise and Blame in Renaissance Rome: Rhetoric, Doctrine, and Reform in the Sacred Orators of the Papal Court, c. 1450–1521*. Durham, N.C., Duke University Press, 1979.

Plett, H. F. *Rhetorik der Affekte. Englische Wirkungsästhetik im Zeitalter der Renaissance*. Tübingen, Max Niemeyer Verlag, 1975.

Schweyen, R. *Guarino Veronese, Philosophie und humanistische Pädagogik*. Munich, Fink, 1973.

Sloan, Th. O. and Waddington, R. B., eds. *The Rhetoric of Renaissance Poetry. From Wyatt to Milton*. University of California Press, 1974.

Stolt, B. *Wortkampf. Frühneuhochdeutsche Beispiele zur rhetorischen Praxis*. Frankfurt/Main, Athenäum, 1974.

Struever, N. S. *The Language of History in the Renaissance. Rhetoric and Historical Consciousness in Florentine Humanism*. Princeton University Press, 1970.

Tasso, T. *Discourses on the Heroic Poem*. Translated by M. Cavalchini and I. Samuel. Oxford University Press, 1973.

Valentin, J. M. *Le Théâtre des Jésuites dans les pays de langue allemande*. 3 vols. Bern, Frankfurt, Las Vegas, Peter Lang, 1978.

Verdu, J. R. *La retórica española de los siglos XVI y XVII*. Madrid, Consejo Superior de Investigaciones Cientificas, 1973.

*Weinberg, B., ed. *Trattati di Poetica e Retorica del '500*. 4 vols. Bari, Laterza, 1970–4.

Wesseler, M. *Die Einheit von Wort und Sache: der Entwurf einer rhetorischen Philosophie bei Marcius Nizolius.* Munich, Fink, 1974.

Zumthor, P. *Anthologie des grands rhétoriqueurs.* Paris, Union générale d'Editions, 1978.

Le Masque et la lumière. La Poétique des grands rhétoriqueurs. Paris, Seuil, 1978.

V. MODERN (SINCE 1700)

Battistini, A. *La degnità della retorica. Studi su G. B. Vico.* Pisa, Pacini, 1975.

Fisher, W. R. and McBath, J. H., eds. *British Public Addresses, 1828–1960.* Boston, Houghton Mifflin, 1971.

Gumbrecht, A. U. *Funktionen politischer Rhetorik in der französischen Revolution.* Munich, Fink, 1976.

*Howell, W. S. *Eighteenth-Century British Logic and Rhetoric.* Princeton University Press, 1971.

IJsseling, S., Steel, C. and Perelman, Ch. *Grondvragen van de Retorica.* Leuven, Wijsgerig Gezelschap, 1979.

Perelman, Ch. and Olbrechts-Tyteca, L. *Traité de l'argumentation. La Nouvelle Rhétorique.* Editions de l'Université de Bruxelles, 1970; third edition 1976.

The New Rhetoric. A Treatise on Argumentation. Indiana, University of Notre Dame Press, second edition, 1971.

Perelman, Ch. *L'Empire rhétorique. Rhétorique et argumentation.* Paris, J. Vrin, 1977.

The New Rhetoric and the Humanities. Essays on Rhetoric and its Applications. Dordrecht, Boston, London, D. Reidel, 1979.

VI. JOURNALS

Communication Monographs (formerly *Speech Monographs*), 1934– (Speech Communication Association, 5205 Leesburg Pike, Falls Church, VA 22041).

Philosophy and Rhetoric, 1968– (Department of Philosophy, Pennsylvania State University).

Quarterly Journal of Speech, 1915– (Speech Communication Association, see above).

Rhetoric Newsletter, 1978– (International Society for the History of Rhetoric; Centre for Renaissance Studies, ETH Zentrum, CH 8092 Zürich; *or* Department of Rhetoric, University of California, Davis)

Rhetoric Society Quarterly, 1968– (Rhetoric Society of America; Department of Philosophy, St Cloud State University, St Cloud, Minnesota).

Rhetorik. Ein Internationales Jahrbuch, 1980– (Stuttgart, Frommann-Holzboog).

Bibliography of comparative literature in Britain

The bibliography has been compiled by Dr Paula Clifford (Reading). It is based in the first instance on information supplied by the members of the British Comparative Literature Association, and by respondents to a wider inquiry. Although entries have been checked against the British National Bibliography, it is not possible to claim completeness or guarantee accuracy in every case. There is no section on translation and translators, as work in Great Britain is already covered by the bibliography of translations in the *Yearbook of Comparative and General Literature* edited by Henry Remak (Bloomington, Indiana). The headings used are those of the full annual bibliography, discontinued in 1971, in the *YCGL*, which were adapted from Fernand Baldensperger and Werner P. Friederich, *A Bibliography of Comparative Literature* (Chapel Hill, North Carolina, 1950). We should like to thank Professor Ulrich Weisstein, editor of the *YCGL* bibliographies, for his generous advice.

In this bibliography, place of publication is London unless otherwise stated. In the case of the university presses the place of publication is omitted.

1978

I. COMPARATIVE, WORLD AND GENERAL LITERATURE

Bergonzi, B. 'Further Thoughts about Marxism and Literature', *Critical Quarterly*, 20 (4), 49–54.

Coulthard, M. *An Introduction to Discourse Analysis*. Longman.

Courtney, C. P. 'French Prose Fiction in the Second Half of the Eighteenth Century: A New Bibliography', *French Studies*, 32, 278–84.

Eaton, T. 'Literary Semantics: Modality and "Style"', *Journal of Literary Semantics*, 7 (April), 5–28.

Eliot, T. S. *To Criticize the Critic and Other Writings* (first published 1965). Faber.

Fekele, J. *The Critical Twilight: Explorations in the Ideology of Anglo-American Literary Theory from Eliot to McLuhan*. Routledge and Kegan Paul.

Forster, L. W. 'Literary Studies as a Flight from Literature?' *Modern Language Review*, 73, xxi–xxxiv.

Harvey, J. R. 'Criticism, Ideology, Raymond Williams and Terry Eagleton', *Cambridge Quarterly*, 8 (Summer), 56–65.

Howard-Hill, T. H. *Literary Concordances*. Oxford, Pergamon.

Macherey, P. *A Theory of Literary Production.* Translated by G. Wall. Routledge and Kegan Paul.

Meidner, O. 'Semantics and Literature', *Journal of Literary Semantics*, 7 (October), 78–89.

Morton, A. Q. *Literary Detection.* Epping, Bowker.

Murray, P. *Literary Criticism: a Glossary of Major Terms.* Dublin, Smurfit Books and Longman.

Norris, C. *William Empson and the Philosophy of Literary Criticism.* Athlone Press.

'Theory of Language and the Language of Literature', *Journal of Literary Semantics*, 7 (October), 90–8.

Olsen, S. H. *The Structure of Literary Understanding.* Cambridge University Press.

Pearce, R. *Literary Texts: The Application of Linguistic Theory to Literary Discourse.* Edited by M. Coulthard. University of Birmingham.

Poole, R. 'Men with scissors', *English*, 27 (Summer/Autumn), 274–81.

Rickword, E. *Literature and Society: Essays and Opinions (II) 1931–78.* Edited by A. Young. Manchester, Carcanet New Press.

Ricoeur, P. *The Rule of Metaphor: Multi-disciplinary Studies in the Creation of Meaning in Language.* Translated by R. Czerny *et al.* Routledge and Kegan Paul.

Ritchie, J. M. and Last, R. 'A Bibliography of German Expressionist Drama in Translation', *New German Studies*, 6 (1), 59–70.

Rose, M. *Reading the young Marx and Engels: Poetry, Parody and the Censor.* Croom Helm.

Routh, J. and J. Wolff, eds. *The Sociology of Literature: Theoretical Approaches.* Sociological Review Monograph, University of Keele.

Scott, A. F. *Current Literary Terms* (first published 1965). New edition. Methuen.

Steiner, G. *On Difficulty and Other Essays.* New York and Oxford University Press.

Watson, G. *Modern Literary Thought.* Heidelberg, Carl Winter Verlag.

Whitehouse, J. C. 'Catholic Writing: Some Basic Notions, Some Criticisms and a Tentative Reply', *Modern Language Review*, 73 (April), 241–9.

II. THEMES AND MOTIFS

Atkins, J. *Sex in Literature, Volume 3. The Medieval Experience.* J. Calder.

Bersani, L. *A Future for Astyanax: Character and Desire in Literature* (first published 1976). Boyars.

Carroll, M. G. 'Realism and Whimsicality in *Tristram Shandy* and *Jacques le fataliste*', *Comparison*, 7, 45–55.

Davie, D. *A Gathered Church: the Literature of the English Dissenting Interest, 1700–1930.* Clark lectures, 1976. Routledge and Kegan Paul.

Edwards, G. *The Prison and the Labyrinth, Studies in Calderonian Tragedy.* Cardiff, University of Wales Press.

Feingold, R. *Nature and Society: Later Eighteenth-Century Uses of the Pastoral and Georgic.* Hassocks, Harvester Press.

Flavell, M. K. 'Vice and Virtue on the German Stage, 1770–1800', *Forum for Modern Language Studies*, 14 (April), 165–82.

Fletcher, J. 'Cheating the Dark Gods: Iris Murdoch and Racine', *International Fiction Review*, 6 (Winter), 75–6.

Forster, L. W. 'Meditation in a Garden', *German Life and Letters* (N.S.), 31, 23–36.
Gillespie, G. 'Dream and Calculus in European Baroque Drama', in *Critical Dimensions: English, German and Comparative Literature Essays in Honor of Aurelio Zanco*. Cuneo, Saste, 154–73.
'The Function of Myth in Lohenstein's Arminius: The Case of Egypt and Prometheus'. *Argenis*, 2.
'Primal Utterance: Observations on Kuhlmann's Correspondence with Kircher, in View of Leibniz's Theories', in *Wege der Worte: Festschrift für Wolfgang Fleischhauer*. Cologne and Vienna, Böhlau.
Green, A. 'Salammbô and the Myth of Pasiphaë', *French Studies*, 32 (April), 170–7.
Grylls, D. *Guardians and Angels: Parents and Children in Nineteenth-Century Literature*. Faber.
Howells, C. A. *Love, Mystery and Misery*. Athlone Press.
Kilborn, M. C. 'The Theme of Suffering in the Works of Louis Guilloux', *Nottingham French Studies*, 17 (2), 44–59.
Knights, B. *The Idea of the Clerisy in the Nineteenth Century*. Routlege and Kegan Paul.
Linder, C. A. *Romantic Imagery in the Novels of Charlotte Brontë*. Macmillan.
McDonald, W. C. 'King Mark: Gottfried's Version of the Ovidian Husband-Figure?', *Forum for Modern Language Studies*, 14 (July), 255–69.
Murdoch, B. O. 'Thematic Analogues of *Paradise Regained*', *Études anglaises*, 31, 203–7.
Newton, J. and Fol, M. 'Edmond de Goncourt et Robert de Montesquiou: une amitié littéraire', *Nineteenth-Century French Studies*, 7 (Winter), 85–103.
Pasley, M. 'Kafka and the Theme of "Berufung"', *Oxford German Studies*, 9, 139–49.
Pickup, I. 'Réflexions sur le régime pénitentiaire dans le roman sous la monarchie de Juillet', *Revue de science criminelle et de droit pénal comparé* (N.S.), 2 (April/June), 309–19.
Round, N. G. 'The Shadow of a Philosopher: Medieval Castilian Images of Plato', *Journal of Hispanic Philology*, 3, 1–36.
Smith, D. *Socialist Propaganda in the Twentieth-Century British Novel*. Macmillan.
Woods, M. J. *The Poet and the Natural World in the Age of Góngora*. Oxford University Press.
Worton, M. 'Obsessional Theatre? The Role of the Father-Figure in Arthur Adamov's Early Plays', *Nottingham French Studies*, 17 (1), 71–7.

III. LITERARY GENRES, TYPES AND FORMS

Bann, S. 'Meredith's Plain Story', *Literatur in Wissenschaft und Unterricht* (Autumn).
Barclay, G. St J. *Anatomy of Horror: The Masters of Occult Fiction*. Weidenfeld and Nicolson.
Bergonzi, B. *The Situation of the Novel* (first published 1970). Second edition. Macmillan.
Blackall, E. A. *Goethe and the Novel*. Cornell University Press.
Bradby, D. and McCormick, J. *People's Theatre*. Croom Helm.
Brewer, D. 'The Nature of Romance', *Poetica* (Tokyo), 9, 9–48.
Brown, C. C. and Pina, M. 'William Browne, Marino, France and the Third Look at *Britannia's Pastorals*', *Review of English Studies*, 29 (November), 385–404.
Colley, I. *Dos Passos and the Fiction of Despair*. Macmillan.

Davies, C. 'Art within a Tradition: *Wuthering Heights* and the German *Novelle*', *Brontë Society Transactions*, 17 (3), 197–204.

Davis, J. *Farce:* The Critical Idiom 39. Methuen.

Donald, M. *The American Novel in the Twentieth Century*. Newton Abbot, David and Charles.

Esslin, M. *An Anatomy of Drama* (first published 1976). Abacus.

Fletcher, J. 'Parvenu Genre, Genre of Parvenus', *Comparative Literature Studies*, 15 (June), 193–202.

Fowler, F. M. 'The Dramatic Image', in *Tradition and Creation: Essays in Honour of Elizabeth Mary Wilkinson.* edited by C. P. Magill, B. A. Rowley and C. Smith. W. S. Maney, Leeds, 63–76.

Gillespie, G. T. 'Heroic Lays: Survival and Transformation in Ballad', *Oxford German Studies*, 9, 1–18.

Howarth, W. D., ed. *Comic Drama: the European Heritage.* Methuen 'Tragedy into Melodrama: The Fortunes of the Calas Affair on the Stage', *Studies on Voltaire and the Eighteenth Century*, 174, 121–50.

Jenkins, C. 'Realism and the Novel Form', in *The Monster in the Mirror*, edited by D. A. Williams. Oxford University Press, 1–16.

Kennedy, A. *Meaning and Signs in Fiction*. Macmillan.

King, J. *Tragedy in the Victorian Novel: Theory and Practice in the Novels of George Eliot, Thomas Hardy and Henry James*. Cambridge University Press.

Marullo, T. G. 'Bunin's *Dry Valley:* The Russian Novel in Transition from Realism to Modernism', *Forum for Modern Language Studies*, 14 (July), 193–207.

Nicholls, P., ed. *Explorations of the Marvellous: The Science and the Fiction in Science Fiction*. Fontana.

Porter, D. 'Stendhal and the Impossibility of Autobiography', *French Studies*, 32 (April), 158–69.

Prendergast, C. *Balzac: Fiction and Melodrama*. Edward Arnold.

Richards, I. A. *Verse v. Prose*. Presidential Address. English Association.

Rowley, B. A. 'To Define True Novellen... A Taxonomic Enquiry', *Publications of the English Goethe Society*, 47.

Seldon, R. *English Verse Satire, 1550–1765*. Allen and Unwin.

Skelton, R. *Poetic Truth*. Heinemann.

Thompson, D. *The Uses of Poetry*. Cambridge University Press.

Wain, J. *Professing Poetry*. New edition. Harmondsworth, Penguin.

Williams, D. A. 'The Practice of Realism', in *The Monster in the Mirror*, edited by D. A. Williams, Oxford University Press, 257–79.

Williams, I. 'The Imperfect Idea of the Novel', *Modern Language Review*, 73 (January), 1–16.

IV. EPOCHS, CURRENTS AND MOVEMENTS

Bann, S. 'Historical Text and Historical Object: The Poetics of the Musée de Cluny', *History and Theory* (Autumn).

Buxton, J. *The Grecian Taste: Literature in the Age of Neo-Classicism, 1740–1820*. Macmillan.

Cadogan, M. and Craig, P. *Women and Children First: The Fiction of Two World Wars*. Gollancz.

Carsaniga, G. M. *The Age of Realism*. Hassocks, Harvester Press.
Conrad, P. *Shandyism: The Character of Romantic Irony*. Oxford, Blackwell.
Coupe, W. A. *The Continental Renaissance, 1500–1600* (first published 1971). Hassocks, Harvester Press.
Cunningham, G. *The New Woman and the Victorian Novel*. Macmillan.
Donoghue, D. *The Sovereign Ghost: Studies in Imagination* (first published 1976). Faber.
Forster, L. W. 'Some Examples of Petrarchism in Slavonic Lands', *Humanistica Lovaniensia*, 27, 1–9.
Harper, A. J. 'Renaissance Verse-Reform and the German Poetry of the Seventeenth Century', *Neuphilologische Mitteilungen*, 79 (4), 426–37.
Hollington, M. 'The Fantastic Paradox: An Aspect of the Theory of Romantic Realism', *Comparison*, 7 (Spring).
Lucas, J., ed. *The 1930's: A Challenge to Orthodoxy*. Hassocks, Harvester Press.
Nadeau, M. *This History of Surrealism*. Translated by R. Howard. Harmondsworth, Penguin.
Reed, T. J. 'Theatre, Enlightenment and Nation: A German Problem', *Forum for Modern Language Studies*, 14 (April), 143–64.
Rogers, P. *The Augustan Vision* (first published 1974). New edition. Methuen.
Rutherford, A. *The Literature of War*. Macmillan.
Sherrard, P. *The Wound of Greece: Studies in Neo-Hellenism*. Collings.
Skrine, P. N. *The Baroque. Literature and Culture in Seventeenth-Century Europe*. Methuen.
Thacker, M. J. '*La desordenada codicia de los bienes ajenos* – A *Caso Límite* of the Picaresque?' *Bulletin of Hispanic Studies*, 55, 33–41.
Tillotson, G. *A View of Victorian Literature*. Oxford, Clarendon Press.
Watanabe, H. *Melancholie und die melancholische Landschaft. Ein Betrag zur Geistesgeschichte des 17. Jahrhunderts*. Berne, Francke Verlag.
Williams, D. A., ed. *The Monster in the Mirror. Studies in Nineteenth-Century Realism*. Oxford University Press.

V. THE BIBLE, CLASSICAL ANTIQUITY

Arkins, B. 'The Originality of Catullus'. *Liverpool Classical Monthly*, 3, 65–9.
Shaffer, E. S. 'The Ironic Mode in Biblical Criticism: Samuel Butler's *The Fair Haven*' (summary), *Victorian Studies Association Newsletter* (Toronto).

VI. INDIVIDUAL COUNTRIES

Butt, J. *Writers and Politics in Modern Spain*. Hodder and Stoughton.
Forster, L. W. Review of U. Bornemann, *Anlehnung und Abgrenzung. Untersuchungen zur Rezeption des niederländischen Literatur in der deutschen Dichtungsreform des 17. Jahrhunderts* (Assen, 1976), *Spiegel der Letteren*, 20, 197–204.
Gatt-Rutter, J. *Writers and Politics in Modern Italy*. Hodder and Stoughton.
Griffiths, G. *A Double Exile: African and West Indian Writing between Two Cultures*. Boyars.
Lough, J. *Writer and Public in France: From the Middle Ages to the Present Day*. Oxford, Clarendon Press.

Lough, J. and M. *An Introduction to Nineteenth-Century France*. Longman.
Mawby, J. *Writers and Politics in Modern Scandinavia*. Hodder and Stoughton.
Perry, N. 'Voltaire in London', *The Times*, 22 April 1978.
Rayfield, P. D. 'The Heroic Ethos of Russian and Georgian Folk Poetry', *Slavonic and East European Review*, 56 (October), 505–21.
Sharratt, P. 'Edmund Wilson and France', in *An Edmund Wilson Celebration*, edited by J. Wain, Oxford University Press, 60–85.
Sims-Williams, P. '"Is it fog or smoke or warriors fighting?": Irish and Welsh Parallels to the Finnsburh Fragment', *Bulletin of the Board of Celtic Studies*, 27 (May), 505–14.
'Thought, Word and Deed: An Irish Triad', *Ériu*, 29, 78–111.
Thorpe, M. *Doris Lessing's Africa*. Evans Bros.
Waller, R. E. A. 'L'Homme de lettres en France et en Angleterre (1700–30)', *Dix-huitième Siècle*, 10, 229–52.
Worth, K. *The Irish Drama of Europe from Yeats to Beckett*. Athlone Press.

VII. INDIVIDUAL AUTHORS

Ashton, R. D. 'Coleridge and *Faust*', *Review of English Studies*, 28, 156–67.
Bair, D. *Samuel Beckett: A Biography*, Cape.
Bance, A. F. 'The Intellectual and the Crisis of Weimar: Heinrich Mann's *Kobes* and Leonhard Frank's *Im letzten Wagen*', *Journal of European Studies*, 8, 155–74.
Beckett, S. *Six Residua*. Translated by the author. J. Calder.
Beer, J. B. *Wordsworth and the Human Heart*. Macmillan.
Belmore, H. W. 'Two Romantic Poets of Solitude: Leopardi and Mörike', *German Life and Letters*, 31 (July), 313–18.
Bradbrook, B. R. 'Chesterton and Karel Čapek', *The Chesterton Review*, 4 (Fall/Winter, 1977–8), 89–103.
Brewer, D. *Chaucer and His World*. Eyre Methuen.
Carr, C. T. 'Carlyle, Goethe and the St Andrews Chair of Moral Philosophy', *German Life and Letters*, 31, 4–12.
Constantine, D. J. 'Hölderlin's Pindar: The Language of Translation', *Modern Language Review*, 73 (October), 825–34.
Dekker, G. *Coleridge and the Literature of Sensibility*. Vision Press.
Donno, E. S., ed. *Andrew Marvell: the Critical Heritage*. Routledge and Kegan Paul.
Faletti, H. 'An Aesthetic Perspective on Gide and Nietzsche. The Problem of Decadence for Creative Effort', *Revue de littérature comparée*, 52, 39–59.
Fletcher, B. S. *et al. A Student's Guide to the Plays of Samuel Beckett*. Faber.
Fletcher, D. J. 'Une lettre inédite de Maupassant', *Revue d'histoire littéraire de la France*, 78 (July/August), 628–9.
Fletcher, J. and Spurling, J. *Beckett: a Study of His Plays* (first published 1972). Second, revised and expanded edition. Eyre Methuen.
Gaskill, P. H. 'Edwin Muir as a Critic of Hölderlin', *Forum for Modern Language Studies*, 14, 345–64.
'Hermann Broch as a Translator of Edwin Muir', *New German Studies*, 6, 101–15.
Gilbert, A. J. 'The Influence of Boethius on the *Parlement of Foulys*', *Medium Aevum*, 47, 292–303.

Green, D. H. and Johnson, L. P. *Approaches to Wolfram von Eschenbach*. Bern.
Gunny, A. 'A Note on Voltaire's Use of English Men of Letters', *Comparison*, 8, 32–41.
Hammond, P. F. 'Dryden's Zimri and Juvenal', *Notes and Queries*, N.S. 25, 26.
Harvey, A. D. '*Clarissa* and the Puritan Tradition', *Essays in Criticism*, 28 (January), 38–51.
Hesse, H. *Hermann Hesse and Romain Rolland*. Wolff.
Hollington, M. 'Dickens and the Dance of Death', *The Dickensian* (May).
Hunt, T. 'Alissa-Elioissa', *Orbis Litterarum*, 33, 183–90.
'Chrestien and the Comediae', *Medieval Studies*, 40, 120–56.
Jefferson, A. 'Imagery versus Description: The Problematics of Representation in the Novels of Nathalie Sarraute', *Modern Language Review*, 73 (July), 513–24.
Jones, M. V. 'An Aspect of Tolstoy's Impact on Modern English Fiction: *The Kreutzer Sonata* and Joyce Cary's *The Moonlight*', *Slavonic and East European Review*, 56 (January).
King, J. *Garden of Zola: Émile Zola and His Novels for English Readers*. Barrie and Jenkins.
Knowles, A. V., ed. *Tolstoy, The Critical Heritage*. Routledge and Kegan Paul.
Knowlson, J., ed. *Samuel Beckett: Happy Days/Oh les beaux jours*, a bilingual edition with afterword and notes by James Knowlson, Faber.
Le Comte, E. S. *Milton and Sex*. Macmillan.
Little, J. P. 'Form and the Void. Beckett's *Fin de partie* and Ionesco's *Les Chaises*', *French Studies*, 32 (January), 46–53.
Little, R. 'Le Pseudonyme de Saint-John Perse', *La Nouvelle Revue française*, 304 (May), 126–7.
'Saint-John Perse and Denis Devlin: a *compagnonnage*', *Irish University Review*, 8 (Autumn), 193–200.
Little, T. E., 'Mervyn Peake and Nikolai Gogol', *Essays in Poetics* (University of Keele), 3 (September), 87–104.
Lowes, J. L. *The Road to Xanadu: A Study in the Ways of the Imagination*. Second revised edition. Pan Books.
McGowan, M. 'Sprache, Gewalt und Gesellschaft: Franz Xaver Kroetz und die sozialrealistischen Dramatiker des englischen Theaters', *Text und Kritik*, 57, 37–48.
Marshall, J. H. 'Imitation of Metrical Form in Peire Cardenal', *Romance Philology*, 32, 18–48.
Martin, G. D., ed. *Jean-Claude Renard: Selected Poems* (bilingual edition), Oasis Press.
Mooney, M. E. 'Molloy, Part I: Beckett's "Discourse on Method"', *Journal of Beckett Studies*, 3, 40–55.
O'Neill, T. 'The Figure of Alfieri in *Dei Sepolcri*', *Italica*, 55 (3), 321–37.
Pasley, M. ed. *Nietzsche. Imagery and Thought*. Methuen.
Pilling, J. 'The Significance of Beckett's *Still*', *Essays in Criticism*, 28 (April), 143–57.
'The Case of Andrey Biely', *PN Review 8* 5 (4), 19–21.
Pontiero, G. 'Estranhos itinerários: Julio Cortázar e Clarice Lispector', *O Estado de São Paulo* (*suplemento cultural*), 29 October 1978.
Simpson, D. 'Pound's Wordsworth; or Growth of a Poet's Mind', *E.L.H.*, 45, 660–86.
Thorpe, C. 'Walter Map and Gerald of Wales', *Medium Aevum*, 47, 6–21.
Ward Jouve, N. 'Entretien imaginaire avec Doris Lessing', *Femmes en mouvement*, 3.

Waring, A. G. 'Science, Love and the Establishment in the Novels of D. A. Granin and C. P. Snow', *Forum for Modern Language Studies*, 14 (January), 1–15.

Wimsatt, J. I. 'Guillaume de Machaut and Chaucer's Love Lyrics', *Medium Aevum*, 47, 66–87.

Windeatt, B. A. 'The "Paynted Proces": Italian to English in Chaucer's *Troilus*', *English Miscellany*, 26–7 (1977–8), 79–103.

VIII. LITERATURE AND THE OTHER ARTS

Atkins, S. 'Heinrich von Kleist and the Fine Arts', *German Life and Letters*, 31 (January), 166–74.

Bann, S. *Heroic Emblems*. Introduction to and commentaries on emblems by Ian Hamilton Finlay, Vermont, Z Press.

Brady, P. V. 'From Cave-Painting to "Fotogramm". Brecht, Photography and the *Arbeitsjournal*', *Forum for Modern Language Studies*, 14 (July), 270–82.

Brown, H. M. '*Zwischen Erde und Himmel:* Kleist and the Visual Arts, with Special Reference to Caspar David Friedrich', *German Life and Letters*, 31 (January), 157–66.

Cardinal, R. 'Soluble City: The Surrealist Perception of Paris', *Architectural Design*, 48 (2/3), 143–9.

Daniels, G. 'Emma Bovary's Opera – Flaubert, Scott and Donizetti', *French Studies*, 32 (July), 285–303.

Fletcher, J. 'The "Metamorphosis of Reality": Film and Narrative', *Comparison*, 7 (Spring), 56–97.

Gervais, D. 'On Reading Ruskin', *The Cambridge Quarterly*, 8 (2), 97–112.